Ritual Ground

Ritual Ground

Bent's Old Fort,
World Formation, and
the Annexation of the Southwest

Douglas C. Comer

UNIVERSITY OF CALIFORNIA PRESS

Berkeley / Los Angeles / London

University of California Press
Berkeley and Los Angeles, California

University of California Press
London, England

Copyright © 1996 by The Regents of the University of California

Library of Congress Cataloging-in-Publication Data

Comer, Douglas C.
    Ritual Ground: Bents Old Fort, world formation, and the
annexation of the Southwest / Douglas C. Comer.
        p.   cm.
    Includes bibliographical references and index.
    ISBN 0-520-20429-8 (cloth: alk. paper).—ISBN 0-520-20774-2
    (pbk.: alk. paper)
    1. Bent's Fort (Colo.)—History. 2. Bent's Old Fort National
    Historic Site (Colo.)—History. 3. Frontier and pioneer life—
    Colorado—Bent's Fort. I. Title.
    F782.A7C67 1996
    978.8'95—dc20   96-8766
                                                            CIP

Printed in the United States of America

1 2 3 4 5 6 7 8 9

To Elizabeth, Samantha,
Margaret, and Jacob

Contents

Illustrations

Acknowledgments

This project began with excavations I conducted in 1976 at the two trash dumps in front of Bent's Old Fort. The first shard of historic ceramic was retrieved by Roxie Hoss, an energetic and altogether delightful local woman, who exclaimed, "Is *this* what we're looking for? My grandmother has some of this stuff!" We had a discussion about the importance of context at that point, one so intellectually provocative to me that I have been thinking about it for all of the intervening years. What did we—I, Roxie, any of us—expect to learn from material, oral, behavioral, and written manifestations of the past? What could and should we expect? Why did we care? My search for instructive context led me eventually to the ideas that give form to this book. Roxie went on to work many years for Bent's Old Fort National Historic Site, so perhaps the excavation and our conversation were as provocative for her as for me.

I have been fortunate to have encountered many people who, like Roxie, have been very helpful, interesting, and intellectually stimulating. This book was, at a point in its history that now seems rather distant, a dissertation. Mary Corbin Sies, the chair of my committee, encouraged me then and has encouraged me since to refine my theoretical approach, particularly in regard to the problematic concept of cultural hegemony. Mark P. Leone has been gracious enough to meet with me many times to discuss, and sometimes debate, this approach. The intellectual excitement of my conversations with Mary and Mark, and their patience, I shall always recall with gratitude. Fred Nicklason generously shared his knowledge of Native American history and the trans-Mississippi West with me. John

Caughey tutored me in the methods of ethnographic fieldwork, and the achievements and approaches of the New Ethnology. I was guided by Myron Lounsbury's knowledge of poststructural and postmodern work.

Especially helpful to my research have been the staff of Bent's Old Fort National Historic Site, including the current Superintendent, Donald Hill, and the Superintendent of the site when I did my archaeological field-work, John Patterson, as well as the current Chief of the Division of Inter-pretation and Resource Management, Alexandra Aldred, who was an administrative assistant there when I first came to the fort. Other park staff to whom I owe a debt include Steve Thede, Chief of Interpretation and Visitor Services; Ranger Interpreter Craig Moore; Volunteer Inter-preter Betty Wesley; Curator Carol Maass; and Park Aide (and retired archaeologist) Gerald Dawson. I also thank Jack Wise, Executive Direc-tor, Bent's Old Fort Historical Association for several informative and enjoyable conversations.

Many libraries and archives have permitted me to examine their man-uscript collections. I am grateful to the National Archives in Washing-ton, D.C.; the Western History Room of the Denver Public Library; the Southwest Museum, Los Angeles, California; the Library of the Colorado State Historical Society, Denver, Colorado; the University of New Mex-ico Library, Albuquerque, New Mexico; and the Huntington Library, San Marino, California. Some individuals at several libraries and archives shared not only their manuscripts, but also their personal knowledge. I am espe-cially appreciative of Peter J. Michel, Director of Library and Archives, Missouri Historical Society, St. Louis, Missouri; Thomas Chavez, Direc-tor of the Palace of the Governors Museum, Santa Fe, New Mexico; and Richard Salazar, Senior Archivist and Ronald Xavier Montoya, Archivist, State Records Center and Archives, Santa Fe, for the time they spent with me. I would like to convey a special thank you to the staff of the Techni-cal Information Center of the National Park Service's Denver Service Cen-ter, especially Edie Ramey, Jody Notch, Barbara Harris, and Jolene Lindsey. Finally, I owe an enormous debt to Research Librarian Pat Her-ron at my "home" library at the College Park Campus of the University of Maryland.

A number of people shared their knowledge of the Santa Fe trade, the role of the Plains Indians in the fur trade, and the nineteenth-century his-tory of the Southwest with me. Authors and historians Marc Simmons, Mark Gardner, David Lavender, and Jerry Greene suggested useful direc-tions for my research. Susan Calafate Boyle, William Patrick O'Brien, and William Gwaltney, all of the National Park Service, were particularly informative in regard to the Santa Fe Trail: Susan about the Mexican end of the trade, Pat regarding Independence and St. Louis, and Bill about Bent's Old Fort's connection to the trail. Other National Park Service employees, archaeologist Douglas D. Scott and historian Jere Krakow, were kind enough to act as discussants in a symposium Pat O'Brien and I chaired at a Society for Historical Archaeology Annual Conference, titled "Nineteenth-Century Trails and the Cultural Landscape." Their comments caused me to rework some of the points in this book. Two archaeologists discussed prehistoric trade in the Southwest with me and suggested pertinent literature: Douglas McFadden of the Bureau of Land Management office in Kenab, Utah, and Timothy Baugh, presently Chief of the Repatriation Office of the Smithsonian Institution. Charles E. Hanson, Jr. and the late Carlyle S. Smith advised me on nineteenth-century firearms. Louanna Lackey provided me with information about ceramic production and trade in Mexico.

Craig Moore, an interpreter at Bent's Old Fort National Historic Site, arranged several times for me to meet with members of the Southern Cheyenne. I spoke most frequently with Ann Shadlow, Mickey Pratt, and Henry Whiteshield. The story about the origin of the Big Dipper, which I relate in chapter 2, is as told by Mrs. Shadlow.

My wife, Elizabeth, has an enthusiasm and talent for living that I find energizing. I am sure that I could not have completed this project without her support, which was constant. An interest in somewhat arcane matters can be isolating, and I feel fortunate to be married to someone who understands both the excitement of research and the discomfort one inevitably encounters along the way. My very young children, Margaret and Jacob, suggested several aspects of the theoretical approach employed in what follows in ways that would require yet another book to describe, much less explain. The construction of reality is a collective affair accomplished by innumerable human transactions, most of them subtle and unnoticed, and so was the construction of this book.

CHAPTER I

Hearts and Minds

Whoever fights monsters should see to it that in the process he does not become a monster. And when you look long into an abyss, the abyss also looks into you.
                    Friedrich Wilhelm Nietzsche, *Beyond Good and Evil*

The most fascinating terrae incognitae *of all are those that lie within the minds and hearts of men.*
                    John K. Wright, in his presidential address before
                    the Association of American Geographers, 1946[1]

Frontiers, Alienation, and the Alien

The southwestern Plains have seemed to many, as Walter Prescott Webb noted about that high and arid region, strangely "oceanic."[2] It is a vast, flat landscape where the horizon merges with the sky, where no points of reference are offered except the ephemeral. Dust devils skitter and vanish, massive black clouds sweep in with lightning and gusts of rain and are gone just as quickly, rain evaporates before reaching the ground. An occasional car or truck can be seen miles away. It shimmers in the distance, whines along an absolutely straight road, and flashes by. In the next moment all is again silent, as if the vehicle had been imagined. The land seems empty, yet awesome and overwhelming.

Webb held that the American sojourn on the Plains had shaped the national "insides." In his seminal work, *The Great Plains,* he quoted from the writings of the painter John Nobel, who was born in Kansas. From

1

his expatriate home in France, Nobel recollected an incident on the south-western Plains:

Did you ever hear of "loneliness" as a fatal disease? Once, back in the days when father and I were bringing up long-legged sheep from Mexico, we picked up a man near Las Vegas [New Mexico] who had lost his way. He was in a terrible state. It wasn't the result of being lost. He had "loneliness." Born on the plains, you got accustomed to them; but on people not born there the plains sometimes have an appalling effect.

You look on, on, on, out into space, out almost beyond time itself. You see nothing but the rise and swell of land and grass, and then more grass— the monotonous, endless prairies! A stranger traveling on the prairies would get his hopes up, expecting to see something different on making the next rise. To him the disappointment and monotony were terrible. "He's got lone-liness," we would say of such a man.[3]

The topography around Bent's Old Fort struck me, almost two decades ago now, as *terra incognita,* in the sense that Mircea Eliade, probably the most influential of all historians of religion, has used that term. This is the land, found in myth worldwide, that is beyond the boundaries of the known world; it is unfounded, chaotic, and unsanctified. As such, it serves perfectly as the backdrop for that most American of creations, the alien-ated hero. "Our heroes have always been cowboys," according to a recent American ballad. In the sense that the cowboy is the loner guided by his personal sense of values, this could not be better stated.

The loner continually reemerges in American art forms. He is Humphrey Bogart in *Casablanca,* an alienated individual who has no apparent code of ethics . . . yet in the midst of his despair he finds a source of direction in a world without fixed points of reference. In the end his vision might be nos-talgic, even morosely sentimental: "We'll always have Paris." Despite bouts of self-pity, he displays a quiet strength borne of will and determination. A stranger, rebel, orphan, or seeker, the loner is characteristic of the most popular American heroes from John Wayne to James Dean, from Dustin Hoffman to Clint Eastwood.

The loner is no less ubiquitous in more intellectual American cultural expressions. As America matured and assumed a leading role on the world stage after the First World War, the most remarkable of a generation of American intellectuals and artists, including John Nobel, quit the coun-try for the moral void of Europe. Ernest Hemingway, Ezra Pound, John Dos Passos, Ford Madox Ford, Gertrude Stein, and others of the "Lost Generation" chose to live where the center had not held, in the Paris of the 1920s. They gloried in it, and found glory there. Existentialism and nihilism became them. They searched out nothingness and stared it down.

Their lives no less than their works are generally recognized as mythic epics. The most important myths, including American ones, are about transcending the fundamental isolation imposed by human consciousness; they are important because they teach us how this is properly done. There is strong similarity in this regard between the artistic expressions described just above and the history written by Frederick Jackson Turner.[4] In his Ur-history of the American West, Americans seek and transform the wilderness.

The transformation of Nietzsche's abysmal emptiness to a settled world, one laid out with reference to all of the reassuring benchmarks of modernity, constitutes one of the most important chapters of the American creation myth. We tend to view "the frontier" as primeval, dormant, awaiting the inspiring touch of civilization. This influences us even as we know on another level that the trans-Mississippi West was peopled when Europeans arrived, and that these people had formed distinctive ways of life. It is the way of creation myths to gloss over such details. Creation myths make certain ontological demands, one might say: they have to start from scratch. The cosmos before the advent of the organizing agency must be, as expressed in Genesis, "without form."

Of course, what Turner and the European settlers for whom he spoke overlooked was that "frontier" is a matter of perspective. To the Romans moving into what is now Great Britain, those isles were the frontier. They were nonetheless inhabited, as was the Biblical promised land. To understand how indigenous populations can be so conveniently overlooked, one must bear in mind that to all human groups, unknown land is unsanctified land, land that does not fit into the forms our assumptions about the world have so far taken. It is unfathomable and threatening until it is sanctified, until our belief and value system has been stretched to make room for it or, more likely, until we tailor the land to our preexisting notions of what the real world should be.

The real world to all peoples is the homeland, which is the geographic center of the known earth. It is made sacred by its connection with heaven, usually visualized as a vertical axis that runs from heaven through earth to the underworld, and connects the three planes of existence. This, the *axis mundi,* can be a natural formation, like Mount Fuji, Temple Hill, Ayers Rock, Mount Meru, or the Black Hills (the last of these sacred to the Lakota). Or, it can be of human construction: the pyramids in Egypt and Mesoamerica, Babylonian ziggurats, henges in ancient Europe, the Kaaba in Mecca, Angkor Wat, Borobudur, any number of Christian cathedrals and churches or Buddhist, Islamic or Hindu temples. Eliade said that even the house was designed after this pattern of the world; he called it an "imago mundi." The Plains Indians of North America, who were nomadic in historic times, regarded the sky "as a vast tent supported by a central pillar; the tent pole or post of the house is assimilated to the Pillars of the World and is so named. This central pole or post has an important ritual role; the sacrifices in honor of the celestial Supreme Being are performed at the foot of it."[5] On the secular front, edifices like the spires of the Kremlin and the Washington Monument, although not geographically central, aspire to political centrality.

The rest of the earth is legitimated by reference to the center. Topographic and other important features are located according to cardinal direction and sometimes distance from the center. Cardinal directions are associated with gods, colors, holy places, and a host of other phenomena that appear in the mythology of the occupants of the homeland. Peaks, valleys, lakes, and so forth are typically scenes of mythical activities of gods subordinate to deities who utilize the *axis mundi* as a passage between heaven and earth. Such is the feeling of a people for their homeland that, as an example, "When Rome decreed that Carthage should be destroyed, the Carthagenians beseeched the Romans to 'spare the city' and instead to 'kill us, whom you have ordered to move away. . . . Vent your wrath upon men, not upon temples, gods, tombs, and an innocent city."[6]

When one passes beyond the boundaries imposed upon the land by the cosmological framework, one is in uncertain and dangerous territory, *terra incognita*. It may be inhabited by unknown gods or by creatures beyond human ken. European sailors, typically, imagined monsters. And they feared that they would fall off the edge of the world. Our human response is to establish benchmarks as quickly as possible that harken back to the known. A new *axis mundi* is fixed: A cross is planted on a foreign shore, a flag is planted on the Moon. The new world replicates the old: In the New World we have, to mention only a few examples, New Orleans, New York, New Brunswick, Nova Scotia, New Mexico. The Masai, moved from their homes in East Africa, "took with them the names of their hills, plains and rivers; and gave them to the hills, plains and rivers in the new country."[7] The deities that sanctified the homeland are transplanted: San Diego, Santo Domingo, Santa Fe. Humans bring with them their architecture as well, which mirrors the sublime pattern of the cosmos, just as the homeland does. Polynesian societies erected the supporting posts of their structures in alignment with the cardinal directions, placing sacrifices beneath them. Astronomers in the sophisticated civilizations of India showed masons where to place the first stone; at that spot the mason drove a stake into the ground in order to fix the head of the mythological snake supporting the world, the snake that symbolized chaos, the formless.[8] The Dutch, settling into the luxuriously forested river valleys of the strange North American continent, mined clay and built ovens for the bricks necessary to construct dwellings properly. Creation and habitation had to be done according to the proper form in order to produce form.

The people who occupy the *terra incognita,* those who are indigenous, are strangers and less than human until we establish their humanity. They are until then like the human figure God pressed from dust in Genesis (chapter 2, verse 7) before he breathed life into them. They must either prove themselves human in our terms, or our terms must be expanded. If this cannot be done, they will be regarded as especially cunning creatures, but treacherous because they cannot be expected to behave in human, predictable ways. Many in "our" group will argue that we should eliminate "them."

We know our kin are human (whatever else we may know or feel about them). The safest course is therefore to establish kinship with unknown peoples. While our fathers and father's fathers may be different, if our gods, who are ancestors even more venerable than our grandfathers, are the same, our kinship is established. Joint participation in ritual that refers, even obliquely, to such gods may be enough to establish kinship. The anthropological term for this is *fictive kinship*.

Kin, fictive or biological, may quarrel, may even come to blows, but nonetheless will recognize the basis for a continuing relationship and in general feel bound by a set of ongoing obligations. The behavior of kin is predictable to a degree that humans find reassuring, especially because life in most other respects is unpredictable. This is so even when behavior is predictably irritating, as with the stereotyped behavior of mothers-in-law in many societies.

Kin will also in almost every case form an alliance in conflicts that arise with others, including more distantly related kin. Kinship does not in every instance do away with conflict, but it does manage and direct it in certain ways. As the Arab proverb goes, "I against my brother, my brother and I against my cousin, my cousins and I against the village, my village and I against the world." This sort of predictability also is reassuring.

The dominant culture in the United States is one that has been carried by unsettled persons, confronted by the alien and unpredictable on all sides. Frederick Jackson Turner's "frontier" of the American West and the creations of the "Lost Generation" of American artists and intellectuals are metaphorical expressions of the human confrontation with nothingness. Anxiety about the uncertainties of life, a nagging suspicion that human existence is without meaning and that a universal chaos will at any moment erupt through the veneer of humanly contrived order has been, almost certainly, a concern of all humans in all places and times. This anxiety is rooted in the human capacity for reflective thought, which is the ability to visualize oneself as a discrete entity in the world and, therefore, something subject to the uncertainties and finalities therein. Such anxiety in modern America, however, has been exacerbated by the circumstances of immigration, the separation from the massive reality of homeland with its reassuring sensory and cultural benchmarks firmly tied to a traditional apprehension of the world. Anxiety has been further heightened to angst by the efforts of modernists to debunk the myths and discredit the traditions, in all their variety, that have imbued humans with a sense of meaning and purpose. It continues today with certain postmodern schools of thought that deny any intrinsic meaning or coherence to the past.

Whatever the merits of the postmodern project, it has met with dubious success. According to a Gallup poll taken in 1991, 90 percent of Americans prayed at least every week and had never doubted the existence of God, 80 percent believed in miracles and expected to be judged for their behavior after death. More than half believed that the Devil existed, compared to 39 percent who reported this belief in 1978. Some observers of religious behavior, in fact, have suggested that the United States is today undergoing yet another "Great Awakening," like those of the mid and late eighteenth centuries and early nineteenth century. Many have puzzled over why, as Lawrence Wright has put it, "in the Western world, religion is an especially American phenomenon."[9]

It seems likely that the reason for the constant resurgence of evangelical fervor in the United States has to do with the sorts of experiences offered by religious organizations, which are ones of ritual interaction. The rites, regalia, and emotionally laden ceremony of formal religion hold great attraction to the alienated since they reduce their sense of isolation.

Americans throughout the history of the country have had reason to feel alienated from both the traditional realms of home and community (which are at present especially fragmented and unstable) and the modern world of capitalistic intercourse. Successful participation in the latter usually requires a tool kit of rational skills unavailable to many. Success in the world of capitalistic exchange also typically requires a single-minded commitment to participation. Many have allegiances that curtail this kind of participation, such as women with commitments to their families that prevent them from pursuing a career full time, those with strong personal interests of little value in the marketplace, anyone not willing to relocate for career advancement; generally, those who fail to assign the highest priority to developing and marketing their skills. Exclusion from effective participation in the capitalistic marketplace engenders alienation in itself, but exclusion also opens up the individual to economic and political exploitation, which deepens that sense of alienation. Today and historically, the socially excluded and alienated are those most likely to become involved in evangelical movements.[10]

This book is about a time and place on Turner's "frontier" where alienated groups, "strangers in a strange land," met and interacted in ways that I call "rituals" to form a common world for a time. As we shall see, alienation was rife on the frontier, not only among those of European ancestry like the Bents and their partner Ceran St. Vrain, who were scrambling for a secure position in the burgeoning capitalistic order that was replacing that of inherited privilege, but also among the Native American and Hispanic populations.[11]

The world that was jointly constructed by these three cultural groups was eclipsed, eventually, by the ambitions of political and business interests in the East. Tragedy befell the architects of the common world, especially the Plains tribes, who, in the perception of Eastern immigrants in the latter half of the nineteenth century, became the demons that dwelled in the Nietzschean abyss. The builders of Bent's Old Fort fared poorly too. Charles Bent lost his life; William Bent lost many of those most dear to him as well as his "castle on the Plains." By that time, however, the world they had created had gained a tenacious hold. Indeed, multiculturalism is still the hallmark of the Southwest. The "middle ground" constructed during the years of Bent's Old Fort's occupation has been diminished, but is still firm enough so that no serious attempt to separate the Southwest from the United States has been made since the signing of the Treaty of Guadalupe Hidalgo.

Bent's Old Fort and the Cultural Landscape of the Southwestern Plains

Before the arrival of Europeans, the broad Plains just east of the southern Rocky Mountains was an area sparsely occupied by pedestrian nomads. For thousands of years small groups of hunters and gatherers followed the banks of major rivers and streams like the Arkansas and its tributaries. Staying close to the water and its plant and animal resources, they seldom ventured into the inhospitable countryside. The names of these groups were never recorded. What became of their descendants we do not know.

After them came the wide-ranging equestrian Plains tribes. These populations had been displaced from ancestral lands much farther to the east by European intrusion: by the disease, social dislocation, and ensuing tribal warfare that became rampant during the seventeenth and eighteenth centuries. Among them were the Cheyenne and Arapaho, the Native American tribes most prominent in the history of Bent's Old Fort, who had been forced from their homes in the vicinity of the Great Lakes. The acquisition of the horse presented opportunities eagerly grasped by these refugees. Mounted buffalo hunting, raiding and warfare, and trade became the essential elements of a way of life which then developed.

The names of these tribes have been etched indelibly into the cultural landscape of the entire southwestern Plains. On maps one finds Cheyenne County and Cheyenne Wells in Colorado, Cheyenne County in Kansas, Cheyenne, Oklahoma, and Cheyenne, Wyoming. Colorado has Kiowa County, Pawnee and Comanche national grasslands, and the city of Arapaho. There are, as well, Brule, Arapaho, and Oglala, Nebraska; Comanche, Oklahoma; and Kiowa National Grasslands in New Mexico.

There are also names from a later, darker period in Native American history, when these peoples were violently obliterated from the landscape of the Southwest: Chivington, Colorado, memorializes the man most responsible for the Sand Creek Massacre. This atrocity took place only a day's march from Bent's Old Fort and Bent's New Fort. By the time of the 1869 massacre, William Bent was one of the few whites in Colorado willing to speak against the extermination of the Native Americans. Not far from Chivington is Sheridan Lake, named for General Philip Henry Sheridan, famed for saying, "The only good Indians I ever saw were dead."

For the most part, however, it is as if the cartographers were most active during the few years of the early nineteenth century when one could say that the Cheyenne and Arapaho were north of the Arkansas River, the Kiowa and Comanche to the southeast, the Shoshoni to the west, the Ute to the northwest, and the Apache to the south (see fig. 1). This arrangement of Native American occupation of the land, though, was contingent partly upon European and American interaction with Native American groups, interaction that grew in frequency and intensity as trails were developed and the trickle of emigration through these courses grew to a flood. It was also determined by the military prowess and fortunes of the various tribes. After the introduction of the horse in the latter half of the eighteenth century, the once sparsely inhabited region became the arena of ceaseless conflict between now mobile groups of Native Americans.

For more than one hundred years, from about the mid eighteenth to the late nineteenth centuries, all Plains Native American groups were transformed into something very like light calvary units. Striking out in all directions, they attempted, as Lewis and Clark noted of the Shoshoni, to "keep up the war from spring to autumn."[12]

The presence of the Spanish was one of the principal reasons for Native American interest in the southwestern Plains—the Spanish brought horses. The Comanche in particular quickly grew adept at "harvesting" horses from the Spanish herds. In the equestrian culture of the Plains Indians, the horse was not only an essential part of the technological basis of that culture; it was also, as Frank Roe and others have documented, the basic form of power and wealth.[13]

The horse played a large role in Comanche mythology. The traditional view of the world is one less segmented than (or segmented in ways different from) the modern one, and so the horse was seen as "valuable" in all ways. Regard for the horse was also religious. Horse riding provided a way to reenact mythological occurrence. The horsemanship of the Comanche awed all who observed it, even other Plains tribes. A Comanche could ride a horse bareback at full gallop in such a way as to conceal himself completely from an observer. To accomplish this, he could crawl under the belly of the horse and back up over either its head or tail. Because of such skill and their proximity to the herds of the Spanish, the Comanche generally held trade in disdain, unlike most other Plains groups and in sharp contrast with the Cheyenne and Arapaho. The Comanche felt they had no need of trade, they simply took what they wanted.

In no small part because of the depredations of the *indios barbaros,* the barbaric Indians, including not only the Comanche but the Apache, Kiowa, Cheyenne, Arapaho, and others, colonization on the northern

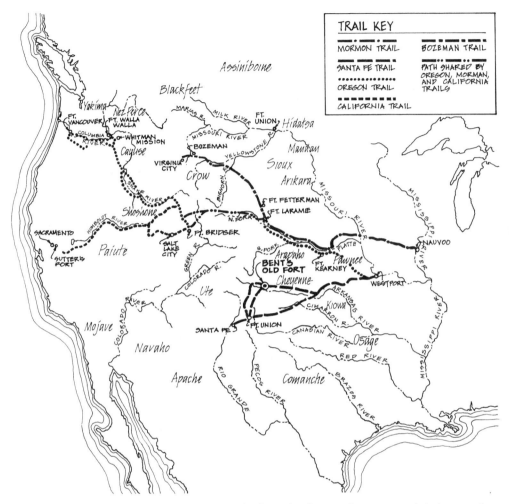

Figure 1. Location of Native American groups in the early nineteenth century and their westerly immigration trails. (Map by Steven Patricia.)

frontier of Spain's New Mexico territory was a very tenuous matter. The strategic importance of Spanish settlement (later, Mexican settlement) here was well recognized, however, by the seats of government farther to the south. Spain's anxiety regarding the security of her northern colonial boundaries was dramatically intensified by the purchase of the Louisiana Territory by the United States in 1803.

Despite Spanish efforts, the preservation of ties to these settlements or even of social order at the northern outposts proved extremely difficult. Of the Spanish who inhabited the northern frontier of colonial New Mexico, Father Juan Augustin de Morfi could only despair. In his report to church officials, "Account of Disorders in New Mexico, 1778," he observed that settlers "live isolated with no one to observe them [and] there are those who have no inhibitions about running around stark naked. . . . [O]ther moral disorders proceed which shock even the barbarous Indians. . . . [R]obbery is looked upon as a tolerable expedient . . . blatant violence is the rule."[14] Here we can see the contingency of occupation working in contradictory directions: The Native Americans were present because of the Spanish, but the hold of the Spanish and (that of the Mexicans after their independence in 1821) on the area was made tenuous by that very presence.

Beginning about 1831, with the construction on the northern bank of the Arkansas River of the trading post eventually known as Bent's Old Fort, American traders undertook what proved a pivotal role in the theater of events in the Southwest. Operating from this post, just over the northern border of Mexico (see fig. 2), the Americans formed trading alliances with Native Americans. In doing this they encouraged raids upon Mexican settlements, if only by offering a ready market for livestock stolen in raids on *rancherias*. The resulting destabilization of the northern Mexican borderlands helped pave the way for the 1846 American takeover of the Southwest.

Previous forays by Americans into the area had been unsuccessful. Not only the Spanish had resisted but also Plains tribes that, unlike the Comanche, had developed a stake in the exchange of European and Native American goods. The Cheyenne and Arapaho in particular feared that the American newcomers would usurp their position in this trade. For their part, Spanish authorities routinely jailed or otherwise detained and harassed American traders and trappers attempting commerce in Spanish New Mexico, beginning with Zebulon Pike's visit in 1806. In doing so, they were heeding the warning given by the former lieutenant governor of Spanish Louisiana who said, in 1804, that the Americans were intent

Figure 2. Location of Bent's Old Fort. (Map by Steven Patricia.)

upon expanding "their boundary lines to the Rio Bravo." His immediate superior, Baron de Carondelet, the Spanish governor of Louisiana, had been greatly concerned with American attempts to expand their fur trade through "control" of Native American groups.[15]

As early as 1803 Spanish officials had come to see the Plains Indians as an essential buffer to American encroachment, provided their loyalty could be obtained through participation in the *Spanish* fur trade.[16] By the second decade of the nineteenth century, the Spanish were trading with the Kiowa on the Arkansas, the Pawnee on the Platte, and the Arapaho in the area between the Arkansas and the Platte. Near the confluence of the Arkansas and Purgatoire Rivers, almost at the spot where Bent's Fort would soon be built, the Spanish engaged in a regular trade rendezvous with the Plains Indians.

In the first thirty years of the nineteenth century, then, the Plains Indians who frequented the territory of the southwestern Plains were enmeshed in a tenuous trading alliance with the Spanish. Even though this alliance was not enough to end raids by the Native American trading partners on Spanish settlements, it seems to have ameliorated them. The cautious alliance was enough to forestall American entry into the region, and this was of strategic importance to the Spanish. For example, in 1811, Manuel Lisa, renowned founder of the St. Louis–based Missouri Fur Company, sent Jean Baptiste Champlain to trade with the Arapaho in their southwestern home and the Spanish traders in Santa Fe, hoping to open the Southwest for this American company's trade. The Arapaho killed Champlain and two of his party. The Arapaho attacked many such contingents from the north who ventured into or near the Southwest in the years that followed. As late as 1823, several American trappers were killed near Taos. The resistance to American traders by Native Americans (particularly by the Cheyenne, their close allies the Arapaho, and the Kiowa) in the southwestern Plains, and in the Southwest, seems to have peaked in the 1820s.[17]

The buffer between Spanish and later Mexican (southern European) and Anglo (northern European) territories, judged crucial by Baron de Carondelet, was removed with Mexican Independence in 1821. Without Spain's strict prohibition of commerce with the United States, the floodgates were opened for American influence. The tide of American power surged, alarming the newly independent Mexican state and prompting efforts (described in chapter 4) to replace the barrier.

In the 1830s Native American resistance to Anglo-American presence in the southwestern Plains diminished. This can be attributed to the construction of Bent's Old Fort in about 1831. A fictive kinship relation-ship was forged between the Anglo builders and their principal trading partners, the Cheyenne and Arapaho. The man most responsible for the fort's construction and operation, William Bent, then established actual kinship relations with the most influential family among the Cheyenne by marrying Owl Woman, daughter of White Thunder, the Keeper-of-the-Sacred-Arrows and therefore the Cheyenne's most important holy man. To White Thunder, the marriage of William Bent to his daughter may well have seemed an eminently logical extension of his control over sacred objects. For the Cheyenne, this kinship ensured an unending sup-ply of European trade goods such as firearms, ammunition, knives, beads, and other manufactured items as well as providing a source of the power associated with these goods—the white man's medicine.

The alliance established a new order in the region. The Cheyenne and Arapaho realized major gains in military power and social prestige from their ties to Bent's Fort and became preeminent among the Native Amer-icans in the area. They used this power and prestige to the advantage of the Anglo owners of the fort—and coincidentally to the advantage of United States interests—by imposing a roughly territorial arrangement on the nomadic, warlike tribes of the region. They laid claim to the im-mediate vicinity of the fort, north of the Arkansas River. The Kiowa were kept to the south, the Pawnee to the northeast, the Shoshoni and Ute to the east, the Sioux to the north, the Apache to the south. Within the trad-ing empire of the Bent & St. Vrain Company—an area encompassing most of present-day Colorado, northern New Mexico, the panhandle of Ok-lahoma, the northern tip of Texas, southern Wyoming, southern Ne-braska, and western Kansas—a measure of stability reigned, despite con-stant skirmishing among Native American groups. Depredations upon the Bent & St. Vrain Company, their wagon trains, and their employees and associates were minimized. At the same time, the Native Americans' trade-based ties with the Mexican population to the south were largely sundered as the Bent & St. Vrain Company usurped the position of the southern traders. Raiding on southern settlements increased (sometimes at the explicit urging of Anglo traders), further jeopardizing Mexico's hold on its northern borderlands.

In contrast to the Mexicans' inability to maintain order, the Bent & St. Vrain Company, operating from the fort that was called a "castle on the Plains" by the press of the day, *embodied* the notion of order. The implicit comparison of the Bents and their close associates with feudal lords is un-derstandable. In their letters, the Bents speak of whipping those who had violated the rules of the fort. The trappers and other employees of the company as well as the Cheyenne and Arapaho on several occasions served as a private army. The fort and grounds were a model of and modeled a new world—a world of modernity, capitalism, and individualism.

The construction of Bent's Fort tipped the balance of power in the southwestern Plains, and ultimately in the Southwest. By the time General Kearny's Army of the West marched to Bent's Fort in 1846 to reprovision and repair before the invasion of Mexico, the New Mexico territory had been won. The army marched into Santa Fe and raised the American flag without firing a shot. The New Mexican governor, Manuel Armijo, had fled with the army that might have provided organized resistance. It is almost certain that Armijo, along with his second-in-command Colonel Diego Archuleta, had met shortly before the invasion with the American trader James Magoffin, who negotiated the terms of the Mexican military withdrawal under orders from President James Polk. Magoffin raced to catch General Kearny's army at Bent's Old Fort and advised Kearny to wait there before marching into Mexico, giving Magoffin time to meet with Armijo and Archuleta.[18] Juan Bautista Vigil, the lieutenant governor (and former employee of American traders), remained in Santa Fe and gave a speech that warmly welcomed the American troops. From Santa Fe, Kearny's troops marched westward to help secure the California territory for the United States.

In early 1847, months after the American victory in Santa Fe, authorities in Chihuahua sent cadets from the military academy there to Taos, to foment a revolution against the American occupation.[19] Charles Bent and other American traders and entrepreneurs were assassinated during the subsequent disturbances. Most of those killed were associated in one way or another with the Bent & St. Vrain Company. This selectivity was that of a planned military operation, although the incidents which transpired during the insurrection were portrayed then, and were even construed by the surviving members of the Bent & St. Vrain Company, as the behavior of an enraged local mob.

In the early morning of January 19, 1847, at Taos, groups of the local populace, many of them Pueblo Indians well primed by liquor and demagoguery, were directed to the homes of influential Americans and American sympathizers. Charles Bent, by then the first governor of the newly established New Mexico Territory,[20] was shot with many arrows and scalped in front of his family. His New Mexican wife and their children and New Mexican in-laws who were present (including Kit Carson's wife) were left unharmed. In the days that followed, other property owned or associated with the Bent & St. Vrain Company was attacked, including ranches at Ponil and Vermejo. But by the end of January, the revolt had subsided, never having engaged the New Mexicans beyond those with special grudges against certain influential Americans. The disgruntled included individuals who had figured highly in the now crumbling power structure of New Mexico, particularly those representing the Catholic Church. Padre Martinez, for example, was always thought by Ceran St. Vrain and Kit Carson to have been involved in Charles Bent's death.[21]

The Bent & St. Vrain Company never recovered from the consequences of the American victory in the Mexican War. Charles Bent's death was one of many blows to the company, and was felt especially by William Bent himself. The fortunes of William Bent's allies, the Cheyenne and Arapaho, rapidly declined. As immigrants streamed into the territories secured by the Treaty of Guadalupe Hidalgo, signed on February 2, 1848, they brought sickness and depleted the herds of buffalo upon which the Native Americans depended in so many ways. Conflicts became increasingly bitter and violent. Many of William Bent's children sided with the Southern Cheyenne in the struggle that soon followed and became some of the most feared warriors in the tribe. One of William's sons' rage was such that he vowed to kill his father. The Plains tribes were soon regarded as demonic by the new Anglo majority, and attempts were made to eradicate them. The most infamous incident in the genocidal effort was the horrendous Sand Creek Massacre, in which many, including women, children, and old people, were killed and dismembered. Those Southern Cheyenne, Arapaho, and members of other Plains tribes who survived the violence were relocated over the next decade to reservations in what is now Oklahoma. In 1849, a year after the treaty that ended the Mexican War, William Bent abandoned Bent's Old Fort. By many accounts he attempted to destroy it as he left.

Beyond History: Cultural Dynamics and the Human Past

The geopolitical boundaries of the United States were dramatically expanded by the Treaty of Guadalupe Hidalgo. The southernmost border of the United States would now run along the Rio Grande instead of the Arkansas River; from the Rio Grande the boundary line would continue westward to the northern shore of the Gulf of California, then on to a point on the Pacific Ocean just south of San Diego. The nation was embraced by the two great oceans of the world, and Manifest Destiny was realized.

The United States annexed what are now the states of California, Nevada, and Utah, almost all of Arizona and New Mexico (the rest was acquired by the Gadsden Purchase from Mexico in 1853), about half of Colorado, and portions of Wyoming, Kansas, and Oklahoma. Even today the area annexed constitutes about 25 percent of the continental United States. The treaty also confirmed American title to Texas. And only a month after the formal declaration of war with Mexico in 1846, the United States came to an agreement with Britain on the division of the Oregon Territory. American resolve, and the likelihood of American success in its military adventure far to the south, probably had much to do with prompting a cooperative attitude on the part of the British.[22]

These are the facts of an American history replete with the dates of wars and treaties and the actions of prominent men; American history as it has been commonly taught in high school and undergraduate courses, the history of history books. But the annexation also signaled changes in the *cultural* landscape of the United States that were no less important than the magnitude of territorial expansion. Sweeping changes had taken place among and between the three distinct cultures that met in the Southwest and on the southwestern Plains prior to the beginning of the Mexican War in 1846: the Native Americans, the Anglo-Americans who came from the Eastern United States, and the Spanish (later Mexicans) who came from the south. Without them the war would not have fulfilled the territorial ambitions of political and business leaders in the United States. The Southwest could not have been won and held.[23]

In a widely quoted passage from his *On War* (first published in 1833), Karl von Clausewitz wrote, "War is not merely a political act, but also a political instrument, a continuation of political relations, a carrying out of the same by other means."[24] He was a spokesman for the *rationalization* of warfare, seeing it as a tactical means to larger, strategic ends. Clausewitz was very influential among the political and military leaders of nations in the nineteenth century (and has been so since that time). These leaders in the United States were sophisticated enough to capitalize upon the cultural juggernaut set in motion when the Bent & St. Vrain Company constructed their fort. Their military objectives, and the strategic ends, could not have been achieved had the cultural phenomena not first occurred.

Despite the Americans' superior technology and armed force, a determined resistance by the Mexicans would have presented formidable and probably insurmountable logistical challenges. The distance of New Mexico from the gateway cities of Independence and St. Louis would have precluded a massive, sustained assault. The relatively primitive overland transportation technology available then, as well as the dangers from the harsh environment and warlike tribes over almost 1,000 miles of the Santa Fe Trail, meant that soldiers and supplies could only move slowly and with great difficulty. Given this, ongoing guerilla activity would probably have won back the province for Mexico.

It was not American military power, per se, which prompted the Mexican government to rapidly withdraw from New Mexico. It was, instead, the inroads made by the culture of modernity that had rendered the Mexican position there untenable. Compare the response of the New Mexican populace with the strong resistance met by the United States military as it penetrated more deeply into Mexico later in the war. There, foreigners were deeply distrusted. Periodic riots were fomented against foreigners throughout the first half of the nineteenth century in this more southern area, and the belief was widespread among the peons there that foreigners were devils, "heritics with tails who plotted to enslave honest Mexicans or lead them off to Hell."[25] Such regions were relinquished under the treaty of 1848.

Histories that have dealt with the annexation of the Southwest have recognized the desire that existed among the New Mexicans for continuing and expanding trade, but they tend to see this in terms of abstract economic interests. What this approach does not sufficiently respect is the way life was experienced by the New Mexicans in the second quarter of the nineteenth century. Trade, almost entirely connected with Bent's Old Fort, was seen as constituent of a new way of life. Its importance to New Mexicans had to do with the creation of new identities in a new world.

New identities were constructed by means of social relationships based in marriage, membership in secret societies, and friendship and kinship, as we shall see, but increasingly all of these relationships derived from those initially established by participation in the Santa Fe Trail trade. Further, playing a role in this trade involved one in a truly global grid of economic transactions. While this subjected one to market forces over which one held little control and that might be manipulated, such drawbacks were not apparent. In any case they were more than counterbalanced by the expansion of parochial horizons.

In the handbill issued by the governor of New Mexico, the Mexican Donaciano Vigil, who replaced George Bent after his assassination, we can see the impact of the new ideology (fig. 3). The handbill, issued by a Mexican and presented in Spanish, refers to aspects of modernity espoused

TRIUNFO DE LOS PRINCIPIOS CONTRA LA TORPEZA !

EL GOBERNADOR INTERINO DEL TERRITORIO,

● A LOS HABITANTES DEL MISMO.

CONCIUDADANOS:—Enfatuada la gabilla de Pablo Montoya y Cortéz en Taos y
Mora, con hacer sacrificado a su capricho al E. S. Gobernador y á otros ciudadanos
pacíficos, y comenzado su grande obra de robar,—con el saqueo de las casas de sus victimas
y cuyos principios han proclamado para hacerse proselitos; ayer presentaron accion en los
Suburbios de la estancia á las fuerzas—del Gobierno restauradoras del orden y de la paz,
desgraciadamente para ellos, en el que el lugar, acabó su brio, pues fueron derrotados con la
perdida de muchos muertos y cuarenta y cuatro prisioneros, sobre quienes recaerá el fallo
de la Ley. De la crueldos y perdidas se componian sus huestes, de forma que puede decirse
que la guerra hera de la canalla contra los hombres honrados y juiciosos; no se señala hasta
hoy uno solo de estos ultimos, injerido entre esa caterba de fuciosos, si no es acaso forzado
por temor de ser muerto en sus manos, ó robados sus bienes de fortuna. El Gobierno
tiene tales datos, y se complace de que dentro de diez dias acabará la inquietud en que os
ha puesto la voz de alarma proclamada en Taos, volviendo la paz precursora de la felicidad
de la patria, á tomar su asiento en el altar de la concordia y confianza reciproca.

Los principales fautores de la conspiración, si pudieren aprenderse recibiran el premio
merecido a tamaños crímenes y el Gobierno que ahora se ha visto forzado á proceder ener-
gicamente para quebrantar la cabeza de la tira rebolucionaria que habia comensado á aso-
marse en Taos; tomará despues medidas lenitivas para consolidar la union de todos los habitantes de este hermoso paiz bajo la egida de la ley y dela razon.

Yo espero pues, que tranquilizados ya los animos de los temores pasados, no penseis si no
en las seguridades y proteccion de la Ley, y uniendoos á vuestro Gobierno le participeis
vuestras luces para ayudado por vosotros, participaros el engrandecimiento que os
desea vuestro conciudadano y Amigo.

DONACIANO VIGIL.

Santa Fé, Enero 25, de 1847.

PROCLAMATION OF JANUARY 25, 1847
by Donaciano Vigil, Provisional Civil Governor

TRIUMPH OF PRINCIPLE OVER LEWDNESS

The Civil Governor of the territory to the Inhabitants of the Same

FELLOW CITIZENS: Angered by the tax (burden), Pablo Montoya y Cortez of Taos
and Mora, having sacrificed to the whim (killed) the ES Governor and other
peaceful citizens, and commenced his grand act of robbing - with the sacking
of the houses of his victims, and whose principles proclaimed him a proselyte;
yesterday fought in the yards and cattle sheds with the forces of the governor
who restored order and peace, disgracefully for the insurgents, in that place
it all finished with vigor, then were routed with the loss of many dead and
forty-four prisoners, on whom will fall the judgement of the law. His forces
were composed of rogues and misguided persons, of such types that it is
possible to say that the war was against honorable and judicious men; it was
determined today that no honest or judicious man entered that crowd of
(fuciosos), even if faced with fear of dying by the insurgents' hands or being
robbed of their wealth. The Governor has such data and is assured that within
ten days the insurrection that has caused the voice of alarm to be proclaimed
in Taos will finish, and we will return to the previous peace and happiness of
the country, taking its seat at the altar of reciprocal concord and
confidence.
    The principal authors of the (illegible) have learned that they will
receive their just deserts for such large crimes and the Government, forced to
proceed energetically to crush the head (illegible) revolutionary that had
started to appear in Taos, will then take lenient action to consolidate the
union of all the inhabitants of this beautiful country under the aegis of law
and reason.
    I thus hope, that the spirits of the past fears are calmed, you will
think in the security and protection of the law and uniquely in your
Government who participated in your fights to help you, we will take part
together in the growth you desire with your fellow citizen and friend.

Santa Fe, January 25, 1847   Donaciano Vigil

Figure 3. Proclamation of January 25, 1847, by Donaciano Vigil. (Courtesy New
Mexico State Records Center and Archives, Santa Fe, Historic File 193, TANM 98;
translation by Melinda Berge.)

by the new government. This can be seen in the use of the terms "principle," "reciprocal concord and confidence," "aegis of law and reason," and "security and protection of the law." These, the handbill implied, offered more advantages to the general populace than did the old, corrupt form of government dominated by a hereditary class structure. The Hispanic archivist at the New Mexico Archives who copied the handbill for me commented that such sentiments had been gaining ground among the citizens of New Mexico prior to the invasion, and so the appeal was probably effective.

Evidence of the crucial role played by the Bent & St. Vrain Company in advancing such sentiment can be seen in the lack of resistance met by American forces in precisely the areas where the company had been most active. The determined resistance farther to the south was on the far reaches of, or beyond, the company's area of operation. It was in this southern area that virtually all United States casualties were sustained. It was from there as well that the short-lived uprising against the newly installed American government in New Mexico that claimed the lives of Charles Bent and his close associates was instigated.[26]

Most histories have given scant attention to the role played by the other, very distinct, precapitalist cultures in the annexation of the Southwest. The Native Americans, particularly the Plains tribes, acted as a kind of "wild card" in what *became* a political game for the control of the Southwest. They were motivated by considerations of value and wealth not readily appreciated from a modern viewpoint. Nonetheless, Bent's Old Fort, which through modern eyes was an economic institution, was instrumental in making allies of the Plains tribes at a crucial point in time. Again, this was done through trade—but more precisely though rituals associated with trade.

Overall, it was as if Anglo-American culture had established outposts in the "hearts and minds" of the members of what might have otherwise been competing cultures. More than one hundred years after the events described here, the American invasion of Vietnam would be compared by some historians to the Mexican War. The similarities are evident. Each was an attempt to extend American control into territories occupied by cultures with very different views of the world, and each severely strained logistical lines because the territories to be occupied were so distant. Unlike the ambitions of the United States in Southeast Asia, though, the American effort in the Southwest was successful.

Furthermore, the transformation was a part of global process, one that continues today. Culture is what is known in physics as a *dynamical sys-*

tem, a system that in changing precipitates still more change. It exhibits in this way something like a "life" of its own. It is also a *complex adaptive system,* one that carries with it schemata, compressed information with which it can "predict" the environment. Murray Gell-Mann notes that "in biological evolution, experience of the past is compressed in the genetic message encoded in DNA." Gell-Mann suggests that institutions, customs, traditions, and myths are comparable schematas operating within human societies.[27] This is the stuff of culture, which provides the "worlds" in which humans (with the possible exception of those in schizophrenic states) must dwell.

The joint project of world construction in the Southwest was made necessary by the dissolution of key social relationships *within* the cultures that met on the southwestern Plains in the nineteenth century. Father Juan Augustin de Morfi wrote to church officials of the breakdown of a colonial social system isolated and under attack not only figuratively, by competing belief and value systems but also literally, by the *indios barbaros.* The *pobladores* of the small Spanish settlements, in de Morfi's view, lived without the social order of even the wild nomadic Indians and were much less civilized than the settled agricultural Pueblo Indians.

Native American groups in the southwestern Plains like the Cheyenne and Arapaho had been displaced from the Great Lakes area by the pressure of other groups migrating from farther east, who themselves had been displaced by the Europeans. Their populations had been greatly decimated by war and disease, and the structures of their society, accordingly, had suffered great dislocations.[28]

Anglo-Americans, whatever their motivation for venturing west—be it to escape an untenable social situation or to advance an entrepreneurial scheme—typically suffered from their dissociation with the social institutions they had left behind. There is abundant documentation of the conflict, violence, and alcohol abuse rampant on the "frontier."

Few forms of constructive social interaction were available with which to knit these diverse, fragmented groups together, especially when they first met. There were no formal institutions in which all might participate, like churches, schools, or governments; they had no sports or forms of theater in common. The most important form of interaction available was trade, which formed the basis for fictive kinship relations. In the eyes of the Native Americans, the practice of ritual exchange established a common, mythological ancestry. Exchange with Mexican trading partners operated in a similar way to establish social as well as business relationships. The Anglos became "known" and "human" to both their Native

American and Mexican trading partners, as did Native Americans and Mexicans to Anglos. This accomplished, Anglos often took Native American or Mexican wives, as did all most involved with the Bent & St. Vrain Company, further solidifying relationships between groups. These three groups formed for a time what Richard White termed a "middle ground," a realm of "shared meanings and practices."[29]

Part of this formation included the acceptance of certain basic, modern assumptions about the world. The most important of these is that the world is better apprehended and manipulated by the individual, as opposed to the group. It is, then, the task of each individual to construct an identity seen as personal, as opposed to social. This results in a "high-grid, low-group, ego-centered" society, as described by cultural anthropologist Mary Douglas, one marked by a relatively low sense of collective solidarity and an emphasis on position within a hierarchical social "grid."[30] Mobility depends upon competence and luck. The degree to which an individual possesses these characteristics determines his or her success in amassing quantities of significant items, valuable in exchange. If the cultural transformation of the Southwest was and is not complete, it has been at least thorough enough that no serious attempt has been made to alter the political boundaries established in 1848.

Culture and Identity:
The Formation of New Worlds

Succeeding chapters in this book will describe and explain how the project of "world formation" in the southwestern Plains and the Southwest proceeded and will deal also with the historical consequences of that project. Ritual operates to sustain or alter the human "world" that culture provides. Ritual behavior that altered the cultures of the Southwest included the protocols inherent in the architecture of the fort and the use of the landscape surrounding the fort. This humanly altered landscape constituted "calcified ritual." We can identify more obvious ritual associated with the fort, too: the rituals of exchange associated with the trade itself, drinking and feasting, gaming, the marriages and other long-term relationships established between individuals belonging to the various cultures that met at the fort, the ceremonies so much a part of the secret societies to which the Anglos and Hispanics belonged, and ritual aspects of warfare.

Ritual occurs at the nexus of subjectivity and objectivity, where the individual is especially receptive to socially assigned meanings. Often, ritual is not recognized for what it is, and thus is "fugitive." Nonetheless, it is through ritual that "realms of meaning" are created. In chapter 2, I look at these realms as they appear and are formed in both "traditional" and "modern" societies.[31] The many similarities between the traditional and the modern worlds that we will discover in this book argue strongly for a fundamental sameness despite superficial differences.

In ritual behavior people influence one another by expressions of all kinds, including alterations they make to the physical world. Most of this is nonverbal. Nonverbal information is often remarkably effective in the long run because it affects how we *feel* as much or more than how we *think*. We hear our national anthem and we are frequently moved both emotionally and physically; we may feel a bit giddy, tears may even spring to our eyes. Similar sorts of reactions may occur when our team wins, at weddings, walking through the Sistine Chapel, visiting our senator in his or her office in Washington, at evangelical religious services, watching the sun set over the mountains, at concerts, accepting an award, touching a loved one, smelling pine needles on Christmas morning or incense in a temple.

All these experiences are fraught with *meaning*. But the meaning is almost always inchoate. If we plumb deeply enough into the meaning, however, what we will find is that it has to do with relationships with other humans, membership in a group. The archetype for any human relationship and for any human group is the family, in whatever form it might occur.

Humans are notoriously neotenic. To an extent much beyond other animals, they retain childlike characteristics throughout their lives. They play and learn as long as they live. They desire attention from their social superiors; they will compete with and battle each other for it. They seek out "charismatic" leaders, people who appear bigger, stronger, more competent, and more knowledgeable than they about arcane matters. Conversely, they are attracted to childlike qualities in other humans, in animals, in imaginary figures. They feel affection and delight in the presence of such characteristics, and are often moved to nurture whom or whatever displays them. In doing this, they are acting out the role of the idealized parent.[32]

Reenactment of such idealized roles (the cast drawn from actors enmeshed as well in historic contingencies) is the basis for ritual. All cultures practice ancestor worship of one kind or another. "Traditional" societies openly regard the ancestors as gods. Virtually every Thai household, for example, has a shrine in which images of the Buddha are positioned next to photographs of parents and grandparents, other kin, and the king. There are complex and sophisticated societies today in which the leader of the society is revered as a deity. In Japan, for example, the king is taken by a large percentage of the population to be in a lineage that began with the Sun Goddess Amaterasu Omikami, the prime mover of the universe. In a real sense, all parents create the universe for their children, and this kind of belief can be seen as a poetic statement of that fact. Many people in modern Western nations that no longer have kings take remarkable interest in surrogate royalty, following the antics of Princess Di and Prince Charles closely, or those of the "kings" and "queens" of the entertainment, sports, and business worlds, the "stars" in the popular heavens. People copy the appearance and behavior of such trendsetters, very much as a small child unselfconsciously and proudly models herself or himself after caregivers. Or they consciously and willfully act out their rejection of such role models through their appearance and behavior. A great number of people spend considerable time in genealogical research, hoping to discover some godlike individual in the family tree. Though leadership is not hereditary in modern societies, most citizens then act out in numerous ways a paternalistic relationship between societal figureheads and themselves. In the United States, virtually every action and utterance by the President or First Lady accessible to the public will be eagerly scrutinized and will evoke an intense emotional response from some quarter of society.

A certain definition of ritual is used throughout this book, one that recognizes the pertinent connections between neoteny, collective human activity, and the alterations to the material world produced by such activity. Chapter 3 introduces ritual as *the reenactment of the actions of the ancestors and gods that transformed primordial chaos into the order of the world*. Mythology is most concerned with these sorts of actions by the ancestors and gods, too, and while myths are verbal expressions, they are almost always offered in a ritual context.

Ritual, on one level, is an expression of nostalgia, the nostalgia of the lost worlds of the womb, the breast, and childhood. This nostalgia for "paradise" is common among all human groups—and is felt no less by those modern man considers to be primitive.[33] Our desire for "oceanic oneness" is a neotenic one, and therefore ubiquitous among humans. The neotenic nature of this desire structures ritual behavior in predictable ways, ways that conform to universal childhood experiences and perceptions.

Societies considered by modern observers to be traditional often have already been altered by contact with more modern cultures. As a case in point a ritual that is one of the most celebrated symbols of "Indian-ness" in both anthropological literature and popular culture, the Sun Dance, can be shown to have been shaped in no small part by early European influence; I explore this in chapter 3. It occupies a liminal position in many ways, including that it attends to a concern for individual "redemption" as well as the traditional preoccupation with the restoration of universal harmony. It does this by implying a timeless model of paradisiacal harmony that incorporates these modern concerns.

In part because of this, the Sun Dance seems strangely familiar to modern observers. It expresses the competitive, warlike, and individualistic culture of the Plains tribes. This culture has been appropriated by modern American culture, in which it operates, in turn, as a paradisiacal model by which to legitimate unbridled concern for self and self-advancement. The effect of this model is likewise made through ritual, although this is done covertly in the personalized experience of novels, motion pictures, television epics, other artistic representations, and historical accounts. In considering the uses to which the Plains Indian culture has been put, it becomes obvious that ritual operates in both traditional and modern societies, albeit in disguised forms in the latter case.

I want to emphasize in this book that ritual, operating from its neotenic base, is the primary means by which culture in all of its aspects is constructed, including those aspects of culture we have relegated to the realm we commonly term ideology, like symbol and myth, as well as to social and economic realms. The way ritual reconfigures and reconveys symbol can be observed in the case of the central symbol in the Sun Dance, the Sun Dance pole (or medicine pole).

The Sun Dance pole is the *axis mundi,* the connection between heaven and earth, between what is mundane and transitory and what is sublime and eternal. From the pole hangs a Sun Dancer (or Sun Dancers), a scene which evokes memories, among some, of Christ on the cross. I favor an historic connection (as do others), the reworking of an ancient ceremony in the eighteenth century by the Plains tribes who were attempting to infuse it with a renewed potency in the face of societal trauma brought about by European disease and European encroachment on many fronts, cultural as well as territorial. I think it likely that the Sun Dance was reworked to more closely resemble the crucifixion scene. But I also think there is more to the connection: Both symbols follow a logic peculiar to ritual. Sir James Frazer's classic anthropological work, *The Golden Bough,* deals in part with the rituals of sacrifice and renewal that so often occur at sacred trees. Christ and the "tree of the cross" can be seen as an instance of this. So is the Sun Dance, which employs a medicine pole that originated as a tree selected, blessed, and cut by shamen. Simon Schama, in his book *Landscape and Memory,* provides a listing of sacred trees from cultures around the world (and often these were bedecked by human bodies as sacrifices or were the dwelling places of sacred animals, spirits, or demigods). He includes

the Persian Haoma, whose sap conferred eternal life; the Chinese hundred-thousand-cubit Tree of Life, the Kien-mou, growing on the slopes of the terrestrial paradise of Kuen-Luen; the Buddhist Tree of Wisdom, from whose four boughs the great rivers of life flow; the Muslim Lote tree, which marks the boundary between human understanding and the realm of divine mystery; the great Nordic ash tree Yggdrasil, which fastens the earth between underworld and heaven with its roots and trunk; Canaanite trees sacred to Astarte/Ashterah; the Greek oaks sacred to Zeus, the laurel to Apollo, the myrtle to Aphrodite, the olive to Athena, the fig beneath which Romulus and Remus were suckled by the she-wolf, and, of course, Frazer's fatal grove of Nemi, sacred to Diana, where the guardian priest padded nervously about the trees, awaiting the slayer from the darkness who would succeed him in an endless cycle of death and renewal.[34]

These I take, as I do all symbols, as having been contrived according to the dialectics of a peculiar culture, but referring finally to a relationship shrouded by the haze that accompanies emerging consciousness in infancy, the relationship between child and caregivers. It is a relationship charged with awe, adoration, fear, love, feelings of dependence, nostalgia, longing, shame, and a host of other, even more inchoate emotions, or emotions peculiar to certain cultures for which we have only awkward terms in English. It is also the relationship that creates the (individual) world for every human, and must be replicated in order that the (collective) world continue. It is the only really ubiquitous human experience (all humans were born and were once infants, all who reach adulthood were given some care by someone), and so provides the common ground upon which a society constructs meaning.

The *axis mundi* is a necessary prop in the ongoing collective renegotiation of the terms of human existence, a material manifestation of the renegotiation that occurs everywhere in much the same way because it refers to the most basic parameters of human existence. Considering this, it seems little wonder that it is given form, in similar ways in many places, as "living" spires, links, or columns between the ancestors and gods that by this connection make earthly beings human and real. The connection is sometimes imagined as phallic, sometimes umbilical, often both. At the axis, individuals and societies are "reborn," and so the birth passage is often represented as well.

The human body in its imagined spatial relationship to the ancestors and deities becomes a model for generative symbols. Richard Sennett, in *Flesh and Stone*, noes that "vast as the Pantheon is, the building seems uncannily to be an extension of the human body."[35] The *oculus* (literally, eye) at the top of the dome forms a column of light at precisely the correct astronomical moment on the central square in the floor of the Parthenon, the *umbilicus* of the building and of the Roman world. Indeed, replicating the umbilicus in conquered territories became an essential ritual in the cobbling together of the Roman empire. Sennett says, "To found a town, one sought on the ground a spot that reflected directly below the point where the four parts of the sky met, as if the map of the sky were mirrored on the earth." His further comments reveal the significance of this:

The umbilicus had immense religious value. Below this point, the Romans thought the city was connected to the gods interred in the earth; above it, to the gods of light in the sky—the deities who controlled human affairs. Near it, the planner dug a hole in the earth, a hole called the *mundus* which was "a . . . chamber, or two such chambers, one above the other . . . consecrated to infernal gods" below the earth's crust. It was literally a hellhole. In making a city, the settlers laid fruit and other offerings from their homes in the mundus, a ritual to propitiate these "infernal gods." Then they covered the mundus, set up a stone square, and lit a fire. Now they had "given birth" to a city. Writing three hundred years before Hadrian, the Roman Polybius declared that the Roman military camp must consist of "a square, with streets and other constructions regularly planned like a town"; conquest was meant to induce that birth.[36]

The symbols here, as everywhere, are constructed by ritual behavior; ritual, everywhere, ascribes to the ancestors and gods human acts of creation and recreation, accomplished through the media of the human body and human intercourse, both sexual and social.

In chapter 4 I begin to examine in greater detail events associated with the establishment and operation of Bent's Old Fort, as recorded by historic documents, historians, and ethnohistorians. Bent & St. Vrain Company was of truly impressive dimensions, a fur-trading enterprise second only in the United States to the giant American Fur Company (with which it maintained close ties). Of the fort, itself, David Lavender, author of the definitive history of Bent's Old Fort, says that "from the Mississippi to the Pacific there was no other building that approached it."[37] Those associated with the fort, particularly the Bent brothers, Ceran St. Vrain, Kit Carson, William Fitzhugh, and Uncle Dick Wootton, were legends in their own time. Eastern newspapers and pulp novelists reported, and embellished, their exploits to an audience that looked upon them as explorers and heroes. They were regarded much as later publics admired Charles Lindbergh or the astronauts of the early American space program.

Bent's Old Fort operated within a previously existing trading network, one with its roots in a prehistoric trade between villagers and nomads of at least 600 years ago, or well before European intrusion. Much of the success of the company was due to the intercultural skills of the principals, by means of which they found a position within that network and linked it to the global capitalistic trading network.

In chapter 4 I look also at the initial entry of Europeans into similar trading systems in the East, almost three hundred years prior to the establishment of Bent's Old Fort. The entry produced profound effects in the Native American cultures before permanent European settlements were established. Cultural dislocations that followed even the first exchange of goods, incidental to European fishing along the Northeast Coast, generated intense competition for positions as middlemen within that trade.

The culturally transformative and constitutive effect of trade is the subject of chapter 5. Daniel Miller, in *Material Culture and Mass Consumption,* took note of "a major tradition in anthropological theory, where it is exchange, often viewed in terms of the polarity of gift and commodity, which is seen as constitutive of society itself."[38] Anthropologists who have attended closely to this polarity include those as varied as Claude Lévi-Strauss and Marshall Sahlins.[39] Most follow Marcel Mauss in constructing a dichotomy between the gift—generally seen as an episode in an "endless" series of exchanges—and the commodity, the sale of which carries with it no (obvious, at least) further implications.

Certainly there is much to this. On the southwestern Plains, it is obvious that for the Cheyenne, Arapaho, and related Plains tribes exchange established the "fictive kinship relations" of classic anthropological theory and set in motion ongoing cycles of mutual obligations. Anglo-Americans, in contrast, engaged in trade as a part of an entrepreneurial scheme, which was tied into a worldwide market system. The ultimate motive here was not so much the forging of immediate social ties as it was profit. Wealth is as essential to the formation of a viable, socially based identity within a market economy as fictive kinship relations are to the formation of identity in a traditional, or gift, society. There is no doubt that the trading practices of the Anglo-Americans and the Native Americans differed sharply.

But the tendency to construct dichotomies often obscures crucial similarities. Mary Douglas points out that gifting continues in market societies and continues to set up obligations.[40] Moreover, even exchanges in market societies are conducive to ritual behavior, because in all societies, even capitalistic ones, trade acts to validate or alter identities. The effectiveness of these rituals can be seen in regard to the groups who met at Bent's Old Fort. The Bent brothers and the other principals of the company, for example, formed genuine and lasting relationships with those in the groups with which they traded.

The symbolic meanings attached even to those items that might appear overtly functional are also taken up in chapter 5. Our modern assumptions about the primacy of function obscure our perception of this symbolic importance. Objects come to symbolize relationships based in fictive kinship, or imaginary relationships. These meanings are ritually assigned. Symbols may be arbitrary, but they refer to ubiquitous human relationships.

Archaeological evidence, supported by firsthand accounts taken from individuals who were at the fort, indicates, for example, that firearms traded to Native Americans there were of minimal functional value. Certainly they were no improvement over the indigenous bow and arrow for use in either warfare or buffalo hunting. Nonetheless, they were much desired trade items. They were valued, like peace medals and beads, more for the ways they were employed to constitute new identities in a world increasingly dominated by modern, Anglo interests than for their more obvious function. They were tokens of relationships with the "Great Father," a term commonly used by Native Americans to refer to the President of the United States, and other fictive kin among the Anglos.

We live in the world our parents and, by extension, our ancestors and gods, created. Ritual maintains that world and in some cases transforms it. In doing so, it shapes the material world. Chapter 6 discusses how the shape of the material world then directs behavior into ritualistic patterns, and so reinforces our cultural assumptions regarding the world of our ancestors.

Yi-Fu Tuan describes how ritual was and is, in a sense, calcified by increasingly sophisticated technologies, including writing and architecture:

A ritual dance, while it lasts, converts a meadow into a sacred space, but as soon as the dance ends the space reverts to a meadow. As distinguished from story-telling and ritual, writing and architecture are typical achievements of high civilization. They make it possible for human beings to greatly multiply, elaborate, and refine separate worlds out of inchoate experience, and to make these worlds a permanent part of the human environment. Pericles' funeral oration faded into thin air, but the written version remains effective to this day in lending glamour to Athens. Ancient Greek activities and ceremonies, which partitioned space, have long since disappeared, but the segmented spaces themselves remain in the landscape as ruined temples and agoras. Behavior is evanescent, but its architectural shell may endure. In the modern world, almost every human activity and state of being has its special architectural frame. Clearly defined and marked places exist for eating, defecating, and sleeping, for playing volleyball and badminton, for rich and poor, for drivers and pedestrians. These places have a high degree of integrity. They are reserved for special functions, and departure from the accepted practice is strongly discouraged. Incommensurable no more mix in physical space than they do in the structures of logical thought.[41]

The fort and the surrounding landscape operated, in a way analogous to the "medicine lodge" of the Plains Indian Sun Dance, to ritually convey both the new social order and the legitimation of that order embedded in the seeming "naturalness" of the massive and imposing structure.

Ritual took the form of *panopticism*, a system of surveillance that results in each individual monitoring and controlling his or her own behavior according to the pattern set by a central authority. The fort was an effective model of a panoptic structure, a reflection of the set of behaviors associated with panopticism, behaviors that were imposed by the architecture of the fort on all who lived and visited there. This system of surveillance eventually advanced the economic and political interests of the United States in two ways (as well as operating more generally to propagate modernity). It produced intelligence by which to direct economic, political, and eventually military incursions. At the same time, it tied the operation of the fort to the larger political agenda of the United States as directed by the federal government. It is of more than passing interest here that once Bent's Old Fort secured its position within the *overall* panoptic system that tied Washington, D.C., to its interests on the frontier, the interests of the individuals associated with the Bent & St. Vrain Company became subordinate to the federal agenda.

In chapter 7 I look carefully at how the panoptic connections between political and economic interests in the East and the trading partners of the Bent & St. Vrain Company were finally accomplished. In all cases, this was done through ritual means. Ritual exchange between the Bents and Native Americans established fictive kinship relations that were frequently strengthened by means of marriage or adoption, that is, by establishing real kinship relations.

What perhaps comes as more of a surprise are the fictive and actual kinship relations between the principals and others associated with the Bent & St. Vrain Company and the Europeans on both ends of the Santa Fe Trail. These ties were established to economic and political leaders in the East, particularly St. Louis, and to those politically and economically influential in New Mexico, especially in Santa Fe and Taos. Fictive kinship relations were expanded even further by the participation of company principals in nineteenth-century secret societies, specifically the Masons. Explicitly ritual interaction here cemented relations between those with common economic interests, a phenomenon that can be traced to its origin in eighteenth-century Britain. Modern ends were thereby realized through traditional means.

With the establishment of American political hegemony in the Southwest, ritualistic cultural interchange broke down between Anglos and Native Americans (although not between Anglos and Hispanics, because many of the latter by now were assuming roles in the rapidly burgeoning capitalistic economy). What transpired next is the subject of chapter 8. Political hegemony opened the way for economic interests that did not depend upon trade with Native American groups. Without the ritual exchange by which to reaffirm a common humanity, Native Americans were increasingly regarded as the "other," the "red devil," a less-than-human impediment to progress. A further rationale for ascribing this alien status was supplied by the Civil War, when Native Americans were considered by many to be "red rebels." The cessation of ritualized relations with Native Americans culminated in a campaign of extermination, typified by the horrendous massacre at Sand Creek, where men, women and children were killed and mutilated in ritualistic ways that denied their human status.

The symbolism of this atrocity was to have a profoundly destructive effect upon Native American–Anglo-American relations. The Cheyenne and Arapaho became implacable foes of the Anglos, and they were ultimately removed from the vicinity of Bent's Old Fort to reservations in Oklahoma. Other Plains tribes met a similar fate. Native American cultures today continue to suffer the effects of this debasement. Native American groups displaying the most severe social ills today are those that suffered most from such humiliation, notably the Cheyenne, as well as the Sioux, who experienced a massacre similar to Sand Creek at Wounded Knee.

New Mexicans, however, had formed an embryonic middle class, with the social resources required to continue to participate in the capitalist economy that had fully emerged. Though New Mexico became a part of the United States, the Hispanics were not removed from their land, as were the Native Americans. Hispanics as a group continue to function more effectively in the modern environment, which demands the discipline of capitalism and individualism.

Today, the reconstructed Bent's Old Fort and its landscape, as well as replicas of items traded there, are employed in ritualistic ways. The discussion of this in the epilogue is intended in part to offer additional evidence for the persistence of ritual as an effective social mechanism in a patently modern environment. In the mythology of individualism, recognition of the "cult of the individual," as it was labeled by Tocqueville—recognition even of ritual itself and its power in the modern world—may be perceived as threatening. Ritual is essentially collective, and it usually operates at realms below the threshold of individual consciousness, that is, at a preconscious level. Neither of these qualities fits easily within the ideology of individualism. But regardless of the presence or the absence of recognition, the power of ritual remains.

This ritual operates in a number of ways, serving a variety of purposes. Perhaps the most evident is that the fort serves as a nationalistic symbol, but the situation is more complex than that. Certain groups associated with the reconstructed fort, particularly the voluntary history association, resist what they see as bureaucratized, regimented history. These groups organize opportunities to "relive" the past through a rigorous reenactment of it. This approach is termed here "evangelical" and is symptomatic among groups that feel excluded from more privileged social strata within a high-grid, low-group, ego-centered social organization. A more direct access to primordial, and thereby a more essential, reality is claimed by such groups—their approach is more "real" and the experience gained thereby more valid and important.

Some consideration is also given to Victor Turner's ideas about the transformational (as well as validating) uses of ritual, as these operate at the National Historic Site. Minority groups at the fort, as well as those identifying with such groups, are attempting to utilize the reconstruction as a "medicine lodge," a locus for rituals of inclusion.

The rebuilt fort was demanded, in a sense, by dramatic necessity. The very existence of the National Park Service's reconstruction of the fort is an unusual departure from that agency's policies, which generally allow only restoration or stabilization of existing structures. Without the reconstruction, however, ritual activity at the site would be much less effective. Each generation, after all, has the task of bridging the Nietzschean abyss between "I" and "others," between "we" and "they." When this is not done, the monsters emerge from the abyss once more.

CHAPTER 2

Realms of Meaning

The World in Traditional and Modern Terms

It is a July evening in 1992, and I am driving north on Colorado Highway 71 on my way from Bent's Old Fort to Stapleton Airport in Denver. I have stayed too long and am in danger of missing my flight, the "red-eye" back to Baltimore. On the advice of the superintendent of Bent's Old Fort National Historic Site, I am taking this shortcut, a two-lane road instead of the interstate, I-25. The superintendent has assured me I can make good time this way, and he is right. As he explained, "It's a straight road with no traffic. There's one little jog about fifty miles north that tells you to slow down for Punkin Center." I've been a little high on fatigue and caffeine for hours, but I am getting a bit drowsy now, so I pull over to get yet another Diet Coke out of the trunk of the rental car.

As I step out, I am struck by the silence. There are no headlights in either direction; there are no artificial lights *at all,* I realize. On an impulse I switch off the engine and headlights. The stars in the night sky, seen through this dry, clear air without ambient light, are brilliant. I am always surprised in a place like this that there are so many.

I think about the meteor shower of 1833, which the Cheyenne regarded as a sign that the world was about to end. Cheyenne warriors rode about on their war ponies, dressed and painted for battle, singing their death songs. From inside the walls of the newly completed fort, the Bents and their employees watched.[1] To the Cheyenne, as to people in all traditional societies, the heavenly bodies and their cyclical movements were the ultimate and most reliable benchmarks in their system of cultural meanings. Mircea Eliade has presented a strong case that such celestial phenomena are archetypal to the arrangement of territories, cities, and religious edifices in traditional cultures worldwide.[2] Of course, this works reflexively: Meaning has been previously *assigned* to celestial phenomena through their inclusion in ritual and myth. Further, by attaching their value and belief system to the arrangement and movements of the heavenly bodies, traditional peoples are linked to the eternal, the predictable; what is cyclical appears to change but is eventually proved immutable. If the connection is convincing, a traditional people finds refuge against the vicissitudes of time.

On the narrative level, the Big Dipper in Cheyenne mythology, for example, is the form taken by seven orphaned children. The eldest child, a young woman, was to be the bride of the White Buffalo. The other children did not want their sister, who provided for them, to leave, and so they took refuge in the limbs of a tree. The White Buffalo sent his herd to butt the tree. When the tree was about to go down, the children shot arrows into the sky and were drawn up behind the arrows to form this constellation.[3]

On the physical level, the stars in what we call the Big Dipper, the constellation Ursa Major, move. One can easily *watch* them move here on the Plains if one is outside and takes the time on any clear night (and nights are rarely not clear). But one can also watch them move back to where they were before, making a complete cycle. A line drawn through the two stars that form the far side of the cup of the dipper will connect with a star nearby, the star at the end of the handle of the Little Dipper. This star, which we call the North Star, does not move. The Big Dipper will make a complete circuit around the North Star every twenty-three hours and fifty-six minutes. As mariners in the Northern Hemisphere have known for centuries, the North Star offers an unchanging point of reference for navigation. Likewise, in the flat landscape of the Plains, as wide and changing as a sea, the North Star and other celestial bodies offered the Cheyenne orientation not apparent in the daylight hours.

This orientation was more than spatial, it was cultural and integral to the Cheyenne's sense of how the world was constructed. I can't help but wonder if the myth about the creation of the Big Dipper is a dreamlike reference to the relationship between the Cheyenne and the Anglos. This relationship became central to the Cheyenne way of life in the early nineteenth century. For about one-quarter of a century, while the Bent & St. Vrain Company operated their big trading post on the Arkansas River, there was a kind of marriage between the two groups. The Cheyenne were newcomers to this land, a long way from their ancestral home. In the traditional way of looking at human life, this is something like being orphaned.

A lifetime is filled with the changes and uncertainties that come with the passing of time, while myth is timeless and therefore eternal. Myth is thus the realm of the sacred. By participating in the rituals that mold the social world—the world of human events—after the sacred, each person finds consolation for the uncertainty and unfairness in his or her life and for the knowledge that individual life must end. Against what Eliade termed the "terror of history," traditional man arrays his myths, rituals, and symbols which, he believes, provide him access to a higher reality, one impervious to the ravages of time. Eliade observed that "an object or act becomes real only insofar as it imitates or repeats an archetype. Thus, reality is acquired solely through repetition or participation; everything else which lacks an exemplary model is 'meaningless'; i.e., it lacks reality." Such "primitive" ontology has a Platonic structure: "Plato could be regarded as the outstanding philosopher of 'primitive mentality.'"[4] According to such an ontology, celestial phenomena offer the archetypes— the "ideal forms"—and all else is only a reflection of these. The world would, indeed, seem to be coming to an end when the archetypes appeared to be falling from their exalted positions.

Standing alongside the empty road, I find myself remembering a conversation I had a few years before with a very modern friend, a lawyer living in Washington, D.C., who was going through a divorce from her equally busy and competent lawyer husband. Facing life alone, she said, was like looking up at the stars and thinking that there were more stars beyond the ones that you could see . . . and more stars beyond those . . . and more beyond that, endlessly. Doesn't this describe the estrangement from a traditional system of meanings that is so much a part of the modern condition?

From a modern, existentialist point of view, as Eliade has pointed out, "the man of traditional culture sees himself as real only to the extent that he ceases to be himself (for a modern observer) and is satisfied with imitating and repeating the gestures of another. In other words, he sees himself as real, i.e., as 'truly himself,' only, and precisely insofar as he ceases to be so."[5]

Modern man, in contrast, claims his "reality" by acting alone. He eschews a traditional basis for his behavior and takes delight in the intellectual exercise of debunking myth as illusion, portraying ritual as reactionary, and revealing the use of symbol to be manipulative. He constructs the world on his own, drawing from his "own" resources (not realizing that they are a part of his culture). In doing so, he recognizes implicitly, at least, that this task—to create oneself, to become the American "self-made" man, for example—is daunting to all but the most adept at modern life. Traditional peoples, in this scheme, are relegated to the ranks of the unenlightened. The enlightened, it is true, must cope with chronic existential anxiety as best they can, although they are sustained somewhat by the knowledge that this very anxiety anoints them as a member of a kind of cultural elite.

It is to this point, the point of absurdity, that modern Western thought has come. Modern man must validate his existence by proclaiming that such validation is not possible. In the *post*modern world, which many social critics say is at hand, all must avail themselves of the "bricolage" approach to world creation that Claude Lévi-Strauss once attributed to traditional cultures.[6] As traditional man once picked through the ruins of a traditional world, a world destroyed by modernity, salvaging fragments and fashioning them into a makeshift universe, so now modern man must adopt the postmodern strategy of mining the debris of the world he has turned against itself.

Reconciling Traditional and Modern Realms of Meaning

The nihilistic strain of postmodern thought purports that the best one can hope for in a world that does not refer to a higher realm of meaning is to amuse oneself by arranging the bits of wreckage in clever ways. A problem with such nihilism is that meaning is tenacious. It is really inevitable, a prerequisite to human existence. Humans are self-evidently social creatures—they must coordinate their actions to survive. In doing so meanings are constructed, and not only linguistic ones. Other meanings reside in conventions of behavior that organize in myriad ways the shared and therefore external world. The most essential of these are learned by children as they imitate the actions of their caregivers. The dependency of the child on the caregiver for sustenance, approval, and attention is later projected into other relationships and provides the basis for social cohesion as well as the impetus for social change. Participation in society by the individual is regarded by her or him as meaningful insofar as it seems relevant to the pattern for human relationships set in childhood.

Because humans construct meaning in collective and largely noncritical ways, neither God nor history is really dead, despite the statements of Nietzsche a century ago and despite postmodern assaults on "metanarratives"—the grand overarching stories, such as broad recountings of history, that can validate or trivialize personal stories. Nietzsche's nihilism was strangely optimistic: It foresaw a new ground for knowledge in reason rather than faith. His God, anyway, had been dispatched earlier in the nineteenth century by Ludwig Feuerbach, who coined the aphorism "theology is anthropology." Although not as striking as Nietzsche's more famous maxim, it nonetheless evidences the replacement of a theological with a scientific order. Postmodernity, with its hyperawareness of perspective and mode of expression, questions science itself and, of course, anthropology and history. It is perhaps most succinctly what Lyotard has said, "incredulity toward metanarratives."[7] Such skepticism is common among thoughtful persons. How far is this statement from the philosophical starting point proclaimed by Socrates: "One thing only I know, and that is that I know nothing"? It is a mistake in any case to think that metanarratives are constructed only by thoughtful persons or, for the most part, in thoughtful ways. Critical evaluation, even deconstruction in the postmodern mode, of a metanarrative is not the same as the construction of one. Whatever incredulity may result is not sure to destroy the metanarrative or to alter it in important ways. Equally likely is that the metanarrative may be transformed in ways unforeseen by the critic.

For example, Nietzsche suggested "will" as the antidote to the sense of universal isolation that the modern viewpoint frequently engenders; he reasoned that man's existence in a cosmos without ordained order gave him the capacity to become whatever he determined to be, to become, finally, a "superman." Of course, Nietzsche did not have the final word, as no one ever does. Theologians, like Paul Tillich in his *The Courage to Be,* found ways to accommodate Nietzsche's intellectual position, building upon Feuerbach's legacy as Nietzsche himself (and Karl Marx) did, but in a different direction. Tillich argued that God exists apart from "theism," and that the courage to face this draws one nearer to the truth, a line of reasoning not dissimilar to the Eastern expression that "the Buddha you can name is not the Buddha."[8]

It should be evident, too, that for most who are unengaged with philosophical or theological niceties the proposition that human life is essentially without meaning is not a durable one. Perhaps it did not serve even Nietzsche well, who suffered from delusions of grandeur and persecution, and near the end of his life was put into an asylum. Lawrence Wright, a journalist who specializes in the foibles of religious leaders, described his own reflections on the matter:

"There is nothing more," I said to myself once in the middle of the night when I was forty years old and struggling once again with the questions that life poses at that hour. . . . I had an image suddenly of the spinning planet; behind it was a great screen, like a portable home-movie screen that rolls out of a tube. It was there to capture my projections. Then the screen snapped and rolled itself up, and I was looking into the stars. It was if I had never seen them so clearly. I realized that the screen had always blocked my view. I think it was also there to protect me from the coldness of space. . . . Atheism forced me to focus on the life I was actually living. Never before had I savored the sweetness of existence so intensely. . . . I felt comforted by the thought that I was living with the truth and not flirting with possibilities. I lived for a year in this state of crystallized certainty. Then doubts crept back in.[9]

Wright's doubts stemmed from his being "open to mystery." He pondered the unified field theory after reading an article about it. He began to think of all attractions as in some sense emotional, the sort of emotion he felt for friends, nature, community, ideas, and values. Then he realized that for him this emotional network was merely another way to envision God. It made him wonder "why the God idea is so resonant it keeps echoing inside me."[10]

In fact, God and history in this era of accelerated modernity continually reemerge in new forms that often are not recognized as such or appear twisted and perverted to those accustomed to the old versions. The recent evangelical movements sweeping the New World, emptying, for example, Catholic churches in South America, are such forms. So are "careerism," the environmental movement, the New Age, the "human potential" movement, the manias that people often develop about everything from railroads to the Civil War to Corvettes to soccer and baseball teams, the resurgence of concern with ethnic identity, and reform movements. These sorts of collective efforts strive to transform the condition of the world (or the world according to the group in question) from mundane to sublime. All implicitly recognize that history has not come to an end, that there is still work to be done and improvements to be made. All are driven by the concern that the human world is less than perfect; all imply that standards exist by which such judgments can be made.

The model for ultimate glory is always in the past. The classic Corvette, the New York Yankees in their heyday, human compassion before the church was corrupted or capitalism introduced, the purity of the race before mongrelization began, the human condition before ancient wisdom was lost or repressed, gracious living in the American South before the Civil War, Atlantis, Camelot (where the "rain never falls 'til after sun-down"), the Ottoman Empire to the Turks, ancient Rome to Italians, the American West to "rugged individualists" in the United States and else-where, the kingdom of Sukhothai to the Thais (when "the fields were full of rice and the rivers full of fish and the king took care of the people"), the fourteenth-century trading center of Malacca to present-day Malays, paradise before the Fall—nostalgia for lost worlds spurs us onward to an imagined future that is really an idealized past.

Modern politicians know this. We may not be privy to their reflections on the subject, but we can see that they deploy this knowledge in a practi-cal way at every opportunity. Mussolini, de Gaulle, and Thatcher, to men-tion only a few, explicitly or implicitly promised to reclaim national great-ness, and Hitler provides perhaps the most notorious example. John F. Kennedy was more subtle in his calls for a "New Frontier," which he por-trayed as an era of selfless patriotism animated by the spirit of American frontiersmen. At the 1992 Democratic convention, Bill Clinton went to great efforts to attach *his* programs for American revitalization to Kennedy's, which, in part because of Kennedy's assassination, have now attained nearly mythical status.

The Transformation of Time

I'm back on the road now and looking forward to the few hours of sleep I'll get on the plane. I'm weary, but I value these long soli-tary drives because they give me time to think. Not that this is entirely pleasant. When I am less preoccupied with the immediacies of work and conversation, anxieties that have been submerged by my hectic routine come bubbling up to my attention. I begin to worry about my family, my job, my research. These obligations, for all their rewards, require what my parents readily identified as "sacrifices," a term that I regard with both amusement and curiosity now, given my interest in the structure of reli-gion. I frequently sacrifice sleep.

I often sacrifice the "nowness" of life, too. And this isn't because as an archaeologist I spend a good deal of time thinking about the past. It is easy for me to relate the past to the present; my appreciation of the pres-ent is enhanced by my regard for the past. What takes me away from the present is the future. Even now I am engaged, as I so often am, in calculating how long it will take me to drive somewhere and to do what I need to do when I get there, when I should leave *there,* how long it will then take to travel to somewhere else, how long to accomplish what is needed at that locale, when I should leave *there,* and so on into the week, month, year, and years ahead. I have an urge to look at my appointment book, which I can't reach while I am driving, to plan with even more precision—and to see what I am forgetting. I, like so many inhabitants of the modern world, am obsessed by time.

This modern obsession with time has it roots in traditional concerns. The Cheyenne, like all premodern human groups, saw in the cyclical movement of the heavenly bodies reassurance that the world would go on despite the mortality of each human in the world. The path to immortality, predictability, and certainty in what humans can see to be a world replete with unpleasant surprises could only be gained through access to such eternal cycles. Access was through ritual, but in order to most effectively marry the fate of the individual with the eternal cycles the ritual had to occur at propitious moments in the astronomical calendar. Personal transition was tied to instants of cosmic change, so a great deal of attention was paid to the skies.

Societies everywhere have built devices by which to enhance their understanding of this calendar; these constructions are observatories, in effect. Being nomads, the Cheyenne built observatories that were not large in scale. They were constructed of durable materials, however, and so many remain today. They are called "medicine wheels," and they dot the Plains (see figs. 4 and 5). In plan view they are circles of stones; spokes and other features on the circle align with specific celestial objects as they rise over the horizon. The appearance of these objects, the sun and various stars, mark the summer and winter solstices, the fall and spring equinoxes, and other calendrical events. The sun and stars were associated with various mythological characters and occurrences.

It is not likely that astronomical devices were developed to aid the proper timing of subsistence activities. Traditional peoples are familiar with their environments to a degree that precludes the need for the kind of rigid precision provided by calendrical time. The !Kung of Africa, for example, can recall the location of a particular edible root or a place where they cached water from year to year as they travel their nomadic rounds. Also, the optimal time for hunting, gathering, planting, harvesting, and other subsistence activities varies a bit each year according to the weather, so it is not productive to begin such activities at the same calendrical date each year. Finally, in the case of nomads like the Cheyenne, the territo-

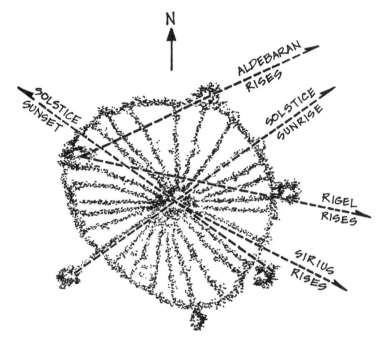

Figure 4. Plan view of a medicine wheel. (Illustration by Steven Patricia after map of cairn alignments by D. Grey; reported in John A. Eddy, "Astronomical Alignment of the Big Horn Medicine Wheel," *Science* 184, no. 414 [1974]: 1040; courtesy *Science*.)

ries within which they range are exceedingly large. The Cheyenne typically traded as far east as the Great Lakes and as far west as the Rocky Mountains. Since their observational devices were generally not portable, they could not be used as these nomads ranged over their broad territories.

What is more certain is that the astronomical observatories were used to schedule ritual. Ritual is the preeminent social mechanism, marshalling and organizing human energies in many ways. It is significant that groups with more sophisticated and complex social and technological systems constructed correspondingly more elaborate observatories. The Mayan civilization of Mesoamerica, to mention only one example from the many sophisticated ancient civilizations around the world that did likewise, built magnificent pyramids that functioned as components of an observation apparatus; one is still the highest humanly constructed edifice in Belize. With this apparatus the Maya identified cycles of time, varying in length from 52 to 256 to thousands of years. Pyramids were built collectively, and

Figure 5. Sunrise at Big Horn Medicine Wheel, aligning with cairns and spokes. (Illustration by Steven Patricia.)

so construction was a ritual of sorts. Each served as an *axis mundi* and therefore a center of ritual. These rituals were social mechanisms that stemmed from religious impulse but were appropriated for "practical" purposes. The Mayan civilization, like our own, has been described as being "obsessed with numbers and time." Whatever the practical benefits to society of this obsession, which might include the ability to better coordinate specialized societal components as society increases in complexity, in order to understand it one must see that the concern with and valuation of quantified time is neither wholly rational nor inculcated by means of the human capacity for critical thought.

Function and Meaning

At present, the practical, or functional, aspects of ritual are widely recognized in traditional societies. It is standard fare in ethnographies to document that subsistence activities in traditional societies, like hunting, planting, and harvesting, are accompanied by ritual. For example, in Thailand, the king, who in the minds of most Thais is holy, sows the first seeds of rice each year. Based upon such evident connections between ritual and function, many anthropological studies have emphasized, to the exclusion of other interpretations, how ritual works to distribute food or organize human labor or accomplish many other practical tasks. These studies have not only seeped into popular consciousness, they are *in accord* with modern popular consciousness that sees the world operating on a practical, functional basis.

Consciousness is largely determined by a complex of habitual behavior, though, and so modern consciousness, while it sees the function in ritual, is largely blind to the ritual in function. Driving down the road right now, most of what "I" am, objectively speaking, is occupied by habit or by convention, which is social habit. I am at this place at this time engaging in what archaeologists, who are sorts of anthropologists, conventionally do (even if the field by convention is unconventional). My driving habits are so firmly in place that I guide the car down the road on "autopilot." If I don't occasionally make a conscious effort to check where I am, I will probably drive right past some important intersection — and miss my plane. Both habit and convention are like that: They are convenient, even necessary (overall, people are safer drivers after driving skills become a habit), but they easily lead one to overlook important phenomena.

So it is with the habit of looking at the world from a "functionalist" perspective. From this angle, one can scarcely see that not only do functional activities conform in pattern to ritual ones, but that functional behavior depends upon ritual; it is socially inscribed by it. What motivates us to engage in the functionalist activities of the modern world is the traditional desire to locate ourselves in relation to culturally determined benchmarks. Ritualistic behavior reassures us that these benchmarks are of paramount importance, unchanging, and natural, and at the same time they establish our place among them. By ritual, "reality" is socially constructed.[11]

Even the most practical and "modern" actions must be to some degree ritualistic to be regarded as meaningful. They must conform to a pattern of what has transpired before, of what was *supposed* to have transpired before. Meaning is predicated upon pattern established in the past. As a rule of thumb, the more distant the past, the more profound the meaning, no less in modern than in traditional societies. Ultimate legal precedent, for example, is constitutional. Moral laws — drawn from natural or supernatural orders — are generally considered superior to civil or criminal ones, as in civil disobedience, conscientious objection to the military draft, or refusing to obey an immoral command issued within the context of a governmental bureaucracy. Geometry is based upon axiomatic statements (and the ancient Greek Pythagoreans saw a mystical significance in geometry, as have others, a significance that derived from reference to eternal truths). The most important inventions and discoveries are commonly considered those that occurred "first." In the arts and literature, what is important is usually determined by how closely a work approximates or how radically it departs from what is regarded as "classic." One may argue with the desirability of these attitudes but cannot dispute that they exist.

Modernity, then, is an amplification of certain trends that one can notice early on, as in the obsession of the Maya with "numbers and time." In fact, this obsession is an essential part of modernity, of the culture of capitalism, industrialism, quantification, abstraction—and individualism. We have internalized the modern view of the world and the basic values and beliefs that shape it and at the same time motivate us to sustain it.

Individualism and Identity

The burden of modernity is carried on the shoulders of the individual. As my parents were kind enough to tell me clearly, this involves sacrifice. Each of us caught up in modernity is supposed to emulate the central figure in the formal religion most associated with modernity, Christianity. We separate ourselves from the communion of humans (as we at least imagine this to exist in the traditional world) to pursue a higher path and thereby serve humanity better. As Yi-Fu Tuan has pointed out, individualism typically generates a sense of independence, a belief in the untrammeled freedom to ask questions and explore, a notion that the world can be assayed without illusion and from a rational standpoint and that the individual is responsible for his destiny. One might say (although Tuan does not put it this way) that individualism holds out the promise of achieving a godlike status, that of Nietzsche's "superman." At the same time, individualism is also characterized by a sense of isolation, loneliness, and disengagement; a loss of vitality and, as Tuan reflects, "of innocent pleasure in the 'given-ness' of the world, and, most oppressively, that the world has no meaning other than what a person chooses to impart to it."[12] In his opinion, modernity is essentially the Western response to the demands of civilization: "A civilization, unlike simpler cultures, is constrained to acknowledge explicitly the problems of society and individual, and to review periodically the relationship of the whole to the parts." A response in China was Confucianism, which did not stress this sort of segmentation of the world and saw "no conflict" among self, society, and nature.[13]

In the Western response, however, society is seen as "a strenuous theater in which each person must be adept at various roles played before a constantly alert and critical public . . . the constant need to be 'on one's toes,' of living in an artificial world, that is, a world that does not, like nature, run on its own but must be constantly maintained."[14] It may be argued (and I for one would argue this) that the "world" in the sense Tuan uses the term is, for the most part, socially constructed by all human groups. It, therefore, must always be socially maintained. What is not recognized is that the construction and maintenance of the world is largely accomplished through ritualistic means in both traditional and modern societies. It is the complexity of modern society that makes of these rituals "strenuous theater." Modern ritual may be found in the realms of business, law, academe, politics—in every sector of modern society. Specific sorts of training are required for roles in this theater, and training in skills for which there may be differences in aptitude is not equally accessible to all. Particular kinds of temperaments are more amenable to these than others. Some people are simply unwilling to make the "sacrifices" required by participation in the theater, sacrifices of communal lifestyle or of innocence, for example. And certain groups have been largely excluded, or excluded from consideration for the most prominent roles.

Females, for example, have not been regarded as suitable for certain roles. After working many years in a notoriously male-dominated industry and rising to the rank of vice president in the corporation, my sister was passed over for a senior vice president position. When she asked why, the CEO told her that "I wanted someone in the slot who, when I gave him the ball, would know what to do with it." The man chosen for the senior post was someone who had been a professional football player.

Those excluded from meaningful participation in high-grid, low-group societies either find the basis for an identity elsewhere or fall into *anomie*. My sister, after the discrimination she had sensed for some time was made explicit, quit her job. Although her work had once seemed to her to be an exciting and challenging part of her life, it had ceased to be meaningful. She then treated herself to a two-year hiatus, a time "away from it all." During this period she went birding. A birder keeps a list of each species she or he has observed. Observing 600 species within the boundaries of the United States is remarkable, 700 species is exceptional. My sister set herself a goal of 700 species. In a two-year period, she traveled to every state in the union (excluding Hawaii, which is "out of bounds") to accomplish this. But leavening this obsession with time and numbers was another aspect of birding: My sister enjoyed the fact that she could go almost anywhere worth birding and find human communion.

Her new avocation, like her old job, provided a structure based in tradition that could accommodate the modern preoccupation with rationality. Birders reenact the exploits of nineteenth-century naturalists, Charles Audubon among them. They are scrupulous in their record keeping. My sister tells me that ornithologists are often vague about bird locations, but a birder can direct you to the tree and the limb where a particular type of species might be observed.

Such specificity reminds me of discussions I have had with members of groups that would like to use the national parks in special ways. In addition to birders, such groups include, but are not limited to, rock climbers, Civil War buffs, French and Indian War reenactors, environmentalists, Native American groups, local historians, backpackers, and advocates for the preservation of old houses, bridges, machinery, and railroads. The activities of these groups have always struck me as being ritualistic in the way that birding is. A national park is especially attractive for this because it is a national theater and thereby provides recognition in a very public way and place. Each group has a pantheon of individuals with heroic accomplishments that will never be matched; all can relate the details of their fields of interest in astounding detail. Rock climbers can tell you who first climbed El Capitan and who set the first permanent piton. Railroad preservationists can tell you where to find the handful of craftspersons still able to repair rolling stock manufactured fifty years ago.

Local historians, notably genealogists and military buffs, are similarly attracted to national battlefields, and they have comparable knowledge of detail. Civil War enthusiasts often speak of troop movements as if they had been a part of the battle and of the participants in these battles with the familiarity one associates with relatives or close friends. Not infrequently, genealogical and military history interests converge. As a descendant of Turner Ashby, of "Ashby's Raiders" fame, once told me, "I don't know why other people get so excited about Ashby. *They* are not related to him." The speaker was implying, of course, that psychological identification with Ashby did not constitute as valid a relationship as her familial one. Nonetheless, such identification can be intense. At a reenactment of the Battle of Monocacy I attended a few years ago, each reenactor had been encouraged to conduct painstaking research into the life of the person they played in the battle. If the person had been a male soldier, they knew the names of the man's wife and children, where he had lived, his medical history, where he had served, and as many other details of his life as possible. If the soldier had been killed or wounded in the battle, the reenactor attempted to fall when and where he had, remaining in the hot sun or crawling slowly through the tall grass, as the role demanded.

Such interests are attempts to reclaim an identity threatened by the ways personal knowledge is trivialized in the face of global modernity. Knowledge of one's kin, family history, and the environment in which one lived once was both intimate and essential. Such knowledge is much less important in the modern world. Each person's grasp of the world is less sure because no one can know the whole, vast array of knowledge that modernity has to offer (even specialists, or perhaps especially specialists because they are so narrowly focused). For these reasons, knowledge is, as Anthony Giddens calls it, "disembedded." Giddens continues: "For the ordinary individual, all this does not add up to feelings of secure control over day-to-day life circumstances."[15]

To regain a feeling of control, one must reappropriate abstract knowledge and reembed it within one's span of sensuous control, in the *now* of the massive reality of one's immediate environment. What is true for avocational activities holds as well for vocational ones. Clifford Geertz observes that, "like sailing, gardening, politics, and poetry, law and ethnography are crafts of place; they work by the light of local knowledge." When one pursues these interests as a profession, one is bound to attend to the broad themes of the global, capitalistic network that ultimately supports one's profession. At this point, one becomes "absorbed in the artisan task of seeing broad principles in parochial fact."[16] Success depends upon the ability to apply one to the other. If one is able to do this in one's vocation, he or she has succeeded within the "grid" of capitalism; the rewards for this are such (in money, power, and recognition) that one can often sustain at least a limited sense of control.

The emotional rewards when one succeeds in applying principle (which in the modern world is similar to arcane, sacred knowledge) to experience are heightened when the element of risk is added to the undertaking. Risk is a constant factor in high-grid, low-group capitalistic societies. I recall sailing near a hurricane (before I was as enmeshed in the capitalistic grid and had time to sail). Because of stinging rain and huge waves it was impossible to know with any certainty where shoals or low islands might be lurking. The desire to know my position in relation to what were now essential benchmarks was truly urgent. After the storm abated a bit and the danger passed, someone on board said, "Why are we doing this?" No one had an answer. But I remember vividly the sense of wild euphoria we shared. I have since suspected that the Bents and the Cheyenne had a proclivity for this kind of experience.

Geertz, borrowing the term from Jeremy Bentham, has examined "deep play." "Deep play" means "play in which the stakes are so high that it is, from [a] utilitarian standpoint, irrational for men to engage in it at all."[17] Geertz made his comments as a part of his consideration of Balinese cock fighting, where men bet much more than they can afford to lose and where "in seeking earthly analogues for heaven and hell the Balinese compare the former to the mood of a man whose cock has just won, the latter to that of a man whose cock has just lost."[18] Nonetheless, Geertz was implying universal application. In part, the sense of what he says about this is like the American notion that "it's not if you win or lose, it's how you play the game." What is important is the demonstrated ability to play the game properly—and to be permitted to play the game.

But "deep play" tells us more than this. We can see that the value of reembedding activity increases as the emotional intensity associated with it rises. So it is with ritual. Explicit content, conveyed primarily with words, may be minimal, clearly secondary, or entirely lacking. What is important is that "sentiment" be generated, as Emile Durkheim, the "father of sociology," would say, and that this be accomplished according to an "ancient" pattern, one that mimics the behavior of the gods and ancients as they founded the world.[19]

Ubiquitous Mechanisms
in World Construction

Durkheim mistakenly associated the power of ritual and sentiment too exclusively with traditional peoples. And how strange it is, given the constant religious fervor in the United States as well as the popularity of quasireligious self-improvement groups and group psychotherapy, that this mistake has been perpetuated by academic and other thoughtful treatments of modern society. From about the time of Freud's publication of *The Future of an Illusion,* religion and what have been regarded as its trappings, including ritual and myth and to a lesser extent symbol, have been relegated to the realm of the unenlightened, the traditional, or, at best, "folk" worlds.

Rituals of initiation provide an example. Mircea Eliade has observed that "all pre-modern societies (that is, those that lasted in Western Europe to the end of the Middle Ages, and in the rest of the world to the First World War) accord primary importance to the ideology and techniques of initiation."[20] Most scholars minimize the importance of initiation in modern societies, although they recognize that it survives in the Christian baptism, Jewish bar and bat mitzvahs, and in other patently religious rites. What this modern point of view overlooks is that rites of initiation persist in fugitive forms.

C. G. Jung proposed, for example, that *individuation*, which he regarded as the ultimate goal of human life, was accomplished by ordeals which were initiatory in nature—*privatized* initiations, as it were, which were occurring in individual lives but were not generally recognized as what they were, and therefore were not usually discussed. Also, initiatory themes are common in artistic works, including novels, poems, works of plastic art, and film. Again, an experience once easily observed now occurs in a much less obvious way.[21]

Even more obvious forms of ritual in modern societies have not been given much scholarly notice. In a recent book, *Secret Ritual and Manhood in Victorian America,* a work that is one of the few that deal in a scholarly manner with the subject, Mark C. Carnes made a number of observations that seem surprising because of the lack of academic attention. Carnes noted that at the turn of the last century, between 15 and 40 percent of American men belonged to one or more of 70,000 fraternal lodges that had as their main order of business at every meeting the conduct of secret rituals. These rituals were arranged by degrees, each permitting entry into higher levels of belonging and realms of arcane knowledge. A majority of these men were middle class and often included the most influential men in a given town. Carnes quoted a contemporary observer, who wrote for the *North American Review:*

Members intent on "gratifying their desire" to accumulate initiatory degrees neglected work and wasted huge sums of money. He concluded that men joined the orders and attended lodges because they felt a "strange and powerful attraction" to the ritual. He explained, "There is a peculiar fascination in the unreality of the initiation, an allurement about fine 'team' work, a charm of deep potency in the unrestricted, out-of-the-world atmosphere which surrounds the scenes where men are knit together by the closest ties, bound by the most solemn obligations to maintain secrecy."[22]

Eliade, in fact, has repeatedly argued for the "irreducibility" of religious structure, saying that sociology and anthropology are often reductionist when they attempt to describe what are essentially religious phenomena in other terms. Modern, irreligious humans, even when they are determinedly irreligious, retain "a large stock of camouflaged myths and degenerated rituals."[23]

Why should this be so? It is because these are essential mechanisms for making sense of the world and manipulating meanings. When I board my airplane this evening, all around me will be people arguably as steeped in the rituals of exchange as any "native" group studied by anthropologists in Mesoamerica, Africa, or the Western Pacific. Their world was founded by Ford and Edison. They will be reading tales in the *Wall Street Journal* about demigods named William Gates and Donald Trump. The in-flight magazine will offer them products—time organizers, briefcases, plaques with inspirational phrases, books and cassettes with formulaic approaches to "management"—which will, according to advertisements, contribute to their success in what amount to magical ways. They will sleep and dream about establishing trading relations with powerful social organizations like Honda, 3M, Marriott, and Disney.

That we don't see the profoundly ritualistic nature of modern enterprises like business and science is due in no small part to the pattern laid out by Emile Durkheim . . . but more than that, to the world in which Durkheim formed his own, subsidiary world. This was the world of colonialism. Western nations developed interests in every part of the globe. This was not by any means the first time one human group had exploited others, but it had never occurred on this scale. Nor had it occurred in this way, one that was largely capitalistic. That meant that a region's resources could be transformed into money, and that this could continue as long as there was a market for those resources, or until the resources were depleted.[24]

Sociology, growing in the hothouse of colonialism, incorporated some of its basic assumptions. These assumptions provided the means, the motivation, and the justification for the exploitation of humans and the environment. Part of the justification involved the amplification of differences between exploiter and exploited human populations. These were projected in a reasonable way—rationality, after all, is a hallmark of modernity, and colonialism grew out of modernity. Sociology did not say, for example, that the exploited were infidels or innately inferior. Sociology (and anthropology) merely said that the exploited were "traditional" or "primitive" peoples. These terms, in the way they are most often used, gloss over the fact that tradition persists in the most technologically advanced societies and that modernity does not arise from a cultural vacuum, but is the result of an exaggeration of cultural characteristics and social practices that commonly exist among largely traditional groups.

I turn on the car radio now, to punctuate the sameness of the night countryside rolling by my windows and listen to music associated with one of the exaggerated social practices of modernity. Until the juggernaut of modernity determines the course of a society, its music generally deals with religion. In contrast, music in modern societies deals most frequently with romantic or, at least, physical intimacy. Romantic love is a watershed between being "traditional" and "modern." An arranged marriage today is looked upon as a sort of barbarism. Witness the public's fascination with the mass marriages orchestrated by religious cults. In fact, we accept as a hallmark of cults what these marriages demonstrate: the subordination of individual choice to that of the group. Romantic love establishes a person's independence from group authority. Parental authority is the archetype for this. I reflect that many of the fairy tales to which my daughter is exposed tell the story of a princess who falls in love with someone the king thinks to be inappropriate.

But romantic love, as the Romantic poets and other artists have pointed out many times, is a particularly thorny rose. Right now on the car radio a singer is lamenting his "achy-breaky heart" in a song that has been the one most frequently played for the past month on a jukebox in a La Junta restaurant, according to a waitress I talked with earlier today. I can believe that; I heard it three times during lunch. Romantic love well represents the problems faced by those who utilize reembedding strategies of the sort needed to maintain one's bearings in the modern world of change and movement. In societies usually described as traditional, each person is embedded by affinity to place, kin, and others with whom one cooperates throughout the course of one's life. Religion offers a poetic expression of these connections. With the collapse of the traditional community as a familiar place that offers daily opportunities for the face-to-face, often ritual interactions that reinforce one's place in the world, one must select "access points" to the modern social network.

These access points are relationships with others, and because there are in the modern world relatively few, one invests a much greater portion of one's attentions and energies to them than one would have to any single relationship in a traditional society. Friendship and, even more, romantic love require a level of intimacy rare in the traditional world, where such relationships are to a much greater degree prescribed. These intimate relationships are notoriously difficult to maintain—hence the singer's chronically "achy-breaky heart." As Giddens has said:

Personal trust demands a level of self-understanding and self-expression which must itself be a source of psychological tension. For mutual self-revelation is combined with the need for reciprocity and support; yet the two are frequently incompatible. Torment and frustration interweave themselves with the need for trust in the other as the provider of care and support.[25]

"Self"-knowledge, then, is a prerequisite for this and many other tactical maneuvers in the overall strategy of reembedding. It involves the knack of looking at all parts of the world "objectively" and of expressing one's operant principles and the facts pertinent to the phenomena in question (a relationship, or whatever it might be) in explicit ways. The linguist Basil Bernstein has called this an "elaborated" mode of communication and has marshalled evidence that indicates that this form of communication is learned, and learned primarily through the relationships a person has had in his or her family of origin. Families in which one's influence upon others is structured largely according to traditionally determined roles typically do not engage in explicit forms of communication; Bernstein calls this a "restricted" mode. On the other end of this communication continuum are families in which influence is determined by the content of speech, families which communicate in the "elaborated" mode. Communication in the latter families has more frequently to do with principle and fact, and less frequently to do with familial obligations.[26] The person in a family or a society which does not have habitual practices (and beliefs about the operation of the world) appropriate to modernity will likely experience difficulty with reembedding in the modern world. And reembedding will become increasingly necessary for each individual as modernity continues to make inroads all over the globe, as the juggernaut careens on its way.

I have borrowed the term "juggernaut of modernity" from Anthony Giddens, who comments that "the term comes from the Hindi *Jagannāth*, 'lord of the world,' and is a title of Krishna; an idol of this deity was taken each year through the streets on a huge cart, which followers are said to have thrown themselves under, to be crushed beneath the wheels."[27] With this image in mind, the term conveys even better some of the awesome power of modernity. This power is especially evident in transitional societies all over the globe in which populations from the countryside are rushing headlong into urban areas, where they exist in poverty and escalating anomie.

Pierre Bourdieu, an eminent sociologist, has looked at such societies, those in transition from "traditional" to "modern" status, including his own. About France, generally regarded as a modern nation by others in the world, many have observed that traditional values hold close sway over the peasantry even to the present. In the 1960s, Bourdieu investigated an increasing dissatisfaction among peasants that so many of their young people were unable to find marriage partners. These unattached individuals were termed "celibate." The poignancy of their condition had provoked the attention of the urban population in France (among whom it is somewhat fashionable to be able to claim peasant roots).

Bourdieu's research showed, surprisingly, that marriage was no less frequent among the peasantry in the 1960s than it had been in 1881. The dissatisfaction among the peasantry resulted from changes in demographic patterns of marriage and in changes in *attitudes* about celibacy. In the past, the youngest children had frequently emigrated to find marriage partners or had remained celibate, living with and caring for their parents as the parents aged. Marriages were less likely to be arranged for the youngest children. Because marriages were arranged, peasants had no need to develop skills required by courtship—in other words, to be able to present the "self" attractively to the opposite sex. When marriages were no longer arranged, those who married were those who had best mastered these skills, and these individuals could as well be the youngest in a family as any other in the birth order. Contributing even more to the dissatisfaction was that once the traditional pattern had been broken, there was no longer social recognition and support for the role of the celibate who cared for his or her parents during old age. The traditional order had changed, and those displaced had been unable to secure a position in the new one.[28]

Those who are threatened by modern practices and values but have less connection to the net of global modernity are in even worse positions. French peasants, after all, garner respect through the nostalgia of the more urban populations of the country, and they participate in the economy, sometimes in characteristically "French" ways, as with the production of wine or other "French" products, that resonate with nationalistic sentiment. But what of those relegated by the shade of colonialism to the status of "pure" primitives?

Bourdieu terms these groups the "sub-proletariat." These groups, such as those he studied in Algeria, live in traditional countries undergoing modernization. They become estranged from their customary lives and eventually must seek out work to obtain capital. Having few or none of the habits associated with modernity, they consider employment to be a result of luck, like winning the lottery. One of the habits the sub-proletariat has not developed is the exercise of applying rational analysis to the "objective" world, and so these people do not have the means by which to understand the basis of their position. It is among such groups that anomie is especially rife. Observing this, Bourdieu predicted that they might "slip into complete disaffection, marginality, and despair which might be fueled into militancy by self-seeking demagogues, or they might be encouraged positively to participate in the construction of a new society which would integrate their old values with modern, capitalist pressures."[29]

How interesting it is to consider Bourdieu's comment about Algeria in the 1960s in terms of the position of the Cheyenne in the early nineteenth century, as well as that of the Mexican peons to the south of the Arkansas River at that time. The Cheyenne world, in a manner of speaking, had fallen apart many times prior to the 1833 meteor shower, and each time the Cheyenne were faced with the task of piecing it back together. The most vulnerable to the plagues introduced by Europeans during the previous centuries, and so the first to die, were the old and the young. These were, respectively, the past and the future of the Cheyenne, both necessary to a meaningful present. In societies without writing, the old were key to the propagation of culture. The old were keepers of the mechanisms whereby the knowledge could be inculcated to society at large—the myths and the rituals. The young, as in all cultures, were the rebirth of the world; without them there was only death. There have been few more militant groups in history than the Cheyenne, who had risen from despair determined to defend as much as possible of their culture.

The most important Cheyenne leaders were charismatic ones, those who possessed "medicine." In an uncharitable mood an anthropologist might term them demagogues. Such leadership, no matter how it is termed, led the Cheyenne to a position that for a time was "embedded" in global modernity, as middlemen in a global exchange network. When the juggernaut of modernity careened in a different direction, however, the Cheyenne were excluded.

The Hispanics in New Mexico were not so easily dislodged. Marginalized first by New Spain and then by Mexico, their response to the American-borne expansion of modernity was not militancy but one that did, in fact, "integrate their old values with modern, capitalist pressures." But the Hispanics did not suffer at the hands of the Anglo newcomers as did the Cheyenne, in ways that denied their status as human beings.

Archaeology and Meaning

I imagine the presence of Sand Creek, somewhere in the darkness to the east, and feel the revulsion and sorrow that I experienced when I visited the massacre site by the cottonwood-lined dry creek a few days ago. The mood this precipitates reminds me that the story of Bent's Old Fort ended badly for both the Cheyenne and the Bents. It strikes me now that there is a tragic, poetic significance in the fact that a son of William Bent, Robert, was forced at gunpoint to lead Chivington's troops to the Indian encampment. Though he did his best not to play a role in the tragedy, even leading the troops through a deep river in the hopes that ammunition would be damaged, he could not prevent the massacre by his efforts. The script had been written. The story it contained was of the destruction of the traditional by the modern. It is one that has been told in myriad ways so many times since the advent of the colonial era that, until very recently, it seemed completely unremarkable to most.

But how true are such stories? Are there metanarratives and themes in history, and are they deterministic? Increasingly such ideas have come into doubt, particularly by postmodern social critics. François Lyotard says bluntly, "Simplifying to the extreme, I define *postmodern* as incredulity toward metanarratives."[30] Another who has done much to generate this doubt is Michel Foucault. He sees the process by which the past can be understood as operating like archaeology—an idea of great interest to me, having been an archaeologist for twenty years. In *The Archaeology of Knowledge,* Foucault says:

There was a time when archaeology, as a discipline devoted to silent monuments, inert traces, objects without context, and things left by the past, aspired to the condition of history, and attained meaning only through the restitution of a historical discourse; it might be said, to play on words a little, that in our time history aspires to the conditions of archaeology, to the intrinsic description of the monument.[31]

History, according to Foucault, depends upon metanarratives; archaeology is concerned with the means by which knowledge is created. "Knowledge" includes what we know, or think we know, about the past. About archaeology Foucault says, in part, that it

tries to define not the thoughts, representations, images, themes, preoccupations that are concealed or revealed in discourses; but those discourses themselves, those discourses as practices obeying certain rules. It does not treat discourse as *document,* as a sign of something else . . . it is concerned with discourse in its own volume, as a *monument.*[32]

Foucault's statement seems to apply especially well to Bent's Old Fort, where archaeology contributed indispensably in the reconstruction of the monument, the fort itself. The reconstructed fort might be thought of as a working model. I emphasize that the model is incomplete and therefore misleading unless scholars and the public see it in the broader context of the physical and cultural landscape, the latter being the sort of landscape that has not been, and can never be, physically reconstructed. What is needed, then, is an abstract reconstruction. The exercise should not be one of abstracting from the monument (as Foucault would say), but of abstracting to the monument.

The abstract, the order, that was embodied and conveyed by Bent's Old Fort will be visible in yet another form when I look down from the airplane tonight at the landscape below. I will see patterns of lights, which especially out here on the Plains will be arranged in straight lines. Lines as straight as this road I am driving on now. During the day from the air I would see to the far eastern horizon countless squares of brown or green dominating the other shapes lying within the grid formed by them. Those striking landscape features are artifacts of modernity here in the United States. They have been produced by the "most extensive cadastral system in the world," as an historian of land survey systems has noted.[33] The United States rectangular survey originated with the Ordinance of 1785. It laid out six-mile by six-mile townships that form a basic political unit in many of the states over which I will fly. The townships are divided into 36 sections, one mile square. Each section contains 640 acres. Once the land was surveyed into townships, an act in 1804 provided for the sale of public lands to the highest bidder by sections, half-sections, and quarter-sections, with the cost for surveying these subparcels to be borne by the purchasers. The Pre-emption Act of 1841 and the Homestead Act of 1862 were intended to encourage settlement of the western lands by offering it on quarter or even smaller sections at low prices or giving the smaller parcels to those who would occupy them.

The U.S. rectangular survey seems unrelentingly rational in the modern way, but not commonly understood are its origins in premodern thought and the way that kind of thought is compatible with the settlement of the western United States. There are good reasons to think that the American survey may have been derived from the Roman system— in any case the Roman system is a precedent to the American one.[34]

Hildegard Binder Johnson has studied the American system extensively and has commented upon this connection:

We now begin to realize another aspect, the original connection of the Roman system with the religious meaning of the center. To clarify the religious symbolism we must distinguish between two derivations from Latin: square, from *quadra* (also *quadrum* leading to *quadratum*), and quarter, from *quartarius*, or the fourth part, as in "quartering" a circle. The first implies form in equilibrium and has a static meaning in ancient cosmology. The second has dynamic meaning in cosmological schemes. The quartering of the circular horizon by the augur who stood at its center facing east was a religious act by which stability—the orderly delimitation of fields by agrimensores—would be achieved.[35]

Johnson notes also "the old and revealing word for the cross point, *umbilicus* (naval, center of the world)."[36] The *axis umbilicus* is a term used interchangeably with *axis mundi,* the center of the world and the axis connecting heaven and earth. What Johnson describes is called "squaring the circle" among Hindus and Buddhists, which consecrates all of the land that lies in reference to this central, sacred point. It brings the cosmic, sacred, *real* and *true* order down to earth. The spires of temples—called variously stupas, chedis, or pagodas—are located according to a similar procedure throughout Asia and the Indian subcontinent.[37] The procedures of the U.S. rectangular survey resonate with the ancient ones, and so legitimate the new order.

This reminds me of an incident told to me by an archaeologist who was excavating a small area at one of the national parks. He carefully drew the location of his excavation unit on a map showing the locations of historic buildings. But one of the historians at the park, who had seen archaeologists at work in remote locations, asked him why he hadn't used a transit to record the location of his excavation unit. My colleague explained that the procedure was unnecessary; the buildings he had used as reference points were drawn on maps and so could be tied to United States Geological Survey benchmarks that were recorded precisely in terms of latitude and longitude. But the historian visited him several times a day, suggesting over and over that a transit should be used. So he could work in peace, my friend eventually "shot in" his excavation unit with a transit. He unfolded the tripod legs, located the device exactly over one of the corners of the excavation, carefully leveled the instrument with adjusting screws, and then peered through it. He recorded ranges and bearings in his field notebook. The historian watched respectfully, enthralled with the process. "It was like a ritual to him," my archaeologist colleague told me, "we had sacralized the site." "Or," he said after a thoughtful pause, "perhaps we had treated the site with the respect the historian thought it was due. The site was *already* sacred to him because of its history."

Somehow, despite my reveries, I have remembered to turn west on I-70 as it intersects with 71 near Limon. I see the ambient light of Denver in the sky ahead. I think about the "little jog" that told me to slow down for Punkin Center, and realize that I had encountered an irregularity in the township system. The north-south lines on the globe, the meridians, gradually converge. To maintain consistency in the size of townships, a new baseline must be established every fourth township, which is every twenty-four miles. Meridians are shifted along these baselines, forming abrupt off-sets. North-south running section roads must adjust to these. It is a reconciliation of local knowledge with one of the principles of modernity, a "reembedding" of local conditions to a global grid.[38]

The jog indicates that the global, modern grid cannot lay sole claim to "reality." Foucault calls attention to just such "jogs." By doing so, he urges resistance to conceptual systems, overarching themes, and metastories. But the cadastral survey system provides a clue to the way in which such privileged positions are achieved. Mechanisms that create the order of the world are ritualistic and so essentially the same in all societies, whether we term them traditional or modern. Today they are practices like those associated with trade and interpersonal relationships and rituals "calcified" in the built environment of architecture and the landscape—what Foucault might term "monuments."

Foucault speaks favorably of the autochthonous transformation taking place in history, history that springs from its own ground, so to speak. In emphasizing how local orders are appropriated by central authorities, however, he recognizes that national and global networks of meaning and power exist. This, of course, explains the sad ending to the story of Bent's Old Fort. The fort was a mechanism for the imposition of the global network, but the vitalized network had no further need of it. What Foucault ignores is the human *penchant* for creating overarching themes and metastories; all persons are implicated in their creation. His preoccupation with denouncing overarching themes as misleading and exploitative is such that he pays little attention to the sense of desolation typically experienced by those excluded from them. It makes no difference that God is dead if people continue to resurrect Him.

Nonetheless, I think of the dynamic that Foucault implies by his use of the term *archaeology*. It describes Bent's Old Fort's role in the embedding of the Native Americans, Hispanics, and American entrepreneurs in the global world order.[39] The fort acted as a *monument* in Foucault's sense of the word, a kind of discourse. And to Foucault the world is created by discourse.[40] What he calls discourse I would prefer to term ritual, because ritual is more clearly a means of conveying meaning that is not strictly rational. Ritual is multisensory and therefore more experiential; consequently it manipulates the emotions more effectively than might, in contrast, a "dry" discourse. Ritual is therefore more likely to "move" us in the direction of a new apprehension of the world or to reinforce an old one.

The connection between archaeology (at least of the sort that deals with monuments and landscapes) and language is not new. Jean-François Lyotard, another noted postmodern social critic, has used this connection in his work, which likens social bonds to "language games" that operate according to different rules depending upon where one is "located" at the moment. To illustrate, Lyotard uses a metaphor he attributes to Ludwig Wittgenstein, who originated the theory of language games: "Our language can be seen as an ancient city: a maze of little streets and squares, of old and new houses, and of houses with additions from different periods; and this surrounded by a multitude of new boroughs with regular streets and uniform houses."[41]

There is also a long-standing connection between archaeology and "meaning" in a more general sense, one that Sigmund Freud was especially fond of positing and exploring. Although Freud's biographer Peter Gay dismisses it as "genial hyperbole," he quotes Freud in a letter to a friend saying that, "I . . . have read more archeology than psychology." Gay and others have noted that Freud often made comparisons of this sort: "The psychoanalyst, like the archaeologists in his excavations, must uncover layer after layer of the patient's psyche, before coming to the deepest, most valuable treasures."[42] Freud likened human mental life to the landscape one might confront if all components to all landscapes of ancient Rome could be restored at once: "On the Piazza of the Pantheon we should find not only the Pantheon of to-day, as it was bequeathed to us by Hadrian, but, on the same site, the original edifice erected by Agrippa; indeed, the same piece of ground would be supporting the church of Santa Maria sopra Minerva and the ancient temple over which it was built."[43] His point was that the past was preserved in the human psyche. But despite the reference to underlying and deeper meaning, Freud, like Foucault, must have thought that meaning was structured through monuments and landscapes, and revealed by archaeology, by means too obvious to deserve elaboration.

What Foucault, Lyotard, Wittgenstein, and Freud, among many others, intuitively grasped, and made great metaphorical use of, was the ability of archaeology to contribute to our understanding not only of the physical landscape as it has been altered by the actions of humans but also of the importance of that reconstructed landscape to our ability to understand the human world. The landscape is an artifact shaped by ritualistic behavior that conveys the world it reflects in ritualistic ways. It is the calcified ritual suggested by Yi-Fu Tuan.

I wearily go through the routine at the car rental agency, writing the mileage on the rental form, checking the car for my belongings, boarding the shuttle bus to the airport terminal. It feels wonderful to move and stretch. I watch the little blue car that was home for a while disappear as the bus turns a corner and feel a twinge of nostalgia. There are few people on the bus, no line at the ticket counter where I check in, and the plane is only half full for this late flight. That's fine with me; the familiar sequence of events is reassuring and comfortable, but I want to continue with my thoughts and it would be difficult to fit them into a casual conversation. When we're in the air the flight attendant comes by. It's just the level of human interaction I want at the moment. She smiles and is efficient, and I order white wine and ask for extra pretzels. I haven't had time to eat. I sip my wine and munch my pretzels and look out the window at the stars. I remember on a previous flight teaching my daughter her A-B-Cs, using as a prop a pretzel package just like the one I have in my hand now. I was delighted with her ability to recognize the letters, and she was just as delighted with my delight.

On that flight we looked out the window at pretty much the same set of stars I see right now, including the Big Dipper. I told her how to find the North Star by tracing a line through the stars that form the far end of the dipper's cup. That lesson began a chain of questions that continued when we got home. My answers had nothing to do with white buffalo and orphaned children, although had they I'm sure my daughter would have been intrigued. Instead, they introduced for her consideration phenomena equally improbable from the standpoint of everyday experience: the earth's rotation around the sun, the reason that day changes to night and winter to spring, the shape of the earth, gravity, the sun's place in the galaxy, quantified concepts of distance and time; in short, some of the basic knowledge—or basic assumptions—upon which she must build.

I close my eyes and hover at the edge of sleep, thinking about Stephen Jay Gould's statement that neoteny "as a life-history strategy for longer learning and socialization may be far more important in human evolution than any of its morphological consequences."[44] I suspect that effective ritual must involve a suspension of disbelief, sometimes willed, which engenders in participants something approximating a childlike state of trust. The very thought of this is probably enough to provoke profound discomfort among most modern peoples. Nonetheless, it's a step in the learning process all the way through life, one that must occur before each application of critical thought. Striking the proper balance between ritual and critical thought is the real challenge in this postmodern world, I think as I drift off. Learning to recognize and understand ritual is a beginning.

CHAPTER 3

Nostalgia for Paradise

The Sun Dance

All ritual, formal or fugitive, refers to mythological occurrence, recognized as myth or not. In doing so, it somewhat ameliorates the existential dread endemic to the human condition by virtue of the human capacity for reflection. We are able to see ourselves even as we act and, so, to envision the uncertainties of existence and the end to that existence. Entering into the realm of primordial occurrence, the timeless world of myth, is accomplished by reenacting the behaviors of the gods or ancestors who created the world as we know it. Ritual is a return to the eternal, and an escape from the uncertainties of mortal existence.

The primordial behaviors of the gods and ancestors are usually set, mythologically, in a kind of paradise that existed before the advent of death or time. Ironically, we are probably most familiar with the nostalgia for paradise expressed in modern society, the yearning for simpler times, which were somehow more "real" (as in the mythological West, where "men were men"). But this is nothing more than the imperfectly disguised nostalgia for paradise typically found in forms more recognizable to us in "primitive society."[1]

Ritual provides a model of paradise, of the ideal world, which is then employed in several ways. Access to the paradisiacal past is provided through the model, thereby pointing the way to a more "real" and satisfying existence. Ritual also demonstrates how the contingencies of history, the unpredictable and unfortunate events that are a part of human life, may be reconciled with this paradisiacal model. And, ritual provides the way, when it is deftly altered, to redetermine the "correct" means of access to paradise and to redefine paradise itself. In doing this, ritual is able to both accommodate and precipitate cultural change.

Nostalgia for paradise imbues ritual with much of its power to maintain and shape human cultures. This nostalgia appears among all human groups.[2] Some have suggested it to be an expression of longing for the womb or the breast. Such an experiential "oneness" does resonate with the emotional state that accompanies ritual, the sharing of "sentiment," the sense that all involved are "really" parts of one thing.

The appeal of paradise, and some of the implications of that appeal as they regard cultural maintenance and change, is evident in the ethnohistory of one of the most renowned rituals, the Sun Dance of the Plains Indians. In Leslie Spier's classic study of this ceremony, he said that "the original nucleus of Sun Dance rites probably received its first specific character at the hands of the Arapaho and Cheyenne."[3] In any case it is closely identified by anthropologists with these groups, who were the principal trading partners of Bent & St. Vrain Company.

In the history of this ritual one can see the transformative power of ritual, that is, its ability to set groups and individuals on a new course. To explain this, the cultural anthropologist Victor Turner has drawn parallels with the modern-day theater. He has pointed out that one story can be interpreted in a number of ways and that the script may be rewritten to accommodate a new version. So it works also, said Turner, with ritual.

Recent and convincing scholarship by Karl Schlesier revealed that the Sun Dance (along with another important Algonquian ceremony, the Midewiwin) was developed in the seventeenth century.[4] While the Sun Dance incorporated elements from older rituals, even ancient ones dating to the time the ancestors of the Cheyenne inhabited Siberia, the Sun Dance was formulated, Schlesier hypothesized, because "existing religious structures appeared as inadequate for the survival of tribal societies."[5] Existing religious structures surely had been tested by events.

Schlesier noted North American epidemics in the 1580s and in 1617, 1622, and 1631. As an example of the effects of this, he cited evidence that the population of Huron settlements declined from 45,000 or 50,000 in 1634 to 12,000 in 1640, the latter figure including the Petuns. He quoted an eyewitness who said that "there remained only very few old men, very few persons of skill and management."[6] Such a loss may well have lessened the "stock" of traditional practices and would likely have decreased somewhat the confidence in some aspects of contemporary religious practice as Schlesier argued.

The central element of the Sun Dance—the center pole of the ritual or "medicine" lodge, which acted as the symbolic *axis mundi* of the universe—may indeed be ancient. Given the Siberian ancestry of the Cheyenne and the Arapaho and the manner in which the center pole was used, it is at least possible that it has been passed along from Siberian ceremonies. Dennis Stanford, perhaps the most noted of archaeologists now conducting research into the oldest sites in the western Plains, has argued for the extreme antiquity of this element of the Sun Dance ritual. After finding in eastern Colorado evidence of what he regarded as a medicine pole, Stanford suggested that it might indicate "ten thousand years of socio-religious continuity" on the part of groups that hunted herds of bison, as did the Cheyenne.[7] The pole Stanford discovered was associated with the remains of a 10,000-year-old buffalo pound. Offerings and the way they were distributed around the pole led Stanford to postulate that ceremonial practices similar to those of the Sun Dance had taken place at the site. It is perhaps this "deep" grounding that provided a firm base upon which later additions to the ceremony were made.

The Sun Dance, as reported by late-nineteenth- and early-twentieth-century ethnographers who sometimes worked from earlier, eyewitness accounts by informants, displays elements indicative of an increasingly individualistic orientation. Here we see the transformative agency of ritual at work. Joseph G. Jorgensen, who considered the more recent versions of the ceremony, termed it part of a "redemptive" movement, concerned with "the search for a new individual state."[8] This is in contrast to Schlesier's evidence that the Sun Dance began as a world renewal ceremony, one focused on the society as opposed to the individual.

The individualistic orientation noted by Jorgensen had developed after European entry into the New World. Individualism accelerated apace with the increasing intensity of trade relations between the whites and the Plains groups. It eventually flowered into a culture that was obsessed with amassing symbols of prestige and wealth. Thus, we see the preoccupation with counting coup and gaining possession of buffalo hides, horses, and women that was characteristic of the Plains cultures of the nineteenth century. The Sun Dance evolved to accommodate such new cultural traits.

Of equal interest is the way in which the Sun Dance, and the culture of aggression, competition, and rampant individualism that it represented, was adopted by modern American culture as a symbol of the "natural" condition of man. As such, it legitimates these characteristics in today's society. The nineteenth-century world of Plains tribes like the Cheyenne and the Sioux is regarded today as a kind of golden age—not only for Native American peoples but for the United States as well.

Ethnographic Treatments of the Sun Dance

Leslie Spier's 1921 study of the Sun Dance has long been regarded as the benchmark work for the ceremony. He linked it most closely with the Cheyenne, Arapaho, and Oglala Sioux but asserted that it was practiced in modified forms by eighteen Plains tribes. Schlesier termed the Sun Dance an "anthropological invention," arguing that these tribes actually performed different ceremonies that shared certain common attributes. He also considered the term *Sun Dance* to be a misnomer, preferring the Cheyenne word for the dance, *Oxheheom,* meaning "new life" or "world renewal" ceremony.[9]

In the general anthropological and popular literature, nonetheless, the Sun Dance is regarded as the central ceremony for the Plains tribes. It is perhaps because the most well-known aspects of the ceremony resonate so strongly with basic modern cultural assumptions about individualism and individualistic renewal (such as the need for a personal vision and the acceptance of suffering to achieve it) that it is likely that it has been studied and described as much as any "primitive" ritual. There is also a vast popular and academic interest in the tribes that practiced the ceremony, particularly the Cheyenne, Arapaho, and Sioux. Numerous ethnographies have been written about the Cheyenne alone.[10] Some large libraries have almost 1,000 entries in their bibliographic files under the heading "Cheyenne."

And yet, there is no agreement about all aspects of even the Cheyenne Sun Dance. The use of tobacco, for example, is mentioned by some ethnographers and not by others. The precise timing of the Sun Dance is also unclear in these ethnographies. Most mention that it is usually held in July or near the summer solstice, but some place the time of the ceremony later. There are many reasons for these discrepancies and uncertainties. Observers often record only what they have decided beforehand to be important and may not mention aspects that are of small interest to them. Also, informants may be vague or purposely misleading. A woman involved in the preservation of Cheyenne traditions told me recently not to put too much credence in the work of ethnographers, including Grinnell (the most famous of Cheyenne ethnographers), because the Cheyenne sometimes found it amusing to lead ethnographers astray.[11] Most important, rituals change even though they must purport to represent the unchanging. It is likely that no two Sun Dances were ever performed in exactly the same way. Enough ethnographic descriptions of the Sun Dance have been done with sufficient precision to record the fact that they *do* change.

Nonetheless, even a cursory description of the most basic elements of the Cheyenne Sun Dance is sufficient to illustrate several facets of the social mechanism of ritual. The ceremony was sometimes called by the Cheyenne "renewing the earth" or the "new-life-lodge" (terms that again hint at a sacred model for both topography and architecture). Many participated in the various roles demanded by the ceremony. The most important of these roles were held by the priests, the sponsor, and the few young men who desired a vision that would guide them through the balance of their lives. These young men, as I argue elsewhere in this book, were suffering from *anomie*; they were in distress because they could not find a suitable place for themselves in their society. They sought a personal rebirth by participating in the rebirth of the Cheyenne.

Simply attending was a kind of participation. The Cheyenne shared a language and many habits of behavior, but during most of the year were not together. They went about their nomadic rounds in bands made up from as few as one to several extended families. These bands were knit together by the affiliation of individuals in the bands, or sometimes of whole bands, and with clans and special "societies," especially warrior societies. Clans and societies convened for rituals, societies for ritual and ritualistic behaviors (warfare and raiding being among the most important of the latter). The Sun Dance, however, was for the Cheyenne as a whole, and acted powerfully to maintain the Cheyenne as a whole.

The construction of the Sun Dance lodge (the ceremony is also known as the medicine lodge ceremony) reenacted the creation of the world. Searching for the Sun Dance pole, counting coup on the tree that was to serve this purpose, and attaching the medicine bundles and offerings to the tree was the first great spectacle of the ceremony. As Donald Berthrong recorded it, one of the tribal chiefs would address the tree, saying words such as these: "The whole world has picked you out this day to represent the world. We have come in a body to cut you down, so that you will have pity on all men, women, and children who may take part in this ceremony. You are to be their body. You are to represent the sunshine of the world."[12]

The "new-life lodge" was then constructed. The altar in the lodge represented the whole of the earth. On the altar were the paramount things of the earth, including a buffalo skull, strips of sod to represent the four cardinal directions and the sun, and the foliage of useful vegetation such as cottonwoods and plum bushes. The lodge itself referred to the heavens, and appropriate designs were applied there. Bundles of vegetation were tied to the center pole, and dried buffalo meat was secured to one of the bundles by a broken arrow. To this, a rawhide image of a human was also attached. At least one ethnographic account records that tobacco was attached to the center pole. Dancers were painted five times during the fifth and sixth days of the ceremony with colors (yellow, pink, white, black) and designs (the sun, moon, flowers, plants) that referred to the blessings of the earth.

It was also at this time that the young men underwent the self-torture that they had vowed to endure in an attempt to gain special favor or relief from the gods. Two skewers, variously reported as being bear or eagle claws or made of wood, were hooked through the flesh of a man's breast or, less frequently, through the flesh of his back. At times the man was hoisted by a rope suspended from the central pole, the sun pole, where he hung until the flesh tore away (fig. 6). Or, he might remain on the ground, pulling against skewers attached to the sun pole until his flesh tore. In some cases, when a man was suspended for a long time and the skewers held fast, he might attach the skewers by means of thongs to buffalo skulls, which he would drag over the plains until they caught on some obstacle and he broke free. This ordeal was preceded by fasting, meditation, and sleep deprivation, which generally produced a state of religious ecstasy and visions in which a totemic spirit advisor appeared, one that would thereafter be the man's spiritual guide. The totemic advisor, of course, would come from the tribe's cultural stock of mythological figures, and so the man's personal vision would be intertwined with that of his culture.

Attendance at the Sun Dance was compulsory for every adult male, but it is likely that everyone in the tribe attended. It was, after all, a spectacle that evoked a considerable affective response in its audience. This is an essential part of ritual, as Emile Durkheim established many years ago; ritual must evoke an emotional response, a shared "sentiment" in Durkheim's terms, that, by being shared, binds together participants and spectators.[13]

Considerable effort and commitment of resources went into organizing a Sun Dance, and this required a sponsor. In pre-reservation days, a man might pledge to sponsor a Sun Dance if he survived some imminent danger, most likely danger experienced during a raid to acquire horses or as a result of the tensions that arose following such a raid. Later, a sponsor might be a person expressing gratitude that a member of his or her

Figure 6. "Sun Dance, Third Day." (Detail from a painting by Dick West; courtesy Philbrook Museum of Art, Tulsa, Oklahoma; reported in Donald J. Berthrong, *The Southern Cheyennes*, copyright 1963 by the University of Oklahoma Press.)

family had recuperated from an illness or escaped from a physical threat. The sponsor could be either a man or woman but had to have access to considerable resources. Prestige accompanied sponsorship. The sponsor was the principal participant of the Sun Dance, being regarded as more important than those who went through the self-torture. The sponsor became known as the "reanimator" of the tribe, the person through whom the tribe was reborn. In subsequent years, the sponsor joined an elite fraternity of Sun Dance sponsors, who were co-owners of the Sun Dance medicine bundle. Thus, the sponsor was assured an important role in future ceremonies. If the sponsor were a man, an added requirement of his sponsorship was that he pledge his wife to the ceremonial grandfather during the preliminary rites of the Sun Dance. If a man's wife was unable to carry out this role for some reason, or if a man had no wife, he had to find another woman to fulfill this role. Often this was a sister.

All the bands of the Cheyenne tribe were present for the Sun Dance. The camp for this occasion was laid out in a carefully prescribed way. It was always located on the south bank of a stream, with the clan camps ordered in a traditional sequence and forming a circle that was often a mile in diameter. An opening in the circle always pointed east. The six

Cheyenne military societies camped at prearranged locations in the camp circle,[14] and to assume a position different from a traditional one was considered highly meaningful and threatening to the order of the tribe.

The Medium Is the Message: A Phenomenological Analysis

Ritual undoubtedly refers to mythology, but the mythology is stated and reformulated, to a degree, by the ritual; that is, it is ritual—an expression that depends only in part upon words—that conveys the mythology to the participants and observers (and ultimately to the succeeding generations who will bear the culture into the future).

The modern world is dominated not only by print but also by words. We frequently make the mistake of assuming that if something cannot be well articulated, it does not exist, it is not valid, or it is at least unimportant. There is some logic to this in the modern world because modern society can only function properly if ideas are given an explicit form that is understandable to a very wide audience. This may include people with whom one does not frequently associate and who, then, are not accustomed to one's idiosyncratic way of speaking, or even people one may never meet. The sociolinguist Basil Bernstein made this point with his research when he noted that children who are brought up in families where an elaborated linguistic code (or way of speaking) is employed, as a rule, do much better in school and, later, in modern society, than do those from more traditional families. Traditional families, often associated with lower socioeconomic class in the Western world, communicate in many nonverbal ways, which often spring from traditional roles. Such families impart a restricted, less-explicit manner of speaking to their children.[15]

While such evidence explains the social advantage enjoyed by those with command of explicit verbal communication in the modern world, our bias in favor of words has now partially blinded us to the real impact of nonverbal communication. This is a point about which painters, sculptors, dancers, musicians, and even architects and mathematicians comment. It is *lived experience*, experience not limited to words, that conveys meaning, and shared experience that generates Durkheim's "sentiment." And this is how ritual makes its effect.

Fieldwork done by the "new ethnographers," a group that includes James Clifford and James Spradley, employs the tenets of "cognitive anthropology." In this approach, fieldwork is designed to reveal the "cognitive chart" employed by members of a given culture in making sense of, communicating about, and altering the world.[16] The focus here is on performance—the actual behavior involved—be it speech, ritual, or the creation of material culture. As Victor Turner explained in *The Anthropology of Performance*, Noam Chomsky, a linguist, was the first to identify the dichotomy between *competence*, the mastery of a system of rules and regularities underlying communication, and *performance*, or what actually occurs and is experienced.[17] We can only speculate about competence. Performance, on the other hand, is doubly informative, in that it indicates the underlying set of rules and regulations and, also, how these are employed—often to bring about change—in the real world. In emphasizing lived experience, performance theory may be seen to lie comfortably within the philosophical traditions of phenomenology, which concerns itself with such experience, and hermeneutics, which explores how meaning is made from experience.

All of this is in way of saying that ritual conveys mythology more surely than might be done by purely verbal means (if means could be purely verbal, which they cannot be). It is the performance of ritual in its entirety—words, behavior, timing, and so on—that conveys mythology in such a way as to reorder society along the lines suggested by that mythology. It does this by evoking Durkheim's "sentiment." Sentiment embeds a value and belief system in the group participating and observing a ritual—it wins the "hearts and minds" of this group as a reasoned, explicit statement of values and beliefs, a theology or philosophy, might never alone do.

Looking at the Sun Dance phenomenologically, we can clearly see several important components of Cheyenne mythology. The Sun Dance reenacts the creation of the world. It is a statement of Cheyenne ontology, a statement made in part by the construction of a "model" of the Cheyenne universe, a model that replicates the larger world. The center pole (or sun pole) is what Eliade termed the *axis mundi*, the symbolic center of the earth, and also the point at which heaven and earth meet. Whether a landform or a temple or pyramid, the *axis mundi* is the most sacred of locations because it provides access to the realm of the unchanging, the "real."

The Cheyenne rituals that involve the Sun Dance pole are similar to Siberian shamanistic rituals that make use of a central pole. The ancestors of the Cheyenne, the Algonquin, came to North America from Siberia, and many similarities between the religious beliefs and practices of the Cheyenne and Siberian groups have been recorded by historians and ethnographers over the past century or so. (Siberian shamanistic practices are generally regarded by religious scholars to have developed before the Neolithic period.) These observations have been noted by Karl Schlesier and other scholars, yet no one, so far as I know, has mentioned the similarities in the ritual use of a central pole, or *axis mundi,* noted below.[18] The similarities provide clues to the ways in which behaviors associated with an important ritual migrate and are made freshly meaningful as a society evolves. These behaviors often seem only practical to modern observers—their meaning eludes the observers, and the rituals become *fugitive.*

In a Siberian ceremony, a master shaman (or "father shaman") initiated apprentices in a ritual that resembles the Sun Dance in some important ways. A strong birch stripped of its bark was set up in each apprentice's yurt on the day of their initiations, where it projected through the central smoke hole. The apprentice climbed to the top of the birch and shouted for the assistance of the gods. The birch thenceforth was left in the yurt to mark the apprentice as a shaman.

Then, as a party, the master shaman and his apprentices went in a procession to a place where many large birches had been prepared by stripping them and setting them into the ground. After sacrificing a goat to one of the birch poles, the master shaman climbed it and made nine notches in the top of its trunk. The initiate then climbed the birch and "disappeared," reappearing some time later with visions he had obtained from his visit to heaven. Nine birches in all were climbed which, like the nine cuts, symbolized the nine heavens.[19]

An obvious similarity is that the Siberian and Cheyenne initiates (initiates to the status of shaman in the first case and to a more satisfying status in Cheyenne society in the second) sought ecstatically induced visions under the direction of an experienced holy man. Cheyenne initiates experienced visions that were personal but which linked them to the larger cultural agenda of their society.

Other similarities seem relevant to the Plains Indian practice of *counting coup.* As with any set of ethnographic similarities, the exact relationship is problematic given the lack of written accounts of the behaviors in question prior to European contact. While a common origin cannot be proven, the similarities suggest at the least a convergence of behaviors formulated from a related stock of meaningful ritual actions.

The counting coup behavior has puzzled many historians and archaeologists, as it puzzled contemporary observers. It appeared to them to be a sort of individualism gone amuck, to the overall detriment of the tribe. Counting coup usually involved touching an enemy (alive or dead) in battle. Doing this conferred great prestige on a warrior, even more prestige than would be realized by killing an enemy or contributing to a military victory. Stories abound of young warriors who could not be restrained from their attempt to count coup and so ruined the battle strategy of their war party.

Counting coup also occurred in quite a different context, one suggesting the real meaning of the behavior. Coup was counted by the Cheyenne on the tree selected to be the Sun Dance pole—it was struck ritually. Far from symbolizing an enemy, however, the central pole was the most venerated of symbols associated with the Sun Dance.[20] It represented the *axis mundi*, as did the stripped birch trees in Siberia that were ritually struck nine times. Given that the ancestors of the Cheyenne came from Siberia and the well-documented similarities in the religions of the two groups, it is possible that the counting of coup by the Cheyenne on the Sun Dance pole is a survival of the striking of the birch poles in Siberia. In the Asian ritual, the nine notches made in the birches symbolized the nine heavens. The blows given to the Plains Indian medicine pole may also have symbolized this or something similar. Ethnographic observers, however, assumed that the behavior they saw at the medicine pole replicated the activity of ritually striking the enemy, the behavior called counting coup. It is highly unlikely that behavior associated with a more profane activity (by virtue of its occurring farther away from the most sacred locale, the *axis mundi*) would be replicated at the most sacred of all sites, the *axis mundi* itself. Such a conclusion does not follow the logic of ritual as observed worldwide, which indicates that behavior reenacted at the most sacred locales becomes the model for all less-sacred activity (as the celestial provides the archetype for the organization of all earthly affairs).

The Sun Dance behavior of striking the *axis mundi*, then, may have provided the model for counting coup, not the other way around. Counting coup may be fugitive ritual. This explanation accommodates one of the more puzzling aspects of counting coup. In battle, the person who killed the enemy gained coup, but not as much as did the second person to strike a blow on the now dead body. While the blows inflicted by the first warrior may have achieved the practical result, the blow by the second sanctified that result; it was a purely ritual act. The ritual striking of the enemy restored balance and harmony to the universe, a balance that had been upset by the killing. It also restored the balance of a traditional society, a balance that had been upset by one of its members acting in a highly individualistic manner. The ritual was thus made to accommodate the individualism that had been transmitted to Plains Indian culture through its interaction with Anglo culture.

The symbolic material that was arranged around the pole in the medicine

lodge—vegetation, dried buffalo meat, the rawhide figure of a man—
re-created, in miniature, the essential features of the Cheyenne world. It
was a succinct expression of the relationship of the sacred to everyday life.
Sacred power, which flows to the living things of the world, was especially
concentrated in the buffalo (the importance of which to Plains society prior
to the arrival of the Anglos cannot be overestimated—virtually all of the
flesh of the animal was eaten, and from various parts of the animal came
almost all of the clothing, tools, weapons, cooking utensils, and contain-
ers used by the Cheyenne), and this power was accessed by man through
hunting and consuming the animal. Some ethnographic accounts also reported that tobacco was attached to the center pole (in more recent times,
this has in some cases been cigarettes). Tobacco, as we shall see, played a
major role in trade rituals with the Cheyenne, as well as with all other Plains
tribes. It also refers to the shamanistic tradition, in that tobacco has been
used for thousands of years among Native Americans, in both North and
South America, to create a nicotine-induced ecstasy that provided visions.

At a certain point in the consecration of the medicine lodge, tobacco
smoke from a sacred pipe was offered to the medicine pole. The bowl of
the pipe was made of a soft red stone, called catlinite by Euro-Americans,
and was often carved into figures that referred to mythological entities.
True catlinite could be procured only in the Timber Mountains of southwestern Minnesota, the ancestral home of the Cheyenne and other Plains
tribes. By the nineteenth century the homeland had undoubtedly assumed
mythological status. Long trips were taken to acquire the distinctive red
stone. Fig. 7 shows the offering of the smoke to the medicine pole in a
photograph that was possibly taken by Cheyenne ethnographer James
Mooney in about 1903. The gesture shown is similar to that made toward
participants in fictive kinship rituals, including the trading rituals that establish fictive kinship relationships (described in chapter 5).

The altar, by reason of proximity, was only a slightly less sacred locale
than the pole itself. Here, other symbols of the Cheyenne world were ar-
rayed in a particular way. The strips of earth that represent the four cardinal directions and the sun spoke to the importance that all cultures place
in being properly oriented in the world. Clifford Geertz, among other
ethnographers, commented about this, giving as an example that the word
for "not knowing which way north is" among the Balinese connotes profound confusion of the sort which the Balinese fear almost pathologically.
Such is the urgency of being physically oriented in a traditional society,
where virtually all landforms are embedded within the mythological basis for the culture's belief and value system.

Figure 7. Offering smoke to the medicine pole at a Cheyenne Sun Dance, circa 1903. (Photograph possibly by James Mooney; courtesy National Anthropological Archives, Smithsonian Institution.)

The importance of orientation is especially visible in the Chinese practice of geomancy. Geomancy survives even in modern Hong Kong, where huge sums are paid to geomancers to align new buildings according to lines of force that exist only within mythology. The belief that disaster will befall any building not correctly aligned is quite real, however. Similarly, the aborigines of Australia are able to find their way with precision from one side of their continent to the other by following "songlines" while on walk-about. The aborigines sing their creation myths, which tell the origin of the landforms they encounter, linking each with a mythological creature. The aboriginal perspective, however, is that they are "singing" the land-forms into being once more, re-creating the world as they go. Therefore, their walkabouts are essential to the continuation of the world.

The intimate knowledge of the environment that such a belief system promotes does possess functional value. The Pintupi Aborigines of Gib-son Desert in Australia, for example, range over a wide area yet can find their way to small resource points that appear only at certain times of the year. These include specific locations where the *mungilpa* seed plant grows in great proliferation after rains, or where wild yams ripen.[21] There are also social implications to intimate knowledge of the environment. To the Pintupi, travel to resource points through and by means of topological reference points called *ngurra*, "named places" created by the ancestors, makes of traveling companions "one countrymen," even if they are from different homelands.[22] But the urgency associated with "getting one's bear-ings," individually and culturally, cannot be fully understood in terms of function alone. It is simply a prerequisite to making sense of the world in all ways, of making life even in its day-to-day aspects meaningful.

The altar, again, represented the earth, and so the strips of sod placed the earth in its proper relation to the heavens (the lodge itself) and the means of access to the heavens, the *axis mundi*. The produce of the earth, the buffalo represented by the skull and the useful plant life such as cot-tonwood and plum bushes, were sacralized through their contact with the earth, which was made sacred through the *axis mundi*. Dancers moved in and out of the sacred space, expressing physically man's sojourn on earth and the temporality of his association with it.

The basic orientation established by the medicine lodge extended to the camp as a whole. The camp was arranged in a circle, reflecting the Cheyenne belief that everything living is circular (the human body, the sun, the tepee, the camp circle), while everything dead or that brings about death is angular (weapons especially, such as the tomahawk and spear). When a clan or warrior society was in disgrace, the tepees of the mem-bers were not allowed within the camp circle. To be outside of the circle, after all, was to be outside the realm of the living, and to be deprived of the essential source of life. Usually, however, the outcasts camped nearby, and if proper reparations were made and proper conduct was followed, they were allowed after a time back within the circle.

Change: The "Pure Products
of America Go Crazy"

We, as inhabitants of the modern world and especially as Anglo-Americans, cannot understand the Sun Dance unless we understand the role we ourselves have played creating it. I alluded to this phenomenon earlier, noting that Karl Schlesier has termed the Sun Dance an "anthropological invention."[23] In this sense, we—anthropologists being representatives of the modern world—were looking for and finding phenomena we assumed to be widespread. There is a strong tendency among moderns to look to traditional peoples for a primal and unchanging past: the paradise that existed before time and history. This "golden age" in the mythology of our culture (and perhaps all others) is associated with purity because it existed "before the Fall."

James Clifford, perhaps the foremost of the new ethnographers, has attempted to debunk the notion of cultural purity. But the idea of a pristine age is stubborn, and to even challenge the reality of it can be profoundly disorienting to some. Hence the line from a poem by William Carlos Williams, which Clifford quoted: "The pure products of America go crazy."[24] To illustrate this, Clifford took note of a vignette that seems so improbable to the modern American mind that it strikes one as surreal: that the English Pilgrims arriving at Plymouth Rock found waiting for them Squanto, a Patuxet Indian, just back from his visit to Europe. In fact, this incident occurred.

The crucial idea here is that we have segregated the idea of modern, European cultures from our conception of traditional cultures (sometimes called "primitive cultures" if they are without writing and cities) including native American ones. Such a clear-cut division does not exist, although it has pleased Western egos to cast the world in such a mold. Doing so has allowed modern societies to look at "primitive" ones as curiosities, fundamentally different in kind from their own and fit subjects for museums. The transfer of cultural "traits," and more important, of ways of looking at the world, has worked in all directions. Moreover, social mechanisms by which the world is constructed, such as ritual, are common to all societies but are less recognized in modern ones with their bias toward explicit, verbal statement. The real means by which culture operates cannot be understood until these facts are a part of an ethnographic tool kit.

As we have seen in the opening discussion of this chapter, the Sun

Dance itself is not a "pure product" of the New World as it existed before European arrival. It was formulated in reaction to dislocations precipitated by the advent of Europeans. The most persistent element of the ceremony, the medicine pole, was not strictly speaking a New World product either, having come from the tradition of Siberian shamanism. We look in vain here for the purity of an American Eden. What we might discern if we examine the Sun Dance ritual with care is an expression of our "modern" anxieties, which are really associated with manufacturing an identity within a high-grid, low-group, ego-centered society: how to reconcile the need to advance individually and to adapt to a rapidly changing environment while maintaining a necessary degree of group solidarity.

The Sun Dance embodied such concerns. The sixth warrior society, for example, danced with guns, thus legitimating the use of those weapons and the link established with the white man by the use of the guns. Sponsorship of the dance is another case in point. In prereservation days, such sponsorship was generally by a warrior who had survived a situation of great danger likely associated with a raid to acquire horses. Warriors gained prestige by counting coup, but also by owning horses. Horses were highly charged religious symbols and so possessed great medicine. Horses also served as a form of wealth for Cheyenne after they became traders, and remained their primary form of wealth until they became heavily involved with the fur trade, when other more portable forms of "currency"—buffalo robes in particular—gained popularity.[25]

Of course, when it became possible to amass wealth, individualism and an early form of capitalism took hold. By the early nineteenth century, the Cheyenne were undoubtedly preadapted to their role in the fur trade with the whites. This was so, in part, because of their experience in the ritual trade of the Plains, in which they were establishing a position as middlemen by virtue of their mobility and military prowess. But, also, they had developed the habit of thinking in somewhat quantitative terms: The more horses a man had, the greater not only his power (medicine) but his wealth.

This development was accelerated by the presence of Bent's Old Fort. Grinnell recounted one of the Cheyenne stories that includes elements pertinent to this idea in *By Cheyenne Campfires*.[26] Here he described a horse-stealing expedition mounted against the Kiowa in about 1839. The Cheyenne party stopped by Bent's Old Fort to get provisions, which William Bent provided on credit. The leaders of the expedition vouched for the younger members and told Bent the families to which these individuals belonged, so that if the young members were killed, their families could be held responsible for the debt. Thus Bent revealed his role as a crucial participant in the economy of raiding and looting, an economy already developed. In acting as a sort of banker, he facilitated this development. This economy collapsed with the movement of the Cheyenne to reservations. By then, however, other forms of wealth had developed. Such forms were available not only to warriors; both men and women could amass these new forms of wealth and, so, could sponsor the Sun Dance. Of overriding interest here is not that the basis for the economy had changed, but that the nature of the culture had been altered by this experience in the direction of capitalism, modernity, and individualism. The Sun Dance ritual could accommodate and, so, validate and perpetuate this change in ideology.

The most striking feature of the Sun Dance, ritual self-torture, is also the one that displays most clearly the orientation toward individualism. As noted previously, the personal vision quest was artfully woven into the fabric of cultural beliefs. Nonetheless, there is no mistaking the fact that the questors assumed center stage in the drama of the ritual and derived great personal prestige from their role. The Sun Dance balanced the urgent desire on the part of young warriors for personal recognition with the needs of the society in a way that can also be seen in the Cheyenne social institution of the *contraries*. The contraries, or Crazy Dogs, acted in overtly antisocial ways. These included riding their horses backward, dressing backward, washing with dirt, drying with water, and flaunting social mores and conventions. In battle, they acted with complete disregard for their personal safety. They would charge alone into the enemy camp or tie themselves to a stake when the enemy charged. Many died in doing so, but those who survived were rewarded with the highest prestige in Cheyenne society. Self-destructive behavior that could have been destructive to Cheyenne society was channeled into behavior that enhanced the common good. The Sun Dance ritual showed the way this could be done. It transformed aggression and nihilism into behavior meaningful to the individual and valuable to the society.

It is likely that Clifford Geertz would see in the behavior of the contraries, as well as that associated with the Sun Dance, Jeremy Bentham's idea of "deep play,"[27] play for which stakes are so high that it makes no sense from a utilitarian standpoint. Bentham used as an example gambling for very high stakes. If a man has enough to survive, his argument went, winning a great deal of money produces less pleasure than losing a great deal of money would produce in suffering. Geertz said that such behavior cannot be understood at all if it is linked closely to rational processes.

Using the Balinese as an example, he argued that humans engage in deep play because it is so meaningful. In fact, the "deeper" it is, the more meaning it has:

It is in large part *because* the marginal disutility of the loss is so great at the higher levels of betting that to engage in such betting is to lay one's public self, allusively and metaphorically, through the medium of one's cock, on the line. And though to a Benthamite this might seem merely to increase the irrationality of the enterprise that much further, to the Balinese what it mainly increases is the meaningfulness of it all, and as (to follow Weber rather than Bentham) *the imposition of meaning on life is the major end and primary condition of human existence,* that access of significance more than compensates for the economic costs involved. (my emphasis)[28]

The arguments in this book support Geertz's major contention, that "the imposition of meaning on life is the major end and primary condition of human existence." The remarkable fact is that survival itself may be forfeited in the urgent quest for meaning. The young Cheyenne warrior, faced with the urgent necessity to establish a viable social identity, often felt that he had no recourse but to put his very life on the line in order to obtain it. I suggest that desperate moves became more prevalent as opportunities for social recognition for junior members of this society dwindled. The development of more unambiguous and more portable forms of wealth made it possible for older, more established warriors to amass wealth. Using this wealth, they then monopolized the means by which further wealth and prestige might be obtained.

Eventually, it took wealth to sponsor a Sun Dance. This alteration in the way the Sun Dance was organized marked a turning point in Cheyenne culture; it set the pattern for other, key social transactions. Perhaps most importantly, in order to mount a raiding expedition, as numerous ethnographers have reported, it was necessary to have the prestige to attract able warriors to the raiding party. In later years this required wealth with which to equip them and to purchase the sacred objects and ceremonies that would ensure the venture's success.[29]

The Sun Dance displays, according to the terminology utilized by Victor Turner, at least two *liminal* facets. Rituals occur, said Turner, at *limens,* or "thresholds."[30] These are points of change, crisis, or danger in the lives of individuals or cultures. All rituals are, in one way or another, "rites of passage," which involve three phases: *separation, marginality* or *liminality,* and finally, *return.* Note that all three must be by definition collective events, because they refer to the *separation* of ritual participants from the balance of the group (which represents the whole of human society), the symbolic placing of these participants in an ahistorical state. This is the primordial state that exists before the beginning or after the end of time, the sacred state away from the normal concerns of work, food, and sleep, and one that is thus *marginal* or *liminal* to the rest of the group. The culmination is the *return* of the participants to a place in society, but one that has been altered by the ritual. The two facets of liminality in the Sun Dance are that the chief participants of the Sun Dance are separated by their presence in the medicine lodge from the rest of the tribe and that the vision questors are further separated by their ordeal, from the medicine lodge participants as well as the rest of the tribe. The questors become those most imbued with the sacred by virtue of the ritual.

The societal threshold to be crossed by the efforts of the participants in the medicine lodge is the one brought about by the summer solstice, when the day stops lengthening and begins to become shorter. The Cheyenne could determine the time of the summer solstice with the "medicine wheel." Rituals at the summer solstice are ubiquitous throughout the world and include those practiced by Neolithic peoples in Europe (circa 4700–2000 B.C.) with the aid of their henges (larger in mass, but functioning in much the same way as the Cheyenne medicine wheel), ceremonies at ancient Mesoamerican, near Eastern, and Asian temples, the burning of witches on midsummer night's eve in medieval Europe, and the lighting of bonfires and burning of witch dolls today in northern Europe on midsummer night's eve, usually accompanied by night-long celebrations. The fireworks that are so much a part of Fourth of July celebrations in the United States are, most likely, survivals of solstice rituals. Fireworks are utilized in many places in the world at liminal occasions to frighten away the demons that always threaten at such times of uncertainty (one well known example is the Chinese New Year).

Such transitional moments are also sometimes linked to personal transitions brought about by change in status, usually by virtue of age, or by personal crisis. The Mescalero Apache, to cite just one Plains group, perform the rituals used to initiate girls into tribal membership and womanhood on the nights near the summer solstice. As the ethnographer Claire Farrer noted:

The girls enter into their ceremony as unformed as was the universe before Creator initiated order. While each girl becomes a physiological woman upon initial menstruation, she becomes a fully social woman and one who understands she is truly "the mother of a people" as she participates in, or even watches, the full cycle of the ceremonial.[31]

Likewise, the Sun Dance, also held near the summer solstice, is an initiation of sorts. The occasion for liminality here is not physiological change, it is a growing psychological disturbance among the questors prior to their decision to undergo the ordeal. It may be described as a sense of meaninglessness, or *anomie,* and may well be associated with the difficulties which grew ever more daunting to the young man attempting to establish a viable social identity. The questor, if successful, returns to the realm of primordial chaos in order to receive his vision and emerges "reborn" as a man with a purpose. This reveals the more individualistic cast of rites of initiation, which are ubiquitous among traditional people.

In the Sun Dance, the initiation is combined with a *healing* ritual, such as that practiced, to cite just one example out of very many, during a Navajo sing. Here, primordial chaos is also evoked, and then harmony and balance is reinstituted through proper behavior (ritual singing, the assembly of kin), and the ailing person is thereby restored to "wholeness." The Sun Dance ritual as it evolved may be seen in this light as an attempt to restore wholeness to an individual split off from a traditional culture, which heretofore had been sufficient to provide a viable identity to the person. As we shall see, there are similarities between "traditional" Cheyenne and "modern" American conditions of alienation and the use of ritualistic behavior to attempt to correct that alienation.

The Golden Age

Ritual behavior always involves a symbolic return to the primordial conditions of existence, before the advent of time and the uncertainties and finalities associated with time. These primordial conditions are everywhere represented as a kind of paradise without death, suffering, or work; when man lived in harmony with the world, even with the other animals; when he had easy access from his world to the "real" world, heaven; and when he thereby could communicate directly with God. Between this timeless world and the present intervened a catastrophe, sundering ready access to heaven and God and marking the beginning of our present unfortunate condition, one characterized by temporality, death, and suffering.[32]

From a Freudian (one might as well here say "modern") point of view, this "paradise" might be the prenatal or preweaning period, which ends with a catastrophic "infantile trauma." An individual's personality, according to this theory, is fixed by his attitude toward the circumstances of this primordial state. Stephen Jay Gould has developed this idea further, expanding upon the idea of prolonged infant dependency to explain what he sees as the ubiquitous human characteristic of *neoteny*. Some implications of this are that humans retain infantile characteristics throughout their lives. Manifestations include the life-long human capacity for learning and play.[33] Another implication, though, is that we retain the longing for a parental caretaker and "savior," casting our gods into this role and casting our parents (and more remote ancestors) as gods.[34] The importance of this human characteristic only increases as ritual becomes less formal (or "degraded") and "privatized" in the modern world, and each individual must assume more responsibility for constructing a meaningful universe for herself or himself from a cosmology more and more idiosyncratic.

In such a cosmology, parents become increasingly important, and the ability to "differentiate" or "individuate" becomes crucial to successful socialization.[35] Successful socialization includes the ability to conceptualize and express oneself in an "elaborated" (rational and explicit) manner, as opposed to a "restricted" (context-bound and abbreviated) one.[36] Such a task is difficult. It is actually impossible to accomplish completely, as Bowen observed, and all too frequently differentiation is so incomplete as to render the individual dysfunctional in the modern world, in all but relatively structured environments. Reasons for inadequate socialization appear to be both idiosyncratic and cultural. Psychologists tend to focus on the idiosyncratic aspects of socialization. As we have seen, these assume much greater importance in the modern world.

Adequate socialization of the young in a modern industrial world is of interest from a cultural viewpoint. The modern world has been aptly characterized by Mary Douglas as ego-centered; that is, it is a world in which the "competence and luck" of each individual is believed to be responsible for his or her "success" or "failure." These latter terms really refer to whether a person has been able to construct a viable identity. Unsuccessful participants in such a world system are doomed to "social oblivion." Douglas summarizes the inherent problems of such a system as follows:

My own hypothesis is that a society so strongly centered on a structure of ego-focused grid is liable to recurrent breakdown from its inherent moral weakness. It cannot continually sustain the commitment of all its members to an egalitarian principle that favors a minority. It has no way of symbolizing or activating the collective conscious. One would anticipate an ego-focused grid system to swing between the glorification of successful leaders and the celebration of the rights of the masses to enjoy success.[37]

What may come as more of a surprise than this statement by Douglas is her contention that other strongly gridded, ego-centered cultures include such "primitive" ones as those of New Guinea (who display what has been called the "Big Man" system) and that of the American Plains Indians. The ego-centered aspect of the Plains Indian culture, I suggest, derives from the influence of American (modern, capitalistic, and individualistic) culture. Ego-centered individualism was propagated largely by the social mechanism of ritual trade, which produced profound changes in cultures already traumatized by disease, defeat, and despair. Such an explanation is required to clear up confusion such as that expressed by the early ethnographer Robert Lowie at the "rank individualism" inherent in the religious structures of Plains Indians groups like the Crow.[38] Douglas observed:

Lowie pointed to this as an example of a religion that Durkheim's approach could not accommodate. This is the very type of society which Durkheim thought could not exist in primitive economic conditions: low level of economic interdependence combined with highly competitive individualism, and a religion of private guardian spirits for each man.[39]

In this system, whether among the American Indians or in New Guinea or here amongst ourselves, each person is committed to it by the lure of outstanding success (or even just moderate success) for himself.

All cultures, according to Eliade, display a yearning for the lost primordial world, which they regard as paradise. It may seem strange to modern observers that the yearning for paradise is most apparent among some of the most archaic of societies:

The most representative mystical experience of the archaic societies, that of Shamanism, betrays the Nostalgia for Paradise, the desire to recover the state of freedom and beatitude before "the Fall," the will to restore communication between Earth and Heaven; in a word, to abolish all the changes made in the very structure of the Cosmos and in the human mode of being by that primordial disruption. The shaman's ecstasy restores a great deal of paradisiac condition: it renews the friendship with the animals; by his flight or ascension, the shaman reconnects Earth with Heaven; up there, in Heaven, he once more meets the God of Heaven face to face and speaks directly to him, as man sometimes did *in illo tempore*.[40]

Nostalgia extends not only to the realm of the purely primordial but also to the dim reaches of what each group perceives to be its profane his tory. Thus, in the past, it was invariably easier to commune with the absolute: The gods were closer at hand, and shamans were more adept at their business of bringing the sacred to the profane.

Such nostalgia is not, of course, limited to archaic societies. More "modern" religions offer abundant examples: praying toward the east in the Muslim religion, baptism as reentry into paradise, the hope of paradise after death in the Christian religion, and so on. Christopher Columbus believed he had discovered paradise on his third voyage. Ponce de León searched for the fountain of youth, and as William Brandon has documented very well, early in their explorations of the New World the Spanish were guided by their belief in Quivira.[41]

Nostalgia exists in less obviously sacred realms, too. It is important to bear in mind that ritual exists as a social mechanism, and myth and symbol as social phenomena quite apart from the validity of their claim to a higher form of knowledge. Although belief in that higher form is essential, the more meaningful realm may exist apart from contemporary religious institutions. Ritual and myth are primary ways of organizing the world; they are, in fact, essential to "world construction" and so extend into areas where ritual has become degraded and the underlying mythology much more difficult to see or to attach to the obviously "sacred."

Such is the case in regard to the strange nostalgia for Native American culture—strange in the sense that the dominant Anglo culture did everything in its power to obliterate the Native American culture for a time and still behaves in a patronizing manner toward Native Americans. Nonetheless, it is obvious that "mainstream" America considers the Native American heritage to be part of its own. The American stake in Native American identity is particularly strong in regard to the Plains Indians, and, I think, even more especially the Cheyenne. Americans have a certain awe of the nineteenth-century Plains Indian way of life, and it is sometimes held up as a model for a more "wholesome" and "natural" way of life. A recent expression of this can be seen in the popularity of the motion picture *Dances With Wolves*. More revealing, there was little resistance to the idea, on the occasion of the 500th anniversary of Columbus's "discovery" of America, that European colonization had despoiled a Garden of Eden. While American popular attitudes toward Native Americans are ambivalent, it should be apparent that Native American culture, at least the romanticized conception of it, is a part of the mythological American paradise. Recognizing nostalgia for what it is acknowledges that such romanticism may be a part of a social dynamic that relegates Native Americans to a subordinate social position. It is as if we need our "primitives."

The fall 1990 issue of *The American West Traveller,* a "take-home copy" which I picked up in my hotel room in Denver, illustrates well some of the nuances of American romanticism about and nostalgia for the Native American way of life. There is a full-page ad for a bronze statue from the Franklin Mint which depicts an Indian, astride a horse, holding up a buffalo skull. The sculpture, titled "Prayer to the Healing Spirit," is remarkably similar to MacNiel's "The Sun Vow," although the advertised sculpture seems to have added one of Remington's horses and one of Bierstadt's buffalo skulls to the vignette. Christmas cards are offered on other pages, most with Western motifs, many depicting Native Americans. The message on one of the latter is, "May the warm winds of Heaven blow softly on your house, and the Great Spirit bless all who enter there. Merry Christmas and Happy New Year." I am urged to send for the 1990 *Indian Market Magazine,* which will guide me through the Santa Fe Indian Market. The guide not only will direct me to the "Hopi painter who delights in symbolism, and a Comanche couple who create miniature beadwork" but also will explain "why Indian art is hot around the world today."

As I page through the magazine, my attention is caught by a photograph of four men wearing Army fatigues, feathered headdresses, and (three of the four) Ray-Ban–type sunglasses. The photograph is an illustration for an article titled "Something to Crow About." The caption says, "The Crow color guard. The man on the right wears a genuine eagle feather war bonnet. Note the two men in the center wearing the blue and silver Combat Infantry Badge. To this day, the Crows elevate warriors to positions of respect in the tribe," as do Americans as a whole, I think.

The trans-Mississippi West occupies a position in American nationalistic mythology somewhere between what Camelot and Sherwood Forest represent to the English. It is by means of the mythology associated with the West that we have, to a considerable extent, defined our country and ourselves. The importance of the West to our national identity is why so much of Western history begins with Frederick Jackson Turner's "The Significance of the Frontier in American History" and ends with discussions and arguments about this single work. Perhaps Turner would be less misunderstood if he had more clearly identified the West as the Eden of our national origin myth.

The role of Native Americans in the national mythology has unavoidably colored American and European perceptions of Native American groups. A recurring myth, and one that has gained increasing ascendancy in the last twenty-five years or so, is one that employs the dichotomy noted by Claude Lévi-Strauss in *The Raw and the Cooked.*[42] Binary opposition is attributed here to that which is "raw and natural" on the one hand and "cooked and socialized" on the other, between what is "natural" and what is "artifice." That which is natural (cotton, rural life, "natural" foods, no make-up) is regarded as being superior to that which is artificial (plastic, city life, fast- or microwaved food, cosmetic surgery), the latter being not as (or at least less) "real" and valid. The merits or flaws of this position are well beyond the scope of this book; however, uncritically regarding Native Americans as the Noble Savage must impede to some degree the rational apprehension of the past. In reality, the Native American past was not quiescent, not a Garden of Eden nor a Peaceful Kingdom as is sometimes suggested by binary partitioning of the modern from the primitive and traditional. It was, instead, characterized by individual and collective attempts to secure meaning, security, and pleasure, and these efforts unavoidably generated conflict.

Archaeological evidence has clearly shown that these conflicts were often worked out in violent ways, ways which included scalping and other forms of mutilation.[43] Such evidence refutes recurring claims in the popular culture that scalping was a European invention.[44] In other words, the Native American past was a typically human adaptation, with conflicts and alliances arising at least in part from idiosyncrasies of personality and the accidental juxtaposition of individuals and events, rather than being an instinctive and harmonious collaboration with nature.

The images of southwestern Plains Native American groups that have realized popular currency not only in the United States but throughout the world are derived for the most part from observations made in the nineteenth century. These images, and the characteristics associated with them, have been incorporated into the national identity of the United States. Nineteenth-century images of Native Americans or Native American paraphernalia appear on coins (the "Indian Head" nickel), on stamps (the commemorative edition of Native American headdresses), in association with college and professional sport organizations (including the professional football team from the nation's capital, the Washington Redskins), as insignia on the uniforms of youth organizations (such as the Boy Scouts of America "Arrowhead" merit badges), on weapons and weapon systems (Tomahawk, Apache), on all-terrain vehicles (the Jeep Cherokee), and in any number of other places where they are generally intended to associate the bearer of the image with the qualities of independence, physical and especially military prowess, pride, endurance, and masculinity. In turn, there is a general implication that such characteristics are peculiarly American. A. Irving Hallowell has noted that

Carl Jung, who has probably analyzed more persons of various nationalities than anyone else, thought he could discern an Indian component in the character structure of his American patients, and D. H. Lawrence asked whether a dead Indian is nought. "Not that the Red Indian will ever possess the broadlands of America," he said and then added, "but his ghost will."[45]

Not only are these images and characteristics taken from the nineteenth century, they are associated with the period of most intense interaction between Anglo and Native American groups—and that of the most extensive armed confrontation between the two.

Such a "snapshot" view of these groups—most notably the Cheyenne, Arapaho, Sioux, Comanche, Kiowa, Apache, and Navajo—disregards their histories before and after the nineteenth century. These images are ahistorical—timeless. They belong to a mythological "golden age," one that sprang forth fully blown, like Athena from the forehead of Zeus. In the popular conception, these cultures existed in their natural and unchanging form from the dim recesses of the past until they were sullied by their collision with the white man's world. If they exist today, it must be only in some degraded manner.

The influence of nostalgia upon the modern perception of these particular Native American groups obscures popular, and to some extent academic, understanding of Native American groups in general. Not only does it focus on a few years out of many but also it ignores the fact that nineteenth-century southwestern Plains Native American groups developed in anything but a cultural vacuum. Their particular cultural configuration they owe in great part to interaction with the very Anglo-Americans who are often cast as their antithesis. In truth, we are much more alike than different, as Mary Douglas has pointed out. She categorized the Crow, and by extension the other Plains Indians, and the industrialized western cultures, high- and low-group societies that operate according to impersonal rules.[46] We should be alike; we are a part of the same cultural dynamic that has produced the modernity, capitalism, and individualism with which we all have since had to contend. Weston La Barre compared coup-counting and the behavior of the "Crazy Dogs" contraries with that of contemporary Americans, observing the similarities between a successful Crazy Dog and a broker who "makes a big killing on a stock market coup by the age of thirty-five—and then dies young of a coronary attack at age thirty-six."[47] Certainly, many American males would not be unflattered by the comparison of their behavior in business with that of a Plains warrior in battle. And I suspect that were they faced with the same choice that confronted young Cheyenne males, that of risking all for "success" or leading what would probably be a longer life as a "failure," many would choose, as did the braves, the former over the latter. Such is the American way.

CHAPTER 4

Castle on the Plains

New Relationships

The construction of Bent's Old Fort cast the beliefs and values of the modern world into material form. It became a kind of "medicine lodge" for the ritual behaviors—and the material symbols associated with these rituals—that served to established the new ideology in the Southwest. We can see in Bent's Old Fort the "calcified ritual" of Yi-Fu Tuan and in the history of the fort the results of that ritual. One result was the very definite class hierarchy that arose with the construction of the fort: company owners at the top, other free traders next, then trappers, then Mexican laborers, and, at the bottom, the Native Americans. Among the Native Americans, though, the Cheyenne and the Arapaho held by far the highest status, evidenced in part by the fact that they were sometimes admitted inside the fort. Other Native Americans were never permitted inside the boundaries of the fort's walls. The fort served as a "model," if you will, of the new systems of control introduced by the Anglos, but it also functioned to implement those controls. It provided a paradigm for what amounted to the industrialization of the southwestern Plains and, later, of the Southwest.

But the fort was not introduced into a cultural vacuum. Native American and Mexican groups protected and advanced their interests in strategic ways. A visitor to the Southwest today can see what was accomplished by their maneuvering: a modern society that displays a unique combination of Hispanic, Native American, and Anglo cultural traits. It is also a society in which dialogue among groups of different cultural backgrounds and resistance to cultural homogenization commonly occur.

Figure 8. Bent's Fort, as drawn by Lieutenant J. W. Abert in his "Journal from Bent's Fort to St. Louis in 1845." (Courtesy Colorado Historical Society, Denver, file #26318; Senate Doc. 438, 29th Cong. 1st sess.)

Bent & St. Vrain Company

Bent's Old Fort was by far the most impressive of several structures built by the Bent & St. Vrain Company, a partnership formed by Charles and William Bent and Ceran St. Vrain. This partnership is first evidenced by a letter dated January 6, 1831, from Ceran St. Vrain to Bernard Pratte & Co., so it seems likely that the company was formed a bit earlier, probably in 1830.[1] Later, two other Bent brothers, George and Robert, became involved with the company and lived for some time at Bent's Old Fort and the other forts owned by the company. They, however, played relatively minor roles in the general management of the company.

The company had been created to exploit the commercial opportunities offered by Mexican Independence in 1821. Beckoning American traders and trappers were the silver bullion and furs of Santa Fe and Taos, beaver pelts from the almost untrapped streams south of the Arkansas River, and the buffalo hide trade with the nomadic Native American tribes in the vicinity of the Arkansas and Platte rivers. New Mexico had been jealously guarded from the attentions of Americans until that time by the Spanish. Native American groups who were trading with the Spanish also had harassed American traders and trappers in the area north of New Mexico prior to Mexican Independence in order to protect their position in that trade.

There is some evidence that the Bent brothers had constructed a stockade at the eventual site of Bent's Old Fort as early as 1828.[2] By that time the Bents were actively trading on the Arkansas River. The construction of Bent's Old Fort from adobe bricks may have begun at that same time or a few years later. Janet LeCompte, a historian who has specialized in the upper Arkansas River Valley, has argued that work did not begin on the adobe fort before 1833,[3] although archaeological evidence indicates a beginning date of construction of about 1831.[4] Construction seems to have been interrupted by a smallpox epidemic which scarred William Bent for life.[5] A letter written by Ceran St. Vrain to the U.S. Army dated July 21, 1847, attempting to interest the federal government in the property, stated that the fort "was established in 1834," but this was written some years after the fact;[6] the fort was probably ready for business by 1833.[7]

By the time the fort was completed, the Bent & St. Vrain Company was already enjoying truly remarkable financial success. In early November of 1832 the company wagon train arrived in Independence, Missouri, with a cargo valued at $190,000 to $200,000. The silver bullion, mules, and furs had been gathered together over the course of two years.[8]

The massive adobe trading post was known as Bent's Fort and Fort William while it was occupied. It became "Bent's Old Fort" after its abandonment in 1849 and the construction by William Bent of another trading post in 1853 at Big Timbers. William Bent was the sole proprietor of this smaller post, built of lumber and stone. It soon became known as Bent's New Fort. William operated his new fort until 1860, after which he continued to trade from his ranch on the Purgatory River until his death in 1869.

The company of Bent & St. Vrain was dissolved in 1849, the year of the old fort's abandonment, a victim of rapidly changing and sometimes tragic circumstances and the inability of the company's leadership to cope with this. Charles Bent, after being appointed the first American governor of New Mexico, was murdered in Taos in 1847 by an angry mob incited by the outgoing Mexicans. Company leadership became impaired with his death, not only because of the loss of Charles's business acumen and influence but also because of the emotional reaction suffered by the surviving partners. William Bent's anger and frustration at the loss of his brother, compounded by other personal difficulties he was experiencing, may have influenced his decision to abandon Bent's Old Fort. Indications that he tried to destroy the fort as he left support this speculation. But it was Ceran St. Vrain who acted to dissolve the company. Facing up to the general unrest after the Mexican War among the Native American tribes and the changing world market for furs, as well as the death of Charles Bent, the canny St. Vrain probably decided that other ventures held more promise.

Position, Strategy, and Execution

Bent & St. Vrain Company owed its considerable success to the ability of the principals to understand, and to skillfully operate within, the emerging capitalistic world market and the Native American trading systems. The fort was essential to the company's strategy.

Whereas other entrepreneurs had deployed their own trappers or had attended Native American trading rendezvous, Bent and St. Vrain saw that operating from fixed trading posts would be a superior strategy in the trading environment of the southwestern Plains in the early 1830s. Buffalo hides were supplanting beaver pelts as the most desirable of furs in the trade. These could be procured solely from the Plains Indians, who knew not only how to hunt the buffalo but also how to prepare the fur. Various tribes among the Plains Indians, though, militantly protected the positions they had established as middlemen in Native American trade. The fixed trading posts let some of the tribes enhance their position.

Pacifying Native American groups by allowing them an important role in the fur trade permitted Bent & St. Vrain Company to maintain a presence on the international border. New Mexico, with its untrapped rivers and untapped reserves of Mexican silver, horses, mules, and blankets, lay just across the Arkansas River from the fort. The large adobe fort offered an alternate trading locale to the ancient fairs held at Taos and Pecos pueblos and the more recent Spanish and Mexican trade at the cities of Taos and Santa Fe. From the day business began at the fort, the availability of manufactured goods there drew trade from the New Mexican pueblos and cities.

During the height of the favorable market configuration, Bent & St. Vrain Company operated several smaller trading posts on the southwestern Plains in order to maximize their profits (see fig. 9). Intertribal fighting made these posts desirable, since warring Native American groups were cautious about entering territories frequented by their enemies. In 1842, Bent & St. Vrain Company built a log trading post on the south fork of the Canadian River, in what is now the panhandle of Texas. In 1845, they built a more permanent adobe post a few miles from the first. The second post on the Canadian became known as "Adobe Walls" (and was the scene of two famous battles between Anglos and Native Americans after its abandonment). These posts were established to facilitate trade with the Kiowa and Comanche, who were generally loath to venture north of the Arkansas River into the territory of the Cheyenne and Arapaho, despite the Bent & St. Vrain Company's continuing efforts to make a peace between these tribes.

Earlier, Bent & St. Vrain Company had built a substantial adobe trading post on the South Platte, north of the future site of Denver and twelve miles below what would be called St. Vrain Creek. George Bent, the brother who probably supervised its construction, named it Fort Lookout. Later it would be known as Fort George, and finally as Fort St. Vrain, most likely because by that time Ceran St. Vrain's brother Marcellin was frequently in charge there. Fort St. Vrain was more accessible to some of the bands of Cheyenne and Arapaho who preferred to stay north of the South Platte and to the Ute, Sioux, and Shoshoni. The establishment of the fort, moreover, neutralized attempts by several other traders to establish posts in that vicinity.

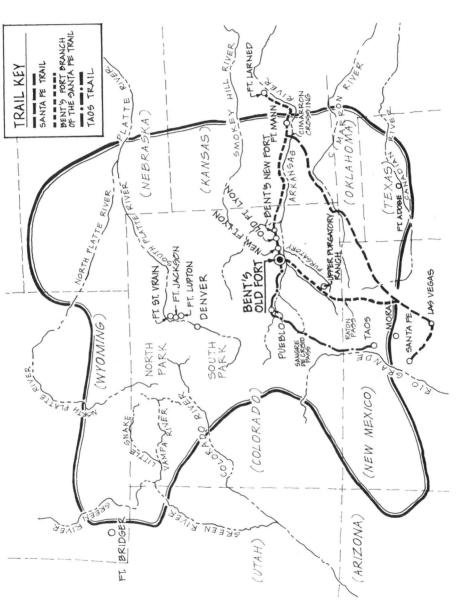

Figure 9. The trading empire of Bent & St. Vrain Company. (Illustration by Steven Patricia.)

Probably for the reason of eliminating competition, Fort Jackson, also on the South Platte, was purchased in 1838 from the firm of Sarpy and Fraeb. The fort had been backed by the powerful American Fur Company. An agreement was reached just after the negotiations for the fort were concluded: thenceforth, Bent & St. Vrain Company would not send trading parties north of the North Platte River, while the American Fur Company would no longer encroach upon the territory south of there.[9] Of the "cartel" thus formed, David Lavender commented, "And so in 1838 big business sliced up the western half of America."[10] There is every reason to think that Ceran St. Vrain negotiated this agreement by means of his close personal relationship with the family of Bernard Pratte, who was the head of the company that served as the American Fur Company's western office.

Bent's Old Fort was the most remarkable structure in the West until the mid nineteenth century and the most dominant feature in the history of the southwestern Plains. As David Lavender has pointed out: "In nearly two thousand miles from the Mississippi to the Pacific there was no other building that approached it. Only the American Fur Company's Fort Pierre and Fort Union up the Missouri were comparable."[11] Matt Field, a correspondent for the New Orleans *Picayune* who visited the fort in 1839 wrote that it was, "as though an air-built castle had dropped to earth . . . in the midst of the vast desert."[12] Did the Bents intend to impress and influence those with whom they dealt by the sheer size of the fort and its architecture, which evoked thoughts of grand castles? We cannot say with certainty, but we do know that the structure itself awed many who visited there. We know also that this worked on numerous occasions to the advantage of Bent & St. Vrain Company. By this and other means, the principals of Bent & St. Vrain were uncommonly adept at influencing persons from many different cultures and backgrounds to act for the benefit of the company. For a quarter-century they exercised control of the region from their fort.

The best presentation of the dimensions of the fort, drawn from at least twenty-six firsthand written observations and three archaeological excavations at the site, was provided by George Thorson, the National Park Service architect in charge of the reconstruction of the fort (see fig. 10). Synthesizing from the various sources, he concluded:

The fort was divided into four main areas: the compound, the inner corral, the wagon room, and the main corral. The compound was essentially a rectangular core of buildings (115 feet by 135 feet) around an inner plaza (80 feet by 90 feet). The inner corral on the east was a wedge-shaped area about 10 feet wide at the northeast bastion, expanding to 40 feet wide at the south. A 15-foot alley separated the compound from the 20-foot wagon house on the south and the 27-foot diameter bastion on the southwest corner. Therefore, the main fort was about 130 feet on the north front and 180 feet on the south with a 175-foot depth. Behind to the south was the main corral at 150 feet by approximately 140 feet (the precise dimension was lost due to earth disturbance). Twenty-nine rooms were identified on the lower level and 9 on the upper level. The enclosed rooms encompassed almost 17,000 square feet. The overall fort proper covered over 27,000 square feet, and the outer corral covered 21,000 square feet for a total of over 48,000 square feet, well over 1 acre.[13]

The fort was built without benefit of architectural drawings, and there was a lack of uniformity evident in numerous aspects of the fort's construction. The thickness of the exterior walls varied from about 2 to 2.5 feet. A National Park Service employee who was on site for several years before reconstruction began has said that the foundations of the fort, previously visible at ground surface, were not straight, but meandered along a generally linear path.[14] Modifications and additions were made throughout the fort at various times during its use, and some discrepancies between documented and observed dimensions may be due to modifications that were made after documentation. Some of the most extensive of these were made during the years 1840–41 and 1846, as activities that culminated in the Mexican War intensified.

Archaeological evidence has indicated that the two most distinctive features of the fort, the towers or "bastions" at the northeast and southwest corners of the fort proper (excluding the main corral) were of different diameters. Although Lieutenant Abert, a skilled illustrator who visited the fort in 1845 with the U.S. Army, recorded the diameter of both bastions as 27 feet, archaeological examination of the remains did not verify this. The southwest bastion is 27 feet in diameter, but the northeast is only about 20 feet.

During the fort's occupation, eight visitors recorded estimates of wall height, and these ranged from 15 to 30 feet, the average estimate being about 19 feet.[15] Only one visitor, John Robert Forsyth, estimated the height of the bastions. Forsyth, who stopped at the fort for a few days in 1849 on his way to California to search for gold, recorded in his journal that the bastions were 25 feet high.[16] The attached main corral walls were not as imposing as the walls of the fort proper, but they could be defended by arms fired from the fort in an attack. The walls here were probably 6 to 8 feet high and, by some accounts, were planted on top with thick

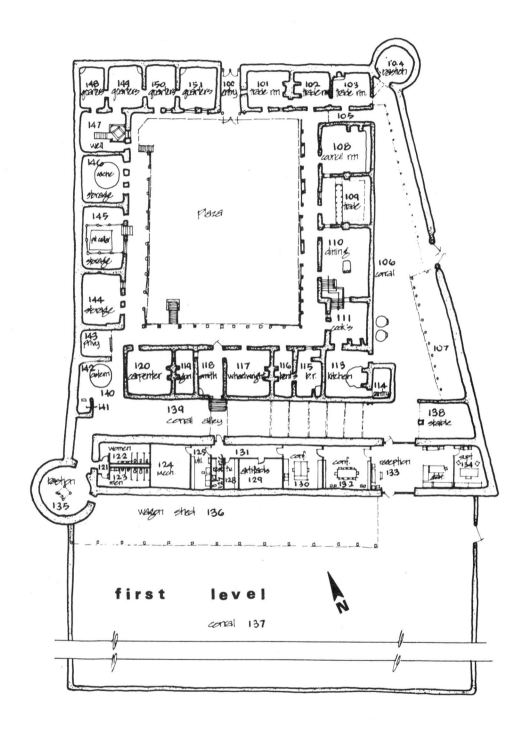

148 quarters 149 quarters 150 quarters 151 quarters 100 entry 101 trade rm 102 trade rm 103 trade rm

104 bastion

147 well

105

146 cache storage

108 corral rm

Plaza

109 trade

145 pit cellar storage

110 dining

106 corral

144 storage

111 jack's

143 privy

107

142 cistern

140

141

120 carpenter 119 wagon 118 smith 117 wheelwright 116 clerk's 115 b.r. 113 kitchen 114 pantry

139 corral alley

138 stable

121 bastion

women 122

men 123

124 mech.

125 util.

128

131

129 artifacts

conf. 130

conf. 132

reception 133

supt 134

135 bastion

wagon shed 136

first   level

corral 137

N

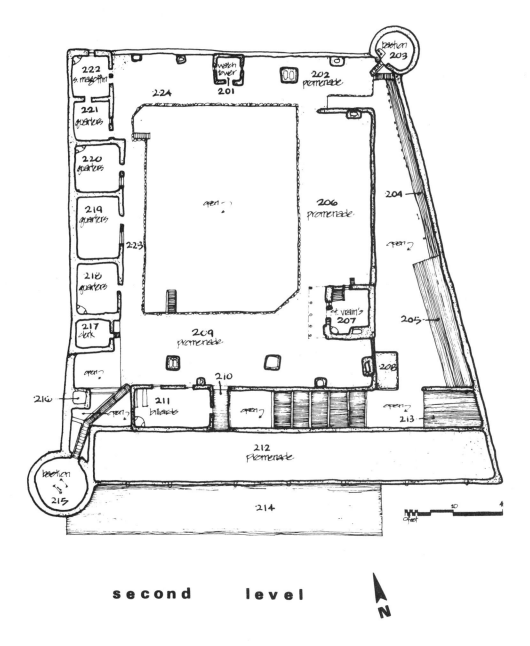

222
s. magazine

221
quarters

220
quarters

219
quarters

223

218
quarters

217
clerk

216

224

201

watch
tower

202
promenade

bastion
203

204

open

206
promenade

open

st. vrain's
207

205

209
promenade

open

208

210

open

213

211
billiards

open

212
promenade

bastion
215

214

10
feet

4

second   level

N

Figure 10. Plan view of the two levels of Bent's Old Fort. (Courtesy Colorado Historical Society, Denver; from George A. Thorson, "The Architectural Challenge," *Colorado Magazine* [Fall 1977]: 112–113.)

Figure 11. Aerial view of the excavated foundation of Bent's Old Fort, taken in 1964. (Courtesy Colorado Historical Society, Denver.)

cactus—a reasonable precaution in a country where horse stealing was an honored occupation.

From overhead, the entire structure would have appeared trapezoidal (fig. 11). The two corners thus produced, one obtuse and the other acute, afforded less cover to a person approaching from the back of the fort than would have two corners of 90 degrees. Without this aspect of the fort's design the corral area would have been less open to surveillance from the bastions and second floor of the fort.

It is plain that the fort was constructed to withstand any attack the Plains Indians might mount, and perhaps an attack from the Mexican army as well. Entry to the fort was restricted to a sort of a tunnel, a *zaguan,* in the front. The door to the *zaguan* was of stout wooden planks, sheathed with iron. Above was a watchtower with windows on three sides and a door on the fourth, providing views in all directions. A telescope assisted the watchman on duty. In the sides of the *zaguan* were small windows, which could be firmly closed or opened, so that goods could be passed to those Indians who were denied full admission to the fort. A brass cannon, mounted atop the northeast bastion, was fired on special occasions with an impressive report. Both bastions were filled with arms. Grinnell claimed:

Around the walls in the second stories of the bastions hung sabers, and great heavy lances with long sharp blades . . . for use in case an attempt should be made to take the fort by means of ladders up against the walls. Besides these cutting and piercing instruments the walls were hung with flintlock muskets and pistols.[17]

A large American flag flew from a pole adjacent to the west side of the watchtower, proclaiming the presence and power of a young country marching westward.

On the inside, the design of the fort showed the influence of both Pueblo and Spanish architecture. Room blocks formed the perimeter of the fort, about twenty-nine rooms on the ground floor, perhaps 15 by 20 feet in size. The tops of these room blocks were flat, and a man could take cover behind the parapet that was formed by the fort's exterior wall as it extended above the roof of these rooms. More rooms were added to form a full second story along the west side of the fort; rooms were also built atop the southeast corner. Huge *vigas,* cottonwood trunks, formed the superstructure of the fort and were visible in the ceilings of the rooms. Almost every room had a fireplace for warmth in the winter and on chilly evenings. During the heat of the summer, the thick adobe walls provided cool shelter.

Some rooms were for sleeping, but more were for other uses. On the first floor were storage rooms, the trading rooms, the kitchen and dining hall, and workshops for tailoring, carpentry, and blacksmithing (where activity was as incessant as in the kitchen). An office for clerks was located on the second floor. Also on the second floor was a special, large room where the fort's owners entertained friends and visitors; eventually this room contained a billiard table and bar. Usually the elite of the fort's rigid social hierarchy lived and socialized on the second floor. It appears that the Bents and St. Vrain may have had rooms on both floors, and may have had access to both by means of stairways located within or just outside their quarters.[18]

When completed, the fort could house about two hundred men and three to four hundred animals. It was staffed by almost every race and nationality that had come to the West. In addition to accommodations for those that slept within the fort's walls, many Indian lodges were frequently set up near the fort, and the numbers of Cheyenne and Arapaho who occupied them added to the activity at the fort during the day.

Bent's Old Fort dominated trade in the Southwest for almost two decades. This trade yielded immense profits in furs and silver, profits that

American businessmen had sought for decades. At the beginning of this period, the fort was a unique American presence; at the end, the area it occupied became a part of the United States.

Many of those closely associated with the fort are well known to historians, and some are familiar to almost all Americans. Perhaps the best known of those who had close ties to the fort is Kit Carson. Popularly known also are Thomas Fitzpatrick, Bill Sublette, "Uncle Dick" Wootton, "Peg-leg" Smith, and other trappers and traders. Virtually every American active in the Southwest who had any influence in commercial or political events in the second quarter of the nineteenth century visited the fort. This included all of the traders and trappers in the region. The fort was used as a staging area by General Kearny's Army of the West just prior to its invasion of Mexico at the outbreak of war in 1846, and the fort had effectively operated as a center for the collection of intelligence for that war for many years before the invasion.

Bent's Old Fort provided rich financial rewards to those associated with it. By 1840, the trading profits of Bent & St. Vrain Company were second only to those of the American Fur Company.

Prehistoric Trade Between Pueblos and Nomadic Groups

The key to the success of the Bent & St. Vrain Company was the ability of its principals to link existing networks of trade with the global system that Bent & St. Vrain represented. Trade networks in the region had been well established in prehistoric times. Some archaeologists suggest that trade between the eastern frontier Anasazi-Pueblo peoples in the Southwest and the nomadic tribes occupying mountain and plain areas may have been initiated because of the need for meat protein by the agricultural Anasazi.[19] Timothy Baugh has noted that agricultural societies in the Southwest were migrating to defensible positions near dependable sources of water and engaging in trade with more nomadic tribes by A.D. 1400.[20]

The process was accelerated by several climatological and cultural occurrences. Around A.D. 1300, a drought caused the relocation of a number of Anasazi-Pueblo villages from what is now southwestern Colorado to various spots along the Rio Grande, in what is now New Mexico. The construction of Taos, along with several other pueblos that quickly became locales for trade with the more mobile Indians, was begun during the fourteenth century. Trade routes were well established with civilizations in central Mexico and with groups on the Pacific coast by that time.[21]

The Proto-Historic Period

European contact began in earnest in the sixteenth century, encroaching upon North America from three directions. From these earliest meetings between Europeans and Native Americans emerged a pattern that would be repeated many times and in many places, including the nineteenth-century southwestern Plains and Southwest.

On the East Coast, European fishermen began exploiting the waters off Labrador, Newfoundland, and New England, putting ashore occasionally to obtain supplies and make repairs. Before long, sailors were making regular summer campsites at which nets were mended and fish were dried and smoked prior to the return voyage. Fishermen soon were engaged in barter with Algonquians, trading European goods for furs. The fur trade, here and across the continent, set off a chain of economic, social, and ideological occurrences that led eventually to European conquest of the continent.

European settlement began early in the seventeenth century with the death of Philip II in 1603 and the end of Iberian control of the Atlantic. In the next thirty years, Jamestown, Quebec, Fort Nassau at Albany, New Amsterdam, New Plymouth, and Massachusetts Bay were founded.[22]

Native Americans quickly discovered that their traditional activities could be more easily, efficiently, and effectively carried out through the use of European goods. Metal implements like knives and axe heads were superior to those made by native technologies. Firearms in some landscapes and situations enhanced the productivity of hunting and offered an advantage in armed conflict. Blankets were lighter, and, for their weight and volume, warmer than furs. Other trade goods had less utility but were soon highly desired; perhaps foremost among these was liquor. Native Americans also wanted items that could be used for decorative purposes.

Competition and conflict among Indian groups turned desire for trade goods into need. Given the voracity of the European appetite for furs, hunting and trapping grounds were soon completely "harvested," leading the natives engaged in the pursuit of furs into the territories of others. This conflict was exacerbated by competition among Europeans from different countries. The English and French, for example, vied with one another for furs that they obtained from Native Americans. In doing so, they formed alliances with specific Native American tribes: the English traded with the Iroquois and the French with the Huron. They encouraged their allies to wage war upon the tribes that were assisting the competing European country. Those attacked could only draw more closely to *their* European allies. Eric Wolf observed that:

Everywhere the advent of the trade had ramifying consequences for the lives of the participants. It deranged accustomed social relations and cultural habits and prompted the formation of new responses—both internally, in the daily life of various human populations, and externally, in relations among them. As the traders demanded furs from one group after another, paying for them with European artifacts, each group repatterned its ways around the European manufacturers.[23]

Wolf also noted that the trade changed both the character and intensity of Native American warfare. Displacement of populations from their habitat and near annihilation of whole populations through the introduction of European disease and military technology began early and continued unabated all along the eastern "front." As just one example of this, the Abenaki of the Maine coast were one of the first Native American groups with which Europeans traded for furs, beginning in the seventeenth century. By 1611, the Abenaki population had declined from about 10,000 to 3,000, most who died having succumbed to the European diseases to which they had no immunity.[24] A great wave of disease, population displacement, and warfare swept west, ahead of the presence of the northern Europeans in the New World.

While the English, Dutch, and French advanced from the east, another group of Europeans was moving into the New World from the south and west. Disease may have been an even greater factor in the social dislocations here. Alfred Crosby cites Spanish records that indicate approximately fourteen epidemics in Mexico and seventeen in Peru from 1520 to 1600. Joseph de Acosta recorded that by 1580, in several coastal areas occupied by Spain, twenty-nine out of each thirty Native Americans had died, and he thought it likely that the rest would soon follow.[25] The susceptibility of the native population to European diseases continued, evidenced by the comment of a German missionary in 1699 that "the Indians die so easily that the bare look and smell of a Spaniard causes them to give up the ghost."[26] Crosby speculates that so great was this susceptibility that the native messengers who brought news of Spanish arrival may have carried fatal infections with them, killing the recipients of the message before they ever saw the invaders.[27]

Ideology and the Europeans

Scholars of all stripes, but particularly historians, have paid more attention to the ideology of the Spanish than of the northern European groups that assaulted the New World from the east. Almost certainly this is because studies have been written from the Anglo-Saxon point of view. The motives of the northern European intruders from this perspective seem obvious: they were "economic" and therefore "rational." Most who have dealt with the subject have not considered northern European motives as ideologically based, although identification as such is implicit in William Cronen's book, *Changes in the Land,* and explicitly made by marxist-oriented theoreticians like Mark P. Leone, who draws from Althusser's treatment of ideology.[28]

Spanish motives, then, in contrast to Northern European ones, have been regarded as less tied to "rational" goals like the establishment of industrial modes of production, and therefore they have seemed more curious. Recently, William Brandon proposed in *Quivira* that the promise of treasure, based in mythology but encouraged by the successes of conquistadors such as Cortez and Pizarro, determined the nature of Spanish–Native American interaction in the New World.[29] The obsession with treasure caused the Spanish to overlook the more "realistic" economic opportunities that might have been enjoyed by taking advantage of Native American trading networks.

Brandon was more charitable to the Spanish than many earlier historians, who subscribed, as David Hurst Thomas observed, to the *leyenda negra,* the "Black Legend," which "systematically overlooked and belittled Spanish achievements." The legend held that Spain was motivated purely by "glory, God, and gold." In pursuit of their ends, the Spanish were cruel, bigoted, arrogant, and hypocritical.[30]

Thomas took issue, of course, with such disparaging remarks about the Spanish national character, yet he recognized the special place of religion in the Spanish occupation of the New World, emphasizing the "Hispanic master plan for missionization as a part of a strategy for controlling the New World."[31] In the eighteenth century, a preoccupation with the establishment of capitalistic enterprise in trade and manufacturing began to displace increasingly moribund traditional religious institutions as primary agencies of social organization in British colonies, but this did not happen in the Spanish-held colonies.[32]

Ray Allen Billington stressed what he saw as the desire of the Spaniards to "save" what they regarded as lost souls while bettering the lot of the natives:

Their task was not only to win souls, but to teach agriculture and industries which would convert Indians into useful citizens. Hence, each missionary was not only a religious instructor but a manager of a co-operative farm, a skilled rancher, and an expert teacher of carpentry, weaving, and countless other trades. The skill with which they executed these tasks attested to their considerable executive talents, just as the ease with which they pacified the most rebellious red men demonstrated their kindly personalities and diplomacy. Only rarely was the calm of a mission station marred by a native uprising; most Indians found the security of life in a station, the salvation promised them, and the religious pageantry ample compensation for the restrictions imposed on their freedom. Usually ten or more years were required to win over a tribe; then the station was converted into a parish church, the neophytes released from discipline and given a share of the mission property, and the friars moved on to begin the process anew. The mission station was a dynamic institution, forever intruding into new wildernesses, and leaving behind a civilized region.[33]

This approach did not succeed against the competition introduced into this area of the New World by other European countries, especially when the Spanish were dealing with the more nomadic Native American groups. In fact, it eventually worked to the disadvantage of Spanish hegemony:

As on other borderlands where Spanish, French, and English civilizations clashed, Spaniards failed to win the friendship of native tribes because their frontier institutions were little to the liking of the red men. They offered the Indians salvation and civilization; the French promised brandy, guns, and knives. The Spanish urged natives to abandon nomadic ways for sedentary lives in mission villages; the Frenchmen learned to live as the natives did and succeeded. Only the French government's failure to exploit its advantage saved Spain's northern provinces during those years.[34]

Billington's interpretation of these events is echoed by others, including Lewis Hanke in an essay on Spanish attitudes toward Native Americans. Here Hanke made the statement that "Spanish conquest of America was far more than a remarkable military and political exploit . . . it was also one of the greatest attempts the world has seen to make Christian precepts prevail in the relations between peoples."[35] Hanke described the debate that raged among sixteenth-century Spanish intellectuals as the colonial era began. It was an elaborate exchange between polar factions that operated within a European value and belief system. The inherent equality of all human groups was propounded by the Spanish Domini-can, Bartolomé de Las Casas; the opposing position that Indians (and, presumably, other non-Europeans) were an inferior type of humanity was argued in the writings of Juan Gines de Sepulveda. The work of Spanish missionaries was consistent with the position taken by Las Casas; the ad-ventures of the conquistadors and later military exploits with that of Sepul-veda. Spanish policy in the New World varied according to the faction in ascendancy.

The Cheyenne and Arapaho

Neither Spain's military nor its missionaries could with-stand indefinitely the economic and ideological assaults launched first by France and then the United States in what became the American South-west. And winning the Southwest was to prove decisive for the United States in fending off attempts to control western North America notably by Spain, but also by France and England.

The highly mobile Plains tribes, who in battle were capable of besting contemporary light cavalry, were the "wild card" in this game for the con-trol of the trans-Mississippi West. Of all of these groups, arguably the most important were the Cheyenne and Arapaho by virtue of their inti-mate association with the Bent & St. Vrain Company and the pivotal role played by that company in securing the dominance of the United States in the Southwest. The Cheyenne and Arapaho had realized the strategic significance of the opportunities presented by the disruption of traditional roles and ways of life that Native American groups experienced with the arrival of the Europeans. These two tribes were then in a position to cap-italize upon the European entry into the already established Native Amer-ican trading network.[36]

The Cheyenne and the Arapaho were once sedentary farmers inhabit-ing areas near the Great Lakes. Historical and archaeological records in-dicate that by the late seventeenth century the Cheyenne were in present-day Wisconsin and Minnesota, while the Arapaho inhabited portions of Minnesota and Manitoba (fig. 12).

Sometime after 1750 the Cheyenne adopted a radically more mobile

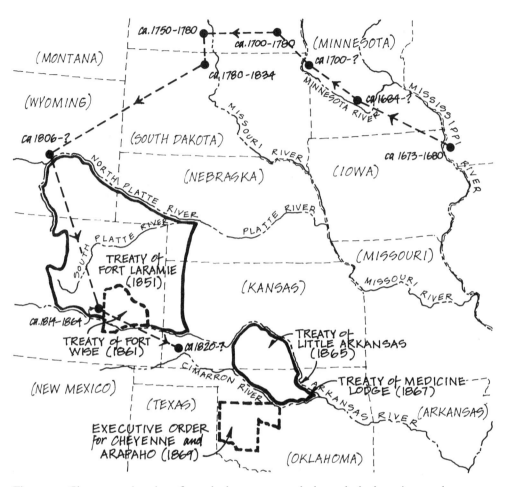

Figure 12. Cheyenne migrations from the late seventeenth through the late nineteenth centuries. (Illustration by Steven Patricia.)

lifestyle. Just before this time they had been living on the Cheyenne River in what is now North Dakota, where they had been semisedentary, engaging in enough agriculture that they were trading corn and vegetables to neighboring tribes. Then they acquired the horse in order to hunt buffalo more successfully.[37] According to Virginia Cole Trenholm, the Arapaho possessed the horse as early as 1760.[38] The introduction of the horse into Cheyenne and Arapaho cultures enabled a dramatic expansion of trading activities for these groups. By 1780, both Algonquian-speaking groups were in the upper Missouri River Valley, where they formed an alliance that has persisted to the present (see fig. 12). The precise reasons for their movements can, of course, never be surely known, but surely the first of these was the dislocation of other Native American populations.

By the 1790s, Baron de Carondelet, the Spanish governor of Louisiana, who had chartered the Missouri Company (properly the "Company of Explorers of the Upper Missouri"), regarded the Cheyenne as the shrewdest of the trading Native American groups with which he dealt. They often represented the Arapaho, who were shy with strangers but who produced buffalo robes much in demand by virtue of their meticulous preparation and the quill work with which they were decorated.[39]

This is not to say, of course, that the Cheyenne, Arapaho, and other Plains groups had not been involved with trade before they acquired the horse. The Plains network encompassed the very large area of the Plains and was linked to trading systems in the Great Basin, the Plateau, and the Southwest.[40] Abundant historical evidence reveals that trade was established between the southwestern Pueblo and the Cheyenne and Arapaho, and also between the Pueblo and the Comanche, Kiowa, Kiowa-Apache, Pawnee, and Sioux.[41] As we have seen, there is also plentiful evidence of *prehistoric* trade between the Pueblo and the Plains tribes.

Donald Blakeslee has hypothesized that the trade system grew out of a need for intersocietal food distribution.[42] Great quantities of food were typically exchanged during a trading visit. Blakeslee cited the work of Fletcher, who observed that the entire meat production of a buffalo hunt was sometimes given away as a part of the calumet ceremony that traditionally accompanied Plains trading visits.[43] In addition, feasting was perhaps the most prominent feature of these trading visits. Goods were exchanged that were used in food procurement; later, these goods included horses.

Trade was carried out in a ceremonial context in which advantage in the short term was not the first priority of either party to the trade. In fact, almost any article of trade could be obtained by a party in need by the simple expedient of sending a delegation to those possessing the desired items to "smoke" with them. After having shared tobacco with the visitors, the hosts would be committing a serious breach of etiquette if they were to deny any request made by the visitors.[44]

Another indication of the ceremonial basis for trade was the redundant nature of much of it: Groups would trade for items that they had already or for which they had little or no need. All trade was accompanied by displays of exquisite etiquette, with those hosting the traders displaying every courtesy. So intense was the desire to engage in trade, so urgent was the need to establish thereby an identity in the fast-changing world of the nineteenth-century Plains Indian, that it produced behavior that might seem bizarre to those accustomed to present-day exchanges in the United States. Plains Indian trading behavior puzzled even the nineteenth-century traveler Lewis H. Garrard, who recounted several trading episodes in the famous journal of his 1847 travel down the Santa Fe Trail. One of these is as follows:

On my neck was a black silk handkerchief; for this several Indians offered moccasins, but I refused to part with it. At last, one huge fellow caught me in his arms and hugged me very tight, at the same time grunting desperately, as if in pain; but one of the traders who understood savage customs said that he was professing great love for me. . . . So pulling off the object of his love I gave it to him.[45]

Garrard also reported an incident in which an Indian brave threw himself on the ground and cried at Garrard's refusal to trade with him.

Such recorded behavior indicates desire for enduring, kin-type relationships established by the ritual of trade much more than desire for the objects that might be obtained by trade. Ceremony not only secured an identity for participants but also had a more long-term practicality than did the sort of exchange in which the object was to obtain the greatest profit per trade. It set up relationships that insured the availability of food in times of famine. Thus Blakeslee saw the well-documented "smoking" for horses and other items as a degradation of a calumet ceremony, in which the smoking of catlinite pipes by leading individuals of two social groups set up a fictive kinship relationship between them.[46] This ceremony was the centerpiece and underpinning of a trading system that Blakeslee postulated, partly on the basis of archaeological evidence, to have evolved during the thirteenth century A.D. He regarded the trading network served by the ceremonialism to be a response to what is called the Pacific Climatic Episode (A.D. 1200–1550), when a markedly drier climate increased the danger of drought and accompanying famine to the groups involved in the network.[47] The greater the distances between trading partners, the greater the insurance, since greater distance would lessen the likelihood that the trading partner would be affected by the same drought. The most effective network, then, would be the largest possible. An environmental impetus for the trade with the southwestern Pueblo in the thirteenth century A.D., incidentally, would accord well with Timothy Baugh's idea that trade between the pueblos and the Plains groups increased as the Anasazi-Pueblo grew more focused on an agricultural technology and lifestyle.

By the early nineteenth century, bands of Arapaho were frequenting the area of the upper Arkansas. Bands of Cheyenne soon followed. There they could harvest Spanish horses and pursue their role as middlemen in the trade with the most remote of the Plains tribes, with the Pueblo tribes, and with the Spanish. They brought to the region British goods, obtained, for the most part, from Missouri River Indians. It was about this time that the Cheyenne split into Southern and Northern Cheyenne, and the Arapaho into Southern and Northern Arapaho. The continuing trade between the southern divisions of Cheyenne and Arapaho and the Bent & St. Vrain Company maintained and deepened their distinct identities. The other Native American groups mentioned were involved in trade with Bent & St. Vrain Company in one way or another, too. The most important pueblos to the Plains trade were those at Taos and Pecos. Bent & St. Vrain Company negotiated a position that usurped in large measure the traditional roles of the Taos and Pecos pueblos (and others) and the more recent role of Spanish Santa Fe. As noted, the company then linked this network with the emerging eastern United States–European mercantile system.

As an illustration of just how well established the Plains trading network was by the time of the American entry into the fur trade of the trans-Mississippi West, consider that Lewis and Clark found iron-headed war clubs among the Pahmap Indians of Idaho—war clubs traded by those on the expedition to the Mandan at their village on the Missouri River while on their way west. In a year the war clubs had moved 700 miles and, as Lewis and Clark reconstructed, through the hands of at least three tribes.[48]

The Native American "Wild Card"

The pattern of increased conflict between erstwhile Native American trading partners who allied themselves differently to competing European (and, in this case, American) factions was as much present in the southwestern Plains and the Southwest as it had been elsewhere, earlier, in the New World. Somewhat exacerbating this pattern was that certain traditional and ceremonial components of trade deteriorated as capitalistic aspects amplified. One instance of this has already been cited: The calumet ceremony, once the highlight of the trading visit, came to be practiced in a much attenuated form, one referred to as "smoking" for desired items. Although trade would still serve as an instrument of interband and intertribal cohesion, it would also provoke competition and conflict. Jockeying for position by dislocated and disarticulated Native American tribal groups would increase.

By the early nineteenth century in the southwestern Plains, the competition between European traders had narrowed for the most part to that between the Americans and the Mexicans, although there was a fear on the part of both of these nations that the British, farther to the west, might be waiting in the wings.

The position of New Spain in this competitive configuration had been, of course, usurped by Mexico. Before the successful revolt of 1821 New Spain had been assaulted by both the French and the Americans. The French gained increasing influence and an enlarging share of trade because they adapted well to Native American ways rather than trying to convert Native Americans to Christianity as did the Spanish. While the Spanish apparently succeeded to some degree with the sedentary Pueblo tribes (much of this conversion was eventually revealed to be superficial), the nomadic groups steadfastly resisted Spanish attempts at salvation.

In 1803, when the United States acquired Louisiana from France, the situation for New Spain turned from bad to worse:

For half a century after New Spain flung its protective wall across the northern approaches to Mexico, the feeble barrier underwent a constant assault. . . . Of the aggressors the most dangerous were Anglo-American frontiersmen, and their shock troops were the fur traders.[49]

Zebulon Pike had made his famous foray into New Mexico in 1806, not long after the American acquisition of Louisiana. This must have confirmed the fears of the Spanish that the Americans had their eyes on New

Mexico, had such confirmation been necessary at all. In 1804 the former Spanish lieutenant-governor of Louisiana expressed what many of his countrymen were thinking when he wrote that the Americans intended to extend "their boundary lines to the Rio Bravo."[50]

The expansionist ambitions of the United States were apparent to the Spanish. So too were the maneuvers that the Americans could undertake preparatory to an actual invasion. The Spanish understood that the Plains Indians could either impede or enhance the effectiveness of the American strategy of infiltrating New Mexico through the fur trade. David J. Weber, in his book *The Taos Trappers: The Fur Trade in the Far Southwest 1540–1846,* reported that Baron de Carondelet worried about American attempts to expand their fur trade through "control" of Native American groups.[51] And Spanish officials by 1803 had come to see the Plains Indians as an essential buffer to American encroachment, if their loyalty could be obtained through participation in the Spanish fur trade.[52]

To this end, during the ten years before the end of Spanish rule in New Mexico, the Spanish traders made a concerted and successful effort to expand their business beyond their traditional trading partners, the Comanche, to include the Kiowa situated on the Arkansas, the Pawnee who then frequented the Platte, and the Arapaho who moved between the south Platte and the Arkansas.[53] They also continued their policy of driving out or jailing any foreign trapper or trader who ventured into New Mexico. One of these, Jules de Mun, learned from the governor in 1817 of the Spanish fear that the Americans were building a fort near the confluence of Rio de las Animas and the Arkansas. The Spanish were frightened enough of this prospect to send troops to the site. When they found nothing, de Mun was released. The Spanish, in fact, were premature in their anxiety by more than a decade, as the site of the imagined fort was very near that of Bent's Old Fort.[54]

Spanish efforts to create a viable fur trade with the Indians were hampered by the structure of Spanish society. There was no middle class to carry out this work. The only persons in Spanish colonial society with enough economic and social sophistication to trade in furs were the very persons formally prohibited from doing so, the governors of the provinces and the clergy. Although many governors and some clergy did engage in such trade, the illegalities rendered their efforts problematic and most likely less effective than they might have been in other circumstances. Later, just before Mexican Independence, would-be Spanish traders were hamstrung by the most practical of considerations: the severe shortage of trade items with which to barter with the Indians. This lack made many attempts at trade with native groups incredibly small-scale affairs. Sometimes traders would endure the hardships and risks of travel to Native American groups with only a few bushels of corn to offer and would receive only a few hides in return.[55]

In summary, the fur trade under the Spanish was not well developed because of three related factors. First, as just noted, there were virtually no fur traders, that is, people trained and experienced in the trade and committed to pursuing it as a way of life. Second, the Spanish found it difficult to accommodate effectively the Plains and Southwest Native American trading systems already in place. To acquire furs, they relied primarily upon the *encomieda* system, a taxing of the Pueblo Indians by Spanish government officials. These Native American groups were sedentary and much more susceptible than were the Comanche, Apache, Kiowa, Ute, and other mobile tribes to Spanish coercion. Weber recorded a monthly payment from Pecos pueblo in 1662 as sixty-six antelope skins, twenty-one white buckskins, eighteen buffalo hides, and sixteen large buckskins.[56] The Pueblo tribes, of course, would have acquired these hides for the most part from Plains Indian groups, through the trade fairs which harkened back to the thirteenth century.

The sorts of furs rendered as tax in this example illustrate the third characteristic of the fur trade in the time period. Almost all furs traded were of "coarse" varieties, as opposed to the "fine" furs which were the main interest of the Americans, English, French, and, much earlier, the Dutch. There was a sense among these parties that pelts taken from southern areas like New Mexico might not be of the same quality as furs from farther north, where animals were subjected to more severe winters. Nonetheless, New Mexican fine furs were valuable. John Jacob Astor himself, while aware that beaver furs from New Mexico were "generally not so good" as those from farther north, still desired the New Mexican pelts because "the article is very high it will answer very well."[57] Perhaps contributing to a certain initial lack of interest in fine furs on the part of the Spanish was that fine furs may not have been as fashionable in Spain and southern European countries as they were in northern Europe.

This, however, did not lessen their value as trade items *with* northern European countries. "Fine" furs—especially beaver, but also weasel, fox, and ermine—were fashionable in northern and many western European countries and so commanded much higher prices in the mid nineteenth century than did the rough variety. Adding to their appeal was that they were more easily transportable than rough furs.

But the Spanish could not really participate in such trade because New

Mexicans themselves were not collecting pelts, and the fine furs were not available through the *encomieda* system because the Plains tribes brought only the coarse variety of furs to the pueblos. Plains Indians had been harvesting the larger skins, much more practical for their uses, for centuries, and a way of life had grown up around these harvesting activities. Bolstered by ideological systems, such behavior patterns are not easily altered. While there are numerous historic examples of Native American societies emphasizing certain economic activities at the expense of others after trade had been initiated by the Anglos, there are few examples of them adopting totally new economic activities. The adoption of farming by Plains Indians, for example, was resisted because it was not perceived as a meaningful activity. It seems likely that trapping beaver was similarly uninteresting to the Cheyenne, Arapaho, Sioux, Ute, and other tribes during the Spanish period, as there are numerous references to the unreliability of Plains Indians as a source for beaver pelt, even when the value of these pelts had been amply demonstrated to them.

American Entry into the Southwestern Fur Trade

The structure of Plains Indian culture worked to the favor of the Bents and their company. The value of beaver pelts dropped dramatically even before the midpoint of the century as the winds of fashion shifted and beaver skin hats grew *passé* among the gentry (they were replaced by silk hats). As the demand for beaver pelts diminished in Europe, there was a coincidental rise in the value of coarse furs such as buffalo, which were used as carriage lap robes, in coats, as rugs, and for other purposes that had become fashionable. Bent & St. Vrain Company, of course, employed the buffalo robe trade as the mainstay of their trading enterprise, achieving a vertical integration through the close ties they so effectively cultivated with the Cheyenne and the Arapaho and, through them, other Plains groups.

But initial interaction between Americans and Native Americans in the southwestern Plains was not auspicious. Unlike the Spanish and English, American fur traders often did their own trapping, rather than relying upon Indians to bring them furs. As noted previously, beaver trapping was not so ingrained in southwestern Plains Indian culture as in the Indian cultures of the Northeast, and Americans were therefore much more efficient at collecting beaver pelts than were the Plains tribes, which provided additional motivation for the Americans to engage in trapping themselves. Another difference between the Americans on the one hand and the English and Spanish on the other was that Americans were often independent businessmen or were grouped in competing companies, whereas the European fur traders were part of monopolistic companies supervised by their governments, like the Hudson's Bay and the Missouri companies. The United States had established government trading posts, called "factories," in 1796 to protect Indians against the unscrupulous practices of many traders, but in 1822 they were abolished. The private sector had complained vigorously that they constituted unfair competition. After the demise of the factory system, which coincided with the opening of Mexico to trade, American entrepreneurs rushed into the frontier and began to rapidly strip it of its wealth.

The Native Americans acted to preserve their position as trading middlemen. The Arapaho, for example, would not allow traders to trade in their country. Not only did the traders present a potential threat to their position, the Arapaho could acquire the goods they desired elsewhere. They visited the Arikira on the Missouri to trade furs and horses they had acquired in the southwest for European goods and corn. Some of these European goods, of course, included firearms, gunpowder, and lead. At the same time, Arapaho were trading buffalo robes and beaver pelts with the Spanish (actually, the Comancheros) to the south for firearms and other goods. When in 1811 Manuel Lisa sent Jean Baptiste Champlain to trade with the Arapaho in their southwestern home and the Spanish traders in Santa Fe, the Arapaho killed him and two of his party. The Arapaho attacked a number of other parties who ventured into this territory for the same reason: to keep intruders out of their trading area.[58]

Between about 1810 and 1820, the Arapaho and the Cheyenne gradually moved south to the Arkansas River, lured by Spanish horses and Spanish trade. Both groups stole horses from ranches in Chihuahua and Durango, which they could now trade to the Americans along with the buffalo robes that the horses helped them acquire. The Americans frequented the ancient trading rendezvous at Taos, where they brought guns, whiskey, and tobacco.[59] The lure of such items, in themselves, was not enough to generate a warm welcome for the Americans among the Cheyenne and Arapaho, since the American presence could threaten the position of the tribes within the trading configuration. Native American traders, after all, ranged as far as Missouri, the Rockies, and Canada, as well as into New

Spain. Such travels provided alternate means of access to manufactured goods. Although the Plains Indians would trade on their own terms with Americans, the tribes continued to harass Americans who entered tribal territory without their permission. For this reason several American trappers were killed near Taos in 1823.[60]

Mexican Independence

Native American hostility toward Americans may have peaked in the 1820s, as increasing numbers of trappers and traders from the young country to the east took their chances along the Santa Fe Trail, lured by the opening of New Mexico that came with Mexican Independence in 1821. Uninvited and underarmed trading parties were quickly divested of their horses, mules, and goods. By 1832 this hostility had begun to lessen.[61]

It is not coincidental that hostilities began to abate as the first trading posts were erected in the area, allowing Native American groups to trade furs (and other items) to the Americans for merchandise. In this way, the Indians' position as middlemen was resurrected and institutionalized. The most notable and successful of the companies who entered the southwestern Plains was Bent & St. Vrain Company. The fortunes of Bent's Old Fort rose with the rising tide of buffalo robe fashionability.

The new profitability of the trade in buffalo robes provided a strong and stable economic base for the relationship between the Bents and their compatriots on the American side, and the Cheyenne and Arapaho on the Native American side. Weber noted, "Unlike beaver pelts, which few Indians trapped, buffalo robes were readily available through trade with the Indians so that the fur trade could be carried out at strategically located fixed trading posts."[62] Thus the Native Americans could pursue activities that they found satisfying *and* retain their position as middlemen.

American entrepreneurs also found a much more cordial reception in New Mexico after Mexican Independence. New Mexicans possessed almost no manufactured goods during the Spanish colonial era. Their society was preindustrial. Just as there was no sector of the populace exclusively occupied with trapping or trading for furs, so there was no one engaged in the production of glass, cloth, pots and pans, ceramics, knives, and other such utilitarian items, except for personal use. Ceran St. Vrain, who ultimately made New Mexico his home, was struck with the evident poverty there, even in the cities.[63] New Mexican dwellings were dark places and rudely furnished, with no glass for windows, often no chairs, beds, or tables, and few ceramics with which to eat. Meals were often cooked in a single pot and eaten by means of tortillas. Furs and blankets took the place of furniture, but even these were difficult to obtain, except by the elite who had the goods to trade for them or the coercive power to acquire them through taxation. Desirous of the products of American and European industry, the victorious Mexicans of 1821 welcomed American traders with open arms.

For a short time this welcome extended even to trapping in New Mexico. By 1824, however, the rush of Americans into the territory had prompted an alarmed central government to decree that only "settlers" be permitted to trap beaver. As it was, in the brief period between 1821 and 1824 when the official restrictions against foreign trapping had been abolished, Americans had been intermittently jailed or otherwise harassed by officials for engaging in trapping in New Mexico. These same officials saw the 1824 decree as an urgent necessity if Mexico were to realize any benefit from this resource inside its borders. Thus the remnants of the old power structure stepped in after a few years to restore what it regarded as a semblance of order to the newly independent state.

Although manufactured goods were earnestly desired from the American traders, there was a chronic shortage of specie during the 1820s with which to purchase such items. Pelts were soon accepted eagerly—indeed, pelts were as desirable as specie if not more so, because profits taken in beaver skins were not taxed. Here was another case in which the leadership in New Mexico saw the American intruders operating outside of the legitimate authority of the new state—and depriving the state of much needed revenue by doing so.

American interest in the opening of New Mexico was intensified because of hard economic times at home. Even farmers in Missouri found that they had to supplement their incomes with trapping in order to acquire scarce capital. Potential for profit in the fur trade was much increased when the United States government abolished its "factories." The bravest of the horde of traders drawn to the Missouri River by the abolition of the factory system ventured beyond, into the newly accessible territory, led on by stories of its largely untrapped streams. Thus, in its early years, trade on the Santa Fe Trail was dominated by traffic in furs. This put additional pressure not only on these resources but also on the New Mexican government to control the activities of these newcomers.

American traders traveled to New Mexico in the summer, traded for what specie and furs they could, then stayed the winter to trap, returning home in the spring. As the political mood in Mexico turned against American trapping, increasing numbers were drawn to the small village of Taos. There authorities were not quite so watchful, and additional furs and other marketable items like blankets were available through the trading network nodules at Taos and Pecos pueblos. Taos was also attractive because it was located in the best beaver trapping area of New Mexico.

American trappers circumvented Mexican restrictions in devious ways, often with the collusion of certain Mexican authorities. Trapping permits for persons with Mexican names, for example, could be obtained by American trappers if a certain number of Mexicans were brought along on the trapping expedition as "trainees." Americans eventually claimed Mexican citizenship and frequently took Mexican brides. They set up households and diversified into other businesses. This strategy was adopted as quickly as possible by Ceran St. Vrain. St. Vrain acquired Mexican citizenship on February 15, 1831, which would have been just a month or two after he established the Bent & St. Vrain Company with Charles Bent. Thereafter, St. Vrain used the name "Severano Sanvrano" in his dealings in Mexico.[64] Simeon Turley, to cite just one other well-known example, also acquired Mexican citizenship. He then built a distillery and set about profiting from the sale of "Taos Lightning," much in demand locally and north of the border. Such expatriate Americans, who retained their patriotism without bothering too much to conceal it, were to play an essential role in the eventual American conquest of the territory.

By the late 1830s, the Mexicans had found a way to profit from the Santa Fe trade, and an embryonic middle class had formed. David J. Sandoval, who in recent years has reexamined the area's history from the Mexican point of view, noted that "as early as 1838 Mexican merchants may have transported the bulk of New Mexico–bound goods on the trail."[65] Sandoval's research indicates also a more sophisticated use of the centuries-old Indian trade fairs by the Mexicans during this time. The one at San Juan de Los Lagos, for example, lasted ten days each December. Trading done during this time was exempted from taxation, except for duties paid to the Mexican government upon entry of the goods into Mexico, and the incipient Mexican middle class used this opportunity to maximize their profits.

Mexican Independence and
Native American Relations

In the quarter-century between Mexican Independence and the Mexican War, the Mexicans suffered much more from the depredation of Plains groups than did the Americans. The situation had been deteriorating for some years even before Mexican Independence, according to David J. Weber, who saw this as a fundamental rejection of Hispanic culture by the seminomadic Native Americans. In turn, the nomadic Native Americans were termed by Hispanic frontiersmen *"indios barbaros,"* *"salvajes," "gentiles,"* or *"naciones errantes."*[66] Thus these "savage" or "barbaric" Indians were differentiated from the Pueblo Indians, who appeared more civilized to the Hispanics because of their sedentary and agriculturally based lifestyle.

It was precisely this sedentary way of life, based in agriculture or ranching, that made the Hispanic frontiersmen, the *"pobladores,"* irresistible prey for many warlike tribes including the Apache, Navajo, Ute, Comanche, Kiowa, and Kiowa-Apache. As a military veteran said of the Apache, "war with this horde of savages never has ceased for one day, because even when thirty rancherias are at peace, the rest are not."[67] This situation very likely obtained with all of the other tribes who engaged in raiding, too; harmonious relations with one band of a tribe did not necessarily mean that another band from the same tribe, or even individuals in the friendly band, would refrain from depredations. The conflict became ceaseless on the Mexican side of the Arkansas after Mexican Independence.

One reason for this further intensification of conflict after Mexican Independence was the waning of Mexican military power, which encouraged raids by the warlike groups. The Americans, however, were clearly involved in the escalating violence: The Mexicans were very aware that they were providing the seminomadic groups with firearms and ammunition. The Spanish had been careful about the numbers of such items and the ways in which they were parceled out, although they had encouraged the Indians to use firearms. In doing so, they attempted to make the Indians dependent upon them, hoping that they would lose their remarkable abilities with the bow and arrow. If this had occurred, the Spanish would have been better armed, because they offered the Native Americans only inferior firearms. Also, the Spanish had hoped that any uprising could be quelled simply by withholding ammunition and replacement firearms. This strategy was not successful because the Plains tribes retained their skill with the bow and arrow, continuing to rely upon their traditional weapons as the mainstay for hunting and warfare. The Mexicans worried about the weapons and ammunition now freely available from the Americans. By the late 1820s, as Weber noted, New Mexicans believed that "American armaments had shifted the balance of power to the Indians."[68]

The American traders who moved into New Mexico after independence in 1821 also exhibited no prudence in supplying another item. This was whiskey, a key ingredient in the general breakdown of order among Native American groups. In the long run, this probably precipitated more problems for the Mexicans than did the greater availability of firearms.

At least as important, the Americans encouraged depredations by providing a ready market for stolen goods, particularly horses and other stock. In some cases this was unintentional, but in many others, it was *not*. In just one of numerous documented incidents, the trader Holland Coffee, in 1835, met with Comanche, Waco, and Tawakoni and "advised them to go to the interior and kill Mexicans and bring their horses and mules to him and he would give them a fair price."[69]

The Plains tribes that traded with the Bent & St. Vrain Company, especially the Cheyenne and Arapaho, became "wealthy." They now had not only plentiful firearms and ammunition but also the tokens of value needed to attract warriors for raiding parties and to equip those parties with the supplies and magical fetishes needed to insure success. They also possessed the "medicine" that went with trade objects, enhancing their prestige and their ability and readiness to attract followers and allies in warfare. This increasing ability to acquire stock through raiding and furs through hunting, and the ready market provided by the Americans, produced some dramatic shifts in trading patterns and alliances—all of them toward the Americans and away from the Mexicans.

David Weber examined this realignment among the Ute. The Ute had been staunch trading partners and allies of the Mexican *pobladores* until about 1830. At that time Antoine Robidoux, an American of French descent, built two trading posts in their territory, one on the Gunnison River, the other on the Uintah River, in the area that is now Colorado. Seduced by Robidoux's guns and ammunition, the Ute no longer had need of the inferior goods offered by the old trading partners, the *pobladores*. It was not long before the *pobladores*, in fact, were seen as appropriate targets for Ute raids. By 1844, the Ute "war" on the *pobladores* had begun.[70]

Finally, we can see how certain sorts of traditional Plains Indian behaviors were amplified through the influences of the Americans. These influences were not only the introduction of exciting new weapons and a large and ready market but also the dislocation of relationships among Native American groups. Westward-moving Americans were pushing Native Americans ahead of them. At the same time, new alliances were forged, for practical purposes, among tribes that might otherwise have warred. Thus Plains Indians like the Cheyenne, Arapaho, Kiowa, and Kiowa-Apache for economic reasons could not wage war on the Americans—or on each other. Among the Plains tribes, though, the most meaningful of activities were those that proved prowess in hunting, raiding, or war. The new alignment of the Plains Indians on the American side (with the notable exception of the Comanche, as we have seen) both directed this orientation of behavior against the Mexicans and intensified it.

Now the rewards for raiding were doubled. One could not only count coup but also could gain added prestige by the acquisition of really substantial booty. The orientation toward raiding and warfare was further intensified as buffalo disappeared. In the absence of buffalo to hunt, there was for a man, according to the Plains Indians system of values and beliefs, little else worth doing than warfare and raiding.

The Preeminence of Bent & St. Vrain Company

By the mid 1830s, Bent & St. Vrain dominated the fur trade in the southwestern Plains and the Southwest, in large part because of the relationship the firm had established with the Cheyenne and Arapaho. Bent & St. Vrain Company had not secured their trading relationship with the Plains tribes unchallenged by other American traders, who were just as aware of the financial opportunities that had arisen with Mexican Independence. Although the precise chronology is fuzzy, the noted historian of the upper Arkansas, Janet LeCompte, believed that a trader named John Gantt was the "first Cheyenne trader on the Arkansas."[71] But this competitor with the Bent & St. Vrain Company was simply not as successful at establishing firm and lasting relationships with the Native American groups of the area.

It seems likely that Gantt alienated the Cheyenne and Arapaho from the beginning of his interaction with them. Although he was licensed to trade with the Indians, LeCompte reported that his real intention was to have his own men trap beaver, thus cutting out the Cheyenne and Arapaho as middlemen.[72] Even after Gantt decided to construct a trading post and deal with the Cheyenne and Arapaho on their own terms, he was out-maneuvered in the establishment of relationships with these potential trading partners.

Many sources record that William Bent made the decision to build his adobe fort near the Purgatoire after a visit by the Cheyenne Chief Yellow Wolf to his temporary picket stockade, which he had located farther up the river. Yellow Wolf is said to have told Bent at this meeting that the Cheyenne would trade with Bent if he would move his operation farther down the Arkansas, into the buffalo range and the traditional wintering ground of "Big Timbers."[73] The significance of this event is heightened in light of Weber's discovery that the Spanish had heretofore been engaging in trading rendezvous with the Plains tribes at this location, even as early as 1818.[74] This might well mean that Yellow Wolf's directions to Bent signaled the intention by the Cheyenne that he would replace the Spanish traders as the Cheyenne's primary trading partner and supplier of manufactured goods. This is a message that, given Bent's probable knowledge at the time, he could understand.

Although Bent did not move quite so far as Big Timbers, he did in essence follow Yellow Wolf's advice, embarking upon a cooperative association with the Cheyenne that would be firmly cemented in 1835. In that year he married Owl Woman, daughter of White Thunder, Keeper of the Sacred Arrows, and thus probably the most respected man among the Cheyenne. By doing this, William Bent became a Cheyenne himself. Many years later, when Owl Woman died, he married her sister, following Cheyenne tradition. Other intimates of the Bents married Cheyenne or Arapaho women. Kit Carson, for example, a friend and associate of the Bent family since childhood, took an Arapaho wife.

Perhaps the most telling incident in the competition for trade relations with the Cheyenne and Arapaho occurred in mid summer of 1834. Gantt had moved his trading operation, like Bent had earlier, downstream, just three miles west of—Bent's Fort. Copying Bent, Gantt was also building an adobe fort, replacing the stockade he had just abandoned. When a party of Shoshoni camped near Gantt's Fort, still under construction, Bent led ten of his men in an attack on the Shoshoni, killing and scalping three of them. He also encouraged the Arapaho and Cheyenne with whom he was trading to steal the Shoshoni horses. The Arapaho and Cheyenne needed little encouragement, being bitter enemies of the Shoshoni. This show of force by Bent had at least two effects. First, it intimidated and shamed Gantt, who was shown to be unable or unwilling to defend his trading partners. It also demonstrated Bent's solid affiliation with the Cheyenne and Arapaho and strengthened that affiliation, since they banded together to defeat a common foe. William Bent may have had more than this rather devious end in mind when he precipitated the attack, since a witness stated that William said the reason for his action was that the Shoshoni had stolen some mules from his brother.[75] Whatever Bent's motivation, Gantt withdrew from competition for the Indian trade in the area not long thereafter.

With that, Bent & St. Vrain secured a powerful position in the fur trade. The friendship of the Cheyenne and Arapaho provided the company with a source of coarse furs and protection for the other aspects of their business, which included the trade in fine furs obtained from "mountain men" who would henceforth gather at the fort for supplies and companionship. The Cheyenne and Arapaho, in return, received manufactured goods and the associated "medicine," which could attract allies and intimidate enemies.

Eventually, the Bents encouraged the Cheyenne and Arapaho peoples to make peace with some of their traditional foes. Such peace benefited the Bents because it facilitated trade with the enemies of the Cheyenne and Arapaho, thus expanding their ready source of buffalo robes. The Comanche, who generally stayed on the south side of the Arkansas, fell into this category. Because of the Bents' alliance with the Cheyenne, the Comanche considered themselves enemies of both parties. One instance of Comanche hostility toward Bent & St. Vrain Company was the murder of the Bents' horse herder and the theft of as many as one hundred horses in 1839.[76] Also, Robert Bent, brother of William and Charles, was killed by Comanche warriors in 1841. Despite such incidents, the Bents were determined to trade with the Comanche, and also the Kiowa, who were not only enemies of the Cheyenne but also traditional trading partners with the Mexicans and, before them, the Spanish.[77] In acquiring these groups as trading partners, the Bents were incidentally moving them closer to the American side of a conflict that had long been developing with the Mexicans.

In 1840, the Bents' efforts paid off. In the summer of that year, at a location on the Arkansas near Bent's Old Fort, peace was made between the Cheyenne and the Arapaho on one side and the Kiowa, Comanche, and Kiowa-Apache on the other.[78] The peace was sealed with an exchange of items that both sides had obtained from Bent's Old Fort, including guns, beads, blankets, cloth and brass kettles. Very probably these were regarded as among the most precious objects the tribes possessed because of their "medicine." With this, the number of individuals with whom the Bent & St. Vrain Company could trade for furs was doubled. By the next year, 1841, Charles Bent wrote to Manuel Alvarez in Taos that he expected 1,500 lodges of Comanche and an equal number of Arapaho, Cheyenne, and Sioux that year. He wrote later that thirty-one Comanche and Kiowa chiefs had arrived in March at the fort, noting, "They have made peas [sic] with us."[79]

After the Mexican War

The principals of the Bent & St. Vrain Company had been greatly involved with the preparations for the Mexican War and were instrumental to the war's success. It is ironic that the war destabilized the area to the extent that the Bent & St. Vrain Company could no longer survive. Newcomers streamed in during the war and after American victory, and buffalo herds decreased rapidly. With these developments, the Plains tribes turned more than ever to raiding.

Comanche hostilities intensified from 1846 to 1849, with severe consequences for the company. In the summer of 1847, attacking wagon trains and troops on the Santa Fe Trail more ferociously than ever before, the Comanche took sixty white scalps, and they destroyed or stole about 330 wagons and 6,500 head of stock.[80] In 1848, the Kiowa responded by informing the Indian Agent for the territory, the old Bent & St. Vrain Company employee Thomas Fitzpatrick, that they would no longer be allied with the hostile Comanche but would join the peaceful Cheyenne and Arapaho on the Arkansas River. Despite their action, the Comanche hostility and the general disruption of activities in the southwestern Plains that it engendered greatly curtailed Bent & St. Vrain Company's ability to carry out trade.

Ceran St. Vrain went to St. Louis in the summer of 1848 to dissolve the company. Charles Bent had been killed in the uprising at Taos in January of 1847. This left William Bent as the sole original principal of the firm, and the only one who remained on the Arkansas. In August 1849, William Bent packed up all that could be moved and set out downstream. After the wagon train had gone several miles, he returned alone.

What happened next is uncertain. What is known both from written accounts from that time and archaeological evidence is that his actions in some way caused a fire that substantially damaged what had been called his "adobe castle." One story was that the cholera epidemic at the fort prompted him to set barrels of tar burning in order to fumigate the fort, and that this set the fort ablaze. Others believed that William Bent, despondent over his recent personal and financial losses, set barrels of gunpowder to explode in several rooms. According to a contemporary, he abandoned the fort because it was "impossible to hold possession of it against the united tribes of Indians hovering around it."[81]

For the rest of his life, William Bent traded with his wife's people, the Cheyenne, at much smaller trading posts he built at Big Timbers. Ceran St. Vrain would make his living at Taos as a merchant, miller, and contractor. Ironically, this was the town the nobly born Frenchman had referred to in a letter to his mother in 1825 when he wrote that he was "oblige[d] to spend the winter in this miserable place."[82]

The favorable relations with the southwestern Plains Indians that the Americans had cultivated with so much benefit for twenty-five years deteriorated rapidly after 1846. As the basis for trade was removed, the rituals associated with the exchange no longer acted to maintain fictive kinship relations. As we have seen, however, the Native Americans during the period of Mexican Independence, 1821–1846, truly weighted the equations of power to the advantage of the Americans. Ironically, the general strife among the Plains Indian tribes ultimately did great damage to some of the Americans who had been most instrumental in organizing the alliance against the Mexicans, including those individuals associated with the company of Bent & St. Vrain. But by this time the war was over, and the Southwest and California belonged to the United States.

CHAPTER 5

Ritual Trade

Sentiment and Conquest

In the sense that the fur traders were the "shock troops" of the American assault on the Southwest, as Billington put it, the conquest of the region occurred with stunning speed. Before 1821, Americans were seldom allowed to cross the Arkansas River, and there was practically no intercourse between Mexico and the United States. But after 1821, with Mexican Independence and the possibility of commerce with New Mexico, American fur traders provided the opening wedge for American influence in the arid plains and green mountain valleys south of the Arkansas. By 1846, General Kearny's army walked unopposed into Santa Fe. There were a few small-scale armed uprisings early on, but within a year any semblance of organized resistance among the erstwhile Mexican citizens had passed. The economy in the region rapidly diversified after this as mining, ranching, and farming replaced the dwindling fur trade in importance. Populations of Americans greatly increased. Roads, railroads, and telegraph lines were constructed. The Native Americans rebelled but were crushed and, by the third quarter of the nineteenth century, were removed to reservations.

This American conquest had depended upon the formation of new alliances and new common realms of understanding between indigenous groups and the Americans. Key Plains tribes had been transformed into allies of the Americans and enemies of Mexico during the period just prior to the Mexican War, and the alliance had been secured by making these Plains tribes trading partners. The role of the Plains Indians in destabilizing New Mexico and, in the case of the Cheyenne, providing a kind of private army to Bent & St. Vrain Company was somewhat tardy confirmation of the Baron de Carondelet's fears about unleashing American influence in the area should trade relations be established by America with the Native Americans. At the same time, resistance to American influence in New Mexico was weakened through the same social mechanism—by engaging Mexican citizens in the trade. Some Hispanics, like Manuel Alvarez, became traders in their own right, traveling to New York, London, and Paris to negotiate more favorable terms for the acquisition of trade goods and cutting out the trading houses in St. Louis from this exchange.[1] Others had become part of an emerging middle class by transporting goods over the Santa Fe Trail.[2] And virtually all New Mexicans were eager for the manufactured goods of the United States and Europe. To a remarkable degree, the Bent & St. Vrain Company provided the agency by which all this was accomplished.

But even this does not tell the whole story. The trading relationship had already wrought fundamental changes to Native American and Mexican cultures alike by the time of the Mexican War. They had been preadapted to inclusion in the emerging global modernity. They were already taking on many characteristics of the high-grid, low-group culture of capitalism and individualism, an ego-centered configuration of society in which each individual must take personal responsibility for manufacturing a viable social identity.[3] Adopting aspects of the ethos of capitalism and individualism was not necessarily immediately beneficial to all individuals in both of these more traditional cultures and often did not fit comfortably with many firmly held beliefs and values. In fact, it set up a cultural tension still not resolved today, especially for many Native Americans. Nonetheless, the cultural dynamics of the time made capitalism and individualism appear highly desirable, perhaps inevitable, and established them as standards that would henceforth be considered natural and normal.

There were essentially two components involved in the transition of these traditional cultures to the new apprehension of life. The first was the destruction of the existing social order. Native American groups had already experienced roughly three hundred years of disease, dislocation, and social disruption. The Sun Dance was formulated in the eighteenth century as an attempt to revitalize a religious structure that then appeared inadequate to the threats to tribal survival. Since that time, dislocation and radical changes in lifestyle had not ceased. For their part, New Mexicans were on the far periphery of the Spanish Empire, generally ignored by the central government, and often living a life of bare subsistence. They

Figure 13. Drawing by Lieutenant Abert in 1846, showing the use of a pipe in a ritual exchange in the trade room of Bent's Old Fort. (Courtesy Colorado Historical Society, Denver.)

were subjected to incessant raiding by the *indios barbaros,* raiding often instigated by the new allies of the Plains Indians, the Americans.

The second component was the initiation of trade. Trading relations provided a means by which to remake the fragmented cultures of the Southwest. Trading was done by these traditional cultures, as we have seen, not only for profit and, in the beginning of the relationships, not *primarily* for profit. Trade was accompanied by ritual that referred to primordial acts of creation. The trade ritual of the Cheyenne, for example, utilized a sacred pipe, the bowl of which was made from catlinite, stone found only in the ancestral home of the Cheyenne. The use of this stone is only one of many references to the creation of the world in the formal calumet trading ceremony. Figure 13 shows a drawing by Lieutenant Abert of an exchange ceremony in the trade room of Bent's Old Fort. The pipe here is almost surely of catlinite. Whether this was a formal calumet ceremony or a more degraded form, such as "smoking over" the trade, the point is that, to the Cheyenne and other Plains tribes, all such exchange referred to a primordial archetype. Those who participated in the exchange, then, were proclaiming a common mythical ancestry and, thereby,

establishing fictive kinship relations. Profit may have been a consideration but was not paramount in importance. Likewise, the reciprocal obligations established by fictive kinship relations may have been useful from
a practical standpoint. It seems unlikely, however, given a traditional view
of the world, that practical considerations were primary. Most important
was the establishment of social relationships. In a traditional world, this
is essential to establishing a viable identity. As time passed, the concern
for profit grew—and this was the key indication that the Plains Indians
had been won over to important aspects of the new ideology. Within the
new ideology, profit was a necessary step in establishing a viable social
identity.

Understanding how trade brought about this cultural change involves
looking at trade and trade goods in a new way. The new perspective recommended here is one that searches for the *meaning* attached to trade
objects, meanings that are assigned through formal or fugitive ritual. In
subsequent chapters, we will look also at how meaning is attached ritually to other sorts of material culture, including the landscape itself, and
how the cultural assumptions and values thereby propagated advanced
the culture of modernity in the Southwest.[4]

The Meaning of Trade Goods

Native Americans profoundly altered their societies in order to acquire European trade goods. They did this in ways that suggest
to me that these goods held meanings that transcended functional value.
I contend that the symbolic significance of trade material is overlooked
in most scholarly and popular works that deal with trade. The value of
goods traded is regarded, usually, as "self-evident": self-evidently functional, prized as a status item, or useful to further trade. Examples abound
and include competent and even notable works of scholarship.[5]

I suggest that the meaning and value (even from a modern functional
or "capitalistic" perspective of value) of trade material is not at all self-
evident, but is entirely dependent upon the context of exchange. Exchange
everywhere in North America established the first relationships between
Euro-Americans and Native Americans and thereby laid the basis for all
future relationships between them. To Native Americans, trade established
certain *obligations* and *rules of conduct*. Often such obligations were ignored
and the rules violated by the Euro-Americans. Successful Euro-American

traders were quick to grasp and manipulate the symbolic importance of trade items, but as the resources—fur-bearing animals—exploited by Native Americans for their part of the trade diminished, these traders were unwilling or in some cases unable to fulfill their obligations.

Participation in this trading relationship cost Native Americans dearly. The firearms introduced by Euro-Americans contributed to the overexploitation of resources and heightened intertribal conflict. Contact with Euro-Americans introduced, time and again, diseases for which Native Americans had no immunity and that killed large percentages of Native American populations. The combination of drastic population reduction and the reorientation of Native American economies toward the production of furs for trade produced massive social dislocations and migrations of population, which further exacerbated intergroup conflict.

The process just described occurred repeatedly over 400 years. The Native American survivors of the nineteenth century, a small group compared to the population at the time of initial European contact, were now operating within a system of beliefs and values that was still traditional in nature, but it was a system that had been much modified by the experiences of the intervening centuries. In the case of the Plains Indians, the system of beliefs and values was now oriented toward a nomadic existence of hunting and warfare. The complete disappearance of even *this* modified traditional way of life—brought about by the end of the trading relationship, dense Euro-American settlement of the continent, and the relegation of Native Americans to reservations—produced an *anomie* which has been manifested in numerous ways. These manifestations of despair range from the Ghost Dance mania of the 1890s to the widespread and chronic health problems brought about by alcoholism and violence in Native American populations today. Such despair is inexplicable without reference to the social relationships and the betrayal of those relationships (which were at best unequal in terms of power) that brought it about. It is the despair of the "disembedded," as Anthony Giddens might put it.[6]

The original Native American–Euro-American trading relationship is important for a related reason. It is no coincidence that the trade goods that provided the focal point of Euro-American–Native American relationships in historic times—alcohol, tobacco, firearms, furs and hides, beads, shells, and various sorts of bodily adornments—are still employed, tragically or creatively, as current touchstones of "Indian-ness" which work to *re*-embed Native American culture within a "cosmic" order. To understand how these items realized their significance, how this was exploited, and why this symbolic power remains, one must look to the original, historic context of their use.

Finally, it is important to understand how traditional values and beliefs attached to trade were altered by exposure to capitalism. The history of the Cheyenne and Arapaho, for example, indicates that while a continuum exists from "gift" exchange on the one side to "market" exchange on the other, these types of exchange are not mutually exclusive. Aspects of market exchange are present in "gift" societies, but, perhaps even more important, aspects of gift exchange are present in "market" societies. In fact, the ritual aspect of any sort of exchange acts to shape social relationships. In the modern world, this is usually overlooked. Paradoxically, as virtually all enduring social relationships have withered away, this has become the preeminent mechanism by which social identities are formed. Ritually assigned meaning, based upon fugitive myth, forms the basis for the much decried "materialism" of the modern world. Material objects still represent social relationships, and most of these relationships are imaginary. A good example of such an imaginary relationship is that which the Native Americans believed to be symbolized by the peace medals, beads, firearms, and other trade objects presented to them by the whites. The Native Americans assumed that such items established a relationship of long-term reciprocal commitments, one essentially alien in the modern world.

Poststructuralism

The social context by which meaning is assigned to trade goods—or any item of material culture, for that matter—operates in a way similar to, but not identical to, that of linguistic context. As Ferdinand de Saussure observed, the relationship between the linguistic *signifier* and the *signified* is purely arbitrary.[7] In the case of trade, the relationship between the object and what it "means" is also arbitrary. A structural linguist would maintain that the meaning of a word is determined by the relationship between that word and others. A relationship of binary opposition is the most obvious. Thus, "black" clearly means the opposite of "white," "love" of "hate," and so forth. But, meaning is really not quite so simple and cannot be adequately explained by this model. Meaning is really determined by numerous relationships, not only between words, but between words and other value-laden cultural phenomena, such as meanings attached to nonverbal symbols, and values and beliefs that are difficult to articulate because they are partially or wholly embedded in the pre- or subconscious (often these are related metaphorically, as in myths, stories, and anecdotes). Richard Harland provided an example. The meaning of the word "rape" depends upon its relationship, in a structural sense, to words like "marriage" and "love"—so much so that feminists have had difficulty in achieving acceptance of concepts like rape within marriage and date-rape.[8] That some acceptance of these notions has occurred is an indication of a change in context larger than a purely linguistic one. It is this sort of a context that concerns "poststructuralists." Generally, as in this example, it is a cultural context that includes changes in role, status, power relationships, and definitions of identity. And, it is just this sort of "poststructuralist" context that must be taken into consideration in order to understand trade goods, although it almost always has not been. Instead, we have had functionalist treatments of trade goods, treatments that have bolstered stereotypes of Native Americans: Native Americans "foolishly" trading away Manhattan for a few dollars' worth of beads, Native Americans incapable of "handling" alcohol.

An Examination of Some Representative Treatments of Trade Goods

Much of our misunderstanding can be attributed to false assumptions about Native American culture. Some of these may be discerned in what is nonetheless an excellent survey of relevant literature by Guy Prentice, which deals with a sort of trade object employed by Mississippian societies from A.D. 1000 to 1400, just prior to European contact. These objects were marine shell beads and columellae. Prentice argued that marine shells should not be regarded as, primarily, status items, the usual interpretation of this material. Instead, they should be regarded as "wealth items of extreme tradeability (i.e., a form of primitive money) and secondarily as status items."[9] In making this argument, Prentice cited the ethnohistoric record and archaeological data and provided what he called a "wealth item model" for marine shell bead use that he thought explained this data better than did the status thesis. Prentice noted that the context in which marine shells have been found at archaeological excavations, often in burials, has encouraged the interpretation of their use as status markers. Commenting on this, he quoted Hodder as saying that we "must not expect simple correlations between social organization and burial."[10] More than status is signified by burial symbolism, he argued, including "ideas concerning death in general, and notions regarding those aspects of social life which should be represented in death."[11] While these comments are a bit vague, they do hint at a value and belief system concerned with more than just status, per se. More convincing for his case is the volume of ethnohistorical evidence he amassed that shows that marine shell items were used by Native Americans, and other traditional peoples, not only as symbols of rank and status but also as a form of wealth. He cited Jane Safer and Frances Gill, who studied the Yurok of northern California:

Tusk shells could purchase a wide range of goods, whose prices were fairly standardized, and virtually all obligations and services from bridewealth to blood debt for murder were valued in tusk string shells.

The Yurok were preoccupied with the acquisition of wealth, in the form of tusk, shell strings, and also woodpecker scalps and obsidian. They believed that if a man fulfilled all religious obligations meticulously, not only would he have luck in hunting, he would draw tusk shells to himself. A large collection of tusk shell strings did not automatically confer prestige, but it was a necessary prerequisite: High status in the community could not be achieved without such a collection.[12]

Safer and Gill also reported on the Pomo of central California, who made shell "money" from the Pismo clam. These cylindrical beads could be owned by men and women and were used to purchase food, bows and arrows, animal hides, baskets, and a host of other things. They concluded, "In most societies where individuals can accumulate wealth, riches and high status go hand in hand."[13] Prentice concluded that "it is this relationship between status and wealth which makes the concept of wealth so important in archaeological and anthropological studies."[14]

Prentice fit all of his data into a body of well-established anthropological theory, most of which posits that the "rise" of less-complex societies to more-complex societies (that is, chiefdom societies from big-man societies, and states from chiefdoms) "may be directly attributable to (although not entirely dependent upon) the ability of the elite to control wealth."[15] Even the very simple big-man society, he noted, depends upon the capability of big men to accumulate and redistribute wealth.

The problem with Prentice's idea concerning the centrality of "wealth" in traditional societies, even the role of wealth in the evolution of society, is that he was using a term that is tied to a very modern notion, that of abstracted, standardized value—a term "steeped" in modernity, abstraction, and the removal of the subject from the object or immediate experience. All objects in traditional societies signify something much more complex than abstract wealth. (I would maintain that they do this also in modern societies, although perhaps to a lesser degree, but I will not make that argument here.) Prentice was using a modern cultural context in his attempt to explain traditional phenomena. To understand more completely, we must try a bit harder to see the world according to tradition.

A way to do this was provided by the early cultural observer, Marcel Mauss, in his classic, but now frequently overlooked, *The Gift*. Mary Douglas speculated in a foreword to a recent edition of this as to why "this profound and original book had its impact mainly on small professional bodies of archaeologists, classicists, and anthropologists."[16] She suggested that Mauss and Durkheim represented a kind of social democracy that opposed (perhaps it would not be too much to say, existed in binary opposition to) an Anglo-Saxon utilitarianism, a Social Darwinism. The debate between these two positions was eclipsed after the First World War by that between social democracy and both fascism and communism. Once political fashions again changed, Douglas saw the chance to utilize Mauss to once more engage and contest the idea of "methodological individualism" (or the idea that the individual is the prime mover in society).

Whatever the merits of Douglas's evaluation of intellectual trends, *The Gift* provided a cultural perspective that more closely approximates the traditional apprehension of exchange and of the material objects involved in that exchange. Mauss noted that exchange in traditional societies (which he also called primitive or archaic societies) is always characterized as gift giving. The giving of gifts is always described by informants in these societies (and, therefore, probably conceived of consciously) as voluntary. In fact, as Mauss's fieldwork and scholarship (since bolstered by any number of other studies) clearly demonstrated, *both the gifting and the reciprocation of the gift in one form or another is strictly prescribed by the traditional culture.* Mauss asked, rhetorically, "What power resides in the object given that causes its recipient to pay it back?"[17] The answer to this, of course, is that the object itself has no "power" or "meaning" (and, for that matter, no "value" in the abstract modern sense, either), power is culturally inscribed — and inscription, for the most part, is achieved through the *ritual* that accompanies both gifting and the reciprocation of the gift.

Mauss referred to this sort of ritual exchange as a "total" social phenomenon, total because it involved all aspects and institutions of society: economic, religious, moral; forms of production and consumption; political and familial units.[18] One might well argue that this occurs, in part, because traditional societies are not as differentiated as modern ones; firm distinctions do not exist between institutions, or between functional segments. In what could well serve as a reply to Prentice, Mauss said this about the exchange practice in traditional societies:

Yet the whole of this very rich economy is still filled with religious elements. Money still possesses its magical power and is still linked to the clan or to the individual. The various economic activities, for example the market, are suffused with rituals and myths. They retain a ceremonial character that is obligatory and effective. They are full of rituals and rites.[19]

There are other differences between *uses* of wealth in traditional and modern societies:

They hoard [in traditional societies], but in order to spend, to place under an obligation, to have their own "liege men." On the other hand, they carry on exchange, but it is above all in luxury articles, ornaments or clothes, or things that are consumed immediately, at feasts. They repay with interest, but this is in order to humiliate the person initially making the gift of exchange, and not only to recompense him for loss caused him by "deferred consumption." There is self-interest, but this self-interest is only analogous to what allegedly sways us.[20]

In part, Mauss drew upon Bronislaw Malinowski's *Argonauts of the Western Pacific* for data with which to bolster his characterization of traditional exchange.[21] Malinowski emphasized the eclectic nature of this; the ritual mixes things, values, contracts, and men together.

The centerpiece of Malinowski's study is the famous *kula ring,* a phenomenon that attracted a great deal of Western attention precisely because it appeared so nonsensical to modernist observers. The kula ring refers to a system of ritual trade of *vaygu'a,* "a kind of money," which is of two sorts. The first of these are the *mwali,* bracelets carved and polished, which are kept in a shell until great occasions when they are worn by their owners or the owners' relatives. The other form of *vaygu'a* are the necklaces called *soulava,* which are carved from the mother-of-pearl of the red spondylus. The chain of islands involved in the kula trade forms a circular pattern. The *mwali* are always traded in one direction, the *soulava* in the other. Only certain persons of high prestige are permitted to own the *vaygu'a,* and these individuals may own them several times over the course of their lives. Ownership, then, is of a particular sort: one may not keep these items too long, and they may only be traded in a *kula* ceremony. The *vaygu'a* eventually build upon a history, a story that is told about who has owned them and the circumstances of their exchange; eventually, each is given a name and is attributed with a personality. Some persons take their own name from that of an especially admired *vaygu'a*. The objects become sacred. Malinowski noted that to have such an object in one's possession is "exhilarating, strengthening, and calming in itself."[22] So strong is their power that *vaygu'a* provide solace to the dying: They are rubbed on the dying person's stomach or placed on his forehead, for example, as if the association with the sacred object could imbue his life, quickly passing away, with meaning. This power appears analogous to the *medicine* of the Plains Indians.

At the same time as the *kula*—at the intertribal fairs that accompany the kula ceremony—the Trobrianders practice the *gimwali,* a much more "capitalist" affair in which an economic exchange of useful goods is conducted. Hard bargaining is done here, of the sort that would be totally inappropriate in a *kula*. Mauss summarized the role of the kula as follows:

The kula, in its essential form, is itself only one element, the most solemn one, in a vast system of services rendered and reciprocated, which indeed seems to embrace the whole of Trobriand economic and civil life. The kula seems merely to be the culminating point of that life, particularly the kula between nations and tribes. It is certainly one of the purposes of existence and for undertaking long voyages. Yet in the end, only the chiefs, and even solely those drawn from the coastal tribes—and then only a few—do in fact take part in it. The kula merely gives concrete expression to many other institutions, bringing them together.[23]

I would like to emphasize certain points taken from the above description of the *kula* exchange, which Mauss held forth as representative of exchange in traditional societies. First, not all of the goods exchanged are imbued with the magical power of the *vaygu'a,* a power which Mauss indicated is enough to give meaning to Trobriand existence, and one that transforms the *vaygu'a* into the most valued of Trobriand objects. The *vaygu'a* derive their power, then, from the *kula ritual.* Ritual, as Mauss's teacher Emile Durkheim stated, produces *sentiment,* an affective response which forms the shared, internalized values and beliefs common to traditional societies. This commonality of belief and value Durkheim termed *mechanical solidarity,* drawing a parallel to the most simple biological organisms, which display a mechanical structure in the sense that each cell in such an organism (for example, a sponge) is so much like all other cells in the organism that a cell or group of cells may be removed without destroying the unity or viability of the parent organism.[24]

Social relationships in such societies are paramount, those between the individual and her or his close and extended family being most influential. Ritual works to reaffirm an individual's place in this constellation of relationships and to create other, fictive kinship relationships. Such relationships are regarded as being cosmically and supernaturally ordained. As Durkheim noted in *The Division of Labor,* "if there is one truth that history teaches us beyond a doubt, it is that religion embraces a smaller and smaller portion of social life. Originally it pervades everything; everything social is religious."[25] Further, as Mircea Eliade has convincingly shown, ritual inevitably refers to mythological occurrence, replicating the actions of the deities and ancestors, and in that way legitimating and sacralizing the relationships reinforced or produced by ritual.[26]

Often, the primordial state in which these mythological events transpired is replicated also. This primordial state is a time and place before the advent of history, in which the bounds of reality as it is now experienced did not apply. Various means are used to achieve such a state, including fasting, sleep deprivation, self-mutilation and torture, and the ingestion of drugs. The Sun Dance of the Cheyenne, Arapaho, and Sioux and the variations of this ceremony practiced by several other Plains tribes include many of these means. Visions that thenceforth provide guidance are experienced in the primordial state.

Some attempt to replicate or, at least, refer to the primordial state is made in rituals of lesser significance, including trading ritual. Plains Indian groups invariably smoked tobacco during exchanges of goods, so much so that the trading of horses was called "smoking over" horses in historic times. Donald Blakeslee and, before him, Joseph Jablow had convincingly established that such behavior is a continuation of the tradition of the *calumet ceremony*.[27] As Jordan Paper noted in his recent, comprehensive study, "the centrality of the pipe to the religious life and understanding of many native peoples of North America can best be compared to the role of the Torah in Judaism and the Koran in Islam; it is the primary material means of communication between spiritual power and human beings."[28] The calumet ritual was a crucial element in the trade at Bent's Old Fort.

Tobacco was, thus, not only an important trade item but also a substance made use of in the trading ritual to replicate the primordial state and enhance the efficacy of the ritual. Its psychotropic, and cultural, effects should not be underestimated. Joseph C. Winter makes a clear case for the use of tobacco as a psychotropic. He begins by reporting on the work of Johannes Wilbert, who conducted a study of the connection between tobacco use and shamanism in South America. Wilbert concluded that "Shamans use enormous amounts of tobacco to achieve effects that confirm the most central tenets and beliefs of their religion."[29] In fact, shamans aim to experience acute nicotine intoxication, stopping just short of using the drug in amounts that would be fatal. The resulting visions are interpreted as legitimizing cultural institutions and normative behavior. Winter goes on to say:

From southern Alaska to southern Chile, tobacco has been used for religious, economic and social purposes, and for many Native American groups, it serves as an important medium of energy exchange. Among the Warao, for example, who live in a region of the Orinoco Delta where it cannot be grown, the acquisition of tobacco for use by heavily addicted shamans, requires a large expenditure of physical energy by the rest of the populace. Trade goods have to be prepared, such as manufacturing hammocks and baskets, catching colorful birds, and training valuable hunting dogs, then the goods have to be exchanged with tobacco-producing groups on long distance trading expeditions. High amounts of energy are also exchanged by the shaman and his people during numerous public ceremonies, rituals, seances, and curing events, all of which involve the consumption of enormous amounts of highly potent tobacco.[30]

The ritual importance of tobacco was perhaps not so exaggerated among North American Native American groups as among those in South America. Nonetheless, as Mary Adair has stated, "no other plant figured so prominently in religion and secular ceremonies, rites of passage, economic and political alliances or social events and relaxation" among North American groups considered as a whole.[31] It is also well documented that tobacco was among the most intensely desired trade items by these Native Americans.

Winter sought to establish the antiquity of the traditional use of tobacco by the natives of North America by dating the spread of the plant in the Western Hemisphere. He noted that the range of the occurrence of some species of tobacco plants moved rapidly southward from North America just after the Pleistocene, that is, just as humans reached those areas of South America. The strong implication here is that humans acted as the agency by which tobacco, which requires cultivated or disturbed soil in which to grow (and is almost unknown in the wild, at present), spread over the New World. Winter suggested that this may have occurred as early as 9000 B.C.[32]

This is supported by a line of ethnological logic, advanced notably by

Weston La Barre, but also by Wilbert, Peter Furst, and von Gernet, that the earliest inhabitants of the New World, the Paleo-Indian big game hunters who crossed over the Bering Land Bridge 12,000 to 14,000 years ago, would have possessed a shamanistic religion.[33] These religions predictably employ psychotropic drugs for visions and out-of-body experiences. Groups with shamanistic religions would have quickly realized the utility of tobacco to that end. Winter went so far as to say that "eventually, even the religions of the Native Americans became organized in one degree or another around it, as even their gods became addicted to it."[34] Winter pointed out another very significant aspect of the tradition of tobacco use by Native Americans: that the deliberate growing of tobacco in Paleo-Indian or even Archaic times would constitute the origins of agriculture; that is, agriculture would have been initiated not for the production of food, but for drugs employed in the replication of the primordial state.[35]

Tobacco was highly valued by Native Americans because of its religious and ritual associations. It seems possible that alcohol held a special appeal to Native Americans for the same reason. There existed among Native Americans a strong tradition of shamanistic ecstasy and a concern with the power associated with visions thereby induced. Native Americans, however, were not oblivious to the double-edged nature of alcohol use. While describing the historic liquor trade with Native Americans along the Arkansas River, LeCompte noted that the Cheyenne disdained the use of alcohol for many years. They were finally persuaded to try it by trader John Gantt in 1832 or 1833, when he added sugar to whiskey in order to make it more immediately appealing to the Native Americans.[36]

Within a decade the Cheyenne had developed major problems associated with the use of alcohol. Already by 1835, the Cheyenne informed a Colonel Dodge at Bent's Fort that "in arranging the good things of this world in order of rank . . . whiskey should stand first, then tobacco, third, guns, forth, horses, and fifth, women."[37] Indian Superintendent William Clark had observed at about the time Gantt deceived the Cheyenne into imbibing alcohol that after a single drink "not an Indian could be found among a thousand who would not sell his horse, his gun, or his last blankets for another drink."[38] LeCompte further noted that whiskey was not only the most demanded, but also, by far, the most profitable trade item. Even "friends" of the Indian, who were on the one hand appalled at the devastation inflicted upon the Native Americans, were, on the other hand, amazed at the profitability of the trade in alcohol and unable to resist participating. Jim Beckworth, known and respected as "Yellow Crow" to the Cheyenne, explained as follows:

Let the reader sit down and figure up the profits on a forty-gallon cask of alcohol, and he will be thunderstruck, or rather whiskey struck. When disposed of, four gallons of water are added to each gallon of alcohol. In two hundred gallons there are sixteen hundred pints, for each one of which the trader gets a buffalo robe worth five dollars![39]

It is interesting that both Euro-Americans and Native Americans succumbed to the seductions characteristic of their respective cultures. LeCompte makes an observation that coincides with my own conclusion concerning the circumstances of traders active in the Southwest:[40] the Anglo trader was not infrequently someone who could not enter economic systems in the East or in Europe. This is exemplified by the principals of the Bent & St. Vrain Company. Ceran St. Vrain was a younger son of a deposed French nobleman who had died insolvent when Ceran was sixteen. The Bents were born into the large family of Judge Silas Bent of St. Louis, a respected man, but one without the considerable financial resources it would require to maintain the social positions of all of his offspring. Such people were born into a society where a secure position and, consequently, an identity were dependent upon amassing wealth. Beckworth, a mulatto, was an employee of the Bents and in a sense their protégé. For all of these individuals, the decision to pursue the difficult and dangerous life of a fur trader could be characterized as a gamble taken to secure a stable identity. It was evidently a gamble desperate enough to cause them to overlook the moral qualms they had about contributing to the misery that alcohol was inflicting upon the Cheyenne. Though there is evidence that the Bents themselves tried to ration alcohol to the Cheyenne, and thereby lessen the damage, there were scores of traders eager to provide alcohol in large quantities (like John Gantt) for every relatively ethical trader, like the Bents.

One can, I think, intuitively understand the appeal of liquor to Native Americans as one becomes aware of the extent to which the sustaining structures of their culture had deteriorated over the previous three hundred years. The disease, social dislocation, and changes in ways of life have been amply documented. Certainly alcohol would have had its customary effect of at least temporarily ameliorating anxiety by inducing an emotional state of Olympian detachment and omnipotence. It is interesting to speculate, too, that in the extreme effects of alcohol the Native Americans might also have been seeking a return to the primordial chaos that was a part of their shamanistic religion, with the hope that a new world might be constructed by means of this experience. Whatever the validity of this idea, it is suggestive that tobacco and alcohol were obviously not desired for their usefulness in any technoeconomic sense, but that they were nonetheless among the most valued trade items.

The ritual aspect of exchange renders it into what Mauss referred to as a "total" social phenomena, in which all kinds of social institutions are given expression simultaneously.[41] Two classic ethnohistories of Plains Indian groups take note, at least implicitly, of this view of trade: Oscar Lewis's *The Effects of White Contact upon Blackfoot Culture* and Joseph Jablow's *The Cheyenne Indians in Plains Indian Trade Relations, 1795–1840*.[42] These works are similar, and neither deals with the more explicitly semiotic aspects of trade goods. Both do, however, clarify that trade prior to and just after contact with Anglos was characterized as gift exchange, that the exchange was accompanied by a variety of rituals, including the smoking of tobacco (so much so that the ritual exchange was referred to as occurring "under the pipe"), and that fictive kinship relations were established. Such kinship relations were often made more important by the practice of cross-adoption: Each group would adopt children from the other. By the early nineteenth century such trade among Plains Indians had become quite complex. More European trade goods, especially firearms, had complicated the equation, as had the increasing friction and competition between groups brought about by jockeying for position within the trade.

Jablow presented an eyewitness account of a three-way exchange between the "Big Bellies" (the literal translation of the Gros Ventres), the "Schians" (the Cheyenne), and the Hidatsa, which occurred in about 1805 at a Hidatsa village in which this tension is obvious. After some preliminary rituals, which had gone well until the unexpected arrival of some Assiniboin who were enemies of the Cheyenne but were nonetheless taken under the protection of the Hidatsa, the exchange began in earnest. The presence of the Assiniboin was an obvious source of discomfort to the Cheyenne:

The Big Bellies brought in some ammunition and laid it upon the shrouds; the son (adopted by Le Borgne, the Hidatsa chief) was directed to lay the stem (pipe) over these articles, which he did accordingly. Our old general was again posted opposite the entrance of the shelter, where he was fully employed in his usual vocation of hanging, inviting everyone to put something under the stem. But all his eloquence was in vain; not a Schian came forward until some of their old men had gone the rounds making long speeches, when a few of the Schians appeared with some garnished robes and dressed leather, which were spread on the ground near the bull's head, which was then laid upon the heap. The Big Bellies then brought two guns, which they placed under the stem. The Schians put another one or two under the bull's head. Our party were each time more ready to come forward with their property than they were with theirs. The latter next brought some old, scabby sore-backed horses for the bull's head. This compliment was returned by our party with corn, beans, ammunition, and a gun. General Chokecherry grew impatient, and reproached the Schians in a very severe and harsh manner for their mean and avaricious manner of dealing, in bringing forward their trash and rotten horses, saying that the Big Bellies were ready to give good guns and ammunition, but expected to receive good horses in return. In answer to this they were given to understand by the Schians that they must first put all their guns and ammunition under the stem, immediately after which the Schians, in their turn, would bring in good horses. As it was never customary in an affair of this kind for either party to particularize the articles to be brought to the stem or bull's head, but for everyone to contribute what he pleased of the best he had, this proposal induced our party to suspect that the Schians had planned to get our firearms and ammunition into their possession, that they might be a match for us, and commence hostilities. To prevent this, no more guns or ammunition were brought forward, and the Schians were told they must first produce some of their best horses; but to this they would not listen. After a few more trifles had been given on both sides, the business came to a standstill on the part of the Schians, who retired to their tents.[43]

Evident here is the breakdown of the ritual aspect of trade that evolved in the nineteenth century. This breakdown had implications internal to trading groups. With emphasis on profits to be derived from trading and the amassing of wealth, rudimentary class differences sprung up among what had been, essentially, egalitarian social organizations among Plains Indians. Horses continued to be a sign of wealth (but one that also signaled a number of other personal attributes about the owner, including prowess in war), but as the trade in buffalo robes grew, men with many horses exchanged them for multiple wives. More wives could process more buffalo hides to robes. There was even an economy of scale in operation: Jablow noted the case in which a Blackfoot chief reported that his eight wives could transform 150 buffalo skins to robes in one year, whereas a single wife could only have processed ten.[44]

Differences in wealth were soon reflected in other areas of society, as Lewis observed.[45] Only the well-off could afford to buy firearms and ammunition, dried provisions, a good horse, and protective war charms needed for raids and battle. The poor, then, rarely led raiding parties and were therefore deprived of the opportunity to establish themselves in more general leadership roles. Even in the realm of the sacral, wealth differences had an effect. War bonnets, elaborate headdresses, medicine pipes, and other sacred objects, while they could perhaps in every case not be bought, were now more accessible to wealthier individuals. The rich could achieve and be recognized by virtue of better war equipment and their ability to draft other individuals of lesser wealth into their war parties.

Ritual in such circumstances becomes less the apparent agency by which meaning is attached to material items. I suggest here, though, that ritual is only, in Mauss's term, *degraded*. (In a more fully modern society, ritual is even better described as *fugitive*.) It still has a great effect, although the effect of ritual becomes more obscure as formal ritual breaks down. Nonetheless, the meaning and value of an object is still determined by its continuing association with a formal ritual, which may no longer be practiced, or by association with a degraded ritual, which refers to mythological occurrences in a manner less formal, less obvious, and perhaps even more within the realm of the subconscious.

As an example of this, consider the ritual of exchange as experienced by the Euro-American trade partners. On the surface, their behavior might appear to be, and may have seemed to them to be, motivated entirely by the "rational" desire for profit. Their behavior nonetheless had as a referent the mythology of capitalism and modernity, associated with what Tocqueville, and others since, have called the "cult of the individual." This value and belief system dictated what was necessary and proper behavior.

When considering trade objects exchanged in the nineteenth century, an era that saw the increasing degradation of trade ritual, it is perhaps easiest to understand the symbolic value of trade objects in general by looking first at those objects associated with the most obvious and undegraded ritual. Francis Paul Prucha's book, *Indian Peace Medals in American History,* provides an example of a class of objects with quite obvious ritual associations.[46] At the same time, these items subverted the ritual Native American "gift" economy. Peace medals manufactured for the Indian trade as gift items were quickly recognized as essential to the establishment of an Indian policy. As the head of the Indian Office, Thomas L. McKinney said in 1829, "without medals, any plan of operations among the Indians, be it what it may, is greatly enfeebled."[47]

The British, French, and Spanish had distributed such medals for decades prior to American independence. The American use of these medals was similar to that of the Europeans: they were given to Native American leaders on ritual occasions such as the signing of treaties, visits to the nation's capital by Indian chiefs, or during tours of the frontier by government officials. The Native Americans were, typically, anxious to substantiate social relations with powerful exchange partners: "When the United States replaced the British, the Indians were eager to obtain symbols of allegiance from the new Great Father."[48] On their side, Americans wishing to establish friendly relations with a tribe would attempt to collect all the medals given to their new trading partners by the former powers, usually the Spanish, French, or British. Americans were well aware that these exchanges symbolized the formal shifting of allegiances. About one such incident, a British officer commented, "Formerly a chief would have parted with his life rather than his medal."[49]

At first the medals used by Americans were struck in silver with the image of George Washington. They were among the most cherished possessions of the recipients and became a symbol of their authority. Often, they were buried with chiefs or passed down from generation to generation. Soon, however, trading companies began to manipulate these symbols to their benefit. They would strike their own medals, with likenesses of American presidents or of company officials. Initially, these too were of silver, but later silver content was much reduced or other metal was used. These medals were often given by trading companies to Native American individuals who might not be recognized as unequivocal leaders among their people but who were compliant to the interest of the trading company. In this way trading companies attempted to act as "king makers," placing in power individuals who would advance the interests of the trading company.

As set forth earlier, ownership or display of trade goods obtained through ritual exchange represented social relationships, ones sanctified by the reference to an archetypical, mythological relationship represented by the ritual. A clear modern example from our own society would be that of a wedding ring. As with a wedding ring, a symbolic object defines not only a social relationship, but the self constructed by means of social relationships. This explains the urgent concern of Native Americans about the display of such symbolic material; through display they defined themselves and their place in the world. Charles E. Hanson, Jr., revealed that the principal users of mirrors, another highly valued trade good, were men (fig. 14). While they were invariably used in preparation for war or ceremony, there are many eyewitness references to frequent and everyday use. A traveling warrior carried his weapons, a bag of red

Figure 14. An early photo of a Sioux man, Louis Dog, using his hand mirror. (Courtesy Museum of the Fur Trade, Chadron, Nebraska; reported in Charles Hanson, Jr., "Trade Mirrors," *The Museum of the Fur Trade Quarterly* 22, no. 4 [1986]: cover.)

paint, and his mirror, according to a colonial observer. A Sioux warrior is reported who rearranged his appearance, including his hair and make-up, five times a day. Hanson quotes the Santa Fe trader Josiah Gregg, who noted in 1844 that no warrior was equipped without his mirror "which he frequently consults. He usually takes it from its original case, and sets it in a large fancifully carved frame of wood, which is always carried about him."[50]

Mirrors were not common European items when the Indian trade began, but as soon as they were made in quantity they were provided to Indian traders. William Pynchon, an Indian trader from what is now Springfield, Massachusetts, had mirrors in his trading stock by 1636. Thenceforth they were a staple of the trade in North America. It is perhaps significant that during the religious and military revival sparked by the Shawnee leader Tecumseh and his brother, Tenkswatawa (the Prophet), in 1812 "the shores of Lake Superior were said to have been littered with blankets, mirrors, and other trade goods." All of this was done in response to the urgings of the revival leaders, who "urged the Ojibway to cleanse themselves of the evil ways of the white men and to turn their backs on tricksters who had used the sacred Midewiwin society to gain power."[51] In casting away the trade mirrors, the Ojibway were arguably ridding themselves of not only the symbols of their relationships with the Anglos but also the images of themselves in those relationships.

Less evidently, but just as surely, more functional trade items represented relationships between Native Americans and Euro-Americans. Thomas Schilz and Donald Worcester noted that although trade goods may have been coveted because they "made life easier," they also endowed their possessor with *wakan* (power): "Middlemen who could acquire powerful talisman like horses, guns, steel tools, and other products of the white men wielded not only economic but also spiritual power over their people."[52]

Elaborating upon the idea a bit more, they stated that the introduction of firearms into the Southwest dramatically altered the balance of power there, and introduced observations that call into question what might seem to be the obvious reason for this, that firearms were a dramatic improvement in the technology of warfare available to the Southwestern Indians. First of all, they observed that these Native American groups never adopted firearms as their primary weapon. They continued to rely upon the bow and arrow.[53] Although Schilz and Worcester did not discuss the reasons for this in any detail, it is generally known that a typical Plains Indian brave could, in a given amount of time, release more arrows than, and as accurately as, an individual with a firearm could fire shots. This situation prevailed until about the third quarter of the nineteenth century, when firearm technology was improved. Before then, the Apache, for example, armed with bows and arrows, were considered by many Western military officers to be as least as good as their light cavalry. While firearms might have been relatively more effective than the bow and arrow in forested areas, in the wide open spaces of the western Plains and the Southwest, firearms held no advantage, at least in the early nineteenth century.

A number of historians have opined that until the Spanish were displaced from the Southwest in 1821, modern, good-quality firearms were not readily available to Native Americans. The Spanish policy was to supply the Indians (especially the *indios barbaros*—the nomads) with outmoded weapons, preferably of inferior steel, which put the Indians at a technological disadvantage and made them more dependent upon the Spanish for replacements and repairs.

It is significant that even with the departure of the Spanish from the southwestern Plains and the entry of the Americans, who would trade virtually any item, Native Americans (along with trappers) evidently continued to use "outmoded weapons." The notion that large caliber, smoothbore, flintlocked firearms were preferred by these groups into the second half of the nineteenth century has been a generally accepted, if not rigorously formulated, notion among fur trade historians for some time. William J. Hunt's analysis of the firearm-related artifacts he recovered from archaeological excavations at Fort Union on the upper Missouri River lends substantial support to this.[54]

There were practical reasons for the predilection: flintlocks were less expensive ($7.00 even in 1861 versus $42.00 for a Henry rifle); flints were much less costly per shot than were percussion caps; if one were to run out of manufactured flints a substitute of sorts could be fashioned from a cryptocrystalline rock; and smoothbore flintlocks could be loaded with almost anything in a pinch, including stones.[55] All this indicates that the Spanish strategy was a dubious one. It also raises questions about the efficacy of such firearms on the southwestern Plains. Given their customary tactics in warfare and hunting, it is by no means certain that the Plains Indians would have been disadvantaged by their absence. The bow and arrow was even simpler to use than the musket, at least to the Native American. It was also a less complicated mechanism and so less likely to malfunction. It was easier to carry, and replacement parts were readily available and cost nothing. It is true that the shock of a musket ball could bring a buffalo, or a man, down more quickly than could an arrow, especially at long ranges. But this advantage did not outbalance those associated with the bow and arrow, especially since traditional tactics were those that dealt with targets at close range.

At Bent's Old Fort, the weight of evidence suggests that more technically sophisticated firearms were not offered at the fort for purchase by the customers, of whom many if not most were Plains Indians. The absence of more sophisticated firearms is borne out by notes the historian F. W. Craigen compiled for a book never published. Craigen reported on an incident apparently relayed to him by a Milo H. Slater, in September of 1903. Slater remembered that during "the regular fall buffalo hunt at Bent's Fort" in 1838, a young man called Blue borrowed a rifle from the leader of the hunt, Ike Chamberlain of Taos, so that he could go along. Two weeks after the hunt began, the lock on the rifle broke and the young man had to return to Taos because only flintlock rifles could be had at the fort at the time that were "useless for buffalo hunting."[56]

Slater may have been overstating the case a bit, but it is enough to again call into question the utility of firearms to the Plains Indians. After all, by 1838 the trading association between the Cheyenne and Arapaho tribes and the Bent & St. Vrain Company was well established. A vital part of this relationship was that the Bents would provide the tribes with the equipment they needed to procure buffalo robes for the fort. Not only are we being told by Slater that flintlock rifles were useless for buffalo hunting, but that Bent's Old Fort did not have anything but these in stock.

Archaeological material recovered from Bent & St. Vrain Company trash deposits includes nothing that might have been associated with firearms well suited for buffalo hunting. Although the account ledger from the fort indicates that 20,000 percussion caps were purchased by Bent & St. Vrain from the American Fur Company as early as 1840, no percussion caps were found in the portions of the two fort dumps used during the Bent & St. Vrain occupation. The percussion caps in the ledger may have been sold to travelers passing through the fort, sent on to New Mexico or elsewhere, or even used by hunters of European extraction who obtained buffalo (often for meat) at some distance from the fort. But had the caps been used by the Native Americans or trappers who frequented the fort, one might expect at least one to show up in the Bent & St. Vrain–period trash deposits. Also, all gunflints found in these deposits were very small. They could have been used only in pocket pistols or small caliber rifles like fowling pieces.[57] Such weapons would have been of marginal utility in buffalo hunting, or for that matter any activity in which a Plains Indian might have been likely to engage at that time.[58]

In summary, the Cheyenne, Arapaho, and other Plains tribes had questionable need of firearms for hunting or warfare. Their bows and arrows were as accurate and almost as deadly as firearms, well into the late nineteenth century. They were also more quickly readied to fire again. Finally, the bow and arrow was more dependable: according to the data that convinced Britain to change to a percussion system, about 1 shot in 6 from a flintlock would misfire, compared to 1 shot in 166 from a percussion cap weapon.[59]

The fact is, however, that firearms were desired by the Indians of the southwestern Plains. As Schilz and Worcester explained, "Nevertheless, all the Indians of the Spanish borderlands eagerly sought firearms for hunting and warfare because of the 'medicine' attributed to such weapons as well as their striking power."[60] Evident here is the symbolic significance of a trade item usually thought of strictly in functional terms.

Horses were another sort of trade good with strong symbolic significance, although the functional value of the horse to the Plains Indian is beyond dispute. It was the acquisition of the horse that allowed the transition from sedentary agriculture to nomadic hunting and warfare. While the horse was generally regarded among the Plains Indians as the most essential measure of wealth, it was also laden with great spiritual meaning; here, again, we see that the two forms of value were not strictly separated. Frank Gilbert Roe's *The Indian and the Horse* contains the statement that "the most profound influences exerted by the coming of the horse into Indian life were in the spiritual realm."[61] Roe noted the various ways in which the horse had become an integral part of the religious existence of the Plains Indian: Shamans utilized the ascribed supernatural powers of horses to influence the fate of the tribe. Young men had visions of the horses that were later to be their own. A warrior's horses were often killed to accompany him to the next world. Horse figures adorned clothing and tepees, imparting in this way their spiritual powers. Most significant, horses were among the most common subjects of poetry and legend.

Ethnologist John C. Ewers looked at three Blackfoot myths in *The Horse in Blackfoot Indian Culture*.[62] One of these myths was called by the Blackfoot informants "Thunder's Gift of Horses." In this, not only horses but also other key symbolic elements of Plains Indian material culture are presented. The story tells of a wise but poor old man who is rewarded for his kind treatment of Thunder's horses. The old man receives the knowledge of how clothing can be adorned with porcupine quills, the power to have visions that reveal appropriate tepee decoration, and two physical objects: smoking ("medicine") pipes and horses. Ewers concluded:

> These myths constitute evidence that to the native mind the horse was a god-send of importance comparable to that of their most sacred ceremonies, created by the same supernatural powers who gave the Indians their chief ceremonial institutions.[63]

The symbolic value of another sort of item, ceramics, was explored by David Burley, in an article about the Metis of the northwestern Canadian Plains.[64] Ceramics were not, strictly speaking, a trade item; that is, they were not usually traded to nomadic Plains Indian groups. Although these tribes had made and used ceramics as sedentary agriculturalists, this aspect of their material culture had been lost as they took up a new way of life as horse-borne hunters and warriors. Quite simply, ceramics (especially very fragile ceramics such as these) had no place in a lifestyle that involved frequent relocation. Nonetheless, the Metis reestablished the use of ceramics, which they incorporated into their nomadic existence. In transient campgrounds, for example, delicate teawares and expensive transfer-printed wares have been recovered archaeologically.

Burley asked why a frequently mobile, semisedentary, hunting and gathering people would maintain such a nonfunctional form of material culture in the face of more durable alternatives. The Canadian Metis were the progeny of Native American women and the European or Euro-American traders who had occupied the area. They lived a life much more closely aligned to that of the Plains Indians than of the European traders, but they remained attached to these traders in two important ways. First of all, they frequently acted as provisioners, as voyagers, or in other capacities for traders. Also, because European and Euro-American women were completely absent from the area until 1830, the women of the Metis were considered to be the most likely marriage partners for the traders. This was particularly true for clerks and officers, for whom, by 1820, Native American wives were no longer considered appropriate.[65] Metis women who displayed the greatest numbers of "civilized behaviors" were obviously the most appropriate marriage partners. Over time, there developed a considerable group of Metis women in the upper echelons of fur trade society. Daughters of these women were further trained in the accomplishments of ladies, including the use of ceramics.

Burley argued that the use of these delicate ceramics spread to "even the most 'poor' and mobile of the hunting brigades" by a process which operates according to what Burley, borrowing from Douglas and Isherwood, called the "infectious disease" or "epidemiological" model.[66] He said that the Metis were known for their hospitality and *joie de vivre* and spent a great deal of time visiting one another, drinking tea, smoking, and gossiping. These visits cut across class boundaries. Burley stated that "as ceramic use spreads from one group to another, social meaning is transferred from visual displays of status to a shared form of material culture."[67] What Burley is saying here, I think, is that the visits were imbued with symbolic significance by means of ritual of the fugitive sort. Burley made it clear that he believed he was following Douglas and Isherwood's thesis:

Instead of supposing that goods are primarily needed for subsistence plus competitive display, let us assume that they are needed for making visible and stable the categories of culture. It is standard ethnographic practice to assume that all material possessions carry social meanings and to concentrate a main part of cultural analysis upon their use as communicators.[68]

Although Burley offered no mechanism for the transmission of social meaning other than his metaphor of contagion, I suggest that the mechanism of transmission is that of ritual. Ritual most certainly produces shared social meanings by means of "sentiment." As Burley observed, "For Metis women, it is important to emphasize that it is not just the acquisition of ceramics that would be important. Rather, it involves the display and use of ceramics with appropriate social protocols."[69] I argue that this is ritual, one that refers to and reenacts the relationships of the European "ancestors." The tobacco-smoking, tea-drinking, and gossiping of the general Metis population are likewise ritual, in this case of a somewhat "degraded" or even "fugitive" sort, since it is less prescribed. It is ritual that resolves a crisis of identity by incorporating the behaviors of ancestors, which are very similar, from two different traditions. The affective response shared by the participants renders the material culture employed important to the participants, in a symbolic sense. It becomes a symbol of their renewed social relationship and, therefore, of slightly altered but essentially stable identities.

Having examined the symbolic value of a variety of trade goods—those that play an essential and obvious role in ritual (tobacco and associated paraphernalia, alcohol), those that at first consideration seem functional (firearms and horses), and those that are functional but which possess a symbolic value more in tune with modern notions of symbol (shells, bracelets, necklaces, mirrors)—we are now better able to appreciate the significance of the quintessential sort of trade good: beads. Columbus, in fact, on his first voyage to the New World, reported exchanging some small green beads for supplies. Beads were a staple of European–Native American trade from that time forward.

The popularity of beads among Native American groups can be explained, in part, because they could be used in a variety of familiar ways. Beads strung or otherwise used as personal adornment have been dated to the Archaic period (6,000 to 1,000 B.C.) in the Great Lakes region.[70] Early colonial entrepreneurs produced "counterfeit wampum" beads, which were similar to true wampum, the prehistoric white and dark purple beads made from shells by the native populations of New England.[71] The varied uses of wampum included: as symbols of treaties and agreements, as accompaniment to formal contracts, as tokens of condolence, as message devices, and as mnemonic devices.[72] As to this last use, the Iroquois, for example, had a Keeper of Wampum who was charged with remembering the significance of each string of wampum in his care. Many contemporary Native Americans claim that because of this, wampum is a sort of historic document, although no one living is sure of how to read the existing strings. At the same time, certain Native American groups have requested the return of wampum from museums and other repositories, saying that wampum belts are sacred objects. From a traditional standpoint, of course, since meaning was assigned by ritual having some mythological referent, such objects are regarded as sacred no matter what the more profane meaning or use attached to them.

Trade beads among Plains Indians replaced the use of porcupine quills for embellishing clothing, although, "when beads first arrived, the most respected Quillworkers refused to use them."[73] Eventually beads were used to reproduce the simple geometric designs favored by the Plains groups. Even so, Powell reported a tradition of reluctance to use anything manufactured by the white man on the most sacred paraphernalia.[74]

Blue trade beads were much in demand by Cheyenne and Arapaho, who felt that the white man had "stolen the blue from the sky." At Bent's Old Fort, the relative frequency of the discovery of blue beads was much higher in areas that were dated to the later period of the fort's occupancy than in those from the earlier period. The greater number of blue beads in the later deposits may evidence a case of supply catching up with the demands of a particular group of consumers.

In considering beads we have come full circle, back to the initial discussion of the prehistoric exchange of shells and columellae. These items cannot be explained solely in terms of how they functioned as instruments by which to amass wealth. This approach is steeped in modernity; it assumes that value is ultimately set by an impersonal marketplace and ignores alternate meanings for material culture. But this is not to say that these meanings do not exist and exert a force. Trade goods could be imbued with meaning through their ritual association with cultural mythos, affecting social behavior in ways that cannot be explained by reference to market value or function. Examples presented here include the use of firearms by the nomads of the Southwest and western Plains when the bow and arrow functioned more efficiently in these locations, the spread of fragile ceramics to nomads in northwestern Canada, the killing of valuable horses to be buried with warriors, and even what seems to be, from a modern viewpoint, the "self-destructive" and compulsive use of alcohol and tobacco by Native Americans. All of these phenomena defy analysis from a stubbornly "modern" perspective that emphasizes function, technology, and economic modeling. This is somewhat curious, since these or similar phenomena are decidedly a part of present-day society.

Native American Trade Goods at Bent's Old Fort

Virtually all the sorts of trade items mentioned were traded at Bent's Old Fort. Liquor, horses, gunpowder, tobacco, blankets, sugar, coffee, and knives were especially popular (and show up in account books, but only very indirectly in the archaeological record). A passage from an early well-researched historical novel provides an idea of the range of items traded at Bent's Fort. All of the items mentioned here have since been corroborated by examination of Bent & St. Vrain Company account books or archaeological evidence:

Shelves were piled with fooferaw, boxes of beads, flints, buckles, finger rings, paints, silver, "hair-money," hawk bells, tubular bone Iroquois beads, steel bracelets, fire steels, hand axes, tin pans, awls, green river knives, pigs of galena, powder, powder horns, beaver and bear traps, looking glasses, combs, needles, thread, pins, ribbons . . . piles of blankets—both trade and Navajo—a few bales of buffalo robes . . . harness, ropes and saddlery, tobacco in great brown twists, chewing tobacco, fringed Spanish shawls, and State's doin's . . . bags of coffee, sugar, raisins, flour, boxes of water crackers, salt pork in barrels, bottles of pepper sauce, saleratus and spices of all sorts. On the lower shelves were stacked bales of calico flannel, domestic cotton, blue and scarlet shrouding, dressed buckskins, 3 point Nor'West blankets, kettles, saddles.

Hardware was in the middle of the room; axes, kettles, spare parts for wagons, horseshoes and ox shoes, hoop iron for arrow heads, lance heads, trade guns, Nor'West fusils, and many a short keg of Pass Brandy, rum and Taos lightening, and kegs of blackstrap molasses.[75]

The trading partners here were principally the Plains Indians; among them, especially, the Cheyenne and Arapaho. Occasionally at Bent's Old Fort, but more frequently at one of the other, smaller forts of the Bent trading empire, trade would be conducted with the Kiowa, Comanche, Ute, Shoshoni, Gros Ventre, Apache, and other tribes. Early in the history of the Bent & St. Vrain Company, trade was conducted with the Sioux, but, after the agreement with the American Fur Company in 1838, the Sioux trading ground was abandoned. Trading goods from Bent & St. Vrain Company probably made their way all over the Plains and beyond, however, as the groups that traded with the company would engage in trade with other tribes. Indeed, the position of middleman in the trade with the Anglos was a coveted one. It made the Cheyenne and Arapaho very powerful indeed among the Plains tribes.

As should be clear by now, the urgent desire for trade among traditional societies, Plains groups included, was initially not so much based in the desire for profit as for the social identity that such trade engendered. The fictive kinship relationships created by exchange, with its attendant ritual, supplied a more secure identity. One grew in prestige as one realized a larger role in such exchange. One's identity was determined by relationships with other humans.

In nineteenth-century Plains Native American societies, including those of the Cheyenne and Arapaho, it became necessary to amass wealth in order to secure this kind of prestige and a social identity. Wealth was required to outfit oneself with horses, firearms, lead, and powder for war and raiding. The charms and rituals needed to assure success in these endeavors had to be purchased. Unless all this could be supplied, warriors could not be obtained for the raiding party. Forms of wealth began to emerge that were closely tied to this system: first, horses—useful in themselves and readily accepted in exchange for anything else desired; as the trade in buffalo robes accelerated, wives also became a form of wealth, since more women could produce more buffalo robes, which could then be traded with the Anglos for the required items. Control of wealth brought more wealth—the essence of capitalism.

For exchange with the Anglos, buffalo robes became the currency. Prices, in numbers of robes, for trade items fluctuated, although they were standardized to a degree. Some prices have been documented by National Park Service historians and the interpretive staff of Bent's Old Fort National Historic Site for the period between 1820 and 1850.[76] One buffalo robe could be exchanged for any one of the following: sixty loads of gunpowder and shot, two gallons of shelled corn, three to four pounds of sugar, two pounds of coffee, one pint of whiskey (raw alcohol diluted with three to six times as much water and variously flavored with tea, tobacco, ginger, red pepper, or molasses), one hank of beads, or one yard of cloth. A trade gun required from six to ten robes, and a blanket several. In this way quantification was imposed upon the exchange by the Americans. In time the way of life of the Plains Indians grew dependent upon the exchange and, even more importantly, the *amassing of quantities* of valuable items, that is, amassing wealth.

Competition for wealth was an important factor in intensifying conflict among Native Americans. Plains Indians no longer procured merely the resources needed by their own and allied group—now they were providing raw materials to an industrial system that serviced millions of people. Demand was practically limitless. As resources were depleted, competition for them became correspondingly more fierce.

Here again is a example of amplification of traditional behavior. It is easy but misleading to romanticize the past; thus it is important to bear in mind that conflict was certainly not unknown prior to European contact. George R. Milner, for one, has amassed evidence from numerous archaeological excavations that amply demonstrates Native American warfare in the time before Columbus' arrival in the New World.[77] Part of the traditional ethos, after all, is that if another group is unrelated—that is, if it does not share the same ancestors, gods, myths, and customs—then that group must not be *as* human as ours, and perhaps not human at all. Most frequently, the term by which bands and tribes refer to themselves translates to something like "the people," with the implication that other beings outside of these small social units might not fully occupy that status.

The alliance between certain Plains tribes and Anglo entrepreneurs also fits within the pattern of traditional behaviors, but this alliance had exaggerated consequences. In the traditional world, trade provided a way of establishing common humanity, of making alliances by which to cooperate, instead of compete in the procurement of resources. Accordingly, in the great social and cultural dislocations that followed European contact, competition for beneficial alliances increased. These alliances secured (at least temporarily) a favorable position within constantly shifting economic, political, and ideological alignments. European trade objects became essential in this struggle—not only for their immediate, utilitarian value, but for their "medicine." The part of this medicine that is easiest for a modern observer to understand is that it demonstrated an alliance with powerful beings. It was, however, more than that: essentially it secured a position in a world that was changing too rapidly and unpredictably for comfort, a world that threatened to spin out of control.

A marriage, uneasy at times, was made between the Anglos and the Native Americans. This is an appropriate metaphor, in several ways. Earlier in this chapter I have suggested that a clear modern example of an item invested with meaning might be a wedding ring. The ring symbolizes a relationship with long-term reciprocal commitments, a symbol based upon a mythological past that sacralizes the relationship. In defining and legitimating the relationship in this way, it defines and legitimates the identities of the individuals involved in the relationship. Identities are *always* socially defined even in the modern world. Because this clashes with our modern mythology of individualism, this is generally not well understood. Nonetheless, it is basic to the social sciences, as Durkheim established one hundred years ago.

Figure 15 illustrates this point in a pertinent way. Shown here is a bride in a contemporary Osage wedding ceremony. (The Osage were occasional trading partners with the Bent & St. Vrain Company.) The bride is wearing items from a United States military dress uniform, one of several uniforms presented by President Jefferson to the Osage delegation to Washington, D.C., in 1803. He also presented the Osage with silver peace medals.[78] Osage chiefs gave the uniforms they received to their wives and daughters, who passed them on to their daughters. The wearing of the uniform by the bride in the Osage ceremony refers in a mythological way to the relationship forged in historic times between the Anglos and the Osage. The Osage, like other Native American groups, invested this relationship with their traditional values, expecting it to be not so much a business interaction but one that involved long-term, reciprocal commitments.

For the most part, trade items intended for the Native American market at Bent's Old Fort were much the same as those that had been traded to Native Americans elsewhere for the previous two hundred years. Many of these items—knives, iron, copper, and brass kettles, axe heads, blankets, and so forth—were eminently useful, but they were desired as much for their *wakan,* their "medicine," the commitment they represented on the part of the Great White Father, as anything else. In this sense, it

Figure 15. An Osage woman, photographed in 1975,
wearing a bridal dress styled from a military uniform.
(From Anne Callahan, *Osage Ceremonial Dance I'n-Lon-Schka*, copyright 1990 by University of Oklahoma
Press.)

made little difference if the items were "fooferaw" or firearms. Each carried with it *wakan*. Thus, when the Cheyenne and Kiowa made their great peace in 1840, they signaled their commitment to it (and the peace was never broken) by exchanging gifts they had acquired from Bent's Old Fort. And when the Cheyenne camped at Sand Creek the night before the massacre there by Chivington's cavalry, they raised the American flag, sure as they did this that it would keep them from harm.

CHAPTER 6

Bent's Old Fort as the New World

Ideology and the Establishment of Political Hegemony

The Mexican War to the south of New Mexico dragged on for two years. Deep in Mexico, American forces were met with strong resistance. In Mexico City, teenaged cadets from *El Castillo* battled the invaders, becoming martyrs. Today, school-aged children are told about *El Niños Heroicas* and how one cadet, rather than surrender, wrapped himself in the Mexican flag and hurled himself from the battlements. Almost 14,000 of 104,000 American troops died in the Mexican War (most from disease), producing a death rate higher than any other war in American history.[1]

The opposition to the American presence below New Mexico makes the war as it occurred in that northernmost province of Mexico quite remarkable. The contrast between the conflict in the two areas is stark. In New Mexico, the war was brief and largely bloodless. Resistance on the part of a very few was more than balanced by support of the change in government expressed by many. For the most part, the populace was quiescent.

The war in New Mexico had been won before General Kearny's Army of the West crossed the Arkansas River in 1846, won by the troubled alliance of Americans and Native Americans and those American traders who had infiltrated deeply into New Mexico and had altered its ideological, social, economic and political infrastructures. Ceran St. Vrain had become a Mexican citizen in 1831 and was an influential businessman in that country even as he worked actively to acquire New Mexico for the United States. The lieutenant governor of New Mexico in 1846 was Juan Bautista Vigil, once a tariff collector whom American traders would sometimes employ to assist in the timely movement of their goods in and out of New Mexico. He lost his job as tariff collector for using his position to help settle a private debt, but he subsequently held various public offices.

The same Juan Bautista Vigil "welcomed the conquerors with an impassioned speech" as General Kearny led the American troops into Santa Fe. Kearny then made a speech of his own, in which he proclaimed that the religious practices of New Mexico would not be disturbed, that his army would pay for anything they took from the populace ("not a pepper, nor an onion will be taken by my troops without pay"), that the army would thenceforth protect them from the Apache, the Navajo, and other predatory tribes, and that their allegiance to Mexico and the Governor of New Mexico, Manuel Armijo, was absolved.

Armijo had fled.[2] A few years earlier, Armijo had made land grants to several American traders who had then become citizens of Mexico, including Charles Beaubien and Ceran St. Vrain. Later, Beaubien and St. Vrain donated parts of their very large grants to the American citizen Charles Bent—and to Armijo, the governor who had provided them with the land in the first place.[3]

Governor Armijo was also General Armijo. Although he had maintained dictatorial control of his people, such control was not enough to stem the cultural sea-change instigated by the trade with the Americans. By the eve of the invasion, Armijo could see that events had moved beyond his control. It is generally believed that both he and his second-in-command, Colonel Diego Archuleta, were bribed in some way by the Americans just prior to the invasion to insure that no resistance would be offered.[4] Howard R. Lamar offered a recap of the evidence for this in his introduction to a reprinting of Susan Shelby Magoffin's diary, *Down the Santa Fe Trail and Into New Mexico.* Susan Magoffin, the teenaged bride of Samuel Magoffin, a wealthy trader, documented her experiences as she traveled west with her new husband on a trading expedition that took place just before and during the Mexican War.[5]

Samuel's brother James had preceded him into the New Mexico trade and was at the heart of the political intrigues that formed one of several subtexts to the Mexican War. James Magoffin had been summoned to Washington in 1845 by Senator Thomas Hart Benton, the man who engineered so much of America's policy of Manifest Destiny. Benton introduced James Magoffin to President James Polk. Polk was enough impressed with him at this and a second meeting that he instructed Secretary of War William L. Marcy to direct General Kearny to send James Magoffin to Santa Fe ahead of his troops. Magoffin's instructions were to strike a bargain with the authorities in Santa Fe for a bloodless takeover of New Mexico.

James Magoffin raced back to Missouri, then down the Santa Fe Trail in a buckboard in order to catch General Kearny's army and his brother's trading caravan. The trading venture would be the "cover" for his presence in Santa Fe. He caught up with both at Bent's Old Fort. General Kearny and James Magoffin consulted there, almost assuredly in the dining room with William and Charles Bent, then Kearny sent twelve men under a flag of truce with Magoffin to Santa Fe.

In Santa Fe, James Magoffin met clandestinely with Governor General Armijo and Colonel Archuleta. Archuleta was to prove the more difficult of the two Mexican military leaders in the negotiations. Armijo and Magoffin were not strangers. Magoffin had married a high-born New Mexican woman and was Armijo's "cousin by marriage." Whether money was given to Armijo as a part of the agreement reached is unclear—but certainly Armijo's dealings with the Americans had resulted in personal financial gains for him in the past. Almost surely Magoffin persuaded him that the American takeover was inevitable and thus any armed resistance would be futile. Colonel Archuleta may have been inclined to fight anyway, being a proud man, but it seems that he was swayed by the argument that the American occupation of eastern New Mexico would clear the way for Archuleta to seize the western half of New Mexico, across the Rio Grande. In the end, Armijo fled with the regular soldiers while Archuleta disbanded the New Mexican volunteers. No military resistance was offered to General Kearny's Army of the West.

By 1846, the Indians had become allies (or were, at least, pacified), and, with Kearny's victory in Santa Fe, the United States had gained a firm hold in the Southwest. This was accomplished through *ideological* means, all of them dependent upon ritual, and Bent's Old Fort had provided a "ritual ground" for the propagation of this ideology, one that resonated with the archetype for all such "monumental" constructions. The structure and grounds of the fort conveyed the form of the new world order. Items traded there facilitated a ritual that altered traditional beliefs. Perhaps, surprisingly, the survival of traditional means for group solidarity among the Anglo elite helped them in their efforts to mount a cohesive and successful campaign of domination in the region.

Nonspoken Definitions and Redefinitions of the World

Modern culture is one of capitalism and individualism. Through capitalism and individualism the world is interpreted and placed in rational categories, quantified, and controlled. The ideological basis of modern culture was and is propagated not only through philosophies, theologies, manifestos, and statements that purport to embody this ideology and therefore to make it available for discussion and criticism, but also by, and perhaps *most effectively* by, material manifestations of that ideology. Bear in mind that ideology determines what is assumed, what is taken to be the normal or natural conditions of society and the "world." These are not infrequently *imaginary* conditions that have been institutionalized and reified. As a part of this process, they have been embodied by the material world, where, for the most part, they are unavailable for criticism. They appear to be *grounded* in nature, in the material, assumed, and natural world around us; that is, they are unavailable for criticism and discussion unless one can interpret material culture by linking it to the mythology to which it refers.

Only in a special and general sense, which I will describe here, does material culture communicate as does language, despite the fact that both are symbolic and can thereby constitute new meanings. Language is a particular case within the general realm of human communication (see the discussion below of Gidden's *structuration*). It is the most explicit means of communication available to us. In the modern world, which depends upon explicit communication to function efficiently, we have fallen into the habit of thinking of it as the only means of communication. This is not so. Nonexplicit, nonverbal communication, in fact, is often more effective for many human purposes. Even with language, metaphor, compared to explicit description, is usually the more effective means of provoking emotional response, sustaining interest in the audience, and motivating this audience to action.[6] It is probably this that Nietzsche had in mind when he said, "Above all I would be master of the metaphor." Provocative ambiguity—between the conditions of this world and the "real" and enduring (mythological) one—is an essential part of ritual. It is achieved through symbol, setting, and linguistic metaphor that refer to primordial creation.

Ian Hodder, to cite one observer, presented a number of differences between how meaning is attached to language as compared to material

culture in "Post-Modernism, Post-Structuralism, and Post-Processual Archaeology." He notes that material culture is less logical and more immediate than language, is often nondiscursive (which, of course, depends
upon the way in which discourse is defined, as Foucault might point out)
and subconscious, and often seems ambiguous. Perhaps Hodder's most
important observation is that while speech and writing are linear—the
reader knows where to begin and how to follow the symbols logically—
material culture is not.[7] To me this suggests that meaning does not in-
here in material culture by means of an internal system of symbolic logic
(since formal logic is associated with material culture only tangentially),
but that its meaning is assigned through social use. This is a major difference. Since it is not possible to identify any formal, logical system of meanings in material culture (in contrast to language), I suspect that meaning
can be assigned to material culture only through a social mechanism that
provokes an *affective response*. Such mechanisms are properly termed ritualistic. Ritual reenacts the primordial relationships, the relationships that
produced order—produced the world—from chaos. As we have seen,
there is good reason to believe that neoteny in humans explains much of
the importance attached by humans to these primordial relationships. The
protracted human childhood, which provides learning opportunities well
into and, in fact, throughout adulthood and the associated lengthy dependency of the child, render such primal relations psychologically paramount. The mythology and rituals of a culture are a collective reworking
of these relationships in symbolic form. Thus, all material culture derives
its meaning by reference to social relationships—and these relationships
are sanctified or legitimated through ritualistic means.

Material culture, like language (and ritual), both *embodies* and *creates*
meaning. Anthony Giddens (although inclined toward neither a postmodern nor a phenomenological viewpoint) developed a theory of *structuration* that covers all forms of symbolic action, including language and
nonverbal communication like material culture. In this, he posited a "practical consciousness" that intervenes between the unconscious and conscious, between our more basic neurological activities and our thoughts
themselves.[8] This practical consciousness is the arena for the innumerable
rules, strategies, and tactics that one must use to understand symbolic expressions or to convey meaning symbolically. An attempt to bring these
conventions to full consciousness would preoccupy one to the extent that
efforts made to understand or convey meaning would be rendered futile.
Knowledge of the rules of linguistic grammar and syntax provide an example. We do not usually decide carefully at a certain point in a conver-

sation that a complete sentence with noun, verb, and direct object would be appropriate and then go about constructing such a sentence with careful attention to the rules of grammar. Rules of grammar are held, at best, semiconsciously, but one "knows," nonetheless, not only what sounds "right," but how to organize sounds in a way that will be understood. Thus, structure is employed by practical consciousness to convey meaning. Depending upon the conversation, this process may be employed to restructure meaning (if for example a new word or language is being learned, or at a different level if a particularly cogent point is made). The process of structuration applies equally to all forms of communication including material culture; language is not privileged here.

Consider a well-known instance of communication via material culture provided by Rhys Isaac in *The Transformation of Virginia*. Between 1740 and 1790, noted Isaac, the "open" floor plan of the typical Virginia house became "closed." Entry into a house at the beginning of this period was usually into a communal hall, a living space into which the visitor stepped immediately. By the end of this period, the hall had been transformed into a much smaller room. This was not a living area, but really a liminal area designed to provide a buffer zone between the "public" world exterior to the house and the "private" realm of the house's inhabitants.[9]

This transitional chamber both reflected the emerging cultural sensibilities in regard to individualism and privacy and acted to institutionalize them. Such sensibilities thereby became a part of the environment. Isaac tied this new architectural style to a variety of cultural changes that he documented to have occurred at about the same time, including changes from a ritualistic to evangelistic form of religion and the move from a plantation to an entrepreneurial economy. He did not identify a mechanism by which the cultural change he had documented found expression in architecture (or, elsewhere, in the landscape). I suggest that the operant mechanism is one of ritual—fugitive ritual to be sure, but ritual nonetheless, in that the architecture expressed the new ideal ("real") order. The order was propagated by the emotional response it evoked in all who were exposed to it. That affective response was undoubtedly complex and, in the end, may have provoked unintended consequences. As a tactic for bolstering the status of the inhabitants of the house, for example, it may not have been fully successful. Nonetheless, the architecture of the house almost surely assuaged the anxieties of those who lived there in just the way ritual would, by demonstrating to the inhabitants, if no one else, their proper place in the world. Others outside the developing mercantile "grid" may have felt excluded.

Nonetheless, the architecture conveyed to everyone something about the ideology to which it referred, despite differences in reaction to that message. One could replace the word "ideology" in the last sentence with "mythology," if thinking about it that way makes it clearer. What is most interesting about the architecture and landscape of Bent's Old Fort is that it expressed a new world order in a way not only satisfying to its builders, but extraordinarily convincing to so many others.

Panopticism

Michel Foucault has termed the culture of modernity, capitalism, and individualism the culture of *discipline*. He compares this to a more simple form of culture which operated by means of "spectacle," that is, a certain kind of ritual and the internalization of shared values and beliefs characteristic of ritual.[10] This culture of shared values and beliefs is one that operates according to Durkheim's *mechanical* solidarity. Every person in such a culture is so alike that society can go on operating in essentially the same manner despite the loss of one or even a group of these individuals. In a modern *organic* society, an industrial one in which there must exist a multiplicity of specialized activities, all of which must be coordinated in order for society to operate effectively, a much greater degree of individual difference must grow up. Socialization becomes problematic since each person must now be individuated or differentiated in order to be successfully socialized. This is all accomplished in a more idiosyncratic context, one in which each individual's particular environment for socialization, especially his or her primary caregivers, can exert the deciding factor on socialization.

"Mistakes" occur. Individuals—imbeciles, criminals, invalids, and so on—are incompletely or perhaps incorrectly socialized. These mistakes exert a destabilizing influence on the intricate balance of the modern society, and some means must be devised to deal with them. Initially, these means were crude, extremely physical, and each in their own way spectacular, designed to attract attention by means of their extreme nature. For criminals they included the extraordinary forms of punishment Foucault described in careful detail: torture, drawing and quartering, and so on. But larger, increasingly diverse, specialized, and more individualized populations could not depend upon spectacle for a number of reasons. Spectacles could not be devised that were accessible to all individuals and segments of large populations simultaneously; further, differentiation of individuals and population segments (especially classes) was conducive to the emergence of a more modern society, while the relatively unreflective sentiment elicited by spectacle was not. In time, means more suited for the control of an increasingly diverse, specialized, and individualized population were devised. These were forms of surveillance.

The embodiment of this form of control, with all of its implications, is found in Jeremy Bentham's architectural innovation, the *panopticon*.[11] The panopticon was a machine for the *amplification* of power, so said Foucault. It was, as such, a way to propagate the modern ideology, for panopticism was also "the abstract formula for a very real technology, that of individuals."[12] In other words, panopticism produced individuals, as defined by the ideology of individualism, through the sanctification of personal discipline.

The symbolic import of the panopticon and its effect upon society requires some discussion to make clear. I think that the ritual value of the panopticon is overlooked by Foucault or, at least, underplayed as he constructed his argument by contrasting this new form of control with the "traditional" forms of "spectacle" and internalized values. It is as if the only sort of ritual were "spectacle." In fact, Foucault is describing another form of ritual, one which operates through the mechanism of the panoptic tower.

Individualism is more than a "technology," it is a belief and value system. It is the aspect of ritual that gives individualism—and capitalism and modernity—the moral force that it has. People subscribe to these ideas not only to avoid negative consequences: They embrace them as concepts that give structure and meaning to their lives. Here religion and ideology are clearly fused, as those concepts have in fact (as Weber pointed out long ago) been incorporated into Protestant belief. Quentin Skinner has pointed out that terms like *frugality* were coined as Protestantism took hold. Other words like *discerning* and *penetrating* were for the first time used in a metaphorical sense to describe talents. Before the rise of Protestantism, to call someone *ambitious* or *shrewd* was to express disapproval; as individualism grew apace, these became admirable traits. Prior to the cultural transformation, to say that someone acted *obsequiously* would be to express approval of that person's behavior; afterward, the same term would be unflattering.[13]

Bentham's architectural invention was a tower surrounded by an annular building (fig. 16). Each room in the ring of rooms extends the width of the building and has windows facing the courtyard and the exterior;

Figure 16. An example of panoptic architecture, circa 1840. (From N. Harou-Romain, "Plan for a Penitentiary"; reported in Michel Foucault, *Discipline and Punish: The Birth of the Prison* [New York: Vintage, 1979], 172.)

exterior windows provide illumination, to put the person in each room "on stage." The tower windows open to the inner side of the ring, and a supervisor standing in the tower can observe activity in all of the rooms. It appears the opposite of a dungeon: light where the dungeon is dark, open where the dungeon is closed, and accessible to observation where the dungeon obscures. But here, "visibility is a trap."[14]

Surveillance can be constant—or not. Those within the cells never know when they are being observed. Observation might be for only a few hours, even minutes, during one day, but the observed have no way of knowing when those hours or minutes might be. They cannot see into the tower, and this is an important point. They must assume constant supervision. Eventually, they must take this task of supervision on themselves. The observer occupies outposts in their minds, so to speak.

The panopticon becomes a machine for surveillance, but one more insidious and far reaching than might first be apparent. Observation, for example, can be delegated to associates, friends, even servants or employees. The person in final charge of the establishment needs only to resume his observation post to see whether the person to whom he has delegated this task has accomplished it correctly. He can tell in a glance if the machine is running smoothly or if the changes he ordered are being implemented according to plan. More important, the panoptic tower is available to inspectors from a central authority. As Foucault stated, "An inspector arriving unexpectedly at the center of the Panopticon will be able to judge at a glance, without anything being concealed from him, how the entire establishment is functioning."[15]

Thus the director of the establishment is himself under surveillance, by the very means that he employs for his observation. Everyone falls under the panoptic gaze. It is this extension of order and the accomplishment of plan that is the final goal of the panopticon. The panopticon was first utilized in situations of deviance and marginality, that is, at hospitals or prisons, where it was especially important to society that the behavior or condition of deviates, who threatened the fine balance of an industrial society, be altered. So the panopticon becomes also an outpost for the scientific method in society—for social engineering, among other things. Treatments in hospitals can be applied to individuals and the results monitored, statistics generated. The routines of prisoners can be altered. The authority can direct more or less reading or medication, a greater or lesser time in solitary confinement, and so forth.

And here we can see something that Foucault did not emphasize: The nature of the reinforcement as well as the intent of the treatment applied by the observer can be positive as well as negative. The picture painted by Foucault was one resembling Orwell's *1984*—Big Brother is always watching and waiting to punish. In modern popular mythology, the watcher is as likely to be a kind of Santa Claus, who "sees you when you're sleeping," and knows when you are awake, bad, or good. Even more to the point is the Biblical depiction of an omniscient God who "knows when each sparrow falls."

Big Brother, Santa Claus, God—real power, the cultural kind, always comes not from contemporary constructs, but from those of the past. Foucault was really talking about the development of something like the superego, the name modern society has attached to that portion of the human "mind" that embodies social beliefs and values and is associated by virtue of human neoteny with parental authority. These beliefs and values are in this way secularized, partitioned off in the society as they are believed to exist in a separate "place" in the "mind." As the architecture and philosophy of the panoptic tower spread—as *panopticism,* as Foucault called it, spread, God became the anonymous observer at the workplace or the university, where modern man must go both in order to survive physically and in order to establish a social identity. Identity can now be bestowed by only this faceless watcher, which many would identify in the twentieth century as the spirit of "Taylorism."[16]

In a manner of speaking, the whole of society becomes a workplace, the work of which is, to quote from Bentham's preface to his *Panopticon,* to accomplish these goals: "Morals reformed—health preserved—industry invigorated—instruction diffused—public burthenss lightened [*sic*]."[17] It is important to see here both that panopticism is linked to the implementation of Renaissance ideals and that this implementation comes about, at base, through ritualistic surveillance that refers ultimately to a ubiquitous aspect of even personalized mythology, the neotenic belief in the legitimacy of parental authority.

Bent's Old Fort was just this kind of device. First, it was a device for surveillance. Surveillance began with the observation and control of the population inside the fort—traders, bourgeois (factors), clerks, trappers, hunters, craftsmen, workmen, herders, laborers, workmen's assistants, and, occasionally, Cheyenne and Arapaho—and the Native Americans outside the fort; but it did not end there. As time went on, the fort was more and more frequently visited by important representatives of the central authority in the East. These were military personnel and traders with political ties, in particular. Visitors could see at a glance that the Bent & St.

Vrain Company had the situation under control. This impression was only enhanced because the observations available at the fort were not limited to those directly made from the bastions there. They included those gathered by the company's representatives on the south side of the Arkansas. These representatives, with the support of the company, had infiltrated the society, economy, and government to the south. To do so they utilized ties forged by trade and marriage—ritual ties.

The fort was a device to advance the agenda of the Renaissance: the culture of modernity, capitalism, and individualism. The principals of the Bent & St. Vrain Company were firm believers in the benefits of rational order to society and the primacy of the entrepreneurial individual in this new scheme. All were members of the Masons, an organization that celebrated these values and strove to inculcate them into society at large. Panopticism provided the design for the circuit of power needed to implement the new order, while ritual and ritualism brought the connections in this circuit into being.

The fort did not conform exactly to Bentham's description of the panopticon; however, there were special conditions at the site of its construction, and the differences from Bentham's basic design were adaptations to these conditions. The central tower was replaced by two towers, the bastions at the northeast and southwest corners of the fort. Supplementing these towers were walkways along the top of the first story of rooms, and the windows facing the central plaza on the second story, rooms inhabited by the upper echelon of the fort. The towers at the opposite junctures of the exterior walls were necessary because surveillance was needed outside of the fort as well as inside (see figs. 8 and 10). The fort occupied alien territory and was subject to attack by Native American groups as well as by Mexicans (particularly since Mexico was located just across the river). Native American groups commonly camped just outside the walls of the fort. Usually these were the Cheyenne and Arapaho, who were only allowed inside the fort's walls at certain times during daylight hours, and then only in certain interior areas such as the trade and council rooms. The presence of the Cheyenne and Arapaho, well armed and equipped by the Bents, was usually enough to discourage visitors from other tribes, except during parlays and negotiations. But skirmishes were not uncommon in the vicinity of the fort. In the late 1830s, as a part of a campaign to eliminate the fort, the Comanche stole all of the horses grazing outside of the fort and killed the man guarding them. In 1841, Robert Bent, a young brother of William and Charles, was killed by Comanche on his way to the fort.

Discipline at the fort was strict, and those who broke the rules were whipped. Banishment from the fort was the most severe punishment and could have fatal consequences in the harsh environment outside of the fort's walls. This discipline supported a strict class system. From highest to lowest, some of the occupational groups within this class system were: the owners of the fort, William and Charles Bent and Ceran St. Vrain; their relatives and distinguished visitors from the East; the bourgeois (the factor); traders; clerks; trappers; hunters; craftsmen; workmen; herders; laborers; workmen's assistants (the last four of these groups were often Mexican); the Cheyenne; and other Native Americans. In all cases, entrepreneurs—independent traders and trappers, for example, who were "free agents"—were accorded higher prestige than were hired traders, trappers, hunters, and guides. A case in point was that Kit Carson, who was originally hired as a hunter and a guide and had worked for the Bents since childhood, was considered socially inferior even after he had achieved wide fame. Ceran St. Vrain would not allow Carson to marry his niece, Felicite St. Vrain.[18]

One measure of the disparity between classes can be seen in the yearly salaries drawn by personnel at the fort. The owners, of course, were not salaried but shared in the immense profits of the fort. By 1846, Bent's Old Fort was the largest of all fur trading posts, except for the outpost owned by the American Fur Company, Fort Union, far to the north on the Yellowstone River. Even in 1832, the Bent caravan from Santa Fe headed east with $190,000 to $200,000 worth of furs, bullion, and other valuables. The fort bourgeois was paid from $2,000 to $4,000 each year, and compensation declined from this high point according to an individual's position on the fort's occupational ladder. Experienced clerks and traders who had mastered Native American languages earned $800 to $1,000 each year. Less experienced interpreters received $500 each year for this service (although they often were paid for other duties in addition to interpreting); an inexperienced clerk might sign on to gain experience for $500 over three years of "apprenticeship," besides which he would receive a suit of fine broadcloth. Hunters were paid $400 each year, but also realized profit from the hides and horns of the animals they killed (which could be an appreciable amount, considering that the fort demanded an average of 1,000 pounds of meat every day).

All of these occupations belonged, at least marginally, to what might be regarded as the "entrepreneurial class." Not only did they provide compensation at a substantially greater rate than did positions of lesser prestige, but the degree of compensation depended upon the measure of "competence and luck" each could demonstrate. As Mary Douglas has argued, competence and luck are the personal attributes most valued and most essential to success in a high-grid, low-group, ego-centered society of the type linked to modern capitalism.[19] Nonentrepreneurial positions carried with them not only much less prestige but also much less pay: craftsmen and workmen might receive $250 a year, a workman's assistant never more than $120 annually, and a laborer or herder about $100.[20] Native Americans, of course, operated in the murky twilight of their traditional society from the point of view of the capitalists at the fort. While trade was of vital concern to them, and profit of increasing interest (the better to amass wealth), trade was always seen by them as ritual exchange or barter, and wealth was not measured in currency, but in horses or, later, buffalo hides and women. Even as late as 1865, when a Cheyenne raid on Julesburg, Colorado, claimed the strongbox with the Fort Rankin payroll, the "green paper" inside was "gleefully chopped up" and scattered to the winds.[21]

The movement of each class was restricted to certain areas within the fort and the immediate landscape of the fort. The Bent and St. Vrain Company controlled access to points of surveillance at the fort: the bastions, in particular, from which activities both inside and outside of the fort could be surveyed, and also the room just above the *zaguan,* the watchtower, which afforded a perspective both inside and outside of the fort. That these locations connoted power is evidenced by symbolic material associated with them. On the northeast bastion was a small brass cannon. This was of limited tactical value in an actual fight but was fired at ceremonial times, such as the Fourth of July, and at the approach of large contingents of Native Americans or visitors from the East. Flying from the watchtower atop the *zaguan* was a very large American flag. The placement of this flag held an important symbolic power. The *zaguan,* after all, was one of the locations in the landscape of the fort most fraught with meaning. It was the most liminal of places, where the transition was made from outside to inside, from the "chaos" always associated with the "wilderness" or the land of the "other," to the creation of the new order. The flag proclaimed this new order to be American. Here we can see, again, the ritual underpinnings of the new culture of panopticism and rational control. It was a ritual woven into the tapestry of everyday life at the fort.

The Company, usually in the person of William Bent, also dictated who occupied the second story of rooms. As an anonymous employee of the fort reported, the "private rooms for gentlemen" were "perched on the very top."[22] This reflected the elite classes' concerns with *privacy,* the privacy of the *individual,* as well as their desire to be in a position from which surveillance could be made (of course, these rooms might also have been quieter and cleaner).

As documented by archaeological research, as well as some contemporary accounts, permanent fort staff like blacksmiths, carpenters, wheelwrights, gunsmiths, cooks, tailors, and, at times, a barber were assigned work and sleeping rooms on the ground floor, as were the lower status Mexican workmen, who slept many to a single room. The trade rooms were also here, accessible for brief periods to newly arrived trappers, mountain men, and Native Americans who were under surveillance constantly while at the fort. Freighters and other transients might be allowed to stay inside the fort's walls but were not assigned rooms. They camped and cooked in the plaza, eating and sleeping just as they did while on the trail.

More elite staff and visitors were quartered in the upper tier of apartments. The bourgeois during the 1840 remodeling of the fort (a time during which Bent & St. Vrain Company was preparing to expand its trading empire and its influence) was Alexander Barclay, who eventually built Barclay's Fort at Moro, New Mexico. Barclay was an Englishman, born to genteel poverty because of an improvident father. According to Janet LeCompte, he was "determined to be independent, to make his fortune, to become a man of property and to live like one—the theme ran through all his letters and impelled all his actions."[23] Another who participated in the remodeling of the fort was Lancaster Lupton, who first visited the fort as a young lieutenant with the First Dragoons under Colonel Henry Lodge in 1835. He later built Fort Lupton on the South Platte River in Colorado. In this we see some of the capacity of the panopticon to multiply and extend the culture of modernity, as was mentioned by Foucault. We recognize this as well in the tenure at the fort and later exploits of "frontiersmen" and "mountain men," the shock troops of this culture, and many of these individuals became iconic figures, contributing images to a mythology for the new culture.

What may not be recognized by many today is that these frontiersmen became symbols of the progress of modernity in their *own* time. In his memoirs, Kit Carson recorded a strange incident in his attempted rescue of a Mrs. White, who had been kidnapped by the Jicarilla Apache. After some hesitation on the part of the officer commanding the rescue party, the fleeing Jicarilla shot Mrs. White with an arrow through her heart. When Carson found her body, it was still "perfectly warm." Carson was stricken with regret, even more so when:

In camp was found a book, the first of the kind I had ever seen, in which I was made a great hero, slaying Indians by the hundred, and I have often thought that as Mrs. White would read the same, and knowing that I lived near, she would pray for my appearance and that she would be saved.[24]

And so, as Foucault also observed, panopticism worked and multiplied itself in two directions: Those who dwelled under the panoptic gaze were disciplined and moved on to discipline others. These were entrepreneurs like Alexander Barclay, Lancaster Lupton, and others, as well as the frontiersmen who acted as the infantry of this invading cultural force. But those who controlled the panoptic "tower" were exposed to the observation of "inspectors," representatives of the central authority who scrutinized the panoptic establishment for conformity with the ideals of the elite culture. In addition to military officers, influential entrepreneurs, bureaucrats, and political emissaries, some who came to survey the fort were writers who cast the events that they observed there into a form compatible with reigning cultural values. These writers included Matthew Field, Frederick A. Wislizenus, Marcus Whitman, Lewis Garrard, Francis Parkman, Thomas J. Farnham, William Boggs, Albert G. Boone, Susan Magoffin, and Lieutenant Abert, who drew as well as wrote what he observed.

Prevalent Eastern attitudes were echoed by these authors, but we can also recognize in their works many approaches to the historic West popular today—ones that they helped to establish more firmly, and to pass on. Lewis Garrard, whose observations were first published in 1850 as *Wah-to-yah and the Taos Trail,* was a young man of means who ventured west to bolster a frail constitution. The West offered a healthy environment and adventure. Garrard was a tourist. Francis Parkman recorded his observations with scientific precision. He was a historian, and his 1849 *The Oregon Trail* is today held in high regard. Other specialists within the emerging modernity were well represented among this group. Matthew Field, of course, was a journalist who would find fame especially during the Civil War. He boiled down experience to essential images, the sound-bites of an earlier age. It was he who coined the term "castle on the Plains" for the fort, one widely quoted and used thereafter.[25] Wislizenus was a naturalist; Marcus Whitman, a missionary; George F. Ruxton, an author.

Susan Magoffin, the young bride of Samuel Magoffin, regarded what no white woman had previously seen with the surprise and a certain disdain appropriate to "a wandering princess," as she referred to herself in her diary. Documentary evidence indicates that she, like many of the other authors, stayed in the upper rooms (although Garrard and some others probably did not). Even though confined to bed in this room because of a miscarriage suffered at the fort (due, one must suspect, to the physical exertion and discomfort she experienced on the Santa Fe Trail), Magoffin remained aware of many of the activities in the fort, to the point of observing, "I hear the cackling of chickens at such a rate sometimes I shall not be surprised to hear of a cock-pit."[26] She was concerned about the gambling at the fort, just as she was about certain habits of the Mexican women: combing their hair in public, showing bare arms and ankles, smoking, dressing their hair with grease. She found it "repulsive to see the children running about perfectly naked."[27] Nonetheless, she recorded this all carefully. Although her diary was probably intended only for her family, Lamar noted that she modeled it after Josiah Gregg's earlier *Commerce of the Prairies.*[28] This very act of careful observation and recording identified her as a member of that class which has as its *duty* to "observe performances . . . map attitudes, to assess characters, to draw up rigorous classifications."[29] This is the culture of discipline, the panoptic culture.

All of this is of no small import as a means by which the *outmoded* culture is criticized and conditions "improved." The incessant collective gambling at the fort, for example, was a survival from an older world, that of rank as opposed to class. Gambling in a modern society does not disappear—it is, rather, enshrined as an egalitarian means of upward mobility, one that depends upon the "luck" that those without access to class-based "competence" must rely upon in order to establish a social identity.[30] But this sort of gambling must be an individual effort, one man against all others, against the "fate" that is the metaphorical expression of the social forces that hold an individual's identity in place (or in check, depending upon how one looks at it). This is the gambling of the poker game or the lottery—winner-take-all. Gambling at the fort, the sort that Mrs. Magoffin could not help but notice (with what seems to me to be a jaundiced eye), even while her life was in danger, was the collective kind, group against group, the gambling of cock fighting and horse racing. Mrs. Magoffin registered no disapproval at the billiard room on the second story, only surprise that such a remote outpost of civilization could claim one.[31] Billiards, after all, was a gentleman's game, one that matched the individual's personal competence against all others. But cock fighting and horse racing were *passé* and now associated with the lower classes. In the eighteenth century they were the passions of tobacco planters, the "old" elite in the East, but had since fallen out of favor as a new way of life emerged, that of middle-class mercantile capitalism. Rhys Isaac noted this in *The Transformation of Virginia:*

Intensely shared interests of this kind, cutting across but not leveling social distinctions, serve to transmit images of what life is really about. The gentry, having the means and assurance to patronize sport and to be seen playing grandly for the highest stakes, were well placed to ensure that their superior social status was confirmed among the many who took part in these exciting activities. In a community where many of the participants could identify each other as personalities or as members of known families—and thus were bound to observe the proper formalities of deference and condescension—the congested intimacy of collective engagement only served to confirm social ranking. In this respect the operations of a face-to-face, rank-structured society differ radically from those of an impersonal "class" society, where such mingling is distasteful partly because it does introduce confusions of relationship.[32]

The appropriate class separation was affected by the segregation of the elite at the fort to the second floor of rooms. Mrs. Magoffin was attended by a physician, Dr. Edward L. Hempstead, who apparently occupied the room next to hers. Dr. Hempstead was more than the fort's physician, he was also the chief clerk there. In an age of less advanced differentiation, of less specialization, this made perfect sense; both occupations were *pre*-occupied by the modern obsession with counting, analyzing, and logically arriving at cures for the conditions that were seen as deviations from the socially defined states of physical and fiscal "soundness." Hempstead was a nephew of Manuel Lisa by marriage and a member of a prominent St. Louis family. Not far away on the second floor was, for a time, a schoolteacher, another harbinger of discipline and the improvement of the "self." The schoolteacher, George Simpson, is known to have habitually dressed in a frock coat and silk hat some years later in the nearby town of Trinidad, Colorado, lest there be any mistaking *his* social identity.[33]

The same sort of segregation was seen in the eating arrangements, a facet of life at the fort remarked upon by many observers (who usually regarded it as another sign of civilization) and one that is striking today in the National Park Service interpretive program at the fort. The owners (William Bent and whoever of the other owners were present), the bourgeois, and the clerks ate before anyone else. They were fed in the dining room with the best food the fort had to offer—the best and most varied cuts of meats, bread, soup, and, on Sundays and special occasions, desserts like pie. Almost certainly, French wines were drunk at this "first table": archaeological excavations recovered numerous bottle fragments and some complete bottles of Medoc and champagne. These were symbols of high status anywhere within the United States at the time. Then, as now, drinking wine is a performance with many and varied rituals (decanting the red wine or popping the cork on a bottle of champagne, savoring and critically assessing bouquet, color, and taste, toasting the host and guests, and so on). The bottles recovered from the site were actually a part of this performance; a "pipe," or keg, of wine filled two bottles, and the bottles were used over and over again.[34] The message of this performance was that discerning wine drinkers were a breed apart from those who drank merely for effect. The ritual of serving and drinking wine became a powerful link to the more refined cultures of Europe. Of these, none was considered more refined than that of France. As Nietzsche, that prophet of modernity, said, "I believe only in French culture, and regard everything else in Europe which calls itself 'culture' as a misunderstanding."[35] (And Roland Barthes calls wine the French "totem-drink.")[36] Served in the context of this outpost so far from Eastern civilization, the symbolic effect must have been considerably heightened.

Finer ceramics were almost surely used at the first table and at other ritualized partakings of food and drink. Such ceramics were found at archaeological excavations at the fort. While porcelain, the most expensive of ceramics, was not found in great quantity at the fort's archaeological excavations, this does not mean that porcelain was not commonly used by the fort's owners. Time and again, archaeological excavations at historic sites like the mansions and townhouses of the wealthy have yielded few fragments of porcelain. It has been speculated by many archaeologists that this means merely that people have in general been very careful with these expensive ceramics (which are often passed down from generation to generation).

More significant is that expensive and *specialized* sorts of earthenwares were recovered that could be firmly dated to the time of the occupation of the site by the Bent & St. Vrain Company (as opposed to its later uses as a stagecoach station and as part of a cattle-raising enterprise). Partial archaeological excavations of the fort's two trash dumps in 1976 yielded a good number of artifacts for which dates of manufacture could be obtained because intermittent dumping and burning had "sealed" the deposits.[37]

Table 1 shows the types and associated vessel forms indicated by shards of earthenware recovered from the trash deposits. Two types of earthenware are especially important. The first of these ceramics is transfer-printed ware. Transfer-printing refers to the rather complex technological process by which these ceramics were decorated. A copper plate was etched with a design and inked, the design was transferred first to thin sheets of paper and then from the paper to the clay body of the ceramic. All of this was done by hand, and difficulties could arise at any stage of the process.

The copper plate had to be prepared in just the right way and the ink carefully wiped from the plate, so that it only remained in the crevices of the etching; the thin paper had to be applied to the irregular shape of the ceramic. Transfer-printed ware was expensive, especially during the early nineteenth century, when it was still relatively rare.[38]

Table 1. Ceramic Types From Bent's Old Fort Main and West Trash Dumps
Presented By Vessel Form (Hollow Versus Flat)

Ceramic Type	Hollow		Flat		Unknown		Total
	#	%	#	%	#	%	#
Annular pearlware	32	100%	0	0%	0	0%	32
Lustre pearlware	44	100%	0	0%	0	0%	44
Spatter pearlware	91	100%	0	0%	0	0%	91
Floral pearlware	182	100%	0	0%	0	0%	182
Blue-edged pearlware	0	0%	34	100%	0	0%	34
Transfer-printed pearlware	33	36%	24	26%	34	37%	91
Miscellaneous decorated whiteware (including pearlware)	0	0%	4	9%	41	91%	45
Miscellaneous undecorated whiteware (including pearlware)	22	4%	27	6%	442	90%	491
Decorated graniteware	0	0%	1	100%	0	0%	1
Undecorated graniteware	3	8%	0	0%	34	92%	37
Yellowware	54	75%	0	0%	18	25%	72
Bennington-type ware	0	0%	0	0%	4	100%	4
Green glaze	0	0%	0	0%	2	100%	2
Porcelain	15	94%	0	0%	1	6%	16
Unknown buff	0	0%	11	100%	0	0%	11
					Total Number		1,153

John Solomon Otto, like many other historical archaeologists, has found that for sites in the early to mid nineteenth century, the presence of a high percentage of transfer-printed shards in a ceramic assemblage is a reliable indicator of high status, much more so than is porcelain which, as discussed, is hardly ever found in any quantity.[39] Adding to its appeal to the upper classes was that with the fine lines permitted by the technology, one could impart detail enough to tell a real story. These stories were usually of significance to the intended "audience," the market for the ceramic. Certainly that seems to have been the case with the transfer-printed ware associated with Bent & St. Vrain Company, as evidenced by the vignette most frequently depicted on the samples recovered from inside the fort and in the fort's trash dumps.[40]

Figure 17. Registry form for the "Gentleman's Cabin" pattern, part of the "Boston Mails" series of English pottery. (Courtesy Crown Publishing Company; from Geoffrey A. Godden, *An Illustrated Encyclopedia of British Pottery and Porcelain* [London: Bonanza, 1965], 159.)

This pattern was called by the manufacturer in Staffordshire, England, "Gentleman's Cabin." It is rife with symbols referring to the new culture of the elite: the culture of panoptic control that implemented, among other social phenomena, colonialism. The scene on the ceramic vessels shows the private ship's cabin of a gentleman and illustrates the privacy accorded to individuals in the privileged group (fig. 17). This is the same sort of privacy provided to the representatives of the elite by the second story of Bent's Old Fort. One might bear in mind that the sailing ships of the early nineteenth century were the technological marvels of their time, on a par in their day with the moon rockets and space shuttles of our own. No other mechanism of that period demanded more precision in its engineering and construction or more competence, both scientific and organizational, in order to be properly employed.

The captain and officers of such a vessel—these might be the four men gathered around the table in the scene—ruled with perfect discipline. Each individual was assigned to his own station, according to his level of competence. The officers were the "natural" masters of the ship, by virtue of their mastery of nature. Nature was harnessed to the ends of this elite group by the use of scientific instruments and knowledge. Gentlemen could use barometers, telescopes, sextants, and other navigational devices. They could read charts, timetables, and almanacs. They could log in careful sequence and detail the events of the voyage, thereby propagating the lessons of their travels to others of their class. The instruments by which all of this could be done are visible or strongly implied by means of the design, which offers us a glimpse into the gentleman's private world, a world of control over nature and lesser men by virtue of his scientific competence. Arranged in a circle around the outside of this central design feature, the view of the cabin, are four large ocean-going vessels, which occupied a position on the cutting edge of maritime technology in the early nineteenth century. The ships are powered not only by sail but also by steam (side paddle-wheels can be seen just below the smokestacks). The names of the vessels are common for trading and whaling vessels of the period: Britannia, Acadia, Columbus, and Caledonia. These ships, however, were the fast mail packets that linked the United States to England.[41] To the owners and traders of the fort, the parallels to their own exploits and ambitions would be obvious. They would surely regard themselves (or at least wish themselves) to be of the same class as the gentlemen portrayed on this ceramic. Also, they considered themselves part of a mercantile, and social, network that extended to England and Europe, a connection symbolized by the representation of the mail packets.

The second sort of ceramic especially noteworthy for its symbolic value at the "first table" and other ceremonious occasions at the fort is provocative not so much by virtue of its cost or decorative motif as by the use to which it was put. Many of the fragments of decorated ceramics recovered from the Bent Period were from tea servings. These included fragments of spatterware and copper lustreware as well as transfer-printed ware. The very ornate copper lustreware was produced almost entirely for tea services.[42] Note in Table 1 that 100 percent of recovered fragments of "lustre pearlware," which in this case is copper lustreware, along with spatter and floral pearlware, are identified as being of "hollow" form. Hollow forms are cups, saucers, bowls, pots, and other vessels designed to serve drink or food in a semifluid state. In these cases, the hollow forms were tea servings. These tea sets were associated with special, even formal, occasions. All this is mindful of what Stanley South has called the "British Tea Ceremony." As South states, "the tea ceremony was an important ritual in eighteenth-century British colonial life, relating to status even in the remote corners of the British Empire."[43] South might well have said *especially* in the remote corners of the empire; the ability to participate properly in this ceremony was a means by which one established one's membership in this colonial force. The ritual both demonstrated and formed a common, mythological "ancestry" and was doubtless employed in that manner at Bent's Old Fort by the elite there.

A "second table" was set for hunters and some workmen. This was the same table previously occupied by the most elite group, but was now set with somewhat simpler fare, including meat, biscuits, and black coffee with sugar. Though those at the second table were members of the entrepreneurial class, it is likely that most would have eschewed the trappings of greater refinement that might have been seen at the first table. Kit Carson on his deathbed asked for "first-rate doings—a buffalo steak and a bowl of coffee, and then bring me my pipe—the clay one."[44] Such were his pleasures, but also the trappings of what he felt to be his proper station. Stripped of effete Eastern conceits, they were appropriate to men of action—plain men with no time for intrigue and politics.

For others at the fort, meals were more bereft of ceremony, and the fare was much simpler. Transients, except for honored guests, were left to their own devices and generally cooked as they had on the trail, although they might be permitted the security of the fort. This in itself was luxurious. After months of danger and uncertainty, where to relax one's guard for only a moment might mean disaster (Plains Indians, even friendly groups, were loath to pass up an opportunity like an unguarded camp), being within this superbly well-defended environment must have been an enormous relief.

Some employees of the fort, too, would not have eaten in the dining room, especially when the population of the fort was at its seasonal peak of between 150 and 200. Such employees included the families of Mexican workmen, who cooked in their rooms or in the plaza. Here there were no individual place settings, in fact, there were no ceramics at all. Eating was a collective affair, and tortillas served as both plates and spoons. Mrs.

Magoffin once participated in such a meal, on the trail south of Bent's Old Fort, and her reaction is instructive:

And then the dinner half a dozen *tortillas* [pancakes] made of *blue corn,* and not a plate, but rapped in a napkin twin brother to the *last* table cloth. Oh, how my heart sickened, to say nothing of my stomach, a cheese and, the kind we saw yesterday from the Mora, entirely speckled over, and two earthen *jollas* [ollas—jugs] of a mixture of meat, *chilly verde* [green pepper] & onions boiled together completed course No. 1. We had neither knives, forks, or spoons, but made as good substitutes as we could by doubling a piece of *tortilla,* at every mouthful—but by the by there were few mouthfuls taken, for I could not eat a dish so strong, and unaccustomed to my palate. *Mi alma* [Susan Magoffin's husband] now called for something else, and they brought us some roasted corn rolled in a napkin rather cleaner than the first & I relished it a little more than the *sopa* [soup]; this and a fried egg completed my meal.[45]

The revulsion expressed here should not, I think, reflect poorly on Mrs. Magoffin. She was a very young woman who was in the midst of a private ordeal. She was merely observing and commenting in the manner to which she had been carefully prepared; hers was a social critique that had real social implications. She objected to the unhygienic and unrefined aspects of the meal, and, in doing so, she gave voice to the concerns of her class. (It is interesting, from today's perspective, that while we might see some merit in terms of hygiene to her objection to eating with one's hands, her delicate palate might have deprived her of an important source of nutrition in the Southwestern environment. The inhabitants at Bent's Old Fort never suffered from scurvy in the way common to populations at other western forts, probably because the chilies used so frequently in Mexican cooking were a source of vitamin C, often the only available source in a diet that depended for the most part on meat.) Had Mrs. Magoffin been in better physical condition at the fort, she could have made these same observations there, without personally participating in the meal, by merely looking out the door of her room into the plaza of the fort, where Mexican families were likely to have been cooking and eating in the same way.

Pierre Bourdieu has written extensively on the ways in which "taste" is employed as part of a strategy of differentiation. This strategy is used by tribes, in the traditional world, to produce distinctions, one from the other, and thereby to help construct an overarching identity *within* the tribe. Bourdieu noted that the same strategy is used in capitalistic societies to establish class differences that are the basis for the classes themselves.[46]

Bourdieu does not much deal with the ways by which "tastes" are es-

tablished. The dynamics of ritual suggest to me that eating together encourages what then appears to be a "natural" intimacy. It is a repetition
of a primal experience. Taste and manners are a kind of communication;
if shared, the message is that "we are alike" in what appear to be very basic ways. This reenactment of a primal experience imbues the foods and
objects involved with a value, tableware included. In the above examples,
we can see what has been indicated in archaeological studies of ceramic
use at historic sites, particularly at plantations.[47] Socioeconomic groups
on the lower end of the scale make more use of bowls (if any ceramics
are used at all). Eating is a more communal affair. An extreme of this, one
might suppose, is the Middle Eastern *mensef,* in which all eat from a single platter, using only their hands. In the Mexican tradition, tortillas are
used to take servings from a communal pot. In New Mexico there were
usually no ceramics associated with the consumption of food, except those
containing liquid. At plantations, slaves ate stews prepared from less expensive cuts of meat, each receiving his or her serving in a bowl.

Among the elite, however, eating becomes a ritual that reinforces the
shared values associated with individualism. Cuts of meat, for example,
are prepared individually. Food is served by means of specialized utensils
and ceramics. Plates provide a frame for several foods, not mixed together
as in a stew but each prepared individually and arranged tastefully. Knowing the "correct fork" marks one as a member of this group. Food is often presented in courses, each course with its own special tableware.
Coffee, tea, and chocolate services are examples.[48] Class lines are more
firmly drawn in this way. People from different classes become uncom-
fortable in each other's presence at mealtime, and so segregation is perpetuated. At Bent's Old Fort, in addition to this mechanism of separation, yet another means of social segregation was implemented: There is
evidence that charges were made for meals (and for the privilege of frequenting the billiard and bar room as well).[49]

In the variety of ceramic shards described in Table 1 can be discerned
the segmentation that is a part of the modern order. Flatware was used
to serve portions to individuals, and much of the sample recovered of this
ware was decorated with the "Gentleman's Cabin" pattern, a vignette of
mythic individualism. Hollowware was used for communal sharing of tea
from the same teapot to the cups of individuals in the upper classes, from
cooking pots to bowls for the lower. Other hollowware was for specialized activities associated with class. Yellowware shards from the trash
dumps appear to represent primarily pitchers and basins. Those in upper
echelons used these as a part of a regimen of personal hygiene. At least

in the upper-class homes of the eastern United States at this time, the basins were emptied and the pitchers kept full by servants. And the few fragments of buff-colored ceramics, which do not appear to belong to any of the English or American ceramic types, hint that the practice of eating and drinking from ceramic tableware was spreading at the fort to those who could not afford (or, perhaps, did not want) factory ceramics. The unknown buff ceramic fragments appear to be a flat form, a saucer or possibly a small plate. It is an extremely soft and porous earthenware with a thick grayish glaze, and it may have been produced in small quantities locally. An alternate possibility is that the ceramics supplemented the service of the upper echelon.

Thus, the panoptic culture (the culture of modernity, capitalism, and individualism) was propagated by several interrelated means. It spread to the south by the actions of the traders and their allied frontiersmen who acted as "missionaries" spreading the gospel of the new culture primarily by means of exchange with its associated ritual. The fort was linked to eastern centers of power by the surveillance of socially influential visitors, who assured the elite in the East that Bent & St. Vrain Company was advancing the agenda of modernity. This association culminated with the use of the fort as an intelligence-gathering post prior to the Mexican War, and as a staging area as the war began. As Enid Thompson noted in 1973,

The relationship of Bent-St. Vrain and Bent's Fort to the Federal Government and particularly, the War Department is slowly emerging, and it is much more important to our history than has been recorded. It was also more costly to the Bents as a family, and to Bent's Fort, than has been realized.

Charles Bent was an American working internally for the overthrow of the Mexican Government in Santa Fe. His chief St. Louis contact was Thornton Grimsley, and his chief contact in Washington was Thomas Hart Benton. Kearny was well apprised of his 5th column in Santa Fe and army officers were instructed to go to William at the fort or Charles in Santa Fe for help if they needed it beyond legal and proper governmental assistance. In plain language, Charles Bent spied for the American conquest of New Mexico, William Bent led the Kearny column to Santa Fe, and many Mexicans, not least Padre Martinez, were aware not only of the danger, but of the actuality. The records of these activities appear in the secret and confidential letters of the Secretary of War in the National Archives. Protests against the activity appear in Mexican Archives of New Mexico in Santa Fe.[50]

A pre-existing network of power relations was reinforced and extended by this surveillance. The intensification of surveillance ushered in the most prosperous days of the fort, the "Golden Years" between 1840 and 1846, which are the focus of today's interpretive program at Bent's Old Fort National Historic Site. During this time, the fort's structure underwent what seem to have been fairly extensive alterations. Fortifications were improved initially during Alexander Barclay's last days at the fort, in 1840, including physical alterations to the building itself. Not long after, the establishment was made more comfortable. The refinement in the way of life at the fort—at least for the elite—would have pleased Alexander Barclay, who complained during his tenure as fort bourgeois that conditions were too primitive for a gentleman of his breeding.

By 1845 the younger Bent brothers, Robert and George, were in evidence at the fort, and they brought with them, for example, the billiard table, which they installed next to a bar they built in the upstairs billiard room. These years also saw an increasing Eastern, particularly a military, presence at the fort.

From 1840 onward, Charles Bent was in frequent communication, through confidential letters, with the United States Secretary of War (these letters are in the National Archives). It is plain from these letters that westward expansion of the country was of mutual interest. Documents in the Archives of New Mexico reveal that Governor Armijo was warning the Mexican government about Bent's Old Fort as a source of subversion by 1840. Authorities in Santa Fe in 1845 made much the same warning to their central government. In 1845, General Kearny arrived at Bent's Old Fort while carrying out a "topographic survey," which all in the region regarded as an intelligence-gathering mission done with the imminent hostilities in mind. In fact, some of his force were "mustered out" at the fort, and one wonders what became of them thereafter. Bent was by now also sending letters of intelligence to Senator Thomas H. Benton. In 1846, of course, General Kearny was back at the fort with his invasion force. It is important to note that this surveillance network was formed and sustained by various ritual means.

It should be clear that manipulation of meaning through the ritual use of symbolically charged material is a social mechanism used not only by traditional cultures. We can see in the use of the Bent's Old Fort landscape the operation of this very phenomenon, one that affected all who visited the fort, whether they were from the American East or New Mexico, or were members of a Plains Indian group.

A similar use of the landscapes and artifacts of modernity have been noted elsewhere. The work of Mark Leone with the eighteenth-century material culture of Annapolis, Maryland, allows us to observe the manipulation of "sentiment" *within* a society that is modernizing. The situation here recalls that which Isaac examined in colonial Virginia, where an elite based in a plantation economy, a group replete with social rituals of hospitality and conviviality, was challenged by an emerging mercantile middle class.

Leone's thesis was that the elite were attempting to maintain control over this society just as it entered the Revolutionary Era by displaying their mastery of natural phenomena in several ways. Important among these were the utilization of objects (and etiquettes) which "were used to observe, study, order, and rationalize natural phenomena": these being, in part, clocks, sundials, telescopes, barometers, compasses, globes, sextants, microscopes, musical instruments, sheet music, and place settings. Such a public use of these devices was intended to establish that this class understood and could control the natural world, and, especially, "modeled daily life's activities on the mechanically precise rules of the clockwork universe."[51] One sort of material culture to which Leone gave great attention is the formal garden of the eighteenth century. It provided a perfect opportunity for the gentry to exhibit their control over geometry and three-dimensional space.

Leone's thesis has been criticized on two counts. First, it assumes that the formal gardens and the use of scientific devices as he described them worked as intended. Was it a conscious strategy? Did all groups (the elite, blacks, Native Americans, and so on) respond to the display in the same way? We have no certain way of knowing. Native Americans, however, were probably not invited to social occasions at formal gardens. Second, he offers no real mechanism here. His case rested, as did Isaac's, on the fact that the material culture and social behavior he observed arose at a time that also saw broad economic and political changes that seem to make the intentions he ascribed to the elite likely.

I contend that Leone was correct in his intuition that the elite were intending to establish their position with the behaviors he observed. He does not however identify the most important audience for this performance, which was *themselves*—not only other members of their elite group, but each individual *self*. To quote Geertz, as done previously, "the imposition of meaning on life is the major end and primary condition of human existence." Just as it might not be practical, from a pragmatic or functionalist point of view, for the Balinese to wager extravagant amounts on cock fighting, so it may not have been practical or effective for the elite in Annapolis to expend large sums in constructing formal gardens. But by doing so the Balinese and elite Annapolitans fixed an identity in terms of the ideologies (or mythologies) that gave meaning to their lives.

The activities of the Annapolitans were obviously ritualistic in nature. I suggest that this is the mechanism Leone implied but did not specify. This is especially clear since they so evidently modeled society after the movements of the heavens. Pursuant to this, very basic to the well-developed theories of Mircea Eliade is the notion of a celestial archetype for society in all its aspects. In a book Eliade said he might have called *Introduction to a Philosophy of History* (actually titled *The Myth of the Eternal Return*), he stated, "for archaic man, reality is a function of the imitation of a celestial archetype."[52] And, as Eliade noted in various places, the "archaic mind" reemerges continually in the modern world. I agree that this occurs continually and that the "archaic mind" is what we may observe among the eighteenth-century elite of Annapolis.

Characterizing gardens in England from early Georgian times and gardens in Annapolis between 1765 and the end of the Revolutionary Era, Leone said they

were built according to the skillful use of the rules of perspective; in England, they frequently carried a particular message, such as individual liberty, through their iconography and *were to so engage a visitor's emotional reaction* [emphasis mine] by entertaining the eye through the illusions and allusions in them, that the message appeared to have a more real existence by being copied in nature. Such copying could, of course, occur only if the rules were assumed to exist in nature in the first place. The connection between the iconography and nature was created by sustaining the "happy enjoyment of Felicities" that help "clear the oppressed Head" of "Vapours" and "terrors," in other words, through the manipulation of the emotions.[53]

Leone provided here a very clear description of the use of the garden as ritual ground, a place that provides in its every aspect reference to the metapast (the mythology) of emergent capitalism and the ethos of a market economy. Elite visitors to the garden were, according to the comments of such visitors recorded by Leone, engaged by the symbolism. The "manipulation of emotions" is the *sentiment* of Durkheim.

The construction of Bent's Old Fort conveyed an effective message to both the Plains Indians and the Mexicans just to the south. In its massive symmetry, it proclaimed the arrival of the Americans in the Southwest. But, much more than that, the fort and the surrounding landscape constituted ritual ground of a sort more powerful than the gardens Leone describes or the architecture dealt with by Isaac. The fort provoked affective responses in anyone moving through the landscape. The experience of negotiating the landscape of the fort would be much different for individuals in each level of the social strata that made up the hierarchy at the fort, and it reinforced that hierarchy every day. In no small part, this difference was due to discrepancies in the ability to see and be seen. Those who controlled the high ground of the fort were able to impose the discipline of modernity there. The owners functioned socially as a kind of superego; they were *in loco parentis* for the central authorities of the flowering modern culture in the East. This was the organizing force that acted upon the disintegrating social worlds of the early nineteenth-century Southwest—disintegration that had been brought about by social and cultural dislocations instigated earlier by the East.

Industrialization and the Landscape

Much of what was transpiring in the East at the time Bent's Old Fort was in operation was linked to the rapid industrialization of the early nineteenth century. As the nineteenth century opened, the United States set forth on a course that would establish the country as an industrial nation and an influence in international affairs. The new direction away from an agrarian and toward an industrial society was set with the real finale to the Revolution, the War of 1812. Particularly after the resounding defeat of the British at the Battle of New Orleans, patriotism ran high in the new country. Patriotic motifs and symbolism in art and on utilitarian objects, like ceramics, became popular. Not only were the British defeated in 1815, the United States also placed itself among the world naval powers with its raid on the Barbary Coast, which freed American ships and hostages.

Having established its military potency, the new nation quickly acted to use it to economic advantage. In 1816, tariffs were introduced to prevent the British "dumping" of manufactured goods in American markets, a move that strengthened emerging American industry. The ground breaking for the Erie Canal in 1817 promised a link between the resources of the "frontier" and the industrial and distribution center of New York. This initial grand attempt to stoke the fires of industry and commerce with fuel from the hinterlands was a magnificent success. As the economic benefit to New York became clear, it sparked what has been called a "canal building mania" among other East Coast cities, an obsession only diverted by the railroads when that technology became available a decade later.

American industrialization and trade thenceforth grew rapidly, and apace. To encourage it further, Congress in 1828 passed what was known in the South as the "Tariff of Abominations," which controlled the import of foreign goods. In that year, also, construction began on the nation's first railroad, the Baltimore and Ohio, intended to link the East with the Ohio Valley. This linkage had been a lifelong goal of George Washington, who had encouraged the National Road and who had been president of the Potomac Company, which had built a series of skirting canals along the Potomac River in 1785. In 1828 Washington's dream found expression not only in the railroad but also through the efforts of the Chesapeake and Ohio Canal Company, which intended to build a canal between the Ohio Valley and Washington, D.C., itself. On July 4 of that year, the President of the United States turned the first shovelful of earth in the construction of the canal, proclaiming it to be an engineering marvel matched only by the pyramids of Egypt.

The two decades between 1830 and 1850 spanned the time of the operation of Bent's Old Fort. The groundwork for massive industrialization had been laid by 1830. In 1850, industrialization was well under way, and the cultural tensions produced by the transition were beginning to weaken the fabric of the nation. There was great disparity now between lifestyles, beliefs, and values along several lines. Gaps widened between the industrial North and the agricultural South, rural and urban areas, the American-born and immigrants, and, increasingly, management and labor. In 1830, the country rode a wave of optimism and patriotism and looked toward a future that appeared bright with the promise of industry. Roads and railroads would be built, water and gas systems installed, police and fire protection instituted. The new country was determined to avoid the class systems of the Old World. The mills of Francis Cabot Lowell would be the prototype; rustics would be exposed to the larger world, and employment there could be the ticket to a morally uplifting way of life. By 1850, the nation was already looking backward with nostalgia to a lost, simpler way a life, a sentiment that would climax with romanticism about the disappearing world of the Southern plantation system. The Lowell experiment had failed, immigrants replaced the farm girls in the mills, class lines were drawn, and conflict along ethnic lines began to rise. Thompson noted that the builders of Bent's Old Fort had patterned their operation along the cultural lines of the 1830s. By 1850, the very forces which the Bents had put in place in the Southwest had overrun them, and "the Fort became not a microcosm, but an anachronism."[54]

Enthusiasm for industry helps to explain certain aspects of the Bent's Old Fort landscape and contemporary reaction to it. As we have seen, it was in most ways an ordered environment, with spaces assigned to the various specialists who were associated with the fort's operation: the traders, trappers, teamsters, workmen, and so on. But this impression of order is countered by the archaeological discovery of two large trash dumps, not hidden from view behind or away from the fort, but located only feet from the fort's front entrance (fig. 18).

The trash pits were initially discovered during archaeological investigations in the early 1960s by Jackson W. Moore. The largest was 70 to 80 feet wide and over 130 feet long, with a depth as much as about 5 feet below existing ground surface. Moore referred to this, because of its size, as the "Main Dump." It was located a mere 40 feet from the fort walls. The other trash pit was smaller—about 25 feet north-south, and 35 feet east-west, with a depth of about 5 to 6 feet. This "West Dump," as Moore referred to it, was as close as 7 feet to the fort walls. The proximity of the trash deposit Moore found "demanding of our credulity," and he concluded that "its presence there must have been truly trying to the occupants of the fort."[55]

A more complete excavation in 1976 revealed a variety of interesting facts about the trash deposits.[56] In both deposits the large preponderance of material was faunal: the bones of animals, which displayed butchering marks. Most of these were buffalo, but there were also deer, antelope, and a wide variety of smaller mammals, fishes, and birds. Though both dumps bore unmistakable signs of repeated incineration, the stench must have been unavoidable to the inhabitants of the fort.[57] Artifacts from the dumps indicated that the west deposit had been made during the earliest period of occupation at the fort. Ceramic dates obtained there indicate that this might have been as early as 1831. Main Dump artifacts suggested that the material there had been deposited after 1841 and prior to 1849, the time period of the most intensive occupation and activity at the fort.

The incongruity of these nuisances with the evident attempts to make the fort a more comfortable, even luxurious place, especially during the period beginning with 1840, is obvious. Perhaps this incongruity is one that might be seen as such only in the present; to the competent owners of the fort the situation may have made more sense. One might guess that the owners regarded the irritating presence of refuse as necessary byproducts of an industrial process. The fort was a kind of factory, after all.

While we may speculate about the attitudes of the fort's owners, it is also true that the tolerance of garbage in close proximity to living (and working) space did not arise with the industrial revolution, as archaeologists who have worked at preindustrial village sites can testify. The

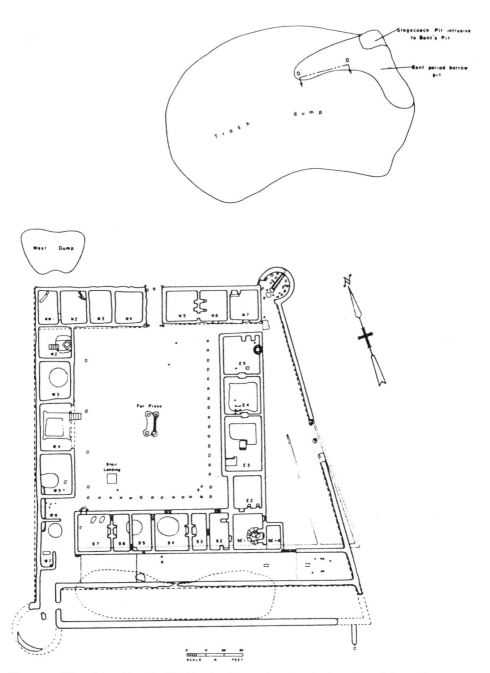

Figure 18. Plan view of Bent's Old Fort landscape showing the location of the trash dumps. (Courtesy Colorado Historical Society, Denver; from Jackson W. Moore, Jr., *Bent's Old Fort—An Archaeological Study* [Denver: State Historical Society of Colorado, 1973], 14.)

agricultural Pueblo Indian (living not far away in the Southwest), for example, not only discarded their trash just outside their dwelling, but buried their dead in these midden deposits, too. Medieval European villages and cities were filthy, and the filth contributed to any number of plagues; just one outbreak of the bubonic plague in England in the fourteenth century killed more than a third of the population there. In the nineteenth-century East, anyone who could arrange to leave the city in the summer did so, not only because the stench arising from the horses, the outhouses, the gutters in the streets where night soil was thrown, and the pigs who rooted in alleyways was unpleasant but also because the threats to health were very real.

This brings us back to panopticism. The plagues of the seventeenth century, brought about by the increasingly dense populations of the cities, prompted the institution of panopticism, according to Foucault. The organization and rigor upon which the central authorities had to depend to counter the devastation of the plague—and the behavioral habits, the rituals that enforced the organization—provided the real archetype for Bentham's eighteenth-century architectural expression of perfect surveillance. I quote at length from Foucault in this regard, since the passage contains the essence of the panoptic system:

The enclosed, segmented space, observed at every point, in which the individuals are inserted in a fixed place, in which the slightest movements are supervised, in which all events are recorded, in which the uninterrupted work of writing links the centre and the periphery, in which power is exercised without division, according to a continuous, hierarchical figure, in which each individual is constantly located, examined and distributed among the living beings, the sick and the dead—all this constitutes a compact model of the disciplinary mechanism. The plague is met by order; its function is to sort out every possible confusion; that of the disease, which is transmitted when bodies are mixed together; that of the evil, which is increased when fear and death overcome prohibitions. It lays down for each individual his place, his body, his disease and his death, his well-being, by means of an omnipresent and omniscient power that subdivides itself in a regular, uninterrupted way even to the ultimate determination of the individual, of what characterizes him, of what belongs to him, of what happens to him. Against the plague which is a mixture, discipline brings into play its power, which is of analysis.[58]

In 1625 the plague struck London with such force that Parliament relocated to Oxford. The next year, 1626, the Dutch purchased the island of Manhattan from the Native Americans for sixty guilders worth of trade goods. Some of the Europeans were fleeing not only the plague, the overcrowding, and the social disruptions that accompanied industrialization on the east side of the Atlantic but also the type of society that had entered into a dialectic with these conditions. Emerging in Europe was Douglas's high-grid, low-group society, the society in which each individual is, eventually, held in place by something like the panoptic gaze but feels little kinship with others. It is also the kind of society in which the less competent and lucky take recourse in millennia movements, fantasies of absolute egalitarianism, magic, and cults; as Eliade might put it, these societies generate an urgent nostalgia for paradise among the less fortunate, an overwhelming desire to rediscover the Golden Age. It is the kind of society that produced the Puritans.

When the Puritans fled their society, they set about immediately to re-create it. They may have thought that they were escaping the dialectic (although, of course, they would not have put it into those terms), but in fact they carried it with them, vectors for modernity. They had been a part of a high-grid society in Europe, and they had benefited in some ways from that grid. Partly these benefits were in the material conditions of their lives, their immediate comfort, which they would not give up.

But I suggest that there was another, broadly ideological, logic at work here (as there always is). Panopticism, rationality, and the modernity that produce high-grid societies are *belief* systems as well as being systems of logical control over the environment. I have described in some detail the ritualistic aspects of panopticism, which produce sentiment and belief. Dissident European immigrants were also believers. They were part of a heretical cult within the belief system, a *counterculture* to the *culture* and thereby dependent upon it. The dominant society served as a foil for them. Now the cult was the society; its members attempted to take control of the grid, not realizing how fully they were enmeshed in it.

The builders of Bent's Old Fort merely continued the dialectic. And they certainly moved to take control of the grid. They were entrepreneurs who went about their business in an eminently ordered way, constructing a landscape in which European plagues could take root. The rituals of modernity, the establishment of the grid in the "wilderness," provided the medium for the plague. Archaeological evidence indicates that what is called the West Dump was a borrow pit from which clay for the making of adobes was taken during the fort's construction in about 1831. Broken or defective adobes were tossed in the fully excavated pit, then trash was deposited there. The Main Dump also began as a borrow pit for alterations to the fort between 1841 and 1846. This time the pit was dug near the river, so that water to mix with the clay would not have to be carried far. Then this pit was used as a trash dump for the duration of the fort's occupation.

Differences in the contents of the two dumps indicates degradation or overexploitation of the riverain environment over a period of about a decade. A reconstruction of diet from faunal remains indicates that buffalo would have been the most common animal source of food during the early occupation of the fort, followed by pronghorn antelope and deer, but then by a riverain assemblage of species that contributed significantly. In order of estimated quantity of meat contributed these were catfish, box turtle, miscellaneous wild birds, wild turkey, and the Canadian goose. By the end of the decade in question, buffalo, antelope, and deer are again most plentiful, but the riverain assemblage is almost absent. Its place in the diet at the fort is taken by domesticated species: chicken, pig, goat, and sheep.[59]

Organizational competence at the fort was enough so that use was made of the excavated pits. They were filled with trash. Sufficient concern for hygiene was felt so that these trash deposits were repeatedly burned. Unfortunately, these measures were not enough to prevent fouling the environment. The Main Dump was surely polluting the Arkansas River during the late period of the fort's occupation. Archaeological excavations have established that by that time the trash from the dump spilled into the river itself.

Humans as well as wild species were affected by pollution from the fort. It is a fact that the final, mortal blow to the fort was not the war that had raged so frequently nearby, not the famine that struck the Native Americans after the Mexican War, not even market forces that changed in the 1840s. The end to Bent's Old Fort came with the cholera epidemic of 1849, a pestilence spread by tainted water. The two wells inside the fort may have been fouled, in addition to the river.

The culture of panopticism outran the panoptic control of Bent's Old Fort in 1849. Panopticism had been instrumental in bringing modernity to the Southwest, and now modernity was setting free the apocalyptic forces so familiar in the Old World. A new era of pestilence, war, famine, and mass death among the Native Americans began, events that the company could not survive. It seems likely that the principals of the company, particularly William and Charles Bent, would have resisted the wave of modernity they had done so much to set in motion could they have foreseen the fates that awaited them. They could not, of course, and so they believed in the new order until it was too late to alter events.

A persistent legend has it that William Bent, disheartened by the recent death of two of his brothers and his wife, the decline in the trade caused by the now incessant warfare, the refusal of the Army to compensate him fairly for the use of the fort during the Mexican War, and the death of half of the Cheyenne because of the cholera epidemic, purposely burned the fort, using barrels of gunpowder to accomplish this. But some historians disagree, among them Thompson:

In spite of the well known legend, no one who knew William Bent believed he burned—Seeley, Carson, or Reynolds. He packed up and left to escape the Asiatic cholera that Yellow Woman had brought inside in panic, and his fumigant, burning barrels of tar, "got away" from him. But perhaps he knew they would.[60]

CHAPTER 7

Circuits of Power

Modern Ends Through Traditional Means

Ritual is the social mechanism that shapes culture and society by producing those preconscious, shared assumptions that are the basis of both. The Western colonial observer sees the role of ritual clearly in what we term "primitive" societies. It is a staple of ethnographies. We proceed from there to assuming that such "nonsense" was left behind by civilized peoples during the Renaissance. This is a symptom of our individualism, what Tocqueville called "the cult of the individual," and is no less a "habit of the heart" than any other mythology.[1]

It is to the realm of affective response that we must look to understand the organizing power of ritual. Society is organized for the *most* part at this pretheoretical level. What is culture if it is not this? Emotional bonds are focused along the lines legitimated by the operant mythology of a society (in modern societies the "stories" told through novels, television, movies, music, the plastic arts, museums, national parks, historic sites, and so forth— as well as maxims, rumors, history, and various "historical" accounts).

In the nineteenth century, certainly no less than today, the national mythology centered to a large degree on the notion of the entrepreneur. The entrepreneur had broken with his past, in the way Euro-Americans, who were dominant in the new country, did when they came to the New World. Americans had thrown off the yoke of Old World tradition and had remade themselves. In the nineteenth century, they were *still* in the process of remaking themselves. As they are now. Like Agonistes, Americans are eternally becoming.

Despite the myth, entrepreneurs had to start from somewhere, like everyone else. And, like everyone else, they were originally defined by the network of social relationships in which they had been embedded by the circumstances of their births. What they became depended upon how this network was extended and transformed, something that could only be done through ritual means. This, of course, is exactly how society operates in primitive cultures as well. In the cultures that we recognize as primitive, social networks are extended through marriage, which establishes new kinship, or exchange, which sets up fictive kinship relations. Both of these extensions of the social network are legitimated through ritual, which acts to sacralize these new relationships by claiming as precedent the behaviors of the gods (or ancestors) who, through that behavior, rescued the world from primordial chaos.

The Bent trading empire was successful, both financially and insofar as its transformative effect on the Southwest, because of these networks. Further, these networks were ultimately linked with a central, panoptic power in the East, one that steered the course of the trading empire to its own ends. The social networks thus became circuits of power. The larger ends of the central authority turned out to be destructive to many of the parties involved in the Bent trading empire—to the Native Americans, certainly, but also to the Bents themselves.

Extending Kinship

David Dary, in a concise and admirable volume titled *Entrepreneurs of the Old West,* made the statement, in a section about the forming of the Bent & St. Vrain Company, that "Ceran St. Vrain, born in Missouri, had been a clerk for Bernard Pratte and Company in St. Louis before entering the Santa Fe trade about 1824, a few years before the Bents."[2] This is true and informative; however, to really understand who St. Vrain was, what he became, and how this affected the fortunes of the Bent & St. Vrain Company, one would need to say much more about his position in a network of kinship and extended kinship, and how, eventually, this fit into the circuits of power in the early nineteenth century.

Ceran St. Vrain's family had been influential in many quarters prior to his birth. His grandfather, Pierre Charles de Hault de Lassus de Luziere, had held a high position in the government of Louis XVI and was forced to leave France during the Revolution, in 1790. His two sons figured importantly in the interests of both France and Spain in the New World. Both of these sons had not accompanied their father directly to the United States but had gone to Spain for four years, where they had "gained prominent places in the armed forces of that country."[3] While his sons were in Spain, Pierre had made contact with his boyhood friend in the New World, the Baron de Carondelet, now governor of Louisiana. Through the governor, he obtained positions for his sons, who then joined him. One of these sons, Charles Auguste, became governor of Upper Louisiana Territory and actually officiated at the transfer of that territory twice: once when it was transferred from Spain to France, and again when it was transferred from France to the United States. His brother, Jacques Marcellin Ceran de Hault de Lassus de St. Vrain, was Ceran St. Vrain's father and, for a time, was in command of the Spanish naval vessels on the Mississippi River.

The family's fortunes declined after the United States gained title to the Louisiana Territory. Although Charles Auguste had officiated at the transfer of the territory, he was now without a job. Pierre lost the land he had been granted by the Baron de Carondelet, and Jacques (Ceran's father) became the sole support of the family, through a brewery he had opened.[4] Nine years later, in 1813, the brewery burned down. Neither Jacques's widow nor his brother had the resources to care for the ten children in the family, and so some were offered for adoption. Ceran was the second oldest child, and at eighteen went to live in St. Louis with General Bernard Pratte, a friend of the family.

Ceran until this point in time had been sustained by a network of kinship, the importance of which was reflected in lengthy formal names of the French elite, which amounted to a description of lineage. Nonetheless, his background had prepared him for membership in the modern, mercantile and political network rapidly assuming form in the United States. Ceran had gained business experience working in his father's brewery, which had supported the family when links to the Old World power structure had been severed. Now, he had been accepted into the family of a key personage in that new system. Bernard Pratte was owner of Bernard Pratte and Company, which was the western agent for the American Fur Company, the largest fur trading company in the United States. Ceran rapidly developed competence in the new system. Assisting him in this was that the new system operated by means of personal relationships only slightly less than did the old. Because of this, much of Ceran's early socialization would hold him in good stead. He was familiar with not just the languages but also the customs of several cultures. Many who dealt with him commented throughout his life on his gentility and helpfulness. He formed many friendships and maintained these relationships for long periods of time. Living with the Pratte family, he developed two associations that, in particular, would have a great influence on his life. One was with Bernard Pratte Jr., the son of the company's owner; the other was with Charles Bent, son of the influential Judge Silas Bent. These friendships continued even as Bernard Jr. and Charles were sent off for more complete schooling than Ceran was able to obtain. Ceran couldn't afford such schooling. This resulted in a deficiency in his education that was evident in his letters, years later.

Ceran worked for Pratte and Company first as a clerk. He then managed fur shipments, and then became involved in the fur trade at the company's posts on the Missouri River. In 1824, Ceran obtained a supply of goods intended for the New Mexico and Indian trade. Trading and trapping opportunities had just opened there with Mexican Independence in 1821. There were several areas of evident business potential. Streams there were still relatively untrapped for beaver, the New Mexicans were anxious for industrial goods from the United States, and there were furs to be obtained from the Native Americans, particularly at the centuries-old pueblo trading centers such as Taos and Pecos. It made good business sense for Pratte and Company to look in that direction for additional profits. Ceran had proven himself competent. With his background he was a logical choice to be sent to the Southwest. He probably had some knowledge of Spanish, and certainly he was familiar with the customs of the Spanish elite. Ceran may have realized that the newly opened region would offer more room for advancement to a newcomer in the trading business than did the much more established Missouri trade.

The Southwest became of enough interest to Pratte Sr. that he sent another of his sons, Sylvestre, to the Taos area to lead beaver trapping expeditions in 1827. On the second of these, with Ceran as his clerk, Sylvestre was bitten by a rabid dog and died painfully of hydrophobia.[5]

Ceran's efforts to assist and comfort the dying Sylvestre impressed the group of trappers on the expedition. When word of this reached Pratte Sr., it could only have strengthened the ties between Ceran and the Pratte family.

In 1831, Ceran became a Mexican citizen by means of a law that permitted foreign traders to do so as long as they lived in New Mexico, were

Figure 19. Portrait of Ceran St. Vrain. (Courtesy Colorado Historical Society, Denver.)

employed and of good character, and agreed to be baptized in a Catholic church. Thenceforth, there would be no legal ambiguity in regard to Ceran's ability to both trap and trade in New Mexico. Also in that year, Ceran, having already been involved in several partnerships, entered into one with his childhood friend Charles Bent. Both he and Charles were experiencing the same problem, one of timing and capital. Both had goods to sell, but currency was scarce at the time they began their venture and prices were low, pending the return of trappers to Taos. Bent and St. Vrain pooled their resources, with St. Vrain buying out half of Bent's goods, which he stored with his own in a warehouse they had jointly purchased. Ceran, the Mexican citizen, stayed in Taos and awaited the return of the trappers, at which time he sold the goods at a profit. Charles, meanwhile, traveled to St. Louis, where he paid Pratte and Company some, if not all, of the money owed them by St. Vrain and acquired more goods from them. In St. Vrain's flawed writing, he explained to the Pratte Company:

I remit to you by Mr. Charles Bent Six hundred Dollars which you will please place to my credit, I am anxious to now the result of the Bever I Sent last fall, and would be glad you would write me by the first opportunity, and let me now what amount I am owing your hous, if you have not Sold the mules I Sent in last and Mr Bent Should want them doe me the favor to let Mr Bent have them, it is posible that I will be able to Collect, Some of the debts due to the estate of S. S. [Sylvestre] Pratte, as yet I have not collected the first cent. there is no news in this Cuntry, worth your notices more than money is verrey Scrse, goods Sells low and duties verrey hie, but Still prospects are better here than at home.[6]

The letter goes on to reveal that Charles Bent had suggested this arrangement (which became Bent & St. Vrain Company).[7] Note that St. Vrain said that he would attempt to collect the debts due to the estate of Sylvestre Pratte, a kindness no doubt appreciated by the Prattes. There are signs that St. Vrain was becoming well established within the political network, too. In 1834, he was appointed U.S. Consul at Santa Fe. In that same year, John Jacob Astor sold the American Fur Company to Pratte, Chouteau and Company of St. Louis.

Some years later, this close relationship with Pratte would again play a role at a crucial juncture of the Bent & St. Vrain Company. In 1836, Ceran St. Vrain sent R. L. (Uncle Dick) Wootton as head of a trading expedition well north of the established Bent & St. Vrain Company trading boundaries, into Sioux country. In exchange for the ten wagons of trade goods they had brought north, Wooton brought back robes and furs worth $25,000. This could have set off cut-throat competition of the kind in which the American Fur Company had engaged against the well-capitalized Union Fur Company, and others, in the Missouri River trade. In the end the American Fur Company, with more resources than the others, had always forced the competition out of business. The Bent & St. Vrain Company was already concerned with the ambitious smaller companies attempting to move into the Southwest. Some of these smaller firms, like Sarpy & Fraeb, were tied to the American Fur Company. And Bent & St. Vrain Company had just suffered the expense of buying, from Sarpy & Fraeb, Fort Jackson and all of its merchandise and peltries, because Fort Jackson was located on the northern periphery of the Bent & St. Vrain trading area.[8]

But instead of conflict, the American Fur Company and Bent & St. Vrain Company entered into a noncompetition agreement, as follows: "Bent, St. Vrain & Co. shall not send to the north fork of the Platte, & Sioux Outfit [acting for the American Fur Company] shall not send to the South Fork of the Platte [sic]."[9] This was done almost casually, by means of a half-page document, with Ceran signing for Bent & St. Vrain.

The agreement, to be sure, was not without benefit to the American Fur Company. Traders seeking to widen their margin of profit by now were attempting to bypass the St. Louis trading houses when purchasing trading goods.[10] Manuel Alvarez, for example, was not only going to New York and Philadelphia, where he could save considerably on the price of trade goods, but was also attempting to make arrangements with houses in London and Paris.[11] Bent & St. Vrain, in comparison, faithfully bought their trade items from the American Fur Company. In May of 1838 alone, for example, the company paid the American Fur Company $13,257.33 for goods and supplies. In return, it received a virtual monopoly on the Southwest trade and the tacit backing of the most powerful of the fur trading firms. By 1840, the Bent & St. Vrain Company was second only to the American Fur Company in the amount of business transacted.[12]

Ceran's ties to other prominent New Mexican traders and to New Mexicans were solidified through marriage. He was first married to a daughter of Charles Beaubien by Beaubien's marriage to a Mexican woman. Beaubien was active in the New Mexico trade as early as 1830.[13] Later, Ceran married Louisa Branch, daughter of Alexander Branch and his Mexican wife. Alexander Branch was another wealthy trader in New Mexico and, for a time, Ceran's business partner.[14]

Kinship Ties to Native Americans

William Bent's upbringing was one of gentility. His father, Silas Bent, had been born in Massachusetts where, according to family legend, *his* father, Silas Bent Sr., had participated in the Boston Tea Party. After studying law in Wheeling, Virginia (now West Virginia), Silas Jr. had received an appointment by Secretary of the Treasury Albert Gallatin as principal deputy surveyor for the newly acquired Louisiana Territory. Moving to St. Louis in 1806, he was appointed justice of the Court of Common Pleas the next year, and later a Supreme Court judge of the Louisiana Territory. Silas Bent was one of the Americans moving into the power vacuum left after members of the French aristocracy, such as Ceran St. Vrain's father and uncle, were removed from positions of authority in the territory. Silas Bent's new importance in the community led to his acceptance by the old guard businessmen, such as Bernard Pratte and Auguste Chouteau—and, eventually, to his son Charles's friendship with Ceran St. Vrain.

William became involved in the fur trade several years after his older brother, Charles, had entered the business. Even before Charles and Ceran St. Vrain formed their partnership in Taos, William had been occupied in building a trading post on the Arkansas. He was doing this in 1828, although whether in that year he was building one of the temporary stockades, beginning the massive Bent's Fort, or both, is unclear. In any case, by 1832 the newly formed Bent & St. Vrain Company met with its first great success, the caravan to St. Louis with at least $190,000 worth of silver bullion, mules, and furs. While some of this was profit from the Santa Fe trade, a good percentage of this value was in buffalo robes. The caravan had reached St. Louis safely, due in part to Charles Bent's legendary skill at organizing and managing such an effort, but also in part to safe passage given through the land of the Cheyenne.

More than anyone else, it was William Bent who was responsible for the amiable relationship of the firm with the Cheyenne and Arapaho. Photographs of him at the fort show an individual who might be mistaken for a Native American, a determined scowl on a dark complected face with high cheekbones (fig. 20). As the French trappers had found, and as William Bent as a young man in St. Louis had in turn learned from their stories, the maintenance of a successful relationship with the Native Americans involved adopting their customs. Part of this was participation in the calumet ceremony. Bent followed this first, essential act of forging kinship ties with an acknowledgment of the continuing, reciprocal com-

Figure 20. Photograph of William Bent. (Courtesy Colorado Historical Society, Denver.)

mitment such a relationship entailed. In fact, William Bent would recognize this throughout his life, acting as an advocate for the Cheyenne and Arapaho until his death.

His allegiance to his new kin was soon tested in several ways. About 1829, a group of Cheyenne came to the trading stockade William Bent had erected. Two of the party stayed on after most had left. A Comanche raiding party appeared on the horizon, and Bent hid the two Cheyenne. The Comanche leader, Bull Hump, saw the tracks of the Cheyenne and demanded to be told where they were. Risking attack by the Comanche, Bent replied that the Cheyenne had left—thereby saving their lives.

Bent was willing to alter his manner of doing business as much as possible to accommodate the traditional behavior of the Cheyenne. This can be seen in his decision to build the large permanent structure that became known as Bent's Old Fort in the general location where the Cheyenne Chief Yellow Hand had indicated the Plains tribes yearly trading rendezvous to have occurred. As mentioned earlier, there is evidence that this general location was also where the Mexicans had been trading with the Cheyenne for furs just a few years before.

Bent was also willing to accept the enemies of the Cheyenne as his own. The incident in 1834 when William Bent joined the Arapaho and Cheyenne in an attack on their bitter enemies, the Shoshoni, illustrates this. The fact that the Shoshoni had been trading with Bent's rival in the fur trade on the Arkansas, John Gantt, and that the attack took place with Gantt looking on and not lending any help, discredited Gantt in the eyes of the Cheyenne and Arapaho.

The most unequivocal evidence of Bent's commitment, from the Cheyenne point of view, would have been his marriage to Owl Woman in 1835 and, when she died many years later, the taking of her sister, Yellow Woman, following Cheyenne tradition. These actions, and the offspring of these unions, transformed fictive kinship relations into actual ones. Other key personnel associated with Bent's Old Fort took Native American wives, also. George Bent, younger brother to William, married a Cheyenne woman named Magpie (although he also seems to have had a Mexican wife). Kit Carson (as a young man) was married to an Arapaho woman who bore him an adored daughter, Adaline.[15] After the Arapaho woman's death, Ceran St. Vrain refused permission for Carson to marry his niece, in part, apparently, because of Carson's half-breed daughter. Carson then married a Mexican woman from a prominent family, who was the sister of Charles Bent's wife.

But it was the continuing ritual exchange with the Cheyenne, repeated many times over, that may have most affected the Cheyenne and Arapaho. Making it all the more impressive was that it took place at the massive adobe fort, which had the look of a natural feature, rising abruptly from the Plains. The panoptic bastions offered perspective into the Indian camps, as well as into the plaza and the room blocks that surrounded it. The bastions also inspired awe because they were well fortified with a variety of weaponry. The layout of the fort resembled in some ways the medicine lodge or tepee with sacred associations to the Plains Indians, but its *axis mundi* was the fur press in the middle of the plaza (fig. 17).

If the Cheyenne did not qualify as the company's private army, it was only because the company staff and allied traders and mountain men better qualified for that title. Resistance from the Cheyenne would have undermined the trading operation. With their help, the resistance of other Native American groups was neutralized and their aggression was turned against the Mexicans. It was only with difficulty that William Bent was able to prevent the Cheyenne tribe from traveling to Taos to avenge his brother Charles's death in 1847.

Secret Societies

Charles Bent, being William Bent's brother, shared a network of kinship with him, which he extended in different directions, although in similar ways. While William saw to the operation of the fort and had as his primary concern relations with the Plains Indians, and while Ceran St. Vrain (although he was a great traveler) attended to the warehouses and stores in Taos and related operations, Charles looked to the east. Initially, this was to the trading houses of St. Louis, but in time his gaze extended to the seat of government in Washington, D.C. As we have seen, by the time of the Mexican War, Charles was in frequent secret contact with military leaders, such as Kearny, and with politicians, including such remarkable characters as Senator Benton and President Polk. It was through these contacts that he was installed as the first American governor of New Mexico.

While Ceran St. Vrain may have had "fictive kinship" ties with the trading houses in the East, it was Charles Bent who suggested how they could be used. After the partnership had been set up, it was Charles who went to St. Louis, taking with him a letter from St. Vrain to his contacts there. Power and politics attracted Charles.

Charles, the first-born of eleven children, was a determined man (fig. 21). Where associates thought Ceran quiet and gracious, they saw Charles as dynamic. A measure of his fierceness can be taken from two of the many letters he wrote to Manuel Alvarez, U.S. Council in Santa Fe. These letters were prepared in February 1841, the first on the nineteenth of that month and the second, although it is undated, probably sometime between the twentieth and the twenty-fifth. In an uncharacteristically sloppy hand, the first of these relates how he had just come from a visit with Juan Vigil, which he made in the company of a Mr. Workman. The visit was to confront Vigil with a copy of certain "false representations" he had made about Bent and Workman to the governor:

I then asked him how he dare make such false representations against us he denied them being false. The word was hardly out of his mouth, when Workman struck him with his whip, after whipping a while with this he droped it and beate him with his fist until I thought he had given him enough whereupon I pulled him off. he run for life. he has been expecting this ever since last evening for he said this morning he had provided himself with a Bowie Knife for any person that dare attack him, and suiting the word to the action drew his knife to exhibit. I supose he forgot his knife in time of neade. . . . I presume you will have a presentation of the whole affair from the other party shortly. . . . I doubt wether you will be able to reade this I am much agitated, and am at this time called to the alcaldis I presume at the instance of Jaun Vigil.[16]

The next letter is much more legibly written and relates how Bent was in fact called before a judge in the presence of Vigil. Vigil, according to Bent, made many threats against both him and the judge: "He particularly threatened to raise his relations and friends if the Justice did not do him Justice, according to his will."[17] Bent was ordered to prison, but he objected that there was no evidence against him except the word of Vigil, who had not actually accused Bent of doing him violence (Workman did the beating, at least in Bent's version of the event). The judge then ordered Bent to Charles Beaubien's house, to be employed in lieu of prison, but Bent again objected on the same grounds. Finally, the judge put Bent under house arrest, in his own home, and collected an undisclosed amount as bail. Bent was still aggrieved at the incident but was obviously much calmer than he had been when writing the first letter. He was waiting for the governor's decision, the judge being about to present the case to him, and he hoped for a favorable one:

I think the Governor is not a man entirely destitute of honorable feelings he well knows there are cases that the satisfaction the law gives, amounts to noth-

Figure 21. Portrait of Charles Bent. (Courtesy Colorado Historical Society, Denver.)

ing. I had rather have the satisfaction of whiping a man that has wronged me than to have him punished ten times by the law, the law to me for a personal offence is no satisfaction whatever, but cowards and women must take this satisfaction. I could possibly have had Vigil araned for trial for slander but what satisfaction would this have been to me to have him fined, and moreover I think he has nothing to pay a fine with, he is a vagabond that lives by fletching his neighbor.[18]

This was still the age of the duel, and Bent was a man of his times.

Bent, who became governor of New Mexico six years after this incident, had run afoul of New Mexican law before. One of these occasions was associated with the 1837 insurrection against an unfortunate named Albino Perez, a governor who had been sent to New Mexico by Santa Anna, the president of Mexico. To put down the rebellion (instigated in part by Manuel Armijo, who had been governor in the 1820s and was miffed at recently being removed as customs collector), Perez obtained supplies from American merchants in Santa Fe with promissory notes. The supplies were not enough, and Perez's force was defeated. Perez himself was beheaded. Armijo saw in this the opportunity to regain power, and he forced American merchants to supply his troops. So supplied, Armijo defeated the rebel force and was proclaimed both governor of the province and commander in chief of the army (the position he held at the time of the Mexican War). Since Bent had supplied two factions in this conflict, he was imprisoned in Taos. Ceran St. Vrain led a rescue party to Taos from Bent's Old Fort but was met on the way by Charles, who had gained his release by bribery and by threatening to have his men burn down the town.

A slightly different presentation of these events appeared in *The Builder*, a magazine of the Masons, in an article in the December 1923 issue titled "Governor Bent, Masonic Martyr of New Mexico." The article was written by a Taos lawyer and Mason, F. T. Cheetham, who had earlier done an article for another local Masonic publication called "Kit Carson—Mason of the Frontier." In truth, it appears that Charles Bent and Kit Carson, along with Ceran St. Vrain and William Bent, as well as the ill-fated Albino Perez and Santa Anna himself, were all Masons. (The same issue of *The Builder* points out that twenty-three signers of the Declaration of Independence were Masons, as were eighteen Presidents of the United States—not to mention Benjamin Franklin.) According to Cheetham's article, Bent was imprisoned because he was mistaken for a member of Perez's Masonic order, the "Yorkinos," from south of the border.[19] Perez had instituted progressive reform measures in New Mexico, on the orders of Santa Anna, said Cheetham. One was a decree providing for public schooling and the institution of a direct tax to pay for it. That there is some validity to Cheetham's thesis is supported by David Lavender's research, which confirmed that the idea of the direct tax was likely the major inflammatory issue behind the rebellion.[20]

As may be seen in this particular incident, in the nineteenth century fraternal organizations such as the Masons provided a means by which an increasingly fragmented society could organize itself around values and beliefs that held a high emotional content. The author of *Secret Ritual and Manhood in Victorian America,* Mark C. Carnes, theorized that this was a reaction against the feminization of religion in Victorian America.[21] But Masonry had been in existence before Victorian times, as had the Odd Fellows. The spate of fraternal organizations that seemed to copy Masonry, and which went on to become so popular in the Victorian age, also arose before this time. Many were formed between 1840 and 1870. They shared the qualities of being *ecumenical,* in that they usually favored no specific religion, and *secular,* because many, like the Masons, steadfastly promoted the separation of church and state.

There are some obvious exceptions here, if organizations like the Mormons and the Knights of Pythias are accepted as fraternal orders. But Mormonism and the Knights of Pythias as well as some of the organizations with a more obvious political or special interest agenda that arose later in the nineteenth century—the United Mechanics, the Know-Nothings, the Knights of the Golden Circle, the Grand Army of the Republic, the Ku Klux Klan—capitalized upon the obvious enthusiasm for ritual displayed by members of the older fraternal organizations like the Masons and the Odd Fellows.

This should not obscure the fact that members of the earlier organizations rallied around what they saw, at least, as the implementation of Renaissance ideals. Such ideals held that the application of rationality to the problems of society would result in a better world. Thus, these organizations were opposed to "archaic" and "corrupt" systems, like those their members saw in New Mexico. The overthrow of the old order there by the more enlightened Americans was a matter of principle. Cheetham quoted an observer in New Mexico some years after the Mexican War:

The annexation of New Mexico to the United States brought it under their Catholic ecclesiastical authorities, and they knew well what to expect from any bishop who might come from us. . . . A bishop was sent from the United States. There was a general suspension, unfrocking, dismay and howling among those

Mexican priests (and it would have been difficult to find exceptions), who "kept cocks and fit 'em, had cards and played 'em, indulged in housekeepers of an uncannoncal age, and more nieces than the law allowed."[22]

These hypocrisies had been enough to stir righteous indignation among the Masons in the Southwest—especially Charles Bent and Ceran St. Vrain. They found the church, and especially the infamous Padre Martinez (who all in the Bent & St. Vrain Company later blamed for Charles's death), opposing them and their influence at every turn.

But if the goals of the Masons and other fraternal organizations embraced the application of reason, then why advance such goals with a mechanism so irrational as ritual? Throughout the United States in the nineteenth century, middle-class men, often the leaders of their communities, expended a great deal of time and money on obsessive participation in what seem sophomoric rituals.

It was Carnes's thesis that although there were evident advantages to the creation of a bond with what amounted to the most influential group of individuals in many towns, it was the ritual activity itself that was the great attraction in secret societies. He noted that rituals were typically so elaborate that they left little time for anything but participating in or witnessing them. Contrary to popular belief, secret society meetings, especially during the later nineteenth century, were not given over to drinking and socializing. Carnes thought that, for nineteenth-century males, "in some sense the present had proven barren, devoid of emotional and intellectual sustenance."[23] By looking to a mythological past, fraught with symbolism, men could reclaim meaning for their lives. Even their participation in modernity was transformed into a kind of calling. Opposition from organized religious groups, notably the Catholics, was stimulated when it became known that the Masons and similar organizations taught that redemption depended upon the exercise of the human capacity for reason.[24] Middle-class experience could resonate meaningfully with reference to the mythology provided by the secret societies:

An arch in a railway station might bring to mind the temple of Soloman, an onerous business contract might gain meaning as a form of Babylonian captivity, and a business reverse could be seen as the "rough and rugged road" on the return to Jerusalem.[25]

So must a Cheyenne forced to a life of agriculture have seen the humpbacked shape of bison in every clump of sod turned over by his plow. Ironically, the "free" and egalitarian life of the Indian was held up as a kind of paradisiacal model by some of the secret societies: "The Improved Order of Red Men . . . advised initiates to emulate the children of the forest, who held all wealth and property in common." In commenting upon this subversion of capitalism, Carnes cited Victor Turner's idea that some such rituals are an essential part of the "dialectal process" of society. Certain rituals are permitted that are in "opposition to existing hierarchies and rules." These may eventually bring about change.[26]

John Brewer offered a more functionalist explanation for the origin of Masonic and other secret societies in eighteenth-century England. In that society, the "patrician" class held such sway in the early 1700s that "the middling sort," as Brewer puts it, were driven to pool their resources.[27] The dearth of capital produced a situation in which indebtedness posed a constant threat to any merchant. Merchants, most succinctly, had a cash flow problem. Their clientele consisted of members of the upper class who were habitually late in the payment of their bills. This was considered a prerogative of the class; in time, it was a *mark* of the class. Unfortunately, the merchant's creditors had to be more concerned with punctuality. Debtor's prison was a constant threat. This was especially so as economic cycles seemed to occur in an absolutely unpredictable manner, at the mercy of fad and panic. Clubs were formed as mutual aid societies: to lend financial assistance or social pressure if loans were called, to provide support for widows and orphans, and so on. Brewer noted Dr. Johnson's comment that almost every Englishman belonged to a society, lodge, fraternity or club.

But the stated nature and organization of these clubs as reported by Brewer raises less functional considerations. Some of these clubs were organized along lines of the interests of the members. Brewer mentions "spending clubs" and "drinking clubs." As he put it, "Every taste was catered for: societies were established for literati, the ugly, gamblers, politicians, homosexuals, rakes, singers, art collectors, and boating enthusiasts."[28] Like the Civil War reenactors, Corvette Clubs, and birding societies of today, this segmentation was really the expression of a desire for intimacy and support. Often clubs stressed reciprocal obligations among members who "transcended traditional social, economic, and religious boundaries." Masonic and pseudomasonic societies as well as these interest-based clubs "boasted of the way in which they united Anglicans and dissenters, men from different trades, merchants and gentlemen, whigs and tories, in common association, promoting unanimity and harmony where only conflict had previously existed."[29]

All these clubs provided protection against the "arbitrary nature of misfortune."[30] This strikes me as nothing other than Eliade's "terror of history," the capricious events of the temporal world that can rob a life of meaning, or end it. The traditional response to this is to build a bulwark of ritualistically contrived meaning against the threat of chaos. Interpersonal relationships are configured or reconfigured in time of crisis with reference to and along the lines of eternal archetypes, which are themselves reflections of neotenic fantasies of enduring unity. This occurred no less among the "solid burghers and respectable tradesmen who made up the bulk of masonic membership." Thereafter:

Masons would rally round a brother whose creditors threatened to foreclose on him. The knowledge that substantial friends, as well as kith and kin, would stand by a tradesman increased his creditworthiness and the confidence that both he himself and others had in his business.[31]

This is an apt description of the sorts of relationships Charles Bent developed over the course of his life. These relationships were an integral part of the success of Bent's Old Fort. What Brewer described as occurring in eighteenth-century England transpired in the nineteenth-century United States and, by the second quarter of the nineteenth century, in the Southwest. As we have seen, the Masonic network by then reached all the way to the president of Mexico.

Brewer made a great point throughout his article of the tension between the aristocracy and the "middling sort" in England and saw the establishment of clubs and secret societies as a strategic move on the part of the middle class in the conflict between these groups. Perhaps it would be more accurate to say that it was a social development that held certain economic advantages for many individuals and groups in the middle class. A problem with using the word "strategic" (as I have myself used it upon occasion) is that it calls forth the image of a general on a battlefield with immediate power to deploy his troops and weapons. That was not the case here, and what the word might inaccurately imply is that the Masons constituted a monolithic organization that had as its end the surreptitious control of nations, in the manner of an eighteenth-century "Tri-Lateral Commission." Another drawback to couching the events in question in such terms is that they might obscure that "strategic" moves, with the rationality that the word implies, were implemented by traditional concerns, and were driven by them as well.

If one proceeds from what I consider to be the phenomenological premise that the first item on the human agenda is to make sense of the world, whether the humans in question are in traditional or modern societies, then what stands out in sharp relief is that individuals from all classes were scrambling in the eighteenth and nineteenth centuries to establish new identities. Class lines, particularly in the United States, were not impermeable. Members of the "patrician" class were throwing their lot in with middle-class entrepreneurs; entrepreneurs were seeking upper-class partners for the associated prestige and as well as the access such new partners would have to politically and economically influential people and institutions.

Bent & St. Vrain Company provides an obvious example. Among the attractions held by St. Vrain in the Bents' perspective were in all probability his connections with Prattes and others and his genteel manner, which was conducive to further such connections. St. Vrain, for his part, must have seen the advantages of tying his fortunes to the Bents, with their business and legal acumen, as well as their drive, innovation, and ability to understand and communicate with a variety of people—the qualities of the entrepreneur. Yes, there was financial and social maneuvering here, but this maneuvering was not on the part of nor for the interests of "class." As important, there is no reason to think that the financial benefits were the only, or even the most important, motivation for participation in clubs or secret societies in either eighteenth-century England or nineteenth-century America. Participation might better be thought of as more generally aimed at the establishment of an identity in a society where amassing wealth was important to such ends. The final goal was not wealth, but what the wealth was imagined to represent.

This brings us to the second question posed some paragraphs above. Why advance "rational" goals—the modernizing goals of the Enlightenment, if you will, or the goal of rationalizing the credit structure, if you are functionally minded—with a mechanism so "irrational" as ritual? The answer is that nothing else would do. Social movements require that values be internalized, and there is really no other way to generate "sentiment" and impart values than through ritual. It is also important that however "rational" the goals might have been, the *motivation* to achieve goals is not rational—it is emotional. Among humans, emotions are invariably tied up with making sense of the world and one's place in it.

The rituals practiced by these organizations were, as previously discussed, initiation rituals. Mircea Eliade identified three basic sorts of these, at least in "primitive" societies: rites marking the transition from childhood or adolescence to adulthood, rites for entering a secret society, and rites of initiation into a mystical vocation.[32] The second of these is the one that arises in the most recognizable form in modern society.

Secret societies are historically recorded everywhere. Most often these are men's societies, *Männerbunde*. Eliade acknowledged the theory that has gained wide acceptance among scholars of religion, that masculine secret societies are a reaction to matriarchy. Their object according to this theory is to frighten women and shake off female dominance. But Eliade noted that we do not see this occurring everywhere in reaction to matriarchy, and he pointed out that men's secret societies share many similarities with the initiation ceremonies associated with puberty. Eliade thought that such secret societies might arise, more generally, when notions of masculinity (or femininity, too, for there are *Weiberbunde*) need to be reenforced, as a result of cultural change:

It is for this reason that initiation into the secret societies so closely resembles the rites of initiation at puberty; we find here the same ordeals, the same symbols of death and resurrection, the same revelation of a traditional and secret doctrine—and we meet with these because the initiation-scenario constitutes the condition *sine qua non* of the sacred. A difference in degree has, however, been observed: In the Männerbunde, secrecy plays a greater part than it does in tribal initiations.[33]

The description of such rituals fits exactly those of the nineteenth-century fraternal organizations. Eliade went on to speak of reasons why secrecy is more important in *Männerbunde* than in puberty rituals. Primary among them is the factor of social change. He pointed out that these secret societies never arise where indigenous peoples have retained, unchanged, their ancestral traditions. But frequently,

the world changes, even for primitive peoples, and certain ancestral traditions are in danger of decay. To prevent their deterioration, the teachings are transmitted more and more under the veil of secrecy. This is the well-known phenomena of the "occultation" of a doctrine when the society which has preserved it is in the course of a radical transformation. The same thing came to pass in Europe, after urban societies had been Christianized; the pre-Christian religious traditions were conserved, camouflaged or superficially Christianized, in the countryside; but above all they were hidden in closed circles of sorcerers.[34]

Christianity, as Clifford Geertz and others have noted, became a "world religion," along with Buddhism, Hinduism, and Islam, because its theology could accommodate any number of smaller, regional, and more parochial religions. It used the instrument of rationality to form this durable theology, which was in this way more ecumenical than the religious systems of thought that had gone before. Secularization, after the Renaissance, demanded even more "ecumenical" belief systems, ones more properly in the realm of philosophy, but operationalized as ideology. The search was on for evidence of "natural law," which did not depend upon supernatural explanations for natural phenomena. In many ways, this was the central intellectual story of the nineteenth century, as evidenced, for example, by the zeal with which the concept of evolution was embraced by many upper- and middle-class individuals during that period. Secularization was essential in the rapidly emerging modern world of the nineteenth century, especially for the middle class. Ways had to be found to accommodate this secularization, but also to assuage the growing sense of *anomie* that such rapid social change often produces. Accommodations took a somewhat bizarre form, for they depended upon a mechanism—ritual—that seemed to violate some of the basic tenets of the new ideology of objectivity and rationality. The tensions engendered by these contradictions were such that the ideal of secularization and rationality had to be all the more enthusiastically, and publicly, embraced.

There was obvious anxiety among middle- and upper-class American men in the nineteenth century concerning their proper identity in the rapidly changing society. This is evidenced in any number of ways, including the strict codes of honor and the many duels in many regions of the country; we see these at work in Charles Bent's letters about his fight with Juan Vigil. It had to do with the general breakdown of traditional social structures and value and belief systems. While not as acute as that transpiring among Native American groups, or among the populace of New Mexico, the American populace was undergoing the same sorts of stresses. These were all the more severe in the Southwestern frontier. Conditions were extremely uncertain there; danger to life was a real factor in the equations of everyday experience. There was no family structure of the sort in which most of these middle-class individuals had grown up. The danger and hardship of the frontier rendered it an unfit environment for Anglo women, to this way of thinking. It was anything but a "normal" environment for the Easterners.

With the displaced American males, as with the Plains Indians, there was really nothing left with which to make up a life other than trade and warfare, and the panoptic culture of modernism and the fictive kinship system of the secret societies easily accommodated these interests. They were, in fact, a perfect match. The panoptic system provided the means by which the new order could be implemented; the "kinship" systems provided a way of reinforcing both that system and the values and beliefs that made the implementation seem important. In this sense, panopticism was the *how*, the secret societies the *why*.

The combination proved very powerful; it set in place the "circuits of power" that implemented the agenda of the central authority in the East. As Foucault could have predicted, the state eventually took over the panoptic mechanism. In England and France, what had been in the hands of private religious groups or charitable organizations soon was taken over by the state, once panopticism was established, producing a single authority responsible for all social order. Foucault provided a quote from an enthusiastic Parisian official: "All the radiations of force and information that spread from the circumference culminate in the magistrate general. . . . It is he who operates all the wheels that together produce order and harmony. The effects of his organization cannot be better compared than to the movement of the celestial bodies."[35]

Here is evidence of the sacralization of panoptic power, a sacralization just as evident in the rituals of the middle-class, male secret societies of the nineteenth century. Such power becomes sacred, or "natural" in terms of modern ideology, when it claims as its referent the endlessly recurring cycles of nature and the mysteries that were known to the ancestors. But now in the celestial archetype is seen the grids of logic; the "clockwork universe" becomes the "music of the spheres." This grid was imposed on the landscape as the panoptic power, facilitated by ritual means, became firmly entrenched. Along with trails came telegraph lines, railroads, fences, settled lines of private property, and political boundaries. All of this tended, too, from the tangible to the more abstract. Trails and railroads gave way to political boundaries, which today yield to lines of communication and authority accessible to only those who have been grounded in their peculiar workings. The land, again, assumes fewer obvious points of reference.

Such logical grids have as an aspect of their control the power to locate and to settle. Foucault put it this way: "One of the primary objects of discipline is to fix; it is an anti-nomadic technique."[36] Among the first casualties of the new order were the nomads: the Plains Indians, the free-ranging trappers, and the traders with their caravans.

CHAPTER 8

Victory and Defeat

The Demise of Bent's Old Fort

After the brief, abortive uprising in 1847, there was never again a serious challenge to American political control of New Mexico. New Mexico society had been poised on the brink of modernity for some time before 1846, with much of its populace eager for the plunge. The lack of resistance during the Mexican War in New Mexico evidenced a willingness to take "initial steps away from a traditional politics of piety and proverb" and to get on with a modern agenda, which would include "the overthrow of established ruling classes, the popularization of legitimacy, the rationalization of public administration, the rise of modern elites, [and] the spread of literacy and mass communications," as Clifford Geertz has said of the movement of society from a grounding in religion to one in ideology.[1] A middle class soon developed there, the New Mexicans having learned from their trade with the Americans many of the skills of modernity, along with the ideology that would drive them to employ and further hone these skills. All of this would be maintained because the basis for continuing exchange was now assured.

Ironically, victory for the United States brought ultimate defeat to the two groups that had probably played the largest role in the transfer of political power in the Southwest. The successful conquest of New Mexico by the United States, which Bent & St. Vrain, particularly Charles Bent, had worked so hard to assist, opened the area to new interests that would destroy the company and drive out William Bent's adopted people, the Cheyenne.

The principals of Bent & St. Vrain Company were not completely responsible for either their success or their undoing. Equally, they were neither the masterminds nor the pawns of a conscious scheme to produce the domination of more traditional cultures by a more modern one. In their behavior they were as opportunistic as a biological species as it interacts with its environment. They were not merely traders in fine furs or buffalo hides. They were involved with every sort of economic activity available to them: selling oxen to immigrants for their wagons, selling provisions to the military, buying horses from the Cheyenne and other Plains groups who had stolen them during raids in New Mexico, selling goods in their stores in Taos and Santa Fe, trading Navajo and Mexican blankets to the Cheyenne, bringing Mexican silver to St. Louis, and so on. They were also involved in every sort of social arrangement available to them: they took Native American and Mexican wives, acted as guardians for children of friends, were active in secret societies, did all they could to make and influence powerful friends in Santa Fe (evidenced by Charles Bent's frequent letters to Alvarez), and cultivated similar associations with sources of credit and politicians in the East.

In this range of behavior, we see the somewhat frenzied activity of the "Big Man," an example taken from a "primitive" society found among the tribes of New Guinea that Mary Douglas identified as being high-grid, low-group, and ego-centered (as is, of course, modern society).[2] Big Men have no authority other than moral. They live in a society that has neither hereditary nor formally elected chiefs. The organization of the society is accomplished in large part by the efforts of Big Men to "make moka," that is, to cajol, convince, or coerce other members of their society into participating in ritual pig feasts and the elaborate preparations for such feasts. Said Roy A. Rappaport in his classic study, *Pigs for the Ancestors*, "Big men tend to be wealthy, tend to be shamans, and tend to be in possession of knowledge of rituals concerned with fighting."[3] But since they are self-appointed and have no formal status as leaders, their lives are not without frustration. Rappaport told of one aspiring Big Man who, unable to inspire a following and after working alone for three days on the building of a ritual structure, complained "bitterly to those who passed by about the worthlessness of Tsembaga men, their sole interest being gardening and copulating."[4] As this example suggests, they are often frustrated, but nonetheless work ceaselessly in order to be a "player" in the important dramas of their world, as the current phrase has it.

The Bents and Ceran St. Vrain were not unlike Big Men, in some obvious ways. They held no power other than what they negotiated by means of ceaseless business and social activities and what I would suggest to be their intuitive deftness with ritual. In these ways, nonetheless, they helped greatly to inculcate the modern order in the Southwest.

Their talents were not magical, however, and they could not see into the future. They could not see that the networks of kinship and fictive kinship they had established would be coopted by the central forces of the United States. Aligning their interests with those of the federal government surely appeared sensible. The government would be a powerful ally. Moreover, they probably believed in the values associated with the United States. And, to be accurate, it was almost certainly not the U.S. government's intention to bring tragedy to the principals of Bent & St. Vrain Company and their Cheyenne and Arapaho allies.

Politicians in the government, backed by business interests, wanted to expand the boundaries of the United States for a variety of reasons. Some of these were probably not well understood by even those who stood to gain most, at least from our modern point of view. Economic, political, and ideological motivations were perhaps only slightly less mixed than what Marcel Mauss would have described as the "total social phenomena" characteristic of "traditional" societies; this is well expressed in the phrase "Manifest Destiny."

But those who rushed into the newly acquired territory did not engage in the same sorts of ritual interactions between Native Americans and Anglos as had been an essential part of the fur trade. Without such continuing ritual, there was no way to reconcile different values and beliefs, or work out common meanings. As we shall see, without a means by which to *humanize* the Native Americans to the newcomers who streamed to Colorado and New Mexico after the Mexican War, the Native Americans remained foreign and worse: They were the demons of this strange and unformed land.

Richard White, in his recent book about the fur trade in the Great Lakes region from 1650 until 1815, emphasized that when Native Americans and Europeans first met, they "regarded each other as alien, as other, as virtually non-human."[5] The point of his history is that over the course of their involvement together, they developed "the shared meanings and practices of the middle ground."[6] White saw both the formation and the loss of the "middle ground" as aspects of a power struggle. He said, "The real crisis and final dissolution of this world came when Indians ceased to have the power to force whites onto the middle ground. Then the desire of whites to dictate the terms of accommodation could be given its head. As a consequence, the middle ground eroded."[7] What the Indians lost here was the ability to claim "a common humanity in a shared world."[8]

Establishment of the grounds for a shared humanity is a part of the essential orientation of each individual to the world, which is really, from a phenomenological point of view (and from a sociological one, I might add), the world of human events. Deciding just who is not human, who is, and to what degree, is a preoccupation among all peoples. This is reflected in many ways, beginning with the fact that virtually all linguistic groups have as their name for themselves a term that they, themselves, translate to something similar to "the humans" or "the people." A few examples among a very great number include the Y'amana (meaning "men" or "humans") of Tierra del Fuego; the Cheyenne, who call themselves *tsis tsis' tas* ("the people"); the Kapauku Papuans of New Guinea, who refer to themselves as *Me* ("the people"); and the Innupiat (meaning "the genuine people") tribe of the Eskimo.

As A. R. Radcliff-Brown observed about the aboriginal tribes in Australia, "in western Australia the first question always asked of a stranger is who is your father's father?"[9] The fact that lineage is a virtual obsession among "primitive" peoples is unchallenged by anthropologists. This is so because it is among the most basic ways of ordering the world. It determines what one's responsibilities are, what one's role is, and what one's proper behavior should be toward another. This acts to fix one's place within the social universe.

Fictive kinship, established by ritual, is important precisely because it makes the unknown known. It transforms the unformed, potentially dangerous other into an ally and a known quantity: a fellow human. The aborigine's question, recorded by Radcliff-Brown, is a clue as to how this is accomplished. Ritual provides the opportunity for joint participation in the reenactment of the behaviors of the ancestors or gods. If one's father's father turns out not to be the same as that of the other person's, a mythological ancestor will serve as well to establish a kinship relation— in this case a fictive kinship relation.

Richard White's argument concerning the development of "shared meanings and practices" does not explicitly present a social mechanism by which this is accomplished. I offer ritual exchange as just that mechanism. As described previously, the calumet ceremony established fictive kinship relations, set mutual obligations, and often generated the affective response that encouraged internalization of shared values and beliefs within the traditional culture. I see participation in exchange ritual, on both the Native American and the Anglo sides, as less a matter of contending for power than of grasping a perceived opportunity for enhancement of "self" in the two increasingly individualistic and "ego-centered" cultures.

What eventually transpired between the Plains Indians and the Anglos arriving in the southwestern Plains from the eastern United States in the middle of the nineteenth century has been called by some a tragic misunderstanding. It was this, but it also was simply a fatal overreaction on the part of the newcomers. The misunderstanding and subsequent hysteria resulted from erosion of what White aptly termed the "middle ground" that the individuals involved with Bent & St. Vrain Company had established. This area of understanding could not be maintained in the absence of ritual interaction, which disappeared with the fur trade. Severe problems between Anglos and Native Americans arose with the war. The increased military activity of the Mexican War had been unsettling to the Plains Indians, and after its successful conclusion, they could see that the way had been paved for many more newcomers, with whom they would not relate as they had with the Bents. The unrest among the Native Americans provoked an increased U.S. military presence, which, perhaps because the military was especially inept, further upset the Native Americans.

The cholera epidemic of 1849, along with the deteriorating conditions for trade, prompted the abandonment of Bent's Old Fort in that year. The stability that had been maintained on this ritual ground for almost two decades was gone. In this chapter we look carefully at these events and, especially, the apocalyptic end to the relationship between the Anglos and the Cheyenne and Arapaho tribes brought about by the attenuation of ritual interchange between the two groups.

Securing New Mexico

With the American occupation of New Mexico in 1846, the United States government moved to secure the area by repacifying the Santa Fe Trail. The Comanche had recently become much more aggressive than they had been over the previous decade or so. The Kiowa had also been troublesome, although they had given late assurance that they intended to mend their ways. Further east, the Pawnee presented a constant threat to travelers on the Santa Fe Trail. Near Bent's Old Fort, the Cheyenne and Arapaho were at peace with the Americans, but given the obvious instability of relations between the numerous interests in the area in this time of change, the government feared that they might become hostile. The government was concerned that it had become overextended, with a huge new area to control and few troops with which to accomplish this. General Kearny's army had moved on; it had been a rag-tag organization in any case. In a few years this unsettled climate would contribute to the demise of Bent's Old Fort, and the removal of this fron-tier institution would further destabilize the area.

Missouri Senator Thomas Hart Benton, the eloquent proponent of both frontier trade and Manifest Destiny, had proposed to Congress in April 1846 that it create an Indian agency to deal with the tribes of the Upper Platte and Arkansas rivers. With the beginning of the war in May, Con-gress assented. The famous trapper, trader, and guide Thomas Fitzpatrick, who had previously been associated with Bent & St. Vrain Company, was appointed as an Indian agent and was stationed at Bent's Old Fort. His duties here were to begin as soon as he was released from his service with General Kearny.

The crux of the problem, as Fitzpatrick saw it, was that the Indians had nothing to lose and everything to gain with their attacks on the Santa Fe Trail traffic. The Indians, of course, were not new to warfare and raid-ing; on the contrary, their long history of such activities had produced many social reinforcements for such behavior. In a letter he wrote to his immediate superior in St. Louis just after assuming his post, Fitzpatrick asserted that the Indians would continue their attacks until the United States proved its ability to punish "some of the worst and most trouble-some tribes." This had not been done so far. Indian attacks against troops were at least as successful as those against the wagon trains of traders. The traders had to be knowledgeable about defensive measures in order to stay in business. The army, in contrast, seemed to have an endless supply of untrained troops and continued to make the same defensive errors. In a spring letter to his supervisor, Fitzpatrick had this comment about a re-cent incident on the Santa Fe Trail:

When we see a government train of wagons manned and in charge of 44 men armed and equipped by the United States travelling across the Plains to New Mexico, and allow a band of savages to enter their lines — cut the harnesses off all the mules, and take them away, amounting to 170 — kill and wound 3 or 4 men — destroy and burn up some of the wagons, and all this with im-punity and without losing a single man, it is hard to foster what may be at-tempted next.[10]

What most in the area were concerned about was that the situation would further deteriorate. Seeing the successes of the Comanche, the Cheyenne and Arapaho might be inspired to take a share of the booty that seemed so readily available on the trail. Unless offending Indians groups could be punished, so wrote Fitzpatrick in his first letter to his superior, they would never "invent other means of gaining a livelihood besides plundering and murdering their fellow human beings." If they could be discouraged from such activities, "Such a course would be the first great step to the settlement, and civilization of the wild and roaming tribes."[11]

Fitzpatrick was destined only to experience frustration in this regard. The troops supplied for the pacification of the Indians were for the most part recent immigrants. Many of them were Germans who spoke no English and were terrified of the Indians, who were like no humans they had ever encountered. These troops, incompetent in battle and impulsive in their dealings with the Native Americans, frequently made bad situations worse. A disheartening example of this occurred at Fort Mann, late in 1847. In the absence of Colonel William Gilpin, Captain William Pelzer, an emigrant volunteer, was left in command of the post. Fitzpatrick later reported that Captain Pelzer and his troops had been so fearful of Indians on their march to Fort Mann that "it required some vigilance and constant watching to prevent them from killing or attempting to kill every Indian they met on the road."[12] Unfortunately, after Colonel Gilpin left, a party of sixty-five Pawnee appeared at the fort, and four leaders rode to the gate with a white flag. When they were in the fort, it was discovered that several hundred more Pawnee were across the river. The fearful Captain Pelzer attempted to take the four leaders hostage, but when the Indians realized what was happening, they tried to escape. Orders were given to fire on them and, as a witness reported,

such a scene of confusion as ensued I never before witnessed . . . the men were firing in every direction. Two of the Indians were killed and a great many wounded. Three of the Indians failed to make their escape through the gate, and ran into Capt. Pelzer's quarters—a guard was placed at the door to prevent their escape. One of their number being bolder than the rest, rushed by the guard, passed the gate, and was shot some forty yards from the Fort. The two Indians who remained in Pelzer's quarters, were afterwards unceremoniously shot.[13]

A hearing the next year decided that, though great damage had been done to U.S. Indian relations, Captain Pelzer had acted out of ignorance rather than premeditation. He and four others were permitted to resign. This was done in spite of the fact that the Pawnee had been assured that the guilty would be punished.[14]

1849: The Gold Rush

Because of their association with the Bents, the Cheyenne and Arapaho had enjoyed relative stability, as compared to the other Plains Native American groups in the vicinity, until the outbreak of war with Mexico in 1846. The next few years after the war saw confusion and unrest. The year 1849 ushered in even greater chaos, which had a terrible effect upon these two groups. The sudden mass of forty-niners that swarmed through the Plains eroded the resources there and thereby strained relations with the Indians. But worse, the forty-niners brought cholera.

That summer the Pawnee lost eleven hundred people, swept off "like chaff before the wind." In about early June the cholera epidemic found the Cheyenne who lost about half of their tribe. Berthrong described it this way:

While the Cheyennes moved south from the Platte Rivers, men and women were stricken by "big cramps," or cholera, fell from their horses in agony, and died. They fled in terror all the way to the Arkansas River, and slowly the epidemic abated. At Bent's Fort the Cheyennes joined a peace enclave and celebrated the cessation of hostilities between the Kiowas and Osages. During the dances, a Kiowa warrior and an Osage dropped to the ground clutching their stomachs. Soon the tribes were in flight. . . . Ceran St. Vrain informed the Indian agent at Santa Fe that never had he seen a "worse state" of affairs during all of his time in the Southwest.[15]

This cholera epidemic was the deciding blow to Bent's Old Fort. It seems possible that the cholera was contracted by the Indians at Bent's Old Fort, since the epidemic struck while the tribes were there. Certainly, for the next few years, the Plains Indians gave the site of the fort a wide berth. The general trend had been a decline in revenues for some years, but 1848 had been profitable. Since the war, though, the Comanche and even some of the Arapaho had been openly hostile to the Bents; now, their principal trading partners, the Cheyenne, were devastated by cholera. Because of this, there was probably no real trade in 1849. One cannot discount William Bent's psychological condition when considering why he abandoned his fort in late August of that year. He had lost his brother Charles during the brief revolt in Taos in 1847. Shortly thereafter, his wife, Owl Woman, died giving birth to their fourth child. He was angry at the United States Army for refusing to pay what he considered just compensation for their use of Bent's Fort during the Mexican War. Now, half of his adopted people, the Cheyenne, were dead because of the cholera epidemic. And war parties ranged the countryside. William Bent's world was falling down around him. With the abandonment and destruction of his fort, he was in one way or another acting out this collapse.

The fort's presence was soon missed. Officials at all levels of the Indian Agency were convinced that a treaty with the unsettled tribes was vitally needed. The appropriate place for the gathering of tribes, of course, would have been Bent's Old Fort.

Beginning on September 8, 1851, treaty talks were held, instead, at Fort Laramie. Attending were most of the Plains tribes from north of the Arkansas, including the Cheyenne, Arapaho, Sioux, Shoshoni, Crow, Assiniboin, Minnitaree, and Arikira. The southern tribes would not attend, being reluctant to journey through a land inhabited by "such notorious horse thieves as the Sioux and the Crow"—nonetheless, the number of Native Americans gathered at Fort Laramie was estimated at ten thousand.[16]

Indian Superintendent D. D. Mitchell told the assembled throng that the great father wanted safety for his white children as they passed through the Indian's territory and the right to build forts there. He asked that each tribe select a chief who would control and take responsibility for his people. The great father wanted to assign a territory where each tribe could live and hunt. With this initiative, based in the modern practices of segmentation and private ownership, the settling of nomadic groups began.

It was a festive gathering, although threatened a few times with the outbreak of violence between groups harboring grudges. Tribes feasted each other and adopted each other's children. Jesuit priests baptized many, including 253 Cheyenne infants. There were impressive displays of horsemanship and dances. Many gifts were exchanged, although the treaty goods were three days late in arriving. In the end, most tribes, like the Cheyenne, were assigned to roughly the area they were frequenting at the time of the parlay. Tribes were not actually restricted to those lands but could hunt and fish where they had been accustomed to doing so. The Treaty of Fort Laramie was the first land treaty for the Cheyenne, and most of the other groups as well. We can see in this an attempt to reinstate the relative stability that the area had known during the existence of Bent's Old Fort.

The treaty was accompanied by ritual (the exchange of gifts, feasting, smoking peace pipes) and included explicit promises of long-term reciprocal obligations. The rituals, however, involved only a few representatives of the federal government. Meaningful exchange did not extend to the masses of Easterners now streaming to and across the Plains. The Native Americans remained unknown and terrifying to the immigrants, as the immigrants did to the Native Americans.

The government promised the tribes a total of fifty thousand dollars each year for fifty years (later reduced to ten years by Congress) in compensation for the destruction of buffalo.[17] A similar treaty was signed with the southern groups, the Comanche, Kiowa, and Kiowa-Apache in July of 1853. These developments were probably an inspiration to William Bent to build his new fort at Big Timbers. In the winter of 1852–53, stone cutters began preparing the masonry for his new trading post.

In 1853, however, Thomas Fitzpatrick wrote that the Cheyenne, Arapaho, and Sioux were actually starving: "They are in abject want of food half the year. . . . Their women are pinched with want and their children constantly crying out with hunger."[18] The killing of buffalo and the disruption to trade were beginning to take a heavy toll. More disruption to the nomadic way of life of the Plains Indians rapidly followed. The Treaty of Fort Laramie, as benign as it might have seemed to the Native Americans at first, signaled the advance of surveying parties, increased immigration, and the construction of army posts.

During the next decade, the world that the Cheyenne inhabited became increasingly hostile to them. Immigrants and settlers pressed in. Berthrong noted that "during the 1853 season, fifteen thousand Americans moved past Fort Laramie, destroying game and bringing diseases to the Indians."[19] When the Cheyenne pressed back, the army engaged in punitive expeditions.

One tragic chain of events began in 1854, only months after the Treaty of Fort Laramie was signed. Irritated by increasing numbers of Anglos coming into their territory on the Santa Fe Trail, some Miniconjous Sioux decided to interrupt the flow of newcomers by taking control of a ferryboat near Fort Laramie. Soldiers were sent from the fort to recover the boat. During this operation, the Sioux shot at the sergeant leading the detachment. Word of this was carried back to the fort. Lieutenant Hugh B. Fleming then decided to lead a larger detachment back to the Sioux, demanding that the Sioux who fired the shot be turned over to them. A skirmish developed in which three Miniconjous Sioux warriors were killed, three were wounded, and two were taken prisoner.

Later, a Sioux warrior angry with the Anglos for the casualties taken during this skirmish shot arrows at a Mormon emigrant. Although he missed the Mormon he killed the Mormon's cow. When word of this reached Lieutenant Fleming, he dispatched Lieutenant John L. Gratten with twenty-nine men and one interpreter to bring in the remaining group of Miniconjous Sioux. Lieutenant Gratten had boasted earlier in the year that with thirty men he could defeat the whole Cheyenne nation. Here was his opportunity to demonstrate the accuracy of his judgment. After a brief but fruitless parley, Gratten attacked, employing two howitzers. The Sioux camp, though, contained not only Miniconjous but Brulé Sioux. In the fight that followed, twenty-eight of the soldiers were killed. Lieutenant Gratten's body was found with twenty-four arrows in it and could be identified only by his watch. In retaliation for the "Gratten Massacre," Colonel William S. Harney led six hundred troops from Fort Kearny in the following year to a camp that had been identified by the new Indian agent in the area as that of the hostiles. Little Thunder, a chief implicated in the Gratten incident, tried to talk the soldiers out of attacking, but to no avail. The soldiers killed at least eighty-six men, women, and children, wounded five persons, and took seventy women and children prisoner.[20]

This pattern—confusion and then conflict leading to retaliation and escalating violence that culminated in inevitable tragedy for the Native Americans as a much superior force was brought into the fray—was repeated. "Peace" might follow, but only briefly, until the resentment and bitterness engendered by the pacification produced yet another incident. The bitterness would quickly spread to other Native American groups, even those not involved with the trouble. For example, after defeating the Sioux, Harney took advantage of his presence as a superior force in the area to make demands of the Cheyenne and Arapaho. If they did not withdraw from the Platte route, hunt only on their own land, and make peace with the Pawnee and Sioux, Harney would "sweep them from the face of the earth."[21] In the face of mounting violence, the military could only respond as they had been trained to do, with force.

Anxiety surely increased with each passing year, perhaps with each month. Such anxiety played a role in the increasing intertribal conflict during this same period. Such fighting quickly acted synergistically with the escalating skirmishes between the Anglos and Indians. Relations between the Cheyenne and Arapaho on one side and the Pawnee on the other, for example, were generally hostile and had grown worse after a Cheyenne defeat in 1853 by the Pawnee. The Cheyenne were made even more aggressive by another terrible loss in 1854. In this debacle, an intertribal force that included not only Cheyenne, but also Arapaho, Kiowa, Comanche,

Sioux, Osage, and Crow had started after the Pawnee, but on the way had encountered a hunting party of Sac, Fox, and Potawatomi. Eastern Indians such as these were extraordinarily well armed and, unlike the Plains Indians, used rifles with skill and in carefully coordinated movements. They inflicted a great number of casualties on the Plains Indian war party.

By 1856, the Cheyenne were back in the vicinity of the Platte, looking for Pawnee and eager to avenge these two defeats. The Cheyenne, of course, had been ordered out of this area by Colonel Harney. Soon enough, the Cheyenne found trouble — but not with the Pawnee, who had been intimidated enough by the Cheyenne presence to forgo their annual buffalo hunt in the Platte River area. Instead, some young Cheyenne warriors encountered a mail wagon, stopped it, and asked the driver for tobacco. The driver panicked. After drawing his pistol and firing, he whipped his horses in a desperate attempt to flee. He did not escape, though, before being wounded in the arm by an arrow.

The young men were chastised by their elders for their rash action, but this, of course, did nothing to stop the by now familiar chain of events from proceeding, having been set in motion in this case by the aspiring warriors' lust for glory. The driver had made his escape into Fort Kearny, and soldiers there responded in alarm. The Cheyenne were tracked to a camp on the Platte, where ten of them were killed and eight to ten more wounded.

Thoroughly enraged, the Cheyenne attacked with a vengeance at three locations along the Platte River route. During one attack on a four-wagon train, Almon W. Babitt, secretary of the Utah territory, two other men, and one child were killed. The child's mother was carried off and later killed. Such actions, of course, only seemed to confirm the immigrants' fears that the Plains Indians were savages.

In 1857, William Bent warned the Cheyenne of an army expedition being prepared against them. The Cheyenne were still angry at their own losses and told him of their strategy, to scatter into small bands between the Arkansas and Platte rivers, and to "kill all they want, and get plenty of white women for prisoners."[22]

The American retaliation for the attacks along the Platte River route was led by Colonel William Vos Sumner in late July 1857. His force of about four hundred cavalry and infantry, with four mountain howitzers, found the Cheyenne camped along the Republican River. The Cheyenne had, therefore, made no attempt to escape, despite what they earlier told William Bent. By this time, they had been convinced by their medicine man, Dark, that the white man's bullets could not harm them. Confident in the power derived from the medicine man's dream, they rode directly at the soldiers. For reasons that remain unknown, Colonel Sumner executed an extremely unusual maneuver at this stage of the battle—a saber charge. The Cheyennes were confounded by this. Their protection was from white bullets, but what about sabers? As the cavalry drew close, the Cheyenne broke and fled. Casualties on both sides were few, but Cheyenne pride was severely damaged.[23] This put the Indians in an even worse temper.

There occurred in 1858 and 1859 a lull in the hostilities. The immediate cause for this cessation of violence was probably the influence of the Cheyenne's old friend William Bent. Having interceded between the Anglos and Native Americans on a number of recent occasions, he was appointed Indian agent in the summer of 1859. But events were to occur that same year that made peace a forlorn hope, even given Bent's ties to the Cheyenne. Bent's position in the Anglo world had deteriorated drastically over the last decade. Where he had been liminal, he was now regarded as marginal by the Eastern immigrants. He could no longer mediate between the modern and traditional worlds.

Before proceeding to those events that in the later nineteenth century finally cast the Cheyenne, the other Plains tribes, and most of the Native American population of the United States into the role of unmitigated and incorrigible villains to the settlers of the West, it might be well to pause. It is from about this time in Cheyenne history that one of the persistent, ahistorical images of the American Indian has been taken. The Cheyenne were still hunting buffalo, still free (that is, had not yet been placed upon reservations), still relying upon the bow and arrow for warring and raiding.[24] The Indian agent for the Upper Arkansas Agency in 1855 described his charges in this way:

The total population of the agency numbered 11,470, in which number were included 3,150 Cheyennes and 2,400 Arapahos. From their camps on the South Platte and Arkansas Rivers, the Cheyenne could field a force of 900 warriors and their allies, the Arapahos, 500. The Cheyennes lived in 350 lodges and possessed seventeen thousand horses. The Cheyenne enjoyed an income of $15,000 from the 40,000 buffalo, 3,000 elk, 25,000 deer, and 2,000 bear killed annually whose skins and hides were the staples in their exchanges with the traders.[25]

This picture faded rapidly. Up until 1858, gold seekers had generally only traversed the trails through what would become the Colorado Territory. But in the spring of that year, a small quantity of gold was found in the areas around the Platte and, in the words of George Bent (William Bent's son by Owl Woman), "the whole frontier was thrown into excitement. In Kansas, Nebraska, Missouri, and Iowa, thousands of men began to prepare to set out for the mountains in the following spring. . . . The Indians . . . did not understand this rush of white men and thought the whites were crazy."[26] During the winter of 1858–1859, prospectors moved quickly to acquire title to Cheyenne and Arapaho lands.

William Bent could not hope to maintain peace for long. His evaluation appeared in the *Annual Report* of the Commissioner of Indian Affairs in 1859:

The concourse of whites is therefore constantly swelling, and incapable of control or restraint by the government. This suggests a policy of promptly rescuing the Indians, and withdrawing them from contact with the whites. . . . These numerous and warlike Indians, pressed all around by the Texans, by the settlers of the gold region, by the advancing people of Kansas, and from the Platte, are already compressed into a small circle of territory, destitute of food, and itself bisected athwart by a constantly marching line of immigrants. A desperate war of starvation and extinction is therefore imminent and inevitable, unless prompt measures shall prevent it.[27]

While Bent acted as Indian agent, he pressed for an adequate reservation for the Cheyenne and Arapaho: the entire Fontaine-qui-bouille and Arkansas River region above Bent's Fort. But a treaty was not finalized until Bent was replaced by Colonel Albert G. Boone. There is no evidence that Colonel Boone did not have the best interests of the Cheyenne and Arapaho at heart. Unfortunately, however, he may have lacked influence in the eventual treaty, or he may have overestimated the ability to teach an entirely new way of life to the Cheyenne and Arapaho and their willingness to learn a new way of life. Whatever the circumstances of its manufacture, the 1861 Treaty of Fort Wise soon proved to be only a legalistic maneuver on the part of the American government to disenfranchise the Indians of the lands they had inhabited before the arrival of the Americans on the scene.

Signed by many of the major chiefs (though they quite often denied their signature later), the treaty indicated that the Indians agreed to give up their claims to most of their lands. What remained to them was a barren part of southeastern Colorado Territory with little game. The treaty also promised $15,000 a year to each tribe for fifteen years and assistance in learning and adopting a sedentary way of life. Stock, agricultural implements, mechanic shops, and dwelling houses were to be purchased with a portion of their yearly monetary allotment. Interpreters, millers, farmers, and mechanics to help them learn the skills needed for this new lifestyle were also to be provided.[28]

Defending the Southwest
from Confederate Invasion

More devastating than even this treaty for the Cheyenne and Arapaho, and all of the Native American groups on the southwestern Plains, was the coming of the Civil War to the West. At about the same time the Treaty of Fort Wise was being negotiated, a Confederate army began a long march from El Paso, Texas, with the aim of securing the western territories to the Southern cause. This force met with success, quickly capturing first Albuquerque and then Santa Fe. The next objective was Colorado. The Confederate invasion of Colorado was checked only by superbly executed defensive maneuvers in 1862, one of which involved moving a regiment of Colorado volunteers into position at Fort Union more rapidly than the Confederates could reasonably expect. Linking up with Union forces in New Mexico, the Union troops blocked the Confederate advance at La Glorietta Pass, in a battle sometimes called the Gettysburg of the West.

The Colorado volunteers were a rugged and unruly lot of miners and mountain men, well-practiced in brawling and violence. Fierce once the battle was joined, discipline was a problem in the days leading up to action. That hard discipline was provided by a Major John M. Chivington. Commissioned as a chaplain, he had requested that he be allowed to fight rather than pray. Historic accounts indicate that he presented a formidable physical presence, being over six feet tall and 250 pounds, with a bull neck and a barrel chest. An acquaintance described him as "the most perfect figure of a man he had ever seen in a uniform."[29] Before he would leave military service, he would be marked as a candidate for the United States Congress by the statehood party in Colorado, the Republicans. Eventually, his name would be inextricably linked with the atrocities against the Cheyenne that occurred at Sand Creek, known for a time as the Chivington Massacre.

At the Battle of Glorietta Pass, though, Chivington exhibited all of the characteristics that made him stand out as a military leader.[30] During the first day of the battle, at Apache Canyon, he hurled his volunteers against the Confederates, riding to the heart of the fray as volley after volley of fire was directed at him as the ranking officer. Miraculously, he was not touched. Later, he moved decisively to exploit a vulnerability in the Confederate array of forces, which he discovered while attempting to flank the rebels. Coming across eighty-five Confederate wagons and five to six hundred horses and mules, Chivington quickly evaluated the situation and discovered that these represented the entire number of supplies of the Confederate forces—left unattended. Laying waste to these supplies, Chivington not only won the battle but sent the Confederate forces fleeing back to El Paso.

Red Rebels as Red Devils: Allies to Enemies

As the Civil War increasingly demanded the attention and resources of the Colorado Territory, unruly Native American groups came to be identified more closely with the enemy, the Confederacy. Unlike the fur traders who had come before, the newest inhabitants of the territory engaged in no constructive exchange with the Native Americans. On the contrary, given the well-publicized skirmishes between whites and Native Americans, most newcomers regarded any contact at all as something to be avoided. For their part, the Cheyenne, Arapaho, and other Plains tribes understood what the mounting traffic on trails, the telegraph lines, and the construction of railroads meant to them. It meant that the buffalo would be killed or would move away, and that they would no longer be able to use the lands through which these "improvements" were placed.

By 1862, a new Indian agent for the Cheyenne and Arapaho, S. G. Colley, had discovered that, no matter what the older, less aggressive and warlike chiefs had agreed to in last year's treaty, these groups were finding it difficult to adopt a radically different way of life. As Berthrong paraphrased Colley: "A few mixed-blood Cheyennes could farm, but full bloods could or would not engage in a way of life whose duties, by tradition, devolved upon women. Hoe corn, cultivate gardens—no self-respecting warrior could stand the derision of his comrades even for presents of the agent's approbation."[31]

The newcomers to Colorado Territory, the Anglos, felt themselves to be in a perilous situation. Threatened by restless and increasingly hostile Indians, they could expect little protection as all available military forces were occupied in staving off the threat to the territory from the Confederacy. It seemed a good idea to be conciliatory to the Indians under these circumstances, as the new agent Colley recommended. Colley organized delegations from the Cheyenne, Arapaho, Comanche, Kiowa, and

Caddoe to be sent to Washington in the spring of 1863. There they met with President Abraham Lincoln. This trip was probably intended not only to strengthen friendship between the Native Americans and the Americans but also to demonstrate to the Indian leadership just how many of these white men there were, and how vast and powerful their civilization was.

Such gestures were no more effective in arresting the increasing level of violence than were the peace medals that were occasionally presented to tribal leaders. This was not the meaningful day-to-day interaction of the fur trade. Only some more elderly individuals were influenced by tokens of friendship and could see the inevitability of the new ways of life brought to their land by the whites.

Such elders, though they were leaders, could no longer prevent aggressive acts by young warriors. Native American leadership was based, for the most part, on consensus, and consensus beyond the band and clan level was difficult even in relatively tranquil times, and these times were turbulent. Furthermore, a way of life had developed that valued an extreme form of individualism. Each man acted as his own agent and had as his goal the accumulation of glory, largely through counting coup. Bands in disagreement with the leadership of larger groups often followed a course of action set by themselves.

On the American side, there were also obstacles to peace. There was little control over the daily actions of the rough miners who now flooded the territory. The greatest of all obstacles, though, was the political leadership of the new territories, which was ambitious for statehood and personal influence. This leadership saw the Native Americans as an impediment to the establishment of a more settled way of life and as an ally to the Confederate invaders. However sincere the desire for peace on the part of federal leaders like Lincoln, in the climate of the Civil War local leadership held sway. Washington had to tread carefully; it could not be seen as interfering with local affairs. The Indian issue could not threaten the cohesion of the Union. And at the local level, by 1863, the political leadership and their agents in the militia spoke occasionally about the inevitability of extermination.

Friction between Native Americans and Anglos in the new territory of Colorado took many forms. A special Indian agent, H. T. Ketcham, was appalled at much of what he observed in the spring of 1864. He saw, for example, an Anglo man hit an Indian in the face with an empty whiskey bottle because the Indian had been watching "wistfully and longingly" as he drank. In a letter to Governor Evans, Ketcham said:

While citizens and soldiers are permitted to enter their villages with whiskey in day time & at night; to make the men drunk & cohabit with the squaws, disseminating venerial [*sic*] diseases among them; while the Commanding Officer at the Post [Fort Larned] continues to get drunk every day & insult and abuse the leading men of the Tribes, & make prostitutes of their women; you cannot expect to have any permanent peace with these Indians.[32]

Such treatment of the Native Americans was common, increasingly so as tension mounted. Some Native Americans responded to this treatment with violence. At times this violence was strategic, as when telegraph poles were chopped down and burned or when railroad track was torn up. These strikes at the modern infrastructure reinforced the idea that the Indians were acting as Confederate agents. (Further proof for this was seen in that the "Six Civilized Tribes" of the Southeast had actually signed a treaty with the Confederates.)

The beginning of the final and most intense phase of conflict between the Anglos and the Indians on the southwestern Plains could probably be set in 1864. Attempts to drive Anglos from the territory now amounted to terrorism; responses to this by the Anglos took the form of atrocities. The struggle became a ritualistic denial of human status to the enemy.

The incident that most greatly damaged the Native American cause was called the Hungate Affair. According to a story that became legend in the Colorado Territory, Nathan Ward Hungate was working several miles from his home with a hired hand named Miller on June 11, 1864, when he observed smoke and flames rising from his house. Fearing Indians, Miller rode to Denver for help, but Hungate could not be restrained from rushing to the immediate aid of his family. When help finally arrived, they found the Hungate place devastated, all the buildings burnt to the ground and the stock gone. The bodies of Hungate's wife and two young daughters were found first. Hungate's wife had been stabbed and scalped, and "the body bore evidence of having been violated." The daughters, one four years old, the other an infant, had their throats cut, "their heads being nearly severed from their bodies." Hungate himself was found the next day. His corpse was "horribly mutilated and the scalp was torn off."[33]

The bodies were taken to Denver, to the center of town where the City Hall would eventually be built. Put on display in the back of a wagon, with the children arranged between the two parents, "everybody" saw the remains. In this way, the nightmare of every settler in this troubled place and time was given palpable form. Fear and anger heightened to panic. In a politically popular move, Governor John Evans went directly to the secretary of war, saying in a letter, that "Indian hostilities in our settlements commenced, as per information given you last fall" and demanding the provision of troops or the authority to enlist them.[34]

A few days later, the rumor of an impending Indian attack swept through Denver. Women and children were rushed to secure locations, where they stayed through the night and into the next day. As a witness remarked, "Few houses in the city had been locked that night and many were left with doors and windows open and lamps burned within. But so general was the belief in a fast approaching death, or a still worse fate, that no thieving was done."[35]

In this time of uncertainty and real danger, when concerted effort among a group of new arrivals from diverse backgrounds was essential, the Anglo citizens of the new territory were able to achieve solidarity against what was now regarded as a demonic force from outside the universe of humans. The earlier Anglo arrivals, most notably William Bent and Kit Carson, did what they could to stem the rising tide of hysteria and counsel their friends, the Cheyenne and Arapaho, to avoid what could only be a losing war against the Anglo invaders.

William Bent had probably seen the hysteria coming as early as 1853 when he sent his children by his Cheyenne wife, Owl Woman, to Westport, Missouri, to live with his old compatriot, Albert Boone, and be educated there. Certainly he could see the racism emerging from the friction between the newly arriving miners and settlers on one side and the Native Americans on the other. In contrast to this, the attitude of Bent's contemporaries, the trappers and traders, resembled pluralistic egalitarianism.

The tide of history, however, did not allow Bent to isolate his children from the emerging civil struggle. Western Missouri was full of Confederate sympathizers. William's son George, being of the appropriate age, soon enlisted in the Confederate State Guard, in the cavalry, and fought to keep the Union out of the western part of the state. His brother Charles, though too young to do so legally, also enlisted in the Confederate forces but was released when his age was discovered. When the Union succeeded in taking western Missouri, federal soldiers searched out those with Confederate leanings. Among those suspect were Bent's other children, including his daughter, Mary, who had married an Anglo businessman and was by now quite entrenched in Anglo society. Nonetheless, the home of Mary and her husband was twice attacked, federal looters destroying or taking all property that could be moved. Having no other refuge, Mary, her husband, and children went to live with her mother's people, the Cheyenne.[36] George, Julia, and Charles, too, eventually found that they had no other place to go than back to the Cheyenne. George was captured during the Confederate retreat from Corinth, Mississippi. His father's influence kept him out of a prisoner of war camp, but George was forced to promise that he would take no further part in the war.

Sand Creek

Thus it was that three of William Bent's children, George, Julia, and Charles, were at Sand Creek in the Cheyenne camp attacked by Colonel Chivington on the morning of November 29, 1864. William Bent's other child by Owl Woman, Robert, acted as a guide for Chivington's troops, after having been told by Chivington that he would be shot if he refused.[37] There was no reason to doubt Chivington, who had demonstrated several times his capacity to order summary executions.

Chivington had prepared his attack carefully. He employed the sort of men he had used to such good effect at La Glorietta Pass—"volunteers," that is, not professional soldiers. The men in his Third Regiment of Colorado Volunteer Cavalry were largely "hundred-day men," men from the dregs of Colorado society who enlisted for about three months. These mining camp toughs and gamblers were not even issued uniforms. Many of the officers were elected by the men and had little control over them. Chivington marched this force to Booneville, near Fort Lyon and Bent's New Fort, and stopped all travel and mail downriver in order to prevent word from reaching Bent or others who might warn the Cheyenne of the impending attack. Then he moved on to throw a line of sentries around Bent's New Fort, thus preventing anyone from leaving until the attack on Sand Creek had been completed.

On the evening of November 28, the Third Colorado Cavalry, along with part of the Fort Lyon garrison force, a total variously estimated to be between 650 and 1,000 men, left the vicinity of Bent's New Fort and Fort Lyon, arriving at Sand Creek the next morning.[38] During the night, Robert Bent had led the force through a shallow lake. He may have been attempting to ruin the paper cartridges used by some of the soldiers.

At first light, both the Colorado Third, brought to the scene by Chivington, and the Colorado First, provided by Major Scott J. Anthony from Fort Lyon, were in position. The Cheyenne were unsuspecting, having been told by Major Anthony some days before to go to Sand Creek and wait while he passed on their petitions for peace, made at Bent's New Fort, to those with authority enough to act upon them.

Three companies charged across the creek to cut off the village from the main herd of Cheyenne horses. Colonel Chivington directed the troops into position, shouting for them to "remember the murdered women and children on the Platte!"[39] Firing commenced on the village. Small arms and cannon using grape shot and canister were employed.

Accounts of what transpired next are available from many sources. In letters that George Hyde eventually compiled into a kind of autobiography, George Bent wrote of the battle.[40] Panels of inquiry later took testimony from many of those present at Sand Creek on that day. From this evidence, and from contemporary evaluation of that evidence, it is possible to piece together fairly certain knowledge about a number of aspects concerning the massacre.[41]

At the approach of the troops, and even after firing had begun, the Cheyenne leadership, specifically Black Kettle and White Antelope, were reassuring their people that they would be safe. These individuals had good reason to believe this because of their recent discussions with the soldiers at Fort Lyon, and the fact that they had met with Governor Evans of Colorado Territory and many high-ranking political and military leaders just two months before. In both cases, the Cheyenne were asking for peace, in the face of a number of incidents involving attacks on white persons or their property that had recently transpired. As the troops approached, Black Kettle stood in front of the village, holding a large American flag that had been attached to a lodgepole. White flags were also raised, and for a time Cheyenne clustered around these for protection. As the soldiers continued to attack, killing men, women, and children, and shooting into lodges indiscriminately, White Antelope, who had been urging peace with the whites, decided, in George Bent's words, that "he did not wish to live any longer." He stood in front of his lodge with his arms folded across his breast, singing his death-song:

Nothing lives long
Only the earth and the mountains.[42]

The soldiers were under orders from Chivington to take no prisoners. In one case, three soldiers took turns shooting at a child of about three years of age who was walking through sand approximately seventy-five yards away, making a sort of game out of it, until one of them succeeded in shooting him. There were numerous other instances of women and children being killed after the heat of the battle. Lieutenant Harry Richmond of the Colorado Third came upon three women and five children being held prisoner, whereupon he killed and scalped them all while they screamed for mercy. A boy of about eight was discovered alive beneath many dead Cheyenne in a trench, and a major of the Third Regiment shot him in the head with a pistol. Jack Smith, a half-breed, was executed after Chivington himself indicated that this should be done.

Finally, the bodies of the dead were horribly mutilated. Many witnesses reported that all the bodies they saw, including women and children, were scalped. A number of people said that White Antelope was not only scalped, but that his nose, ears, and testicles (which were used for a tobacco pouch) were cut off. Others told of the butchery of women and the display of their "private parts" and, in one case, a heart on sticks. Rings, it was said, were obtained by cutting off fingers. A man who claimed that Jack Smith had been killed accidentally while looking at a gun, admitted, nonetheless, that "some of the boys dragged the body out onto the prairie and hauled it about for a considerable time."[43]

Charles Bent was captured with Jack Smith, and the Denver volunteers were eager to execute him, too. Some New Mexican scouts who had been garrisoned at Fort Lyon and who knew the Bent family protected him only by threatening to shoot the Denver men. George and Julia Bent escaped the slaughter by running up the bed of Sand Creek along with about half of the Cheyenne and Arapaho who had been camped there. While the firing continued, they dug pits with their hands and huddled in them for cover. George had been wounded in the hip. When the soldiers withdrew to search for other Indian camps, George and Julia along with the other survivors moved further up the creek bed, "the blood frozen on our wounded and half-naked bodies," as George described it.[44] They proceeded for only a few miles before the wounded and the women and children could go no further. Bivouacking on the open plain, there commenced what George Bent called the worst night of his life. It was bitterly cold and windy. Those who had not been wounded worked feverishly to gather handfuls of dried grass for fires that would keep the wounded and the children from freezing. Relatives and friends of the missing crept back to the Sand Creek site to find naked and mutilated bodies.

Before sunrise the next day the survivors started toward Smoky Hill, where the hostile faction of the Cheyenne and Arapaho were camped. Those at Sand Creek, after all, had been those who were anxious for peace. Warriors from the Smoky Hill camps rode out to meet the survivors with food, blankets and buffalo robes. They were put on horses and brought back to camp. Bent recalled that as we rode into that camp there was a terrible scene. Everyone was crying, even the warriors and the women and children screaming and wailing. Nearly everyone present had lost some relations or friends, and many of them in their grief were gashing themselves with knives until the blood flowed in streams.[45]

After Sand Creek: The End of Ritual

Sand Creek achieved notoriety soon after it occurred. It represented a definitive end to an era of cooperation between the tribes of the southwestern Plains and Anglo cultures and produced changes within both cultures. It, of course, had its most profound effect on those most directly involved.

Sand Creek and similar incidents probably contributed to the erosion of optimism associated with westward expansion. The settlement of the West could no longer seem to be unalloyed progress. Jefferson and his contemporaries who had looked to the West so eagerly had espoused the Renaissance ideal of toleration and subscribed to the notion of the perfectivity of mankind through the application of reason. Thus the Native Americans were essentially like the Europeans but had not yet enjoyed the benefits of education and, particularly, science. According to this view, assimilation could not be far off. Incidents like Sand Creek indicated that this ideal was far from being realized.

Sand Creek also became a cause for severe friction between the federal government and the state. A schism formed between federal and Colorado political and military leaders. Federal leaders lined up uniformly against the events at Sand Creek. Committees were formed—first in the House of Representatives, and then a joint committee of the Senate and the House—which condemned the actions at Sand Creek. As the House committee put it in 1865:

As to Colonel Chivington, your committee can hardly find fitting terms to describe his conduct. Wearing the uniform of the United States, which should be the emblem of justice and humanity; holding the important position of commander of a military district, and therefore having the honor of the government to that extent in his keeping, he deliberately planned and executed a foul and dastardly massacre which would have disgraced the variest savage among those who were the victims of his cruelty.[46]

The events that occurred after the empaneling of a military commission to investigate Sand Creek illustrate well the growing federal-state antagonism. A fact-finding military commission set to work in Denver in 1865. The proceedings were not public, but word of them spread through Denver, sparking general resentment about the investigation and those who testified "against" Chivington and the Third Colorado. One of the first to testify, and one of the most outspoken, was Silas S. Soule, who had been a captain in the First Colorado Cavalry. During the investigation, several shots were fired at him from ambush. Finally, he was shot and killed by a soldier from the Colorado Second named Squiers. Squiers was apprehended in Las Vegas, New Mexico, by a Lieutenant Cannon of the New Mexico Volunteers. Cannon brought Squiers back to Denver, but soon thereafter Cannon was found dead in his Denver hotel room. It was suspected that he had been poisoned. Squiers escaped again, and reports later placed him in California.[47]

Relations between Anglos and Native Americans, too, were predictably ruptured. Sand Creek set off a period of violent reprisals on the part of the Cheyenne and Arapaho. Virtually all of the individuals in these two groups now wanted revenge. For a time, Black Kettle's position as leader of the Cheyenne was taken over by two who were more warlike, Leg-in-the-Water and Little Robe, even though Black Kettle himself now wanted war and busied himself rallying half-blooded Cheyenne and Sioux against the white man. When the old trapper and friend of the Cheyenne, Jim Beckworth, urged peace, Leg-in-the-Water replied:

But what do we have to live for? The white man has taken our country, killed our game; was not satisfied with that, but killed our wives and children. Now no peace. . . . We have now raised our battle-axe until death.[48]

All of these groups, including the outcast and extremely warlike Dog Soldiers of the Cheyenne, were brought together on the Republican River. Now more than two thousand warriors could be directed upon selected targets. And selected they were; no longer did small bands raid as opportunity suggested. The actions of the warriors were directed by the war councils of the soldier societies. In the face of the obvious efforts to exterminate them, the Cheyenne and Arapaho put aside for the time being the individualism that had hampered their military operations. Raids on the Julesburg stage station, several large ranches, and wagon trains along the Platte route provided food to the hungry tribes, although George Bent had to instruct the raiders on the use of many unfamiliar items, including how to open tin cans.[49] The night after the Julesburg raid, a victory dance was held "in full view" of the soldiers and civilians huddled together in Fort Rankin. A lieutenant, Eugene F. Ware, watched from the fort all night. The Indians, illuminated by the light from fires built with telegraph poles they had cut down, were

circling around the fire, then separately stamping the ground and making gestures . . . , and finally it was a perfect pandemonium lit up with the wildfire of burning telegraph poles. We knew the bottled liquors destined for Denver were beginning to get in their work and a perfect orgy was ensuing.[50]

But such victories were short-lived. With the end of the Civil War, more troops were committed to dealing with the "Indian problem." Over the next five years, many battles were fought. Treaties were signed (and soon broken), but Anglos gradually asserted their control over the movements of the Cheyenne and Arapaho.

In 1868, Black Kettle and his wife were killed at the Battle of Washita, the army forces there being led by Lieutenant Colonel George Armstrong Custer. Though Custer claimed that 103 Indian men were killed in this battle, more reliable estimates, from three sources, were between 9 and 20 men and 18 and 40 women and children killed. General Philip Henry Sheridan remarked after receiving Custer's report that "If we can get in one or two more good blows, there will be no more Indian troubles in my department."[51]

In the Treaty of Medicine Lodge, signed on October 28, 1867, the Cheyenne and Arapaho ceded their claim to their preferred territory between the Arkansas and Platte rivers. They accepted by this treaty an area bounded by the 37th parallel and the Cimarron and Arkansas rivers. Increasingly, of course, they were in no position to bargain. The land to which they were finally assigned was determined not by treaty, but by executive order in 1869. This land was in the Indian Territories, a good distance east of what had been the prime buffalo grounds north of the Arkansas, and far from where their old friend William Bent had established his trading posts.

William Bent's life ended in the same year that the Cheyenne and Arapaho relinquished their freedom. On May 19, 1869, Bent died of pneumonia, which he contracted while taking a wagonload of goods for trade to Santa Fe, as he had done so many times before. Returning home, he was caught in a late spring snowstorm. He was buried in Las Animas, where later his eldest daughter, Mary Bent Moore, and her husband, Judge R. M. Moore, would be laid to rest beside him. The Pueblo *Chieftain,* in an obituary, estimated William Bent's fortune to be between $150,000 to $200,000 when he died—evidently the years and misfortunes he had endured had not dulled his business acumen.

William Bent's children, other than Mary, chose the Cheyenne way rather than the world of the white man. George and Charles in particular, haunted by what they had seen at Sand Creek, fought bitterly against the increasing restrictions to the Cheyenne way of life. Charles would become, in Lavender's words, "the worst desperado the plains have ever known," pursuing a path of treachery and cruelty. In one instance he staked out a naked captive, cut out his tongue and "substituted another portion of his body in its place," built a fire on his stomach, and howled with glee as the man died in agony.[52] Charles also attempted to kill his father after William disowned him in disgust. George moved with the Cheyenne to their final reservation in what is now Oklahoma. Julia married Edmund Guerrier, another half-breed who had been present at the Sand Creek Massacre. Both George and Julia have grandchildren, great-grandchildren, and great-great-grandchildren still living on the Oklahoma reservation areas as members of the Cheyenne-Arapaho tribe.

Sand Creek, then, marked the real end of the era of cooperation based upon ritual exchange between the Native Americans and Americans. The Bents and Ceran St. Vrain had laid the foundation for this collaboration with the construction of Bent's Old Fort and their willingness to accommodate the traditions of their trading partners. The demise of the fort was the removal of a key element in the ritual interaction between the Americans and Native Americans. Without such ritual interaction, by which to establish a common humanity, each side regarded the other as something less than "real" and "human." The recent arrivals rallied under the leadership of men like Chivington, the Methodist minister-warrior, who was determined to establish the hegemony of his value and belief system. Very quickly, however, Chivington and the more parochial system he espoused were displaced as the federal government reclaimed control of the culture of modernity, capitalism, and individualism.

Mircea Eliade observed that

one of the outstanding characteristics of traditional societies is the opposite that they assume between their inhabited territory and the unknown and indeterminate space that surrounds it. The former is the world (more precisely, our world), the cosmos; everything outside it is no longer cosmos but a sort of "other world," a foreign, chaotic space, peopled by ghosts, demons, "foreigners" (who are assimilated to demons and souls of the dead).[53]

He elaborated on this by saying that unknown, "chaotic" space must be made known through consecration. Without such means, the unknown remains the unformed and terrifying, and those who populate it retain the status of demons. What Eliade says here in regard to "traditional" man is equally true of "modern" man, although the ideology of individualism works stubbornly against this realization. The events we have examined in this chapter are evidence that Eliade was correct in his observation that the "unconsecrated" remains unknown and terrifying. In the absence of ritual between the Plains Indians and the Anglos from the East, each side appeared as demons to the other—demons in the form of the three-year-old boy at whom the soldiers of the Colorado Third took turns shooting, demons in the shape of the Hungate children.

Modern Ritual
at Bent's Old Fort

Ideology and Ritual

Modern man draws a line between religion and ideology, but that line is revealed as a fuzzy one if carefully examined. At first, unreflective glance, the difference seems clear enough. Religion assumes the intervention of supernatural forces in the world, while ideology must make its case for the order of things without recourse to the supernatural. After a more sustained look at the matter, we might notice that those who subscribe to an ideology tend to behave as if supernatural or, at least, sacred forces were at work in the world. Often they seem to be striving for the attainment of some sort of earthly paradise and to regard their lives as meaningful only insofar as they are contributing to that end.

After all, what is regarded as supernatural depends upon one's definition of the natural. In previous chapters I have argued that such notions are socially constructed. "Natural law" often serves as a paradisiacal model. It is what the world was like before the connection between heaven and earth was sundered. The natural order would again be realized if all would behave correctly. A model for correct behavior was provided by the gods and the ancestors—in the case of ideology, one may regard the founders of countries, business or social organizations, schools of thought, movements in art, or countercultures as the gods and ancestors. Present-day leaders are those who most closely emulate such behavior. Human neoteny provides the basis for ancestor veneration and plays a large role in the selection of leaders and our attitudes toward them. The ancestors and gods, as well as present-day leaders, share many attributes with the primary caregivers we knew as children. They tend to appear to be larger, more powerful, and more knowledgeable about the arcane than are we.

Whatever the differences between religion and ideology, they are structured similarly. They are socially constructed models of the ideal. As such, they provide the basis for value and belief systems that motivate the behaviors of individuals and groups. In this way (among others) they are different from theology and philosophy, which deal with the intricacies of value and belief systems themselves. Religion and ideology are in this sense more practical, and theology and philosophy more abstract. As Geertz said of religion, and I think the statement applies as well to ideology, it is the "placing of proximate acts in ultimate contexts."[1]

What I have been arguing for, while describing the history, ethnohistory, and material culture associated with Bent's Old Fort, is the recognition of a means by which both religion and ideology are shaped and propagated that is most essentially nonverbal. I have called this *ritual,* or *fugitive ritual,* the means by which the proximate and mundane is imbued with the sacred or sublime, and placed within an ultimate context. Ritual is inseparable from either religion or ideology: Religion and ideology are what we do, while theology and philosophy are what we think about what we do.

I have been arguing even more specifically that ritual was a crucial factor in the "winning" of New Mexico and the Southwest. As a part of doing so, I have tried to illustrate the essential aspects of ritual as they occur in both religious (traditional) and ideological (modern) societies. All ritual shares the basic structure of the Sun Dance, in that it refers to an ideal pattern that provides the model for the current social configuration and one's place within it. As we have seen, rituals are liminal. They persist precisely because there must be some means by which to adjust for the tension between the ideal and the world at hand. The ideal, the unchanging, sometimes *must* change because it becomes drastically out of tune with contemporary conditions and possibilities. More frequently, one's status in reference to the ideal changes. Both sorts of transitions are accommodated, and facilitated, ritually.

Clifford Geertz's view of ideology was that it provides a symbolic framework to replace the one lost as parochial religious symbolic structures are discarded. Such religiously based structures are abandoned as the world becomes less parochial, and religious symbolism can no longer accommodate the phenomena observed in the larger world. Sense is made of the world, after all, by matching up internalized symbolic structures with external experience. These structures may be thought of as a variety of Kant's *a priori* assumptions. Making sense of the world by means of these assumptions is the first order of business for humans. If such sense cannot be made, anxiety is generated that precludes effective behavior. Anxiety of this sort is unbearable and explains the mad scramble for a workable ideology that Geertz described as occurring in modernizing countries. He gave as an example the French Revolution, which he said was, "at least up to its time, the greatest incubator of extremist ideologies . . . in human history."[2]

There is an urgency here, an intensity that is entirely understandable from a Kantian point of view, a viewpoint more lately called phenomenological. The intensity is acknowledged in both popular and scholarly attitudes toward ideology. To call someone an ideologue, for example, is not to be flattering. It implies that the person is close-minded, that he or she is willfully nonreflective. Such a person clings to his or her beliefs desperately since to lose them, he or she fears, would produce unendurable chaos in his or her life. For similar reasons, any change in the ideology to which he or she subscribes is feared and resisted. The person or group and the events associated with the origin of the ideology assume almost sacred status. Here is one area, as I have discussed just above, in which the line between religion and ideology becomes very blurred.

Freud and Marx, for example, are often regarded as kinds of demigods, beings touched by the infallibility of genius (itself a word with supernatural overtones). Their followers occupy a kind of privileged position and are permitted insights denied to others. Thus, for example, Marxist thought emphasized that ideology obfuscates and prevents an understanding of true social conditions, particularly power relationships between socioeconomic groups. Marxism itself, however, is not recognized as an ideology by Marxists. As Mark Leone explained in his "Time in American Archaeology": "Ideology in the Marxist sense simply does not exist in societies without classes."[3] Geertz commented in a tongue-in-cheek manner, "I have a social philosophy; you have political opinions; he has an ideology."[4]

Similarly, Freudians believe they alone see the world without illusion. Eric Berne, author of enormously popular books based in Freudian psychology (among them *I'm O.K. — You're O.K.*) said in a recent book that

the human race is split during late childhood into the Life Crowd, who spend their lives waiting for Santa Claus, and the Death Crowd, who will spend their lives waiting for Death. These are the basic illusions on which all scripts are based.[5]

This statement prompts this question: If half of the human race believes in one sort of illusion and the other half another, who is illusion-free? Only the Freudian analyst . . . and his patients (who, it is important to note, look upon the analyst as a surrogate parent):

The therapist, with full humanity and poignancy, and with the patient's explicit and voluntary consent, may have to perform . . . surgery. In order for the patient to get better, his illusions, upon which his whole life is based, must be undermined. . . . This is the most painful task the script analyst has to perform: to tell his patients that there is no Santa Claus.[6]

If the "surgery" is completely successful, the patient will achieve a kind of modern nirvana, known among some psychologists and a large portion of the general public as "self-actualization."

These points do not refute self-actualization, nirvana, or the cultural awareness required to see behind the masks of capitalist ideology as ideal conditions to which humanity might aspire, but they should be seen as just that. And what this highlights is that the enterprise of pursuing ideal states, even of the modern sorts, is inextricably bound up with ritual. The patient emulates the analyst (the embodiment of the ancestors), the spiritual novice the sage, the student the Marxist teacher. Because human enterprise (Freudian, spiritual, Marxist, and in general) is entangled with neoteny, there is a tendency to see "our" small group (the surrogate family of origin) as the only one that has access to ultimate knowledge, and one which must battle "their" much larger and potentially overwhelming group that would, if they could, snuff out the flickering flame of truth.

Neoteny in this way colors our perception of all human transactions, even perceptions informed by scholarship. The concept of cultural hegemony was offered by the Marxist Antonio Gramsci to explain how a culture can dominate other cultures or sub-cultures without recourse to overt coercion.[7] Because it assigns central importance to values and beliefs, cultural hegemony might be used as a key to an enhanced understanding of the events and, especially, the material culture associated with Bent's Old Fort; it might explain how the "hearts and minds" of the members of he various cultures of the Southwest were won, and thus how Kearny's Army was able to walk virtually unopposed into Santa Fe. Cultural hegemony could enable the construction of an appealing story for Bent's Old Fort (and elsewhere) with clear-cut heroes and villains all acting according to ideological scripts with which we, from hearing similar stories, are familiar. Nonetheless, such stories ignore problems of motivation and intentionality that a phenomenological approach finds quite relevant to an understanding of collective human behavior. Characters in dramas scripted in accord with cultural hegemony theory are either battling or in league with a diabolical force. The complexities of making real life decisions in the context of competing and conflicting value and belief systems are not well represented in these tales.

To begin with what is a relatively minor point, the Bents and Ceran St. Vrain were not intentionally advancing modern ideology. They were extraordinarily skilled socially. They demonstrated a high level of competency for communicating well, verbally and nonverbally — nonverbal communication including ritual. They honed and exercised these skills to advance their own interests, financial and otherwise, which to some extent coincided with the interests of other groups, including businessmen, and politicians in the East. That these interests were not compatible in the end with their own is evidenced by the demise of Bent & St. Vrain Company, the death of Charles Bent, and the tragedies that befell William Bent and his children. By the end of the fur-trading era, William Bent's interests coincided as much with those of the Cheyenne as with any other group.

More important, by the cultural hegemony model, the Cheyenne and the Mexicans, as well as the principals of Bent & St. Vrain, would be seen as dupes: they were "co-opted," and they sold out for the industrial goods of the Western world. I would say, rather, that they became engaged in a modernization process that began in Europe, reached the Southwest in earnest in the early nineteenth century, and is still occurring in most parts of the globe. Faced with the unavoidable impingement of the modern world, the Cheyenne and the Mexicans replaced at least some of their traditional and more parochial symbolic system with elements of the ideology that was proffered to them by means of the Bents, their fort, and the exchange of trade goods. The rituals involved were, after all, those of inclusion. At a liminal moment in their history, the rituals eased a transformation that most had chosen. This is what ritual is supposed to do, no less in this case than when a Sun Dancer seeks a new vision for a reformed life. As to being dupes — well, there are advantages to modernity, after all. And though the Cheyenne were undone, it was neither the rituals nor modernity, *per se*, that were their undoing. Tragedy occurred when ritual ceased.

I hasten to make two additional points. I am not saying that the annexation of the Southwest was done for purely ideological purposes or by completely ideological means.[8] Ideology is never pure — it is interwoven with all other strands of culture. The political and economic situation in North America in the early nineteenth century was more complex than I have been able to deal with fully in this book. I have mentioned almost not at all the happenings in Texas, for example, or California. Nor have I dwelled much on the threats, perceived and real, from other European powers who might have had designs on parts of North America and how the Mexican War was in part a reaction to that. David M. Pletcher has observed that:

If the United States had not won the [Mexican] war decisively, the power of Britain and France might have increased in the Atlantic and the Caribbean. Thus, the war was a turning point, not only in the internal history of the United States and in its relations with Latin America but also in the relations between hemispheres. Victory in the Mexican War did not launch the United States as a Great Power—this would require another half-century of growth—but it certainly helped to promote the nation from a third-rate to a second-rate power that would have to be reckoned with in its own neighborhood.[9]

The United States had economic and political motives, which were advanced through political and military means. The standard presentation of history, however, leaves out the role of value and belief systems (in this case, ideology) in both setting and achieving such agendas. I am saying that our understanding of history is deficient without a fuller appreciation of how value and belief systems operate in these regards.

My second point is that I am not offering an excuse or apology for the military invasion of Mexico. Quite aside from questions about the morality of the Mexican War, resistance to the American presence in and then its annexation of the Southwest was minimal. Had there been resistance, it seems doubtful that New Mexico, at any rate, would have been won and held.

What transpired after the war, I think, strengthens the case being presented in this book for the importance of ritual in the construction and maintenance of what Richard White has termed a "middle ground," and which I regard as a common world.[10] A resistance or separatist movement did not develop among the New Mexicans. Among the Native Americans it did. The reason for the difference in reaction had to do with more than just economics. The federal government expressed its willingness to support the Cheyenne and other Plains tribes if they would abide by a new set of rules. But life under these terms was meaningless. The new life being proposed was so far outside of the symbolic framework that had organized their lives that it evidently made little sense to the Cheyenne.

It is important to remember, too, that the symbolic structure being used by the Cheyenne was not developed by the Cheyenne and other tribes in isolation. Although it contained ancient elements, it had been shaped in large part by interactions with the Europeans since they intruded upon the continent three hundred years earlier. The Plains Indians' culture often seems strangely familiar to Americans of all sorts, including Anglos, because Americans and the Plains Indians created it together. During its creation, the Plains Indians were partners with the newcomers from the Old World. The traders respected Native American traditions, participated in Native American rituals, and, in so doing, gradually transformed the Native American culture. We have seen, for example, how the Plains Indians thoroughly adopted individualism.

With the end of the fur trade, the opportunity to live in meaningful ways was suddenly removed. Meaningful behavior for Native Americans was reenactment of ideal behavior, the behavior of the ancestors and gods. The Native American perception of such primordial behavior, however, had been shaped by three hundred years of ritual trade with the Europeans. The "traditional" preoccupation with buffalo hunting and raiding had developed in tandem with European and then American interests in the West and Southwest and had found its fullest expression in the relationship between the Cheyenne and Arapaho and the Bent & St. Vrain Company. Without trade, the connection—the ritual exchange—that linked the traditional realm of meaning with the new one was also taken away. From a traditional point of view, the cessation of opportunities for Plains Indians to participate meaningfully in exchange with their White Father constituted a betrayal.

New Mexicans, on the other hand, were not deprived of their traditional activities, nor were their connections with the modern world, based in ritualized exchange, severed. Not only did they remain involved with the Santa Fe Trade, for instance, but their involvement increased just prior to and after the war in a number of ways. David J. Sandoval has estimated that half of the goods moving over the Santa Fe Trail in 1838 were being transported by Mexicans.[11] Other scholarship in progress presents similar business enterprises on the Chihuahua Trail at about the same time.[12] By the time of the Mexican War, many Hispanics were mercantile traders as well. Their more complete acceptance of modern ideology rendered these activities meaningful in their culture. Acceptance of a wider spectrum of modern beliefs and values came quite readily to the emerging middle class in New Mexico, perhaps because they could emulate the traditional behaviors of the elite in their society in regard to mercantile trade.

This argument is the one central to this book: Bent's Old Fort served as a model of modern ideology, and that ideology, or essential portions of it, was then propagated in a ritualistic manner to the more traditional cultures of the Southwest. More of this ideology was adopted by the New Mexicans than by the Native Americans, in part because ritual interaction between the Americans, who were bearing the new ideology to the Southwest, and the New Mexicans was sustained after the Mexican War. Ritual exchange between Americans and Plains Indians decreased drastically after the abandonment of Bent's Old Fort and virtually ceased after Sand Creek. One effect of this was that the Native Americans became anomalous figures in the modern world.

Bent's Old Fort, reconstructed in 1976, operates again today as "ritual ground." In investigating present-day ritual, we have the advantage of being able to observe it firsthand, which allows us to identify some fine points in the operation of ritual that are often lost to historic and ethnographic accounts, as well as to the archaeological record. Treating these fine points constitutes a step along the road suggested by Geertz, toward a reasoned examination of symbolic frameworks—to my way of thinking, these frameworks are rituals. Such examination might lead to the more informed application of ritual. Ritual is inevitable because it is a part of the social structure by which essential cultural meanings are conveyed, manipulated, and altered. A society devoid of ritual is impossible because ritual establishes the connections among individuals, and groups, that are necessary to a society. The question is only how ritual will be employed.

In what follows, I direct the reader's particular attention to two aspects of ritual at the restored fort, which is now known as Bent's Old Fort National Historic Site. The first is the tendency in a modern high-grid, low-group, ego-centered society such as our own for the development of what has been called an "evangelical" faction by Rhys Isaac.[13] This faction is one that, Mary Douglas says, "discards existing rituals and looks for a radical new rite which will usher in a golden era."[14] At Bent's Old Fort, this faction comprises the employees of the history association that is affiliated with the park and some of the volunteer interpreters. Evangelicals, as the name implies, seek direct access to communion with the primordial past, whether the ideal or the sacred, depending upon how one looks at it. They believe that existing, formal structures of ritual impede immediate access, and they do not acknowledge their own behavior as ritualistic. The other ritualistic phenomenon I address is the way interpretation, obviously a kind of reenactment, is being used in an attempt to reform society. There is a very conscious effort to "write in" to the "script" the activities of minorities. The reformation is being attempted by minority employees of the National Park Service, with encouragement from the agency itself.

Independence Day

Jack Wise is selling a great many beads. In the reconstructed storeroom of Bent's Old Fort, he chats with the visitors, explaining the historic uses of the trade goods displayed on the walls and selling handsome reproductions of trade items as fast as can be done without disrupting his narrative. It is Independence Day in 1992, 143 years after the fort's proprietor, William Bent, abandoned and destroyed the massive adobe structure. Whether this was done intentionally or unintentionally is a matter of speculation and debate among the interpretive staff here. The Fourth of July was a grand event during the fort's occupation, perhaps the biggest of the year in that era of patriotism and optimism. Appropriately, this will be the busiest weekend of 1992 for visitation, and the entire arsenal of interpretive approaches is being employed.

Reenactments of certain historic events that occurred here are under way. Ann Shadlow, the great-granddaughter of William Bent and his first Cheyenne wife, Owl Woman, is telling stories to groups of tourists in the tipi just outside the fort's front entrance. Ann is also the granddaughter of Julia Bent and Edmund Guerrier, both half-breeds who survived the Sand Creek Massacre. In fact, she was brought up by Julia Bent, who, having abandoned the ways of the whites because of Sand Creek, taught her no English. Ann spoke only Cheyenne until she was twelve. Nearby, on the banks of the Arkansas, tents have been pitched by reenactors portraying the advance guard of General Kearny's dragoons. In 1846 these dragoons and other troops massed three or four miles downstream from the fort, shoeing oxen and picking up fresh supplies preparatory to their invasion of Mexico. General Kearny and his officers meanwhile received intelligence information from and discussed strategy with the owners of the fort and prominent Santa Fe traders, probably in the dining and billiard rooms of the fort.

Another encampment by the river is that of a Mormon woman and her children. The Mormon woman speaking "in character" tells you that she and her family were displaced from Missouri by the infamous Extermination Edict of Governor Lilburn Boggs. It is somewhat ironic that a Mormon family would seek refuge at Bent's Old Fort, since Governor Boggs had been married to Juliannah Bent, younger sister of William and Charles Bent. Juliannah died after bearing two children by the governor, but he still retained close ties to the Bent family. The Mormon woman says that her husband has taken ill from the journey, probably from the water in one of the streams along the Santa Fe Trail. He is seeing the doctor inside the fort.

Out of character, she will tell you that she is not permitted in the fort because evidence that Mormon women were at the fort is inconclusive. Her real-life husband is even now, between his stints at portraying the doctor's patient, searching through the reconstructed fort's modern library for the evidence that he hopes will someday gain entrance for his wife to the fort during one of these reenactments. They are Mormons in their daily lives, and it is important to them that their church be written into this piece of history.

The man in charge of the administration of all the National Parks in the Rocky Mountain Region, Regional Director Bob Baker, has chosen to spend this Fourth of July weekend at the fort. He and his wife are dressed in period clothing, which, like most of the period dress worn at the fort today, was made four years ago. The design and manufacture of clothing that might have been seen at the historic fort, down to the manner in which it was stitched, was the object of careful research. The clothing being worn now by the superintendent of the fort, Donald Hill, for example, was patterned after the jacket, shirt, and pants taken from the body of a free trader who died in the early nineteenth century. That the superintendent is dressed in the clothing of a free trader, who occupied the uppermost rung in the hierarchy of the fort, seems logical. Bob Baker, though, is wearing the outfit of a trapper. Don Hill tells me later that he had made the offer of trader's apparel, but Bob had been very sure that he wanted to portray a trapper instead. To my wondering aloud about why the regional director would find the role of a trapper more appealing, Don replies that the trapper symbolizes the romance of the era to many. Perhaps the regional director identifies with the independence, freedom, and self-sufficiency of the trapper, he says.

Outspoken and highly animated, Bob Baker earlier this morning told the assembled park staff that their most important task was to impart to the public a sense of what the park should *mean* to them. The Park Service must touch the visitors' hearts with the story each particular park has to tell. At the conclusion of his talk, Bob had played a videotape his office had produced in which the images are accompanied by a popular song, a kind of rock ballad. The videotape is filled with symbols: small children, handicapped National Park Service employees, beautiful views of national parks, and park visitors of all races. I am moved, and then a bit embarrassed to be so. Nonetheless, I consider asking for a copy of the videotape to show to my own office.

After the meeting adjourns, Bob Baker walks the parapets and bastions of the fort, appearing unexpectedly, like Banquo's ghost: now here to watch the reading of the Declaration of Independence in the plaza, now there to observe an interpreter describe the diversions in the billiard room. The superintendent, despite his trader's clothing, has been thrown into the real-life part of Macbeth: his ambitions for his site are imperfectly concealed as he engages the regional director in frequent quiet but intense conversations.

The panoptic mechanism is still at work here, quite obviously, as it was over 140 years ago. The architecture of the fort still serves admirably in this regard. A dignitary, the regional director, has arrived to inspect the operation. If not quite at a glance, he can quickly observe the interpretive program from any number of positions on the second story of the structure, particularly from the bastions and watchtower. He watches the exhibition of bullet making in the plaza, the Cheyenne tipis out in front of the fort, the dragoon camp down by the river, and so on.

Other rituals that support hierarchical divisions, in addition to the inspection itself, are also in place. The regional director will eat at first table with the superintendent and senior park staff. Were there no reenactment, he would probably have lunch with them anyway. It is an eerily reflexive situation: the historical roles the regional director and his staff are playing out are something like their present-day roles. What strikes me as especially strange, as a fellow employee of the National Park Service, is just how natural these roles appear to me.

Ritual and Interpretation

Independence Day conforms in virtually every way to what one would expect as a ritual on the summer solstice. July the Fourth, after all, is only a few days after the actual solstice and probably represents the limits to which historical fact could be stretched in the direction of that precise date. Were the celebration to occur on the actual solstice date, the night would be the shortest of the year. It is, therefore, a liminal event, marking the transition from a period during which days grow longer, to the sixth-month period when they will grow shorter. From the traditional point of view, danger is always present at times of change. Fireworks, an Independence Day tradition, have been used in many places to frighten away demons on such occasions. The fact that Independence Day is thought of as a secular holiday only illustrates that the modern distinction between ideological and formally religious phenomena, while obviously useful, is also misleading insofar as the workings of ritual as a social mechanism are concerned. As Anthony Giddens has observed in regard to one of Emile Durkheim's most noted works, "*The Elementary Forms* demonstrates that the existence of gods is not essential to religious phenomena."[15] With this in mind, we should not be surprised at the various sorts of portrayals of the ancestors (the founding fathers) and the retelling of the origin myth (the reading of the Declaration of Independence and related documents) that are presented in parades and speeches on July 4. At Bent's Old Fort on July 4, 1992, the Declaration of Independence is read in the plaza—as it would have been during the fort's occupation.

Every day at Bent's Old Fort is an Independence Day of sorts, a reenactment of the consecration of the Southwest by its inclusion in the United States. Ritual must replicate the primordial behaviors of the ancestors (or gods) who created the order of the world out of chaos. This activity refers to a mythology, which may be subtly changed by the manner in which the ritual is enacted. The ritual must evoke an affective response; that is, it must induce the "sentiment" that promotes the internalization of the values and beliefs expressed by the ritual and the mythology. As the regional director observed, the ritual must "touch the heart," in this case with the "story each park has to tell," in order to serve the public.

Ritual is transacted only in part by words. Some ritual employs no words at all. Nonverbal aspects of the interpretation can be more convincing than verbal presentations, because they appear natural and obvious, and because they are not explicit and, so, are difficult to explicitly discuss or refute. The architecture, landscape, and furnishing of an historic site like Bent's Old Fort are obvious examples of this. Even *absences* are meaningful here. The dirt, the bad smells, the noise, the illness, the danger and uncertainty, and the coarseness and brutality are not well presented, if at all. There are valid reasons for not replicating such conditions in the present day, but leaving them unrepresented panders to the nostalgia for a lost paradise that is ubiquitous among human populations.

Verbal, ordered, rational, that is to say, *elaborated* presentations of historic context can help here, but even these have ritual components. In the case of national parks, elaborated presentations are bolstered by ritual in two notable ways. First, the authority of the verbal presentation is enhanced because it is the "official" history. Here again, what is left out of the official history might be assumed by the visitor to have not existed. Second, a political—which is as much to say ritualistic—process is used

Figure 22. Dedication of the marker erected by the Daughters of the American Revolution at the site of Bent's Old Fort. (Courtesy Colorado Historical Society, Denver.)

in designating areas as part of the National Park System. I will deal with the second of these two components, then take a closer look at the notion of "official" history.

William Bent abandoned and partially destroyed the fort in 1849. There is no record of its use for the next thirteen years. From 1861 until 1881, the somewhat restored structure was used by the Barlow-Sanderson Overland Mail and Express Company as a home station and general repair shop. Then, for the next three years, many of the rooms were used for cattle stables. After 1884, the fort was unoccupied. The adobe, without constant repair, deteriorated rapidly.

The Daughters of the American Revolution (DAR) dedicated an historic marker at the Bent's Old Fort ruins as early as 1912 (fig. 22). The ceremony drew over two hundred people. Local dignitaries posed for photographs next to the marker and atop a "genuine Overland stagecoach." In 1920, the DAR took over the site and, in 1930, erected a cobblestone gateway arch at a cost of $319.32, "to which . . . schoolchildren, among others, contributed" (as reported in the 1963 DAR "Golden Anniversary Program").[16] Thereafter, the fort was the site of reenactments, plays, and celebrations. By 1954, the financial burden of maintaining the remains of the fort and the grounds had proven heavy enough so that the DAR cheerfully conveyed the deed to the fort property to the State of Colorado for the sum of one dollar. The State Historical Society of Colorado, seeing in the fort potential for emphasizing Colorado's role in American history, began its lobbying effort for federal sponsorship of the site almost immediately. Politicians receptive to this idea included Governor Daniel Thorton, both Colorado Senators, John A. Carroll and Gordon Alott, and Congressman J. Edgar Chenoweth of the Colorado Third District. Particularly effective in enlisting the assistance of these politicians was Dr. LeRoy R. Hafen, the executive director of the State Historical Society.[17]

In February 1958, Acting National Park Service Director Eivind Scoyen advised Colorado Senator Carroll that Bent's Old Fort would fit well within that year's priority theme, Westward Expansion. Scoyen then authorized the preliminary historical and archaeological investigations at the fort that marked the beginning of federal efforts that would culminate in the reconstruction of the fort. Two years later, in 1960, President Eisenhower signed a bill that became Public Law 86-487 of the 86th Congress, "authorizing the establishment of a national historic site at Bent's Old Fort near La Junta, Colorado."[18] The reconstruction was funded so as to be completed by the American Bicentennial, in 1976. At the dedication ceremony that year were U.S. government officials, the governor of Colorado, Native American groups, and mountain men reenactors.

All of the actions that led in 1960 to the fort's designation as a National Historic Site were predicated upon the idea that Bent's Old Fort was a site of premier historical significance to the United States. It, thus, became a part of the nation's official history. This lends authority to the interpretation provided, both verbally and nonverbally, at the site. But what, exactly, do these notions of "significance" and "official history" entail?

Robert Berkhofer has been a leader in the reevaluation of history as it is practiced by the historian; that is, he has striven to make the historian visible in the creation of history, a stance that he argued is more instructive than assuming that objectively significant historic phenomena are waiting somewhere to be discovered. This latter assumption is basic to what Berkhofer termed "normal" history. Berkhofer pointed out that "normal" history is based upon two assumptions: a "Great Story," which is formed according to standard structures and themes, and a "Great Past," which is composed from the Great Story.[19] Clearly, Bent's Old Fort was judged significant because it conformed to a Great Story, identified by the National Park Service and the Congress of the United States as "Westward Expansion." This Great Story is a history that is increasingly out of touch with an ever more pluralistic society (one that does not necessarily reflect social fragmentation or balkanization but, more probably, an ever less parochial world).

When Bent's Old Fort became a part of the "official" history of the United States, it became a part also of its Great Past. The United States, however, had changed dramatically in the years between 1960 and 1976, the date of the dedication of the reconstructed site. What may have been conceived by its early sponsors to be a bit of unalloyed celebratory history—the expansion of the United States into what had been Mexican Territory—held other connotations by the early 1970s. Several revisionist history books had been published that compared the Mexican War to the war in Vietnam. Concepts like "Manifest Destiny" had become anathema to a large section of the United States population in the 1960s, particularly in academia, and sensitivity to the mistreatment of Native Americans at the hands of the United States government was growing. Such mistreatment was obviously relevant at the new historic site given the intimate relationship between Plains Indian history—including the Sand Creek Massacre and the removal of the tribes to reservations—and the story of Bent's Old Fort. Also, the notion of Westward Expansion did not strongly suggest the role of minority groups in Southwestern history, and Hispanics were by the 1970s the fastest growing minority group in the country.

In employing the terms *Great Story* and *Great Past,* Berkhofer identified history as the operant mythology of the modern world (although he may not have intended to do precisely this). While modernity assumes objectivity, Berkhofer and other postmodern or poststructuralist scholars have argued convincingly that objectivity in the realm of human events does not exist. They urge a perspective, in this way, that challenges modern ideology.

We see the mythologizing of the past more clearly in our accustomed role as observers to "primitive" societies. These societies, we assume, have less concern with what "actually happened." In such societies, stories are told as a part of a larger ritual re-creation of the world. The Australian Aborigine "sings" the world into existence by retelling the origin myths. If he did not, he believes that the world would come to an end. In a similar way, telling and retelling our modern histories assures that the modern world is renewed and the existing order legitimated. On some level, which we try hard to ignore, we understand as well as do the aboriginal inhabitants of Australia that without the constant retelling, the world as we know it would cease to exist.

The power to tell the Great Story is the power to control the Great Past, and this is really the power that controls how the world is constructed. All the National Parks are necessarily a part of this mythological history because they represent what is understood to be collective national origin and are infused with what we formally recognize as "significance." From an anthropological standpoint, myth provides the essential pattern for proper human behavior. It tells members of society what is meaningful, even what their own life "means."

The Planning Process

With the relationship of interpretation to ritual and ideology in mind, it seems worthwhile to consider how decisions that affect a formal interpretive program at a National Park are made. The enabling legislation that establishes a National Park, which must be passed by both houses of Congress, contains the rationale for the park's existence. Generally, the legislation is quickly followed by the formulation of a mission statement, which elaborates on the reasons the park was established. It also describes the natural and cultural resources of the park and in general terms presents a plan for their protection. Having laid this groundwork, a more comprehensive planning document is prepared.

Such a comprehensive planning document, a master plan, was prepared for Bent's Old Fort in 1975. It emphasized the fort itself as a kind of museum display, describing the intent to include authentic period furniture in the fort and to reenact events that occurred during its occupation. Interpreters would be dressed and trained to act as key figures in the history of Bent's Old Fort. Interpretive strategy would capitalize upon the most striking, and most controversial, aspect of developing the historic site—the massive physical reconstruction of the fort.

Reconstructions are not often done by the National Park Service because they are only infrequently in conformance with National Park Service policy regarding the management of cultural resources. Exceptions are rare and, inevitably, precipitate a storm of controversy. Opposing positions are argued within the Park Service itself, and an antireconstruction coalition is almost always victorious. A reconstruction usually involves, and more frequently implies, a degree of speculation that the National Park Service finds unacceptable. The visitor to a National Park, so the line of reasoning goes, should be able to depend upon the fact the materials they are seeing represent what was *actually present* at the time being portrayed.

Every effort is made to preserve the original materials, the historic fabric, of the site, for two reasons. First of all, historic fabric is preserved so that the visitor can feel secure that what he or she is seeing is authentic. Each incidence where this policy is not followed erodes the trust the public has learned to feel for the National Park Service and the integrity of its historic sites. The second reason has to do with the preservation mandate of the National Park Service. The original material—the bricks and mortar of a historic structure or the soil matrix of a subterranean archaeological site—comprises a kind of library for future researchers. We cannot foresee the nature of analytical techniques that will be devised in the future. For example, who would have guessed before C-14 analysis how important a fragment of charcoal, wood, or other organic material in association with a cultural feature could be in determining its precise age? Recent advances in DNA research have led to the analytical capability to identify the species of animals killed or butchered with prehistoric stone tools used thousands of years ago from microscopic traces of blood remaining on these tools.

For these reasons, the relatively nonintrusive and reversible treatments of restoration or stabilization are preferred at historic, or prehistoric, sites. These involve the preservation of historic fabric, using present-day materials and technologies very minimally to achieve this result. This, however, does not produce a completely "authentic" presentation. While we may present what falls within the scope of a historic restoration project with a minimum of speculation, other, misleading, factors are inevitably present in this restored scene. First of all, we have no control over what has transpired just outside the boundaries of restoration projects. The restored 1790s building may be located next to an 1840s home and on a modern paved street. The net effect is something quite different than what would have been presented in the late eighteenth century. In addition, while we can control what goes into a restoration project, we always leave many aspects of the true historic scene out. About some we have no knowledge. About others we may know something, but not enough to justify their inclusion in the scene at the risk of misrepresentation. Finally, the original scene itself was constantly changing. It was dynamic, whereas the restoration must pretend that it did not change. Aspects of the landscape were ephemeral: a garden here one year and not the next, a fence constructed and then allowed to deteriorate, plumbing and electricity installed, a porch added or removed, and so on. A certain point in time must be selected to represent the entire history of the site, an action that excludes representations of the site as it appeared at other times.

At Bent's Old Fort, the year selected for representation was 1846, the high-water mark of the Bent & St. Vrain Company and the year the fort was used as the staging point for the Mexican War. The selection of this representative point was done after a careful analysis of the site's purpose, which is of course related to the Great Past. The rationale for the selection of 1846 as the interpretive year is presented in the comprehensive management document, which for Bent's Old Fort was the master plan.

Thus, such decisions form the basic structure of interpretation. They determine what is included and excluded from the historic scene, even nonverbally. The nonverbal scene not only is in many ways the most persuasive form of presentation, it is also the most ideological because it conveys what is assumed, normal, or natural—so obvious as to not be worthy of discussion. Only by further, verbal interpretation and critical discussion can such assumptions be made visible, and the restoration transformed into information as opposed to something like propaganda.

This is not to say that a great deal of critical discussion does not go on *behind* the scenes, and some may involve the public. In 1991, the decision was made to rework the comprehensive management plan for Bent's Old Fort. A new, general plan is produced every ten years or so for each National Park, in recognition of the fact that the social and environmental context in which each park operates changes. Full-scale comprehensive management plans are known as general management plans (GMPs). They require at least two years to produce, in large part because coordination of input to the plans from various National Park Service offices and from the public is time consuming.

The first step in the preparation of a GMP is the formulation of a document called a *Task Directive,* which presents the problems and issues inherent in the management of the park area and the form in which these will be addressed in the GMP. In effect, this is a contract for services between the staff of the park for which the GMP is being prepared and those most actively involved in its preparation. These people are generally from the appropriate regional office and the central planning and design office for the National Park Service, the Denver Service Center.

A team captain is appointed who is then responsible for the preparation of the task directive and the production of the products laid out there. (The team captain for the Bent's Old Fort GMP was Cathy Sacco; she is bright, energetic, and articulate, as people chosen for these lead positions tend to be.) The team captain is responsible for explaining the purpose and, as it takes form, the content of the document to the myriad of offices, "publics," and individuals who will become involved in the preparation of the GMP, and in making sure that their involvement is fairly represented there. Individuals are assigned to the planning team from the various offices that will be involved with the formulation of the GMP; again, these are usually the Denver Service Center, the regional office, and the park. This task directive may go through several drafts. There must eventually be a consensus on the acceptability of the plan by the superintendent of the park, the regional director, the manager of one of the geographically based teams (eastern, central, and western) of the Denver Service Center, the Washington Office, and the manager of the Harpers Ferry Center (the office that has responsibility for producing interpretive materials—films, brochures, posters, and so forth—for all the National Parks).

Once agreement has been reached on this basic document, public input is sought. This input has, at times, resulted in the reformulation of the task directive and necessitated reagreement about the altered document by all involved offices. The team captain and planning team endeavor to notify the public of the impending planning effort in a variety of ways. Besides placing notices in newspapers and at the park, an attempt is made to identify as many as possible of the "publics" who might have an interest in the future of the park. These groups are varied and surprisingly numerous for every park. They generally include Native American groups; naturalist organizations like the Audubon Society; groups interested in the history of the park, such as the Civil War Roundtable or Fur Trade reenactors; those with recreational interests such as organizations of hikers, bicyclists, cross-country skiers, motorcyclists, fishermen, boaters, and snow-mobilers; groups with special needs such as the blind, deaf, or paraplegic; and organizations who want special access to the park for ceremonies or demonstrations. This latter public has included not only the obvious Native American groups that have traditionally attached sacred significance to landforms in National Parks, but also New Age organizations who request access to mountain peaks, and, recently, a neo-Nazi organization that has claimed Zion National Park as their homeland. All of these groups will bring to the park their own version of history.

Brochures based upon the issues and problems identified in the task directive are sent to the various publics. Input is solicited in writing and, almost always, at public meetings where issues and problems in addition to those identified in the brochure are raised by the publics and recorded, as are any comments. This record of the meeting and a reformulated list of problems and issues is made available to all the publics soon after the meeting, along with a request for further input. Several meetings are sometimes held.

The planning team then compiles a number of alternative means by which the issues, problems, and comments so far received might be addressed. This list is reviewed by the concerned offices and frequently the publics. Often another public meeting is held at this point, and input on the alternatives is requested. Following this, the planning team selects a preferred alternative and makes it known, along with a rationale, to the concerned offices, and sometimes again to the publics. All concerned National Park Service offices must agree on the selected alternative. Vociferous objection to the alternative on the part of any public can prompt a reformulation of alternatives or a refinement of the preferred alternative.

Once National Park Service offices have agreed upon an alternative, an environmental impact statement (EIS) is written by the planning team, a document that addresses all of the foreseeable impacts of the alternative's implementation. Such impacts might be on the biological, cultural, or social environment. The EIS is then disseminated to the public for review. Frequently, there follow several cycles of comments, revisions, more comments, and more revisions until the alternative is satisfactory to all concerned and the selected alternative is transformed into a GMP.

Based upon this document, an interpretive plan and then a statement for interpretation are formulated. Each of these goes into progressively greater detail about how the interpretive program at the park will be operated. Nonetheless, the essential aspects of the interpretive program—themes and approaches—are laid out in the GMP.

Bent's Old Fort is located (as are many national parks) in a relatively remote and unpopulated area. The park has many strong supporters who desire to be involved in the planning there, even though they live at some distance from the park itself. The Santa Fe Trail Association membership, for example, tends to reside in areas all along the length of the trail, from Independence to Santa Fe. In part because of this reason, public meetings were not held. Nonetheless, a good deal of input was obtained from interested parties. Over 1,000 brochures describing the draft GMP were sent out, and almost two hundred attached questionnaires were returned.

Not surprisingly, the GMP for Bent's Old Fort emphasized the fort's association with the Santa Fe Trail. The plan also highlighted its role in the "opening of the West" and its impact on the indigenous populations of the area, particularly the Hispanic and Native American groups there.

Local Input to Interpretation

The interpretive plan is prepared by either the park or regional staff, or sometimes jointly by members of the staffs of these two offices. The statement for interpretation is usually prepared by the park. A statement for interpretation has been redone several times at Bent's Old Fort National Historic Site by the park staff over the past eighteen years, reflecting some of the social issues that have become more prominent in that time. (This was done even in the absence of such changes in the master plan.) Many of the park staff are drawn from the local community, providing for additional consideration of local interests and concerns in the interpretive planning process. Also reflected in the interpretive program at the park is the increasing emphasis over the past fifteen years within the National Park Service in recruiting employees from ethnically diverse backgrounds. A greater visibility of the historic role of the Mexican population at the fort is probably due in no small way to the placing of a Hispanic female in the key position of chief of interpretation and resource management at the park. While no Native Americans are on the park staff, at least one of the interpretive staff has very close ties with the Cheyenne and Arapaho tribes, and this is also reflected in the current interpretive approach.

There is every evidence that park staff from all levels of the organization are given a voice in the formulation of the interpretive program, including the statement for interpretation. In November 1991, for example, the supervisory park ranger for interpretation and visitor services at Bent's Old Fort, Steve Thede, met with the interpretive staff—this included permanent employees, the seasonal employees who work only in the summer during peak visitation and who are so much of the interpretive effort at any park (these are often school teachers), and volunteers—to come up with a rough draft of the 1992 statement for interpretation for the fort. The meeting took place away from the fort, to emphasize the idea that new approaches would be welcome and that approaches would be worked out collectively. By design, Donald Hill, the superintendent, and Alexandra Aldred, the chief of the division of interpretation and resource management, did not participate. It was thought that their influence might steer the group toward the interpretive programs of the past as opposed to what might be done in the future.

The longest discussion was the first and most basic: what was the purpose of the park? It was important to the group that the essential theme be "The Opening of the West" as opposed to "Westward Expansion." To Steve Thede's surprise, when he later checked the exact wording of the park's enabling legislation, he discovered that the law had been written using "the Opening of the West," *not* "Westward Expansion." To the interpreters at the fort, "Westward Expansion" expressed an Anglo-centric point of view: what transpired was an expansion only to the Americans from the East. The idea of the "Opening of the West" was much more palatable. In this light the fort was seen by all cultures involved as an institution that offered new opportunities: for trade and for an enhanced standard of living to the Cheyenne, Arapaho, and other Native American groups; for American manufactured goods on the part of the Mexicans. As for the Americans in the East, Steve related, the Bents and Kit Carson were like astronauts. Highly romanticized versions of their exploits appeared frequently in eastern newspapers in the second quarter of the nineteenth century, and their names were known to the general public there.

The interpretive staff then set about brainstorming how the interpretation would be accomplished. Some of the ideas—like holding horse races on a reconstructed race track—were quickly discarded. Living history figured greatly in the staff's thinking, for two reasons. First, it provided immediacy, which involved the visitor with the larger story of the fort, a point of departure from which what Steve called "take-home messages" could be developed. Also, it encouraged the visitor to adopt a point of view appropriate to the nineteenth century. At that time, for example, getting to the fort was not as simple as driving there in a car. It was a dangerous undertaking that required careful planning and the assistance of experts. The resources of the fort were vitally important in this context. A place to repair a wagon wheel or a station that provided food and fresh water could be crucial to survival.

Each interpreter then set his personal goals, the "take-home messages" he wanted to give to the visitors. Interpreters were also encouraged to be as explicit as possible about how to measure their own success by formulating statements such as, "seventy-five percent of the people I talk to will know the names of at least two Indian tribes who traded here by the time they leave."

Such discussions as this also readied the park staff to provide input to the planning team as it went about drafting the various documents preparatory to the GMP. Some areas of consensus about the GMP began to emerge. One was to move away from the more unstructured forms of reenactment that took place at the fort in the late 1970s, before the interpretive program was as well developed as it later became. At that time, troops of "mountain men" would arrive at the fort and relive what they considered to be the frontier experience. Sometimes this would include such anachronisms as leather hand-tooled "holsters" for beer cans (the contents of which, one might assume, would assist them in their efforts to replicate primordial chaos). Reenactors now are, in essence, auditioned and trained. They are invited by an event coordinator from the interpretive staff. Invitations are issued after the decision is made that such reenactors are necessary to the story to be conveyed.

The consensus among those involved with the formulation of the GMP was that reenactments should be put into a larger context. To provide that context, the new GMP recommended that a visitor center be built, where the history of the fort could be presented in a more abstract way. Interpreters typically say that this gives the visitor several choices: they can go to the visitor center first and then visit the historic site, now better prepared to understand what they are seeing, or they can visit the site first, draw their own conclusions, and then compare these to the story the visitor center offers. Alternately, they can decide to only visit the site, missing the official story as presented in the visitor center. Park visitor surveys indicate that some people prefer this last alternative. The same surveys also indicate that almost no one visits only the visitor center; they have traveled to the park, after all, for the experience of visiting the site, even if for only minutes. The visitor center, the plan recommended, should be away from the site, as far as possible, although there is a limit to how far people will (or are able to) walk. Administrative functions would be moved to the visitor center, freeing up more of the reconstructed fort for interpretation. All twentieth-century interpretive devices (like the television and VCR, which in 1991 occupied space in the reconstructed fort) would be moved to the visitor center, too, thus removing a rather jarring intrusion to a portrayal of nineteenth-century life.

The Reenactments

Jack Wise is more relaxed on this Independence Day than is the superintendent. Jack is the executive director of the Bent's Old Fort Historical Association, a private group that has been organized to support the park's activities. Though there are many special events today, his role is unchanged. He and his staff run the store. He feels confident that this is the soul of the fort, just as trade was in historic times. Visitors want to take something back from their visit, almost *demand* it. A National Park Service study of visitor activity at Grand Canyon done some years ago, now legend in the Park Service, revealed that the average visitor spent about twenty minutes looking at the canyon, the rest of the time looking for or checking into hotels, perusing menus and eating, and buying souvenirs. (Though there are, of course, many who depart drastically from this average.) The National Park Service does not operate for profit and so delegates the provision of such services to concessionaires. Some of the concessions are run by private enterprises; others, like the one at Bent's Old Fort, are operated by nonprofit affiliates of the National Park Service.

Jack points out that visitors to the fort in historic times came here to do exactly what current-day visitors do, in one respect—to trade for things. And the things he provides are, to the best of his ability, almost exactly like what was purchased here in historic times (fig. 23). No rubber tomahawks here, he declares. The store stocks Hudson's Bay blankets, the real thing, including the white Bent's Fort blanket made especially for Bent & St. Vrain; custom blacksmithed hand tools, hardware, and cooking utensils; hand-made rifles; powder horns, not plastic but real horn, costing from $100 to $115 apiece ("but people buy them, they buy authenticity," says Jack); museum-quality reproductions of redware pottery; black silk scarves ("I pull them out with a flourish and say, 'for you, from the Orient'—they snap them up"); bricks of tea ("the kids can't get over them"). "It's all in the presentation," says Jack. "If you tell them about the item, how it was used and who used it in historic times, they'll buy it. They want to take home a piece of history."

Sales have increased dramatically since Jack took over responsibility for the concession. He attributes the success of the history association's concession to his ability and that of his staff to go into character. It is plain that they are *very* good. Dressed in period costumes, they seem like professional actors to me. Jack has a thespian's voice; it fills a room easily. He and his association people bring their acting skills to the concession, turning it into a reenactment as surely as is the dragoon camp down by the river.

Still, he is impatient to test the frontiers of reenactment in ways that the National Park Service will not allow. He hands me a flyer for an event he has planned through an organization with which he is affiliated, called Vistas of Time. Each year he has organized a program called "Polk Springs," named for the private ranch where it is held. He tells me that there are half a million people in the United States who have been involved with reenactments, in one capacity or another, and it is from this

BENT, ST. VRAIN & COMPANY

PRICES SUBJECT TO CHANGE

Bent's Old Fort Historical Association

35110 Highway 194 East — La Junta, Colorado 81050

(719) 384-2800

1. **CAVENDISH TOBACCO** We searched long and far for a good blend of historic pipe tobacco that didn't smell of oranges or cherries. This is a good cavendish that won't burn the mouth. Wrapped in a period-looking wrapper marked "Payn & McNaughton." $1.25

2. **NEW ORLEANS SEGARS** These come a dozen to a package and are wrapped in brown paper with a copy of an original label on the front and ends. $5.50

3. **TWIST TOBACCO** This is the old-timey twist tobacco that could either be chewed or smoked in a pipe. It has a good but strong flavor. Very authentic. $2.75

4. **TOBACCO CANTEEN** These are made of rawhide and are sewn while wet, pounded full of wet sand, then allowed to dry. These were used for smoking tobacco but can also be used to carry beads, percussion caps, small caliber lead bullets, etc. Patterned after originals. $9.50

5. **CLAY PIPES** Made the original way by forming wet clay around the proper diameter wire then baking it. These pipes are copies of the many thousands that were excavated at Bent's Old Fort and other fur trade sites. Ready to use and need no breaking in. $6.75

6. **MEDICINE BOTTLE** A clear 8 oz. bottle, very similar to ones used on the frontier to carry medicines. Each comes with a cork. $4.00

TINDER BOXES Made by a master medal worker, Ted Cash, these boxes show attention to detail, craftsmanship and dedication to authenticity. Choose from three styles; the oval hinged-lid (7), the oval with "burning glass" (8), or the square, bulged bottom and top (9). $17.75 each

10. **GOURD CANTEEN** These are the real thing, made from narrow-necked gourds and were used by residents of the early Southwest. These are extremely close to the version shown in The Mountain Man Sketchbook series. $18.25

11. **CASTOREUM BAIT BOTTLE** The Bent, St. Vrain & Co. now has a good reproduction bait bottle. They are patterned after the originals shown in The Mountain Man Sketchbook series. They were used by beaver trappers in the Rocky Mountains to carry beaver scent or castoreum to attract beavers. $8.75

12. **CASE OR GIN BOTTLE** Squared so they could be packed in cases to prevent breakage. They were used for gin or other potables and were in use from the French and Indian Wars to the Civil War. These are handblown into molds and have no seam. $19.25

13. **ONION BOTTLE** This was also a liquor bottle. It is free blown and holds a little over a quart. $18.25

14. **PUMPKINSEED OR SADDLE-FLASK BOTTLE** Approximately 6 inches tall, this clear, hand-blown bottle holds about a pint. This durable, thick-glassed bottle is perfect for a possible bag or the bottom of a chest. $12.25

15. **OAK BARRELS** Available from gallon to 108 gallon sizes. These barrels are made by master coopers from red oak with steel hoops. All are wax lined with a side bung. Complete and ready to use for almost any liquid. Should be soaked prior to use; will not leak after being soaked. P.O.R

16. **RAW CONE SUGAR "PILONCILLOS"** Sometimes called a "hat" of sugar. It is though this is where the expression "I'll eat my hat" originated. Raw cane sugar. $3.00

17. **LEATHER BELT BLANKS** Two inches wide, 44 long. We have plain blanks and ones painted red or black. The painted ones were a great trade item with the Indians. $12.00

18. **"BEEHIVE" SMALL JUG** These are the correct ceramic jugs for the period. The buff-colored cylindrical style were more common in the 1880's and later. Our potter matched these to original drawings Holds a little over one quart. $14.25

19. **MOLDED BEESWAX CANDLES** Similar to the originals that were about 75 per cent beeswax, 25 percent tallow. Burn slowly and evenly and do not smoke or smell. Hand-molded locally. $3.00 pair

20. **HUDSON BAY RATION BOX** We have a fine carpenter who now builds these for us using hand-wrought fittings. Made to specifications in The Voyageur's Sketchbook $160.00

Figure 23. Page from the 1990 sales catalog published by Bent's Old Fort Historical Association.

group that attenders are drawn. The ad runs, among other places, in magazines for reenactors. It reads, in part:

GREETINGS: THIS IS NOT A REENACTMENT!
We are looking for 100 soldiers right from the Civil War battlefields via the prison pen at Camp Douglas, Illinois, to come West with a galvanized Yankee Infantry Company and soldier in the Indian Wars of 1865 for five full days of very real living history.
This is not a club or regiment being formed with dues and meetings nor are you obligated to anyone in any way. This is strictly an in-depth living history experience where you sign up to soldier in 1865 on the southern plains in Comanche country for five full days. Then you are discharged.
Polk Springs is designed to be a "socio-learning" experience which means you will learn history as it happened and that you may enjoy yourself while learning to live in the past.
On Monday morning, prepare yourself mentally to go into 1865 and not return to the present until the following Friday. Conditions will be identical in every way humanly possible to those of 1865; tough, harsh, and bleak. The experience will wear on you physically and mentally.
Experienced as well as novice reenactors and living historians alike need understand that no one should be offended nor take anything personally. If you are shouted at, threatened or punished for some infraction, it is all in the context of the U.S. Army of 1865, not you as a person today. . . .
There will be no dances, no Sutler's Row, no military balls, no bands or canned music, no referees, no "firing demonstrations," no cars, no interpretive talks, no visitors, no tours, and no cam-corders. There will be virtually no 20th century for five days. This is not a typical event. There will be no reenactments of any battles, no one will "be killed" or "wounded."
HOWEVER, YOU WILL BE FIRING LIVE AMMUNITION!
Discipline by the officers and NCOs will be rigid and tough as it originally was. You will be in the Army for five days and you will be expected to follow orders. *You will be in period first person 24 hours a day for five days.* There will be no cession of duties at 4:30 PM or any other time to discuss the day's activities, drink cold beer, or listen to Civil War period music on boom boxes. . . . You will not live history as we or any museum or government agency interprets it. You will live history the way it was. We guarantee it.

The almost evangelical fervor with which a past relived without scripts is pursued here reminds me of Mary Douglas's theory that such sentiments are often generated in high-grid, low-group, egocentric societies, the societies of "impersonal rules."[20] Ritual is disdained by those who feel excluded in such societies in favor of direct communication—communication without symbols—with what is sacred and more real, more "authentic." Rhys Isaac noted this also, as discussed in a previous chapter, in regard to the transformation of Virginia society during the period 1740 to 1790.[21] There was a change in that society from ritual to spontaneity, from hierarchy to egalitarianism, from hospitality to individualism, and from conviviality to privatization. This serves as well as a description of the iconic values of America, values especially related to the American West. Out here on the "frontier" there is disdain for formality, for bureaucracy, for anything, in fact, that limits a person's freedom to do as he or she damn well pleases. Many National Park Service employees who have worked in the "last" American frontier, Alaska, have told me that they were afraid to let people there know that they worked for the federal government. There were stories of nasty, sometimes violent, incidents. Alaskans went north to get *away* from things like federal governments: governments impose licensing requirements for fishing and hunting, environmental regulations, and restrictions on the use of marijuana.

As I talk to Jack Wise, it occurs to me, not for the first time, that the ethos at work here is very much like that of the Plains Indian:

The endurance, courage, independence, perseverance, and passionate willfulness in which the vision quest practices the Plains Indian are the same flamboyant virtues by which he attempts to live: while achieving a sense of revelation he stabilizes a sense of direction.[22]

I would venture to say that Geertz has presented here a list of the qualities that many in America, if not the rest of the modern world, admire most. They are certainly regarded as virtues in the nearby town of La Junta, Colorado, home of the "world-famous" Koshare Indian Dancers (fig. 24). None of the dancers is really Indian. The organization is a Boy Scout Troop. It is much less of an exaggeration to say that the Koshares are world famous. They have danced all over the world and are much in demand wherever the Boy Scouts or similar organizations gather. The Koshares were organized by Buck Burshears, a local man who died several years ago. He was alive when I did my excavations of the Bent's Old Fort trash dumps in 1976, and we had the opportunity to talk several times because he was very interested in what we were finding at the fort. I remember most his conviction that admittance to the Koshares practically ensured a boy's success later in life. Buck could talk at great length about his boys who had become doctors, lawyers, and successful businessmen. In part he attributed these success stories to the discipline it required to be a member of the dancers, but he also felt that the young men were absorbing some of the admirable traits of the Indians: independence, determination, and stoicism.

Figure 24. Cover of the Koshare Dancers' souvenir publication.

In drawing a distinction here between the National Park Service and non-National Park Service approach to interpretation, I do not mean to say that Park Service personnel are immune to the allure of evangelicalism. Recall that the regional director chose to play the role of the independent, free, and spontaneous trapper instead of the wealthier and more powerful trader. And Don Hill has spent a good deal of time searching through military records for references to his Claremont County, Ohio, ancestors who fought in the Mexican War. He eventually discovered that they had gone through Veracruz, but not Bent's Old Fort. He was disappointed because, as he tells me on Independence Day, he was hoping for the sense of "connection" he understands many of his reenactors to be seeking.

And so while a National Park Service employee such as Alexandra Aldred, Bent's Old Fort's chief of the division of interpretation and resource management, might approach reenactment in a more ordered way than does Jack Wise, it is still with a good deal of passion. Alexandra has worked for the Park Service at Bent's Old Fort since 1968, and a conversation with her soon reveals the qualities—organization, initiative, an innovative approach, and determination—that have moved her from an administrative assistant position (which she held when I was conducting excavations at the trash dumps) to her current job, which is second in authority only to that of the superintendent. In 1976 she was generally known by the Americanized "Alex"; today she gently encourages me to call her Alexandra, pronouncing her name in the Hispanic fashion with softened consonants.

Alexandra shares some statistics with me from the 1991 statement for interpretation. In 1990, visitors were largely families and couples traveling at least overnight and were likely to be relatively well educated and secure financially. A full 65 percent were "through visitors," whereas only 35 percent were "home based" (had departed from and were returning to their homes in the same day). A reported 55 percent of visitors were with family groups, and 17 percent were couples without children. Only 14 percent were local residents (and this counts the busloads of children from local schools), 35 percent were regional residents, 48 percent national residents, and 3 percent international residents. There is a great interest in the site among the German and Japanese visitors, but to get to Bent's Old Fort requires a special effort because it is slightly off direct routes between other major tourist attractions. Only 3 percent of visitors were members of minority groups.

Taking into consideration the composition of her audience, Alexandra is particularly interested in portraying the roles of minority groups in the history of the fort through the interpretive program. She thinks that the living history and reenactment programs convey minority participation in the historic activities at the fort very well. Alexandra explains that the initial interpretive emphasis at the fort on the hunters and trappers, the "mountain men," was a bit misleading since by 1846, the year to which the fort has been reconstructed, these mountain men were no longer frequenting the fort as much. This initial emphasis had been evidence of the powerful link that existed in the thinking of many of the "publics" between the fort and mountain men. There seemed to be some compelling symbolism here. Mountain men—the trappers—perhaps more than any other group held a liminal position between the American and the Native American. Through their intimate association with Native Americans (so we are told by both contemporary and current-day popular accounts), the mountain men acquired some of the Native Americans' most remarkable characteristics: toughness, resourcefulness, disdain for authority, and the ability to survive in the wilderness on their own.

Interpretation is now, however, more carefully based upon research into what transpired here at particular times. This shift in the interpretive focus came as a relief to the park staff, Alexandra tells me. Mountain men reenactments could easily get out of hand. There was a good deal of the drinking and carousing that reenactors associated with the behavior of the mountain men. The reenactors insisted upon the same kind of freedom and absence of societal controls they ascribed to the mountain men.

The Independence Day events—breaking the piñata, firing the cannon, making adobe bricks, cooking food in the plaza, reading the Declaration of Independence, the presence of dragoon and Indian encampments, and so forth—were based upon observations made firsthand by historic visitors to the fort on various Fourths of July. Alexandra discovered all these events in the copies of diaries and notes kept in the fort's library. She worked from the observations of Lieutenant Abert, Susan Magoffin, and Alexander Barclay.

Alexandra is especially pleased because this year, for the first time, a local African-American woman, Phyllis Howard, had agreed to play the fort's famous black cook, Charlotte. Alexandra had tried repeatedly over the years to fill this position by contacting black universities in the South, to no avail.

There have been similar problems in filling the "roles" of Native Americans and Mexicans for living history and reenactment purposes. Recruiting from the list of potential employees provided by the regional administrative office, the "seasonal register," had not yielded a diverse pool of applicants. Seasonal applicants are allowed to select two parks at which they would like to work, and those choosing Bent's Old Fort were most likely to be white males. The park has been successful in recruiting for Native Americans on only a few occasions. Each time the recruits were unhappy with being separated from their family groups and went back to the reservations in Oklahoma after a short period. Native Americans at Bent's Old Fort fur trade reenactments are frequently portrayed by Anglos, very talented and dedicated, who bring with them tipis, costumes, cooking equipment, weapons, and other Native American accoutrement they have carefully constructed. Over long reenactment weekends, they will sleep in their tipis down by the river, cooking and living as their careful research indicates that Native Americans did. Meanwhile, real Cheyenne who sometimes come from the Oklahoma reservations to participate in these weekend reenactments usually stay at one of the local motels. Nonetheless, Alexandra never ceases in her attempts to get representatives from appropriate ethnic groups. For the Independence Day observance, she had found a Mexican migrant family from Brownsville, Texas, who were American citizens. Unfortunately, one of the children in the family became ill at the last moment.

Craig Moore, a member of the permanent interpretive staff at the fort, has developed over many years very close ties with the Southern Cheyenne on the Oklahoma reservations. In the spring of 1991, he persuaded the Henry Whiteshield family to come to the fort, where they reenacted the typical manner of ritual exchange in the trade rooms. This proved to be a very moving experience for Craig and many of the interpretive staff, to whom the ritual significance of the reenacted exchange was clear. Henry, gray-haired and distinguished, told me he found it satisfying to be at the fort, and he was gratified at the respect displayed by the visitors who observed the reenacted ceremony.

For the 1992 Independence Day celebration, Craig arranged for the presence of Ann Shadlow and her daughter, Mickey Pratt. Both these women have been very active in the movement to preserve Cheyenne traditions. Ann Shadlow is a storyteller and recipient of the Native American Woman of the Year Award. Her grandmother was Julia Bent, youngest child of William Bent and Owl Woman. Because Julia was present at the Sand Creek Massacre, she, like her brothers Charlie and George, gave up the white lifestyle that William had tried to encourage them to adopt. Julia married another offspring of an Anglo-Cheyenne union, Edward Guerrier, son of famous mountain man Bill Guerrier. Ann lived with Julia from infancy, and Julia attempted to provide Ann with a traditional upbringing, to the extent of never speaking English or permitting it to be spoken in Ann's presence. She also taught Ann as many as possible of the Cheyenne stories, some of them quite likely thousands of years old. Having told the stories to Cheyenne children virtually all of her life, Ann several years ago responded to what she had by then decided to be the sincere interest on the part of non-Cheyenne and attended the National Folk Life Festival in Washington, D.C. This led to a number of engagements all over the country. At the Independence Day observation, she for the first time told a story in Cheyenne to a white audience.

To Alexandra the fort and grounds are a teaching tool, one that is particularly vital because she has learned that what one experiences is retained much longer and in much greater detail than what one merely hears or sees. Her approach to interpretation was greatly influenced, she says, by a visit to Mount Vernon in the 1950s. She was herded through the home of George Washington in an unpleasant way, and she felt that she had learned nothing. It was as if she were expected to feel privileged to have been permitted to enter such hallowed ground. The opportunity to experience the massiveness of the fort itself is important, she thinks. Alexandra had been at the site for six years prior to reconstruction, looking almost every day at the foundations there. Nonetheless, she was astounded by the scale of the fort as the walls began to rise.

She admits that the reconstruction raises some difficult ethical questions. The week before my conversation with her, interpretive specialists from the Harpers Ferry Center had been on site and had followed her and some of her interpreters around for several days as they gave tours. One of the observations the specialists found most remarkable was the number of times people would ask if the fort were real—dating from the previous century, that is. Several different members of the same group of ten to twenty visitors might ask this question in the course of a single tour. The visitors evidently found it very difficult to accept that the fort was a reconstruction. Alexandra feels sure that many people leave the site still believing that the fort is historic fabric, even though she tells the groups at the beginning of the tour and sometimes several times more in the course of the tour that the fort has been reconstructed, that it is all new, with the exception of some hearth stones in the kitchen.

Ritual Ground

To Alexandra's frustration, visitors tend to perceive the reconstructed fort as being authentic because any ancient site is universally regarded by humans as a place more "real" than those they encounter in the course of their daily lives. The architecture of the fort, its massive presence and design, reinforces that impression. In chapter 7 I described how the fort operated as a link in the new circuits of modern power; this is the paradox of the modern agenda being advanced by traditional means. The paradox persists today, and is the source of the frustration felt by Alexandra and many others. The traditional world will not ever be completely reformed because it is part and parcel of a human world in which critical thought is at best intermittent. It is to encounter a heightened sense of reality that people travel—make pilgrimages, if you will—to Bent's Old Fort and other places that play a role in the stories people *will* tell about their past. National parks and World Heritage Sites, the "must sees" in travel books and magazines, and even museums that contain "important" artifacts from such locales are tourist meccas. Implied is the opportunity to participate in or witness the reenactment of an "ancient" order. Humans expect from ritual, from this encounter with the sacred, a model for mundane activities. If the model seems appropriate, these mundane activities are imbued with meaning. If the symbolic framework offered by this model does not work, people often fall into the Nietzschean abyss of despair, alienation, and *anomie.*

For many Plains tribes, including the Cheyenne and Arapaho as well as the Crow, Sioux, and Shoshoni, among the most sacred of sites was the Big Horn Medicine Wheel (see figs. 4 and 5).[23] It is located on a peak in the Big Horn Mountains in Wyoming. After carefully documenting the medicine wheel for several years in the early 1970s, the archaeologist John Eddy decided that it served admirably as a place from which to observe not only the sun at solstice, but the cyclical movements of many other celestial bodies. Before sunrise on the day of summer solstice, cairns in the wheel can be used to locate the brief rising of Aldebaran, the brightest star in what we call the constellation Taurus. Twenty-eight days later (a lunar month or "moon"), other cairns align with the rising of Rigel, brightest star in Orian; twenty-eight days after that, another set of cairns align with Sirius, brightest star in the sky. The span of time from solstice to the rising of Sirius comprises the summer season on this peak in the Big Horn Mountains—snow may be expected either before or after.

Eddy found this topographic situation somewhat puzzling. It could not be explained in terms of observational conditions, which were no better on the mountain peak than on the plains: "The choice of a cold and arduously reached mountaintop in preference to the equally useable nearby plains must be justified on other grounds—possibly mystical or purely aesthetic."[24] I suggest that the mountaintop served as the *axis mundi*, the point around which the human world took form. Its ontological status as such is bolstered by a comment made by a Crow in 1923 that "it was built before the light came."[25] Tree-ring dating of wood taken from one of the cairns suggests a chronological date of A.D. 1760.

The early ethnographer and historian of the Cheyenne, George Bird Grinnell, noted a likeness between the medicine wheel and the medicine lodge in which the Sun Dance is held.[26] They are quite similar in general design, as well as in many details. For example, the central cairn in the wheel corresponds in location to the medicine pole in the lodge, and the twenty-eight spokes in the former are strikingly like the twenty-eight rafters of the latter. Other cairns in the medicine wheel are located where altars and openings appear in the design of the medicine lodge. In 1952, Robert Yellowtail, then chairman of the Crow Tribal Council, mentioned to Forest Service personnel that he thought, based on such similarities, that the Big Horn Medicine Wheel might be a replica of a medicine lodge, being built of stone because it was constructed in a place where timber was not readily available.[27]

What seems more likely, given among other things that the Big Horn Medicine Wheel operates so well as an astronomical observatory, is that the medicine wheel provided the pattern for the medicine lodge, even though there are, as one might expect, some design differences. It might also have provided the pattern for other vital Plains Indian structures. Eddy relates that "a Crow name for the Big Horn Wheel was 'the Sun's Tipi,' and in one Crow legend 'the Sun built it to show us how to build a teepee.' "[28] In this we can see that idealized relationships, the spatial expressing the social, are mirrored first in the most sacred of locales, which may have been frequented only by priests, those initiated into the most arcane rituals of the sacred. Then these relationships are expressed in a design that structured the most important of Plains Indian rituals, one in which all participated, the Sun Dance. And this organizes daily existence along sacred lines; the tipi, the most intimate and private of locales, is seen to reflect the sacred pattern. It becomes an *imago mundi*. In reflecting it, it is also imposed upon daily behavior. Movement through the space of the tipi becomes a kind of ritual.

The ritualized interaction by means of space organized according to a sacred model becomes a ground, an essential point of reference, for all human interaction. The society of humans can be expanded by the replication of this behavior to include other individuals and groups. Figure 7 shows a Cheyenne ritually offering smoke to that most sacred of locales, the *axis mundi* as it is represented in the medicine lodge, referring, probably, to the more "real" center of the world as it occurred on the sacred mountaintop. Figure 13 portrays much the same ritual gesture, this time offered to a trading partner who thereby joins the circle of humanity.

In the sense that the ritual in figure 13 (which took place at Bent's Old Fort) is farther removed than the ritual in figure 7 (which took place at a medicine lodge) from its original (and, in a Platonic sense, ultimate) referent, it has become "degraded," as a sociologist might say. But this does not necessarily lessen its power to organize human relationships, that is to say, to organize human society. Both ritual and symbol become more available for metaphorical extension or outright appropriation (the difference here may be one of perspective) as organization occurs.

An example, taken from the symbolism of the Oglala Sioux, is provided by Paul Radin in *Primitive Man as a Philosopher.* It serves to illustrate well the metaphorical extension of symbols originally given meaning through explicit reference in ritual to the eternal realm. The Oglala Sioux are a Plains Indian group who (like the Crow, Shoshoni, and others) share a great many elements in their symbolic world with the Cheyenne and Arapaho, including the meanings attached to the circle:

> The Oglala believe the circle to be sacred because the great spirit caused everything in nature to be round except stone. Stone is the implement of destruction. The sun and the sky, the earth and the moon are round like a shield, though the sky is deep like a bowl. Everything that breathes is round like the stem of a plant. Since the great spirit has caused everything to be round mankind should look upon the circle as sacred, for it is the symbol of all things in nature except stone. . . .
>
> For these reasons the Oglala make their *tipis* circular, their camp circle circular, and sit in a circle at all ceremonies. The circle is also the symbol of the *tipi* and of shelter. If one makes a circle for an ornament and it is not divided in any way, it should be understood as the symbol of the world and of time.[29]

As Geertz commented, "for most Oglala the circle, whether it is found in nature, painted on a buffalo skin, or enacted in a sun dance, is but an unexamined luminous symbol whose meaning is intuitively sensed, not consciously interpreted."[30] All of this is fine; however, it is the nature of symbols to be so "sensed," by humans in "traditional" *or* "modern" societies. Even words do not "stand for" something, they convey meaning by virtue of the text and context in which they are used, a context that is provided by assumptions of which we are dimly aware, at best. Proximate meanings are influenced by our assumptions about ultimate meaning. Ritual is context *par excellence*. Inevitably, meaning bestowed by ritual is appropriated for use in ritualistic ways, which bestow altered meanings.

The calumet ceremony performed in the context of Bent's Old Fort bestowed new meanings on that ritual and the symbols associated with it, though it did not obliterate the old. Bent's Old Fort was a powerful influence; it was calcified ritual, it enveloped the calumet ceremony. All activities at the fort were ritualized as they were repeated again and again within the pattern into which they were forced by the structure and its landscape. The Cheyenne were thereby provided their place in the new scheme of things along with all others who frequented the fort—the Mexicans and other ethnic groups, work-defined classes, entrepreneurs, and so forth. Bent's Old Fort was not only the blueprint for the new order, it *was* the new order. It provided the order in immediate terms, in a massive reality that could be touched, heard, tasted, smelled, and seen collectively, no less here than in the medicine lodge. The new order, grounded in experience, became the new reality.

In the way that the circle provided a luminous symbol for the traditional world, the symbol for the modern world might be the square, seen in organizational grids with hierarchies and specializations; the order and control of the survey are imposed upon the earth, and the more rigid compartmentalization of human activity is expressed in the architecture of structures and landscapes, and, indeed, in every aspect of modern human behavior. But the square is a model and an ideal nonetheless.

While modernist philosophers have determinedly attempted to debunk the notion of eternal forms (the sort of eternal patterns the Cheyenne and virtually all other traditional peoples believed to be revealed in the cycles of the heavens and nature, as well as Plato's rationally ordered ideals), that has not prevented people from behaving as if such forms exist. In the modern world, cues for performance in the reenactment of archetypical behaviors are provided less by the cycles of nature, often obscured by modern technology anyway, than by the ordered abstractions of bureaucracies. Chapter 2 of this book was intended as a kind of phenomenological exploration of the two realms of meaning formed by traditional and modern reenactments. I attribute the manner in which such "world formation" is conducted to the human characteristic of neoteny, which prompts us all to look to the patterns established by the founders of the world, our ancestors, in formulating the world for our descendants. Mostly this is done in uncritical ways, even by the most critical among us. I suggest, perhaps parenthetically, that it is the portion of such uncritically patterned behavior that best qualifies as human "culture." It is the nongenetically encoded schema that orders human society.

Thus ritual lives on, in fugitive forms that evade modernist scrutiny. The architecture of the humanly contrived landscape is an example. It is often explained in terms of function, with only a grudging, patronizing acknowledgment of something called "style." While we may recognize the "exotic" belief systems associated with the form of the Cheyenne tipi, we do not see the connection between our belief in "the way things should be" and, for example, the design of residential architecture. Around the turn of the last century, with optimism running high in the project of modernity, many cities saw the construction of "apartment hotels," which provided centralized facilities for laundry, cooking, cleaning, and other shared amenities like barber shops and telephone answering services. These soon failed. Today, with families in which both parents work and people on average, married or not, working longer hours (sometimes at two or more jobs), there are obvious, practical advantages to such living arrangements. Yet this patterning of residential space has not proven popular; it seems "dehumanizing," which, of course, reflects our belief in the autonomous, individual human.

The above is not to say that all ritual, and all landscapes, are *deemed* equally important as models for human behavior by the members of a society; they are not regarded as equally sacred or real. The more sacred provide models for the less, but the less, being more integrated in day-to-day life, may have the most influence in shaping society and the values and beliefs of societal members. It is in great part a matter of repetition, of establishing what Bourdieu termed *habitus*. The gradation of the real and the sacred are essential to the societal dynamic that is necessary to the replication of society, or, for that matter, to the reformation of society.

These gradations of reality were described by Plato in his well known allegory of the cave, which appears in *The Republic*. His ideal forms are the base upon which the world is constructed in the traditional manner. They display the world as it should be organized in all ways, from the spatial to the social. This organization is one of relationships that facilitate the eternal cycles of the cosmos. By discerning them, one is better able to participate in them, to link one's society and self to the eternal realm.

The most real, and therefore the most sacred, of all sites is at the center or navel of the earth, the *axis mundi* that unites all realms of being. But as with so much in mythology, this is often understood to be metaphorical. As Black Elk said, "Anywhere is the center of the world"[31]— as long as it displays the attributes that identify it as the center. As did Bent's Old Fort during the fur trading period, and as it does now.

How to best deal with the continuing human penchant for ritual, for mythologizing the past, and for organizing experience around what Geertz has called unexamined luminous symbol is beyond the scope of this book. I have tried here only to make a case for the operation of ritual as it affected a controversial and what I think to be poorly understood portion of history and for its continued operation today. I think that this second point is more important than the first. It implies that we should stop regarding "traditional" or "primitive" peoples as radically different from ourselves, in part because we are at present impaired in our understanding of ourselves and of "them." It also implies that presenting the past will forever be a ritual similar in many respects to theater. The presentation may be blatant or subtle propaganda, it may be thought provoking, it may be well or poorly done, effective or ineffective, but it will always both reflect and propagate certain assumptions about the operation of the world.

I have also argued in a related way in this book that ritual, usually fugitive ritual, is the social apparatus by which humans represent and reform the world in the present. Moderns, especially academics and those aligned with or aspiring to the sciences, are loath to recognize this fact, but its truth should be obvious: Ritual permeates every part of the modern world. The market-driven lifestyles of our world incorporate numerous highly stylized—that is to say, ritualized—behaviors. How and to whom and when and where we speak and gesture are fraught with meanings that frequently overwhelm what we imagine to be "content." Indeed, we are all today more or less engaged in the "strenuous theater" Yi-Fu Tuan claims to be essential to the maintenance of the modern world.[32] This includes the use of many props: the cars we drive, the places we eat, the clothes we wear, the houses in which we live, the places to which we travel. In the more obviously collective realms of modern politics and business, theater is no less essential. For the most part, the communication media offer critiques not of ideas and policies, but of the performances of politicians; not of product quality or production process, but of the theatrical maneuverings of corporate executives. Such critiques, which amount to reviews of actors in their roles, and the performances themselves exert substantial influence on the selection of leaders not only in politics and business, but in academia, the sciences, and many other social spheres as well. Yet, as I have tried to emphasize, giving form to the present or the past is not a matter of choosing between ritual and rationality. Ritual can be informed by rationality and rationality is not infrequently ritualized, as we clearly see in the marketplace and politics alike.

In sum, to ignore the presence and power of ritual is to be willfully naive and to place ourselves at great risk. In the absence of activities in which all can meaningfully participate there develop alienated individuals and factions that often provide an identity to its members through opposition to others. All too frequently this leads to the sorts of atrocities that have been described in this book. In the year just past as I write this, 1995, children have died horribly in Bosnia, Rwanda, and Oklahoma City, demonized by the excluded as surely as were the innocents in the nineteenth-century Colorado Territory. We recoil from the very thought of these events, but unless we find a way to construct a ground that can accommodate us all, one that will fill Nietzsche's abyss, we must know that we are doomed to more tragedies in the future. It is the hope of humanity that we can hope for the understanding we will need for this task.

Notes

Chapter 1: Hearts and Minds

1. Quoted in David Lowenthal, "Geography, Experience, and Imagination: Towards a Geographical Epistemology," *Annals of the Association of American Geographers* 51 (1961): 241.

2. I refer to the "southwestern Plains" as an area comprising the eastern third of Colorado and of New Mexico, the northern extension of Texas, the Oklahoma panhandle, western Kansas, and southwestern Nebraska. The "Southwest" embraces present-day New Mexico, Arizona, southern Utah, southern Colorado, and the southern tip of Nevada—perhaps half of the Mexican Cessation of 1848.

3. Walter Prescott Webb, *The Great Plains* (New York: Grosset & Dunlap, 1931), 488.

4. Frederick Jackson Turner, "The Significance of the Frontier in American History." In *The Frontier in American History* (New York: Henry Holt and Company, 1920), 1–38.

5. Mircea Eliade, *The Sacred and the Profane: The Nature of Religion: The Significance of Religious Myth, Symbolism, and Ritual within Life and Culture,* trans. Willard R. Trask (New York: Harcourt Brace Jovanovich, 1959), 53.

6. David Lowenthal, "Past Time, Present Place: Landscape and Memory," *The Geographical Review* 65 (1975): 12.

7. Karen Blixen, *Out of Africa* (London: Putnam, 1937). Quoted in Lowenthal, "Past Time," 9.

8. Ibid., 54–55.

9. Lawrence Wright, *Saints and Sinners* (New York: Alfred A. Knopf, 1993), xii.

10. See, for example, Rhys Isaac, *The Transformation of Virginia 1740–1790* (Chapel Hill: University of North Carolina Press, 1982).

11. The term *American* is fraught with difficulty in a work like this book. Where I term a group or person who resided in the United States something other than

American, it is only for the purpose of pointing out some affiliation with another group that is pertinent to the book. In some cases I have employed hyphens to achieve this kind of differentiation, as with Euro-Americans and Anglo-Americans. In a number of instances, I have fallen back on the term *Anglo* to designate persons from the eastern United States, especially those who arrived in the vicinity of Bent's Old Fort just prior to and after its demise, when in fact a group so designated may have included African-Americans, Native Americans from eastern groups, Hispanics, and members of other groups.

As to other group nomenclature, in general the collective nouns I use here to designate the human groups that appear in this book are those I think to be ones most frequently employed to refer to those groups. I depart from these common terms only where I think that to not do so would be misleading or when I know their use to be objectionable to the groups involved. I use the terms *Native American* and *Indian* interchangeably because both are typically employed in the literature from which I drew for this work. I have used *Cheyenne* instead of *Tsis tsis' tas* because the former is not objectionable, so far as I know, to the group in question, and again because a large body of literature is attached to the term *Cheyenne.*

In the first draft of this book I took care to employ the plural form when referring to more than one member of any Native American group (for example, "a party of Cheyennes" instead of "a party of Cheyenne,") in order to be consistent with the usage of plural forms for other ethnic groups (Germans, Americans, etc.). This proved to be so distracting to those who looked over the early manuscript that I changed all such references to the singular forms ("a party of Cheyenne") that are used by most anthropologists for Native American groups.

I speak of the *Spanish* as the citizens of the country immediately to the south of the United States prior to 1821; after that date I refer to them as *Mexicans.* Spanish-speaking persons residing in the United States I term *Hispanics,* and in some cases this term is also used to refer to Spanish-speaking people who might have lived at least part of the time south of the border.

I ask the pardon of any I may have offended in my efforts not to be pedantic and so to move the book along. I invite your reactions to my use of the terms I have described above, and any others.

12. Anthony McGinnis, *Counting Coup and Cutting Horses* (Evergreen, Colo.: Cordillera Press, Inc., 1990), 4.

13. Frank Gilbert Roe, *The Indian and the Horse* (Norman: University of Oklahoma Press, 1955).

14. Quoted in Marc Simmons, *Coronado's Land: Essays on Daily Life in Colonial New Mexico* (Albuquerque: University of New Mexico Press, 1991), 127–161.

15. David J. Weber, *The Taos Trappers: The Fur Trade in the Far Southwest, 1540–1846* (Norman: University of Oklahoma Press, 1986), 35.

16. Ibid., 28.

17. Thomas F. Schilz, "Ponies, Pelts and Pemmican: The Arapahos and Early Western Trade," *Red River Valley Historical Review* 7, no. 9 (1982): 28–38.

18. Howard R. Lamar, "Foreword," in Susan Shelby Magoffin, *Down the Santa Fe Trail and into New Mexico,* ed. Stella Drum (New Haven: Yale University Press, 1982), ix–xxxv.

19. Mark Simmons, personal communication, 1992.

20. The United States termed New Mexico a territory and appointed a governor, Charles Bent, before the area was ceded by Mexico in 1848.

21. David Lavender, *Bent's Fort* (Lincoln: University of Nebraska Press, 1954), 281.

22. John S. D. Eisenhower, *So Far From God: The U.S. War With Mexico 1846–1848* (New York, Doubleday, 1989), 68.

23. Similar cultural changes had occurred in California, but the circumstances of these are beyond the scope of this book. The social mechanism that effected these changes were quite surely the same, however.

24. Karl von Clausewitz, *On War* (London: Routledge & Kegan Paul, 1962).

25. David M. Pletcher, *The Diplomacy of Annexation: Texas, Oregon, and the Mexican War* (Columbia: University of Missouri Press, 1973), 50.

26. Simmons, personal communication, 1992.

27. Quoted in Roger Lewin, *Complexity: Life at the Edge of Chaos* (New York: Macmillan, 1992), 15.

28. This is discussed as it relates to the fur trade in Eric R. Wolf's *Europe and the People Without History* (Berkeley: University of California Press, 1982), 158–194, and treated as it deals with Bent's Old Fort in chapter 4 of this book.

29. Richard White, *The Middle Ground: Indians, Empires, and the Republics in the Great Lakes Region, 1650–1815* (Cambridge: Cambridge University Press, 1991), ix–xvi.

30. Mary Douglas, *Natural Symbols* (New York: Vantage Books, 1970), 125–139.

31. That these terms are highly problematic is a major theme of this book, and there will be much discussion of how these terms have been used, what they have meant in various contexts, and how they have been misleading. In general usage pertinent to the topics discussed in what follows, *traditional* refers to belief, practice, or statement transmitted from generation to generation, and often implied is that the transmission was oral, carries the force of convention, has persisted from time immemorial, and is largely uncritical; *modern* is used to refer to that which departs from or repudiates tradition, especially in its use of science and especially critical thought, and the practice of market capitalism, as well as the ideologies associated with science and capitalism. It is in the assumption of the fundamental departure of the modern from the traditional that the central problem lies.

32. Weston La Barre, *Shadow of Childhood* (Norman: University of Oklahoma Press, 1991), 11–51. Also, as La Barre suggests, Stephen Jay Gould, *Ontogeny and Phylogeny* (Cambridge, Mass.: Belnap Press, 1977); and Ashley Montagu, "Time, Morphology, and Neoteny in the Evolution of Man," in *Culture and the Evolution of Man,* ed. Ashley Montagu (New York: Oxford University Press, 1962), 324–342. Yi-Fu Tuan not infrequently alludes to neotenic influences, as in his *Space and Place* (Minneapolis: University of Minnesota Press, 1977), 19–33.

33. Eliade, *The Sacred and the Profane,* 39–45.

34. Simon Schama, *Landscape and Memory* (New York: Alfred A. Knopf, 1995), 218.

35. Richard Sennett, *Flesh and Stone: The Body and the City in Western Civilization* (New York: W. W. Norton & Co., 1994), 102.

36. Ibid., 108. Sennett quotes Joseph Rykwert, *The Idea of a Town* (Cambridge, Mass.: MIT Press, 1988), 59; and Polybius, *Histories,* VI.31, trans. F. Hultsch and

E. S. Shuckburgh (Bloomington: Indiana University Press, 1962), 484; quoted in Spiro Kostof, *The City Shaped: Urban Patterns and Meanings Through History* (London: Thames and Hudson, 1991), 108.

37. Lavender, *Bent's Fort,* 136.

38. Daniel Miller, *Material Culture and Mass Consumption* (Oxford: Basil Blackwell, 1987), 71.

39. See, for example, Claude Lévi-Strauss, *The Elementary Structures of Kinship* (New York: Basic Books, 1969); and Marshall Sahlins, *Islands of History* (Chicago: University of Chicago Press, 1985). Exchange was also carefully treated by Karl Marx, of course; see his *Capital: A Critique of Political Economy* (New York: International, 1967).

40. Mary Douglas, "Foreword," In Marcel Mauss, *The Gift: The Form and Reason for Exchange in Ancient Societies,* trans. W. D. Halls (London: Routledge, 1990), xiv.

41. Yi-Fu Tuan, *Segmented Worlds and Self: Group Life and Individual Consciousness* (Minneapolis: University of Minnesota Press, 1982), 7–8.

Chapter 2: Realms of Meaning

1. A letter signed George Bent to George Bird Grinnell, dated September 24, 1912. George Bird Grinnell Collection, folder 56 (letters of George Bent), Southwest Museum, Los Angeles.

2. Mircea Eliade, *The Myth of the Eternal Return: Or, Cosmos and History* (Princeton, N. J.: Princeton University Press, 1954), 1–34.

3. Ann Shadlow, personal communication, 1992.

4. Eliade, *Myth,* 34.

5. Ibid.

6. Claude Lévi-Strauss, *The Savage Mind* (Chicago: University of Chicago Press, 1966), 16–33.

7. Quoted in Anthony Giddens, *The Consequences of Modernity* (Stanford, Calif.: Stanford University Press, 1990), 49–50. Giddens has doubts about "postmodernity," and thinks that the term is "best kept to refer to styles or movements within literature, painting, the plastic arts and architecture. It concerns aspects of *aesthetic reflection* upon the nature of modernity" (see p. 45). He does not think that modernity has been overcome, only that is it beginning to understand itself (p. 48).

8. Paul Tillich, *The Courage To Be* (New Haven: Yale University Press, 1952), 182–190.

9. Lawrence Wright, *Saints and Sinners* (New York: Knopf), 109.

10. Ibid., 109–110.

11. Peter L. Berger and Thomas Luckman, *The Social Construction of Reality* (New York: Anchor Books, 1967).

12. Yi-Fu Tuan, *Segmented Worlds and Self* (Minneapolis: University of Minnesota Press, 1982), 139.

13. Ibid., 146.

14. Ibid., 175.

15. Giddens, *Consequences of Modernity*, 146.

16. Clifford Geertz, *Local Knowledge* (New York: Basic Books, 1983), 167.

17. Clifford Geertz, "Deep Play: Notes on a Balinese Cockfight," in *The Interpretation of Cultures* (New York: Basic Books, 1973), 432–442.

18. Ibid., 421.

19. As Durkheim described sentiment in *Sociology and Philosophy:*

When individual minds are not isolated, but enter into close relation with, and act upon each other, from their synthesis arises a new kind of psychic life. It is clearly distinct from that led by the solitary individual because of its unusual intensity. Sentiments created and developed in the group have a greater energy than purely individual sentiments. A man who experiences such sentiments feels that he is dominated by forces which he does not recognize as his own, and which he is not the master of, but is led by; and everything in this situation in which he is submerged seems to be shot through with forces of the same kind. He feels himself in a world quite distinct from that of his own private existences. This is a world not only more intense in character, but also qualitatively different. Following the collectivity, the individual forgets himself for the common end and his conduct is directed by reference to a standard outside himself. . . . For all these reasons this activity is qualitatively different to the everyday life of the individual, as is the superior to the inferior, and the ideal to the real.

It is, in fact, at such moments of collective ferment that are born the great ideals upon which civilizations rest. These periods of creation or renewal occur when men for various reasons are led into a closer relationship with each other, when gatherings and assemblies are more frequent, relationships closer and the exchange of ideas more active. . . . At such times the ideal tends to become with the real, and for this reason men have the impression that the time is close when the ideal will in fact be realized and the Kingdom of God established on earth. This illusion can never last. . . . Nevertheless these ideals could not survive if they were not periodically revived. The revival is the function of religious or secular feasts and ceremonies, public addresses in churches or schools, plays and exhibition — in a word, whatever draws men together in intellectual and moral communion.

Quoted in Anthony Giddens, ed. and trans., *Emile Durkheim: Selected Writings* (London: Cambridge University Press, 1972), 228–229.

20. Mircea Eliade, *Rites and Symbols of Initiation* (New York; Harper and Row, 1958), ix–x.

21. Ibid., 132–136.

22. Mark C. Carnes, *Secret Ritual and Manhood in Victorian America* (New Haven: Yale University Press, 1989), 1–2.

23. Mircea Eliade, *The Sacred and the Profane: The Nature of Religion: The Significance of Religious Myth, Symbolism, and Ritual Within Life and Culture,* trans. Willard R. Trask (New York: Harcourt Brace Jovanovich, 1959), 204–205.

24. See William Cronon, *Changes in the Land: Indians, Colonists, and the Ecology of New England* (New York: Hill and Wang, 1983), for a description of this process as it occurred in New England, at the outset of colonialism.

25. Giddens, *Consequences of Modernity*, 143–144.

26. Basil Bernstein, "Elaborated and Restricted Modes of Communication."

27. Giddens, *Consequences of Modernity,* 139.

28. Derek Robbins, *The Work of Pierre Bourdieu* (Boulder, Colo.: Westview Press, 1991), 33.

29. Quoted in ibid., 23.

30. François Lyotard, *The Postmodern Condition: A Report on Knowledge* (Minneapolis: University of Minnesota Press, 1988), xxiv.

31. Michel Foucault, *The Archaeology of Knowledge* (New York: Pantheon Books, 1972), 7.

32. Ibid., 138–139.

33. Hildegard Binder Johnson, *Order Upon the Land: The U.S. Rectangular Land Survey and the Upper Mississippi Country* (New York: Oxford University Press, 1976), 30.

34. Ibid.

35. Ibid., 28.

36. Ibid., 29.

37. Adrian Snodgrass, *The Symbolism of the Stupa* (Ithaca, N.Y.: Cornell Southeast Asia Program, 1985).

38. A conversation with Paul Grout, Region 2 Survey Coordinator for the Colorado State Highway Department, two years later confirmed the association of the alignment of highway 71 with the survey system. In the late nineteenth century, easements of thirty feet on either side of section lines were granted to Colorado counties, and roads were to be constructed within these easements. Jogs in road alignments occurred for a number of reasons. Mr. Grout thought that the pronounced jog south of Punkin Corner might have been to take advantage of a particularly good location at which to cross drainages. A desirable location would be one with relatively shallow grades; steep grades were impossible for wagons drawn by horses.

39. The reader should note that Foucault is simply incorrect in his statements about the methods and aims of archaeology as it is practiced today—he says, for example, that it is unconcerned with the material it deals with as "a sign of something else." In fact, many archaeologists interpret artifacts and structures as if they were texts. This fact, however, has little to do with Foucault's argument or, for that matter, with the potential of the approach that Foucault endorses.

40. Foucault's broad definition of discourse is essential to much of the most influential scholarship at present, of course. Edward W. Said, to mention only one, has used this as a point of departure in his *Culture and Imperialism* (New York: Vintage Books, 1993), in which he presents a "nation" as a kind of discourse, or narration: "The power to narrate, or to block other narratives from forming and emerging, is very important to culture and imperialism, and constitutes one of the main connections between them" (p. xiii).

41. Quoted in David Harvey, *The Condition of Postmodernity* (Cambridge, Mass.: Blackwell Publishers, 1989), 46.

42. Quoted in Peter Gay, *Freud: A Life for Our Time* (New York: W. W. Norton & Company, 1988), 171.

43. Sigmund Freud, *Civilization and Its Discontents* (New York: W. W. Norton & Company, 1961), 17.

44. Stephen Jay Gould, *Ontogeny and Phylogeny* (Cambridge, Mass.: Belknap Press, 1977), 9.

Chapter 3: Nostalgia for Paradise

1. Mircea Eliade, *The Sacred and the Profane: The Nature of Religion: The Significance of Religious Myth, Symbolism, and Ritual Within Life and Culture*, trans. Willard R. Trask (New York: Harcort Brace Jovanovich, 1959), 39–45.

2. David Lowenthal provides some examples that are interesting because they involve "modern" groups, as in "Geography, Experience, and Imaginations: Towards a Geographical Epistemology," *Annals of the Association of American Geographers* 51 (1961): 241–260, 241. Eliade mentions ubiquitous nostalgia in his writings; see, for example, *The Sacred and the Profane*; 91–93, and *Myths, Dreams, and Mysteries* (New York: Harper, 1960), 95–98.

3. Leslie Spier, *The Sun Dance of the Plains Indians: Its Development and Diffusion*, Anthropological Papers of the American Museum of Natural History, vol. 16, pt. 7 (New York: Museum of Natural History, 1921) 453.

4. Karl H. Schlesier, "Rethinking the Midewiwin and the Plains Ceremonial Called the Sun Dance," in *Plains Anthropologist*, 35, 127 (1990), 1–27.

5. Ibid., 1.

6. Ibid., 2.

7. Dennis Stanford, "The Jones-Miller Site: An Example of Hell Gap Bison Procurement Strategy," *Plains Anthropologist*, Memoir #14 (1978): 97.

8. Joseph G. Jorgensen, *The Sun Dance Religion: Power for the Powerless* (Chicago: University of Chicago Press, 1972), 7.

9. Schlesier, "Rethinking the Midewiwin," 9.

10. George Dorsey, *The Cheyenne*, Anthropological Series, vol. 9, nos. 1 and 2 (Chicago: Field Columbian Museum, 1905); George Bird Grinnell, *The Cheyenne Indians: Their History and Way of Life*, 2 vols. (New York: Cooper Square Publishers, 1962); E. Adamson Hoebel, *The Cheyennes* (New York: Holt, Rinehart, Winston, 1960); James Mooney, "The Indian Ghost Dance," *Collections of the Nebraska Stage Historical Society* 16 (1911): 168–182, and "The Ghost Dance Religion and the Sioux Outbreak of 1890," in *Annual Report of the Bureau of Ethnology*, 1892–1893, pt. 2 (Washington: Government Printing Office, 1896); abridged edition, ed. Anthony F. C. Wallace (Chicago: University of Chicago Press, 1965); John H. Moore, *The Cheyenne Nation: A Social and Demographic History* (Lincoln: University of Nebraska Press, 1987); Peter Powell, *Sweet Medicine: The Continuing Role of the Sacred Arrows, the Sun Dance, and the Sacred Buffalo Hat in Northern Cheyenne History: Volumes I and II* (Norman: University of Oklahoma Press, 1969); Karl H. Schlesier, *The Wolves of Heaven: Cheyenne Shamanism, Ceremonies, and Prehistoric Origins* (Norman: University of Oklahoma Press, 1987).

11. Mickey Pratt, personal communication, 1992.

12. Donald J. Berthrong, *The Southern Cheyennes* (Norman: University of Oklahoma Press, 1963), 66.

13. Durkheim considered sentiment to be an essential aspect of the "mechanical" solidarity that he said was characteristic of traditional cultures. Modern cul-

tures, according to Durkheim, were bound together by more rational, functional considerations. These had to do with the specializations necessary to an industrial society. In such a society, because of specialization, the members of the society were mutually dependent upon one another, leading to an "organic" solidarity. The terms "mechanical" and "organic" Durkheim borrowed from the biological theory of evolution that was becoming influential at the time of his writings. "Mechanical" referred to those organisms in which one cell was so much like all others that the loss of one or more cells did not interfere with the functioning of the organism. An example would be the sponge. "Organic" life forms were those with specialized organs. Durkheim attributed the deterioration, or degradation, of ritual to the lessened dependency on mechanical solidarity. Michel Foucault made reference to Durkheim's ideas, although Foucault argued (as we shall see in a subsequent section) that surveillance replaced ritual as the principal binding force of society. What Foucault did not recognize is that surveillance is a kind of ritual. This is evident in the case of Bent's Old Fort. See Emile Durkheim, *The Division of Labor in Society* (New York: The Free Press, 1965), 124–126.

14. In Cheyenne mythology, the holy man called Sweet Medicine had established five of the six military societies. Four of them—the Wolf Soldiers, the Fox Soldiers, the Dog Soldiers, and the Bull Soldiers or Red Shields—he formed by transforming himself into the animals that served as totems for these societies. The sixth society was said to have been created by a warrior named Owl Man after the Cheyenne had made contact with the Europeans. When performing at the Sun Dance and elsewhere, the members of this society danced with guns, to symbolize this association with the white man.

15. Basil Bernstein, "A Sociolinguistic Approach to Socialization, with Some Reference to Educability," in *Directions In Sociolinguistics: The Ethnography of Communication*, ed. Dell Hymes (New York: Rinehart & Winston, 1977), 465–497.

16. James P. Spradley, *The Ethnographic Interview* (New York: Holt, Rinehart, and Winston, 1979).

17. Victor Turner, *The Anthropology of Performance* (New York: PAJ Publications, 1986), 76.

18. Schlesier, *Wolves of Heaven.*

19. Mircea Eliade, *Rites and Symbols of Initiation* (New York: Harper and Row, 1958), 93–94.

20. Berthrong, *The Southern Cheyennes.*

21. Fred R. Meyers, "Always Ask: Resource Use and Land Ownership among Pintupi Aborigines of the Australian Western Desert," in *Resource Managers: North American and Australian Hunter-Gatherers,* ed. Nancy M. Williams and Eugene S. Hunn (Boulder: Westview Press).

22. Ibid., 180.

23. Schlesier, *Wolves of Heaven,* 13.

24. James Clifford, *The Predicament of Culture: Twentieth Century Ethnography, Literature, and Art* (Cambridge, Mass.: Harvard University Press, 1988), 1–17.

25. Several ethnographers have noted this dual importance of the horse. See, for example, John C. Ewers, *The Horse in Blackfoot Indian Culture,* U.S. Bureau of Ethnology, vol. 159 (Washington, D.C.: U.S. Government Printing Office, 1955); Joseph Jablow, *The Cheyenne Indian in Plains Indian Trade Relations,*

1795–1840, Monographs of the American Ethnological Society (Seattle: University of Washington Press, 1950); and Oscar Lewis, *The Effects of White Contact Upon Blackfoot Culture: With Special Reference to the Role of the Fur Trade,* Monographs of the American Ethnological Society, ed. A. Irving Hallowell (Seattle: University of Washington Press, 1942).

26. George Bird Grinnell, *By Cheyenne Campfires* (Lincoln: University of Nebraska Press, 1926), 34–37.

27. Clifford Geertz, "Deep Play: Notes on the Balinese Cockfight," in *The Interpretation of Cultures* (New York, 1973).

28. Ibid., 434.

29. Another reason for decreased opportunity for young warriors was not necessarily related to the Sun Dance or to new forms of wealth. As time went on, the Cheyenne experienced intensified pressure by Anglos to curtail raiding — except on the enemies of the Anglos. When the Cheyenne were placed on reservations, of course, there were no sanctioned opportunities for raiding.

30. Turner, *Anthropology of Performance,* 21–32.

31. Claire R. Farrer, *Living Life's Circle: Mescalero Apache Cosmovision* (Albuquerque: University of New Mexico Press, 1991), 57.

32. Eliade, *Sacred and Profane,* 97.

33. Stephen Jay Gould, *Ontogeny and Phylogeny* (Cambridge, Mass.: Belknap Press, 1977).

34. Weston La Barre, *Shadow of Childhood* (Norman: University of Oklahoma Press, 1991), 102–146.

35. Differentiation is considered by Murray Bowen, *Family Therapy in Clinical Practice* (New York: Jason Aronson, 1990); individuation by M. L. von Franz, "The Process of Individuation," in *Man and His Symbols,* ed. Carl G. Jung (New York: Dell Publishing Co, 1964), 158–254.

36. Bernstein, "Sociolinguistic Approach," 465–497.

37. Mary Douglas, *Natural Symbols* (New York: Vantage Books, 1970), 138–139.

38. R. H. Lowie, *Primitive Religion* (London: Routledge & Kegan Paul, 1925).

39. Douglas, *Natural Symbols,* 136.

40. Eliade, *Sacred and Profane,* 66.

41. William Brandon, *Quivira* (Columbus: Ohio University Press, 1990).

42. Claude Lévi-Strauss, *The Raw and the Cooked: Introduction to a Science of Mythology: I* (New York: Harper & Row, 1969), 336.

43. George R. Milner, E. Anderson, and V. G. Smith, "Warfare in Late Prehistoric West-Central Illinois," *American Antiquity* 56, no. 4 (1991): 581–603.

44. James Axtell, *The European and the Indian: Essays in the Ethnohistory of Colonial North America* (Oxford University Press: New York, 1981), 17–21.

45. A. Irving Hallowell, "The Backwash of the Frontier," in *Beyond the Frontier: Social Process and Cultural Change,* ed. Paul Bohannon and Fred Plog (Garden City, N.Y.: Natural History Press, 1967), 344.

46. Mary Douglas, *Natural Symbols* (New York: Pantheon, 1970), 125–139.

47. Weston La Barre, *Culture in Context* (Durham, N.C.: Duke University Press, 1980), 152.

Chapter 4: Castle on the Plains

1. Ceran St. Vrain, A.L.S. C. St. Vrain to B. Pratte & Company, dated at Taos, January 6, 1831, Chouteau-Maffitt Collection, Missouri Historical Society. See also Harold H. Dunham, "Ceran St. Vrain," in *Mountain Men and Fur Traders of the Far West,* ed. LeRoy R. Hafen (Lincoln: University of Nebraska Press, 1982), 154; and Janet LeCompte, *Pueblo, Hardscrabble, Greenhorn* (Norman: University of Oklahoma Press, 1978), 14.

2. Geoffry A. Godden, *An Illustrated Encyclopedia of British Pottery and Porcelain* (New York: Crown Publishers, Inc., 1965), 31–33.

3. Janet LeCompte, "Gantt's Fort and Bent's Picket Post," *Colorado Magazine* 41, no. 2 (1964): 117.

4. Douglas C. Comer, *Bent's Old Fort 1976 Archeological Investigations: Trash Dump Excavations, Area Surveys, and Monitoring of Fort Construction and Landscaping* (Denver: National Park Service, Denver Service Center, 1985), 174.

5. David Lavender, *Bent's Fort* (Lincoln: University of Nebraska Press, 1954), 139.

6. Ceran St. Vrain, A.L.S. C. St. Vrain to Lieutenant Colonel Enean Mackay, U. S. Army, National Archives-Abandoned Military Reservations Section, box 52, folder labeled "Ft. Lyon (Old) Col. (1847)."

7. Dwight E. Stinson, "Historic Structures Report, Part II," manuscript on file, National Park Service, Denver Service Center, 1965, p. 4.

8. Lavender, *Bent's Fort,* 144; and Samuel P. Arnold, "William Bent," in *Trappers of the Far West,* ed. Harvey L. Carter (Lincoln: University of Nebraska Press, 1983), 223.

9. Pratte, Chouteau & Co. agreement with Bent, St. Vrain & Co., dated July 27, 1838, P. Chouteau-Maffitt Collection, Missouri Historical Society.

10. Lavender, *Bent's Fort,* 136.

11. Ibid.

12. John E. Sunder, ed., *Matt Field on the Santa Fe Trail* (Norman: University of Oklahoma Press, 1960), xii.

13. George Thorson, "The Architectural Challenge," in *Bent's Old Fort,* ed. Cathryne Johnson (Denver: Colorado Historical Society, 1976), 111.

14. Alexandra Aldred, personal communication, 1992.

15. Stinson "Historic Structures," 53.

16. Ibid., 18.

17. George Bird Grinnell, *Bent's Old Fort and Its Builders* (Topeka: Kansas State Historical Society, 1923), 38.

18. Enid T. Thompson, "Furnishing Study for Bent's Old Fort Historic Sites, Colorado," manuscript on file, National Park Service, Denver Service Center, 1973, pp. 52–67.

19. Timothy Baugh, personal communication, 1991. See also John D. Speth and Susan L. Scott, "Horticulture and Large-Mammal Hunting: The Role of Resource Depletion and the Constraints of Time and Labor," in *Farmers as Hunters: The Implications of Sedentism,* Arizona State University Anthropological Research Paper No. 24, ed. David L. Wilcox and R. Bruce Masse (Tempe: Arizona University, 1989), 213–256; and John D. Speth, "Some Unexplained Aspects of Mu-

tualistic Plains-Pueblo Food Exchange," in *Farmers, Hunters, and Colonists: Interaction Between the Southwest and the Southern Plains,* ed. Katherine A. Spielman (Tucson: University of Arizona Press, 1990), 18–35.

20. Timothy G. Baugh, *Edwards I (34Bk2): Southern Plains Adaptations in the Protohistoric Period,* Studies in Oklahoma's Past, No. 8, Oklahoma Archaeological Survey (Norman: University of Oklahoma Press, 1982), and Timothy G. Baugh, "Ecology and Exchange: The Dynamics of Plains-Pueblo Interaction," in *Farmers, Hunters, and Colonists: Interaction Between the Southwest and the Southern Plains* (Tucson: University of Arizona Press, 1991).

21. Richard I. Ford, "Inter-Indian Exchange in the Southwest," in *The Handbook of North American Indians,* vol. 10, ed. William C. Sturtevant (Washington, D.C.: Smithsonian Institution, 1983), 711–712, 719–720.

22. Eric R. Wolf, *Europe and the People Without History* (Berkeley: University of California Press, 1982), 160–161.

23. Ibid., 161.

24. Ibid., 163.

25. Alfred W. Crosby, Jr., *The Columbian Exchange: Biological and Cultural Consequences of 1492* (Westport, Conn.: Greenwood Press, 1972), 38.

26. Ibid., 37.

27. See also Philip L. Walker, Patricia Lambert, and Michael J. DeNiro, "The Effects of European Contact on the Health of Alta California Indians," in *Columbian Consequences,* vol. 1 (Washington, D.C.: Smithsonian Institution Press, 1989), 349.

28. See William Cronon, *Changes in the Land* (New York: Hill and Wang, 1983); Mark P. Leone, "The Georgian Order as the Order of Merchant Capitalism in Annapolis, Maryland," in *The Recovery of Meaning,* ed. Mark P. Leone and Parker Potter, Jr. (Washington, D.C.: Smithsonian Institution Press, 1988), 235–263 (and elsewhere); Louis Althusser, "Ideology and Ideological State Apparatuses," in *Lenin and Philosophy,* trans. Ben Brewster (New York: Monthly Review Press, 1971), 127–186.

29. William Brandon, *Quivira* (Columbus: Ohio University Press, 1990).

30. David Hurst Thomas, "Columbian Consequences: The Spanish Borderlands in Cubist Perspective," in *Columbian Consequences: Archaeological and Historical Perspectives on the Spanish Borderlands West,* vol. 1, ed. David Hurst Thomas (Washington, D.C.: Smithsonian Institution Press, 1989), 3.

31. Ibid., 11.

32. For studies that deal with the ideological shift in the eastern United States, the reader is directed to Rhys Isaac, *The Transformation of Virginia, 1740–1790* (New York: W.W. Norton & Company, 1982); and Dell Upton, *Holy Things and Profane: Anglican Parish Churches in Colonial Virginia* (Cambridge, Mass.: The MIT Press, 1986).

33. Ray Allen Billington, *Westward Expansion: A History of the American Frontier* (New York: Macmillian Publishing, 1974), 356–357.

34. Ibid., 365.

35. Lewis Hanke, "Indians and Spaniards in the New World: A Personal View," in *Attitudes of Colonial Powers Toward the American Indian* (University of Utah Press: Salt Lake City, 1969), 6.

36. Donald John Blakeslee, *The Plains Interband Trade System: An Ethnohistoric and Archeological Investigation,* Ph.D. dissertation, Department of Anthropology, University of Wisconsin-Milwaukee, 1975; Joseph Jablow, *The Cheyenne Indian in Plains Indian Trade Relations, 1795–1840,* Monographs of the American Ethnological Society (Seattle: University of Washington Press, 1950); Brandon, *Quivira.*

37. Donald J. Berthrong, *The Southern Cheyennes* (Norman: University of Oklahoma Press, 1963), 9.

38. Virginia Cole Trenholm, *The Arapahos: Our People* (Norman: University of Oklahoma Press, 1970), 19.

39. Thomas F. Schilz, "Ponies, Pelts and Pemmican: The Arapahos and Early Western Trade," *Red River Valley Historical Review* 7, no. 9 (1982): 29.

40. Blakeslee, *Plains Trade System,* 118.

41. For trade with the Cheyenne, see Elliot Coues, ed., *New Light on the Early History of the Greater Northwest: The Manuscript Journals of Alexander Henry and David Thompson, 1799–1814* (New York, 1897), 378; and George Bird Grinnell, *The Cheyenne Indians: Their History and Way of Life* (New York: Cooper Square Publishers, 1962), 15. For trade with the Arapaho, see John C. Ewers, "The Indian Trade of the Upper Missouri Before Lewis and Clark," *Missouri Historical Society Bulletin* 10, no. 4 (1954): 431. For the Comanche see Edwin Thompson Denig, *Five Indian Tribes of the Upper Missouri,* ed. John C. Ewers (Norman: University of Oklahoma Press, 1961), 164; and Richard I. Ford, "Barter, Gift, or Violence: An Analysis of Tewa Intertribal Exchange," in *Social Exchange and Interaction,* Anthropological Papers, No. 46, ed. Edwin N. Wilmsen (Ann Arbor: Museum of Anthropology, University of Michigan, 1972), 21–45. For the Kiowa, see ibid., 30; and Denig, *Five Indian Tribes,* 164. For the Kiowa-Apache, see Ewers, "Indian Trade," 431. For the Pawnee, see Alice C. Fletcher, "The Hako: A Pawnee Ceremony," in *Bureau of American Ethnology, 22nd Annual Report, Part 2* (Washington, D.C., 1904); Antoine Davis Raudot, "Memoir Concerning the Different Indian Nations of North America," in *The Indians of the Western Great Lakes, 1615–1760,* Occasional Contributions from the Museum of Anthropology of the University of Michigan, No. 10, ed. Vernon Kinietz (Ann Arbor: Museum of Anthropology, University of Michigan, 1940), 403; and George E. Hyde, *Pawnee Indians* (Denver: University of Denver Press, 1951), 103. For the Sioux, see Henry A. Boller, *Among the Indians: Eight Years in the Far West, 1858–1866,* ed. Milo Milton Quaife (Chicago: R. R. Donnelley & Sons, 1959), 158.

42. Blakeslee, *Plains Trade System,* 180.

43. Ibid.

44. Ibid., 165.

45. Lewis H. Garrard, *Wah-to-ya and the Taos Trail* (Norman: University of Oklahoma Press, 1955), 36.

46. Blakeslee, *Plains Trade System,* 145.

47. Ibid., 7.

48. Blakeslee, *Plains Trade System,* 123.

49. Billington, *Westward Expansion,* 370.

50. David J. Weber, *The Taos Trappers: The Fur Trade in the Far Southwest, 1540–1846* (Norman: University of Oklahoma Press, 1986), 35.

51. Ibid.

52. Ibid., 47.

53. Ibid., 30.

54. Ibid., 47.

55. Ibid., 16–27.

56. Ibid., 18.

57. Ibid., 195.

58. Schilz, "Ponies, Pelts and Pemmican," 28–38.

59. Ibid., 33.

60. Ibid.

61. Ibid., 34.

62. Ibid., 210.

63. Weber, *Taos Trappers,* 6.

64. Louis Branch, "Ceran St. Vrain and His Molino de Piedra in the Mora Valley," manuscript on file at New Mexico State Records Center and Archives, file #20, 1981.

65. David J. Sandoval, "Gnats, Goods, and Greasers: Mexican Merchants on the Santa Fe Trail," *Journal of the West* 28, no. 2 (1989): 25.

66. David J. Weber, "American Westward Expansion and the Breakdown of Relations Between Pobladores and 'Indios Barbaros' on Mexico's Far Northern Frontier, 1821–1846," *New Mexico Historical Review* 56, no. 3 (1981): 221–238.

67. Ibid., 222.

68. Ibid., 226.

69. Ibid., 225–226.

70. Ibid., 221–238.

71. LeCompte, "Gantt's Fort," 117.

72. Ibid., 111.

73. Lavender, *Bent's Fort,* 141–142; George E. Hyde, *Life of George Bent, Written From His Letters,* ed. Savoie Lottinville (Norman: University of Oklahoma Press, 1968), 60; Berthrong, *Southern Cheyennes,* 25; and LeCompte, "Gantt's Fort," 118.

74. Weber, "American Westward Expansion," 30.

75. LeCompte, "Gantt's Fort," 121.

76. Janet LeCompte, "Bent, St. Vrain and Company among the Comanche and Kiowa," *Colorado Magazine* 49, no. 4 (1972): 275.

77. Forrest D. Monahan, Jr., "The Kiowas and New Mexico," *Journal of the West* 8, no. 1 (1969): 67.

78. LeCompte, "Bent, St. Vrain and Company," 279.

79. Ibid., 280.

80. Ibid., 289.

81. Ibid., 291.

82. Weber, *Taos Trappers,* 6.

Chapter 5: Ritual Trade

1. Thomas E. Chavez, *Manuel Alvarez, 1794–1856: A Southwestern Biography* (Niwot, Colo.: University of Colorado Press, 1990), 87–103.

2. David J. Sandoval, "Gnats, Goods, and Greasers: Mexican Merchants on the Santa Fe Trail," *Journal of the West* 28, no. 2 (1989): 22–31.

3. Mary Douglas, *Natural Symbols* (New York: Vantage Books, 1970), 125–139.

4. Items traded to Native Americans by Europeans, and between Native American groups prior to European contact, have typically been discussed in one of several places: in museum documents; in the professional publications prepared by historians, archaeologists, and anthropologists; in publications directed at private collectors of such material; and, occasionally, in publications such as newspaper and magazine articles aimed at a more general audience. Although the treatments of Native American trade goods by collectors and in the popular media are not without a certain relevance to our central concern, my attention will be restricted to scholarly studies of trade goods. The works I have selected for evaluation are relevant to the interpretation of the meaning of such material. There is little scholarship that deals with this. That which exists tends to fall within one of two groups: a very small number of highly theoretical works that deal with few concrete examples, and a very large number of descriptive writings that mention the symbolic value of trade items almost in passing.

5. Arthur J. Ray, *Indians in the Fur Trade: Their Role as Trappers, Hunters, and Middlemen in the Lands Southwest of Hudson Bay, 1660–1870* (Toronto: University of Toronto Press, 1974); Frank McNitt, *The Indian Traders* (Norman: University of Oklahoma Press, 1962); and George Irving Quimby, *Indian Culture and European Trade Goods* (Madison: University of Wisconsin Press, 1966).

6. Giddens, 146.

7. Richard Harland, *Superstructuralism: The Philosophy of Structuralism and Post-Structuralism* (London: Methuen, 1987), 13.

8. Ibid., 16.

9. Guy Prentice, "Marine Shells as Wealth Items in Mississippian Societies," *Midcontinental Journal of Archaeology* 12, no. 2 (1987): 211.

10. Ian Hodder, *Symbols In Action: Ethnoarchaeological Studies of Material Culture* (Cambridge: Cambridge University Press, 1982), 211.

11. Prentice, "Marine Shells," 196.

12. Jane F. Safer and Frances M. Gill, *Spirals From the Seas: An Anthropological Look at Shells* (New York: Clarkson N. Potter, 1982), 55–56.

13. Ibid., 97.

14. Prentice, "Marine Shells," 198.

15. Ibid., 194. Among the well-established theorists cited by Prentice are Elman Service, Marshall Sahlins, and Marvin Harris. It is notable, however, that some of these individuals, in particular Sahlins and Service, have retreated from a strictly "processual" position (which assumes cultural evolution driven by increasingly efficient etho-economic adaptation) over the past decade. Nonetheless, Prentice explained accurately the basic ideas common to the cited work of these individuals.

16. Marcel Mauss, *The Gift: The Form and Reason for Exchange in Archaic Societies* (New York: W. W. Norton, 1990), xvi.

17. Ibid., 3.

18. Ibid.

19. Ibid., 72.

20. Ibid., 75.

21. Bronislaw Malinowski, *Argonauts of the Western Pacific* (London: Routledge and Kegan Paul, 1922).

22. Ibid., 512.

23. Mauss, *The Gift*, 27.

24. Anthony Giddens, *Emile Durkheim: Selected Writings* (Cambridge: Cambridge University Press, 1972), 6.

25. Emile Durkheim, *The Division of Labor in Society* (New York: The Free Press, 1965), 143.

26. Mircea Eliade, *The Myth of the Eternal Return: Or, Cosmos and History* (Princeton, New Jersey: Princeton University Press, 1954; *Rites and Symbols of Initiation* (New York: Harper and Row, 1958); and *The Sacred and the Profane: The Nature of Religion: The Significance of Religious Myth, Symbolism, and Ritual Within Life and Culture,* trans. Willard R. Trask (New York: Harcourt Brace Jovanovich, 1959).

27. Donald John Blakeslee, *The Plains Interband Trade System: An Ethnohistoric and Archeological Investigation,* Ph.D. dissertation, Department of Anthropology, University of Wisconsin-Milwaukee, 1975; Joseph Jablow, *The Cheyenne Indian in Plains Indian Trade Relations, 1795–1840,* Monographs of the American Ethnological Society (Seattle: University of Washington Press, 1950).

28. Jordan Paper, *Offering Smoke: The Sacred Pipe and Native American Religion* (Moscow: University of Idaho Press, 1988), 13.

29. Joseph C. Winter, "Prehistoric and Historic Native American Tobacco Use: An Overview," unpublished paper presented at the Annual Conference of the Society for American Archaeology, New Orleans, 1991. Johannes Wilbert, "Magico-Religious Use of Tobacco Among South American Indians," in *Cannabis and Culture,* ed. V. Rubin (Paris: Mouton, 1975), frontispiece.

30. Ibid., 180–181.

31. Mary J. Adair, "Tobacco on the Plains: Historical Use, Ethnographic Accounts, and Archaeological Evidence," paper presented at the 1991 Conference of the Society for American Archaeology, New Orleans, 1991, pp. 1–2.

32. Winter, "Prehistoric and Historic," 10.

33. Weston La Barre, "Old and New World Narcotics: Statistical Questions and an Ethnological reply," *Economic Botany* 24 (1970): 73–80; Wilbert, "Magico-Religious Use"; Peter T. Furst, *Hallucinogens and Culture* (San Francisco: Chandler and Sharp, 1976); Alexander D. von Gernet, *The Transculturation of the Amerind Pipe/Tobacco/Smoking Complex and Its Impact on the Intellectual Boundaries Between Savagery and Civilization 1535–1935,* unpublished Ph.D. dissertation, Department of Anthropology, McGill University, 1988.

34. Winter, "Prehistoric and Historic," 14.

35. Ibid., 10–12.

36. Janet LeCompte, *Pueblo, Hardscrabble, Greenhorn* (Norman: University of Oklahoma Press, 1978), 10.

37. Ibid., 88.

38. Ibid., 89.

39. Quoted in Donald J. Berthrong, *The Southern Cheyennes* (Norman: University of Oklahoma Press, 1963), 91.

40. LeCompte, *Pueblo*, 6, 10, 14, 115.

41. Mauss, *The Gift*, 3.

42. Oscar Lewis, *The Effects of White Contact Upon Blackfoot Culture: With Special Reference to the Role of the Fur Trade*, Monographs of the American Ethnological Society, ed. A. Irving Hallowell (Seattle: University of Washington Press, 1942); and Joseph Jablow, *The Cheyenne Indian*.

43. Jablow, *The Cheyenne Indian*, 48.

44. Ibid., 20.

45. Lewis, *Effects of White Contact*, 56.

46. Francis Paul Prucha, *Indian Peace Medals in American History* (Madison: The State Historical Society of Wisconsin, 1971).

47. Ibid., 3.

48. Ibid.

49. Ibid.

50. Quoted in Charles Hanson, "Trade Mirrors," *Museum of the Fur Trade Quarterly* 22, no. 4 (1986): 3.

51. Carolyn Gilman, "Grand Portage Ojibway Indians Give British Medals to Historical Society," *Minnesota History* 47, no. 1 (1980): 28.

52. Thomas F. Schilz and Jodye L. D. Schiltz, "Beads, Bangles, and Buffalo Robes: The Rise and Fall of the Indian Fur Trade Along the Missouri and Des Moines Rivers, 1700–1820," *Annals of Iowa* 49, nos. 1–2 (1987): 7. Schilz has co-authored several articles about the fur trade.

53. Thomas F. Schilz and Donald E. Worcester, "The Spread of Firearms Among the Indian Tribes on the Northern Frontier of New Spain," *American Indian Quarterly* 11, no. 1 (1987): 1–10.

54. William J. Hunt, "Ethnicity and Firearms in the Upper Missouri Bison-Robe Trade: An Examination of Weapon Preference and Utilization at Fort Union Trading Post N.H.S., North Dakota," *Historical Archaeology* 27, no. 3 (1993): 74–101.

55. John Witthoff, "A History of Gunflints," *Pennsylvania Archaeologist* 36, no. 1–2 (1966): 48; Harold F. Williamson, *Winchester: The Gun That Won the West* (Washington, D.C.: Combat Forces Press, 1952), 35; Hunt, "Ethnicity and Firearms," 77–78.

56. Milo H. Slater, A.L.S. Milo H. Slater to F. W. Craigen, dated 1903, Craigen Far West Notebooks (typescript), Colorado Historical Society.

57. Douglas C. Comer, *Bent's Old Fort 1976 Archeological Investigations: Trash Dump Excavations, Area Surveys, and Monitoring of Fort Construction and Landscaping* (Denver: National Park Service, Denver Service Center, 1985).

58. Hunt suggests in the article cited above, "Ethnicity and Firearms," that at Fort Union the firearms utilizing small gunflints were used by fort inhabitants for sport hunting. This might have been the case at Bent's Old Fort, too, but there is little to indicate that Native Americans would have hunted in this manner.

59. Berkeley R. Lewis, *Small Arms and Ammunition in the U.S. Service* (Washington, D.C.: The Smithsonian Institution, 1965), 160.

60. Schilz and Worcester, "Spread of Firearms," 1.

61. Frank Gilbert Roe, *The Indian and the Horse* (Norman: University of Oklahoma Press, 1955), 376.

62. John C. Ewers, *The Horse in Blackfoot Indian Culture,* U. S. Bureau of Ethnology, vol. 159 (Washington, D.C.: U.S. Government Printing Office, 1955).

63. Ibid., 297–298.

64. David V. Burley, "Function, Meaning, and Context: Ambiguities in Ceramic Use by the *Hivernant* Metis of the Northwestern Plains," *Historical Archaeology* 23: no. 1 (1989): 97–106.

65. Ibid., 102.

66. Mary Douglas and Baron Isherwood, *The World of Goods: Toward an Anthropology of Consumption* (London: Alten Lane, 1979), 101–104.

67. Burley, "Function, Meaning, and Context," 104.

68. Douglas and Isherwood, *The World of Goods,* 59.

69. Burley, "Function, Meaning, and Context," 102.

70. Richard E. Flanders, "Beads and Associated Personal Adornment Among Prehistoric Great Lakes Indians," in Grand Rapids Public Museum, *Beads: Their Use by Upper Great Lakes Indians* (Grand Rapids, Michigan: The Museum, 1977), 2.

71. Charles H. Gillette, "Wampum Beads and Belts," *Indian Historian* 3, no. 4 (1970): 33.

72. American Indian Historical Society, "Belts of Sacred Significance," *Indian Historian* 3, no. 2 (1970): 5–9.

73. Peter Powell, "The Enduring Beauty of Cheyenne Art: Crafts That Reflect a Proud Indian Nation's Traditions, Beliefs, and Oneness With Nature," *American West* 10, no. 4 (1973): 7.

74. Ibid.

75. Walter Stanley Campbell [Stanley Vestal], *'Dobe Walls: A Story of Kit Carson's Southwest* (Boston: Houghton Mifflin, 1929), quoted in Enid T. Thompson, "Furnishing Study for Bent's Old Fort Historic Sites, Colorado," manuscript on file, National Park Service, Denver Service Center, 1973, 241–246.

76. National Park Service, *Bent's Old Fort Living History Orientation Handbook and Sourcebook,* manuscript on file, Bent's Old Fort National Historic Site, La Junta, Colorado (n.d.), 36.

77. George R. Milner, E. Anderson, and V. G. Smith, "Warfare in Late Prehistoric West-Central Illinois," *American Antiquity* 56: no. 4 (1991): 581–603.

78. Alice Anne Callahan, *The Osage Ceremonial Dance I'n-Lon-Schka* (Norman: University of Oklahoma Press, 1990), 116.

Chapter 6: Bent's Old Fort as the New World

1. John S. D. Eisenhower, *So Far From God: The U.S. War With Mexico 1846–1848* (New York: Anchor, 1989), xviii.

2. David J. Weber, *The Taos Trappers: The Fur Trade in the Far Southwest, 1540–1846* (Norman: University of Oklahoma Press, 1986), 94–95.

3. Janet LeCompte, "Manuel Armijo and the Americans," *Journal of the West,* 19, no. 3 (1980): 51–63.

4. Walter Briggs, "Bent's Old Fort: Castle in the Desert," *American West* 15, no. 5 (1976): 10–17.

5. Susan Shelby Magoffin, *Down the Santa Fe Trail and Into New Mexico*, ed. Stella M. Drumm, foreword by Howard R. Lamar (Lincoln: University of Nebraska Press, 1982).

6. See Clifford Geertz's discussion of metaphor in "Deep Play: Notes on the Balinese Cockfight," in *The Interpretation of Cultures* (New York: Basic Books, 1973), 208–213; and also Colin Turbayne's groundbreaking work, *The Myth of Metaphor* (New Haven: Yale University Press, 1970).

7. Ian Hodder, "Post-Modernism, Post-Structuralism and Post-Processual Archaeology," in *The Meanings of Things: Material Culture and Symbolic Expressions*, ed. Ian Hodder (London: Unwin Hyman, 1989).

8. Anthony Giddens, "Action, Subjectivity, and the Constitution of Meaning," in *The Aims of Representation: Subject/Text/History*, ed. Murray Krieger (New York: Columbia University Press, 1987).

9. Rhys Isaac, *The Transformation of Virginia 1740–1790* (Chapel Hill: University of North Carolina Press, 1982), 302–306.

10. Michel Foucault, *Discipline and Punish: The Birth of the Prison* (New York: Vintage Books, 1979), 32–69.

11. See ibid., 200.

12. Ibid., 225.

13. Quentin Skinner, *Meaning and Context: Quentin Skinner and His Critics*, ed. James Tully (Cambridge: Polity, 1988).

14. Foucault, *Discipline and Punish*, 200.

15. Ibid., 204.

16. So named for Frederick Winslow Taylor, known as the "father of scientific management," who gained fame with his time and motion studies. These studies were first used to increase productivity in American mills in the late nineteenth century. His "modern" management techniques became the rage throughout American industry.

17. Jeremy Bentham, *Panopticon, or, the Inspection-House* (London: R. Baldwin, 1812).

18. Enid T. Thompson, "Furnishing Study for Bent's Old Fort Historic Sites, Colorado," Manuscript on file, National Park Service, Denver Service Center, 1973, p. 15.

19. Mary Douglas, *Natural Symbols* (New York: Vantage Books, 1970), 125–139.

20. National Park Service, "Bent's Old Fort Living History Orientation Handbook and Sourcebook," manuscript on file, Bent's Old Fort National Historic Site, La Junta, Colorado (n.d.), p. 35.

21. Donald J. Berthrong, *The Southern Cheyennes* (Norman: University of Oklahoma Press, 1963), 227.

22. Unsigned article in *St. Louis Weekly Reveille*, May, 1846, pp. 167–168.

23. Janet LeCompte, *Pueblo, Hardscrabble, Greenhorn* (Norman: University of Oklahoma Press, 1978), 116.

24. Harvey Lewis Carter, *"Dear Old Kit": The Historical Christopher Carson* (Norman: University of Oklahoma Press, 1968), 125–126.

25. See Lewis Garrard, *Wah-to-yah and the Taos Trail*, introduction by A. B. Guthrie, Jr. (Norman: University of Oklahoma Press, 1955); Francis Parkman, *The*

Oregon Trail, ed. E. N. Feltskog (Madison: University of Wisconsin Press, 1969); and Matthew C. Field, *Matt Field on the Santa Fe Trail,* ed. John E. Sunder (Norman: University of Oklahoma Press, 1960).

26. Magoffin, *Down the Santa Fe Trail,* 61.

27. Ibid., 95.

28. Ibid., xvii.

29. Foucault, *Discipline and Punish,* 203.

30. Douglas, *Natural Symbols,* 125–139.

31. Magoffin, *Down the Santa Fe Trail,* 61.

32. Rhys Isaac, *The Transformation of Virginia 1740–1790* (Chapel Hill: University of North Carolina Press, 1982), 104.

33. LeCompte, *Pueblo,* 261.

34. Thompson, "Furnishing Study," 126.

35. Friedrich Wilhelm Nietzsche, *Ecce Homo,* part 4 in *The Philosophy of Nietzsche* (New York: Modern Library, 1900), 32.

36. Roland Barthes, *Mythologies* (New York: Hill and Wang, 1972), 58–61.

37. Douglas C. Comer, *Bent's Old Fort 1976 Archeological Investigations: Trash Dump Excavations, Area Surveys, and Monitoring of Fort Construction and Landscaping* (Denver: National Park Service, Denver Service Center, 1985).

38. George Miller, "Classification and Economic Scaling of Nineteenth Century Ceramics," manuscript on file, National Historic Parks and Sites Branch, Ottawa, Canada, 1979. Miller, a ceramics expert, has estimated that if undecorated whiteware were given a value of 1, then transfer-printed ware should be assigned a value of 3. On this scale, porcelain would be 4 — not that much more than transfer-printed ware — while most other decorated ceramics would be assigned a value of only about 1.3.

39. John Solomon Otto, "Artifacts and Status Differences," in *Research Strategies in Historical Archeology,* ed. Stanley South (New York: Academy Press, 1977).

The percentage of transfer-printed shards to total number of shards that might be calculated from Table 1 would be deceptively small, 8%, for several reasons. First of all, the trash dumps were utilized by everyone who occupied or frequented the fort, not just those in the uppermost social stratum among residents there, who would have been the most likely to have used transfer-printed ware. Also, a good number of the shards classified as "miscellaneous undecorated whiteware" in Table 1 were probably transfer-printed, because many transfer-printed vessels display large white, undecorated spaces. (Other decorative techniques, like hand-painting, spattering, or lustering, characteristically do not, in part because of the technologies utilized in their production.) In this case, too, many of the shards had been so blackened by the numerous fires set in the dump that decoration may have been hidden. Finally, only a small portion of the two trash dumps were excavated. The sampling strategy employed during the excavations there permitted an estimate of the total number of transfer-printed shards that might be present in both dumps to be made. At an 80% confidence level, one might expect 220 to 478 such shards. When one considers the small number of persons likely to have used transfer-printed ware, the ware seems better represented by these numbers. And, the estimate is based upon the number of shards recovered that were *identified* as being transfer-printed. Those not identified in this way, for reasons just described, would not then have contributed to the range estimated for both dumps; thus, the real number of transfer-printed shards is almost certainly higher than this.

40. Jackson W. Moore, *Bent's Old Fort, An Archeological Study* (Boulder, Colo.: Pruett Press, 1973), 72; and Comer, *Bent's Old Fort*, 47, 65.

41. Donald Shomette, personal communication, 1993.

42. Jeff Miller, personal communication, 1977.

43. Stanley South, *Method and Theory in Historical Archaeology* (New York: Academic Press, 1977), 42.

44. Thompson, "Furnishing Study," 118.

45. Magoffin, *Down the Santa Fe Trail*, 94.

46. See Derek Robbins, *The Work of Pierre Bourdieu* (Boulder: Westview Press, 1991), 117–131.

47. John Solomon Otto, "Artifacts and Status Differences," in *Research Strategies in Historical Archaeology,* ed. Stanley South (New York: Academy Press, 1977).

48. While no ceramics are known to have been produced commercially in New Mexico, far to the south in the Spanish colonial city of Puebla the same was not true. A full range of ceramics was produced there, although these ceramics were fired at a low temperature and therefore were less durable. Louanna Lackey, who has conducted ceramics research in Puebla for over two decades, reports that these included chocolate services and a few tea services. These ceramics found their market with the Spanish elite there and in nearby Mexico City, and some were carried north by Spanish missionaries and traders. See Louanna M. Lackey, "Elite Ceramics: Dishes Fit for a King," in *Ceramic Ecology Revisited: The Technology and Socioeconomics of Pottery,* ed. Charles C. Kolb (Oxford: British Archaeology Reports, 1988), 89–109.

49. Thompson, "Furnishing Study," 21.

50. Ibid., 15–16. She cites: RG 107—Microfilm 6, Federal Records Center, Denver; and Mexican Archives of New Mexico, New Mexico #1128, Santa Fe.

51. Mark P. Leone, "The Georgian Order as the Order of Merchant Capitalism in Annapolis, Maryland," in *The Recovery of Meaning: Historical Archaeology in the Eastern United States,* ed. Mark P. Leone and Parker B. Potter (Washington, D.C.: Smithsonian Institution Press, 1988), 242.

52. Mircea Eliade, *The Myth of the Eternal Return: Or, Cosmos and History* (Princeton, N.J.: Princeton University Press, 1954), 5.

53. Leone, "Georgian Order," 252. He cites Kimmerly Rorschach, *The Early Georgian Landscape* (New Haven, Conn.: Yale Center for British Art, 1983), 1–7.

54. Thompson, "Furnishing Study," 6.

55. Moore, *Bent's Old Fort*, 60.

56. Comer, *Bent's Old Fort*.

57. The incinerations produced many of the "unknown" ceramic shards listed in Table 1.

58. Foucault, *Discipline and Punish*, 179.

59. Comer, *Bent's Old Fort*, 59.

60. Thompson, "Furnishing Study," 6.

Chapter 7: Circuits of Power

1. Alexis de Tocqueville, *Democracy in America,* trans. George Lawrence, ed. J. P. Mayer (New York: Doubleday, Anchor Books, 1969), p. 287. "Habits of the Heart" was used as the title of a book by Robert Bellah, et al., which discussed the fierce individualism characteristic of Americans (Berkeley: University of California Press, 1985).

2. David Dary, *Entrepreneurs of the Old West* (Lincoln: University of Nebraska Press, 1986), 76.

3. Paul Augustes St. Vrain, "The De Lassus and St. Vrain Family," New Mexico State Records Center & Archives, file #97, 1943.

4. Louis Branch, "Ceran St. Vrain and His Molino de Piedra in the Mora Valley," manuscript on file at New Mexico State Records Center and Archives, file #20, 1981.

5. Harold H. Dunham, "Ceran St. Vrain," in *Mountain Men and Fur Traders of the Far West,* ed. LeRoy R. Hafen (Lincoln: University of Nebraska Press, 1982), 151.

6. St. Vrain, "The De Lassus and St. Vrain Family."

7. In this same year, 1831, William Bent may have begun construction of Bent's Old Fort (see chapter 4), and so arrangements may have been considerably more complicated than as disclosed by this letter. Whatever they were precisely, in November of 1832 the first Bent & St. Vrain wagon train arrived in Independence with a fortune in silver bullion, mules, and furs.

8. Receipt of Bent St. Vrain & Co. to Abel Baker, Jr. for Fort Jackson with its merchandise, dated October 24, 1838. P. Chouteau-Maffitt Collection, Missouri Historical Society.

9. Ibid.

10. Peter Michel, personal communication, 1992.

11. Thomas E. Chavez, *Manuel Alvarez, 1794–1856: A Southwestern Biography* (Niwot, Colo.: University of Colorado Press, 1990); and Thomas E. Chavez, personal communication, 1990.

12. Dunham, "Ceran St. Vrain," 155.

13. David J. Weber, "Louis Robidoux," in *Trappers of the Far West,* ed. LeRoy R. Hafen (Lincoln: University of Nebraska, 1983), 38.

14. Louis Branch, "Ceran St. Vrain and His Molino de Piedra in the Mora Valley," manuscript on file at New Mexico State Records Center and Archives, file #20, 1981, p. 6.

15. David Lavender, *Bent's Fort* (Lincoln: University of Nebraska Press, 1954), 184.

16. Charles Bent, A.L.S. C. Bent to Manuel Alvarez, dated February 19, 1841. Alverez Collection, letter 47, New Mexico State Records Center and Archives, Santa Fe.

17. Charles Bent, A.L.S. C. Bent to Manuel Alvarez, undated. Alverez Collection, letter 48, New Mexico State Records Center and Archives, Santa Fe.

18. Charles Bent, A.L.S. C. Bent to Manuel Alvarez, no date. Alvarez Collection, letter 48, New Mexico State Records Center and Archives, Santa Fe.

19. F. T. Cheetham, "Governor Bent, Masonic Martyr of New Mexico," *The Builder* 9, no. 12 (1923): 359.

20. Lavender, *Bent's Fort,* 191.

21. Mark C. Carnes, *Secret Ritual and Manhood in Victorian America* (New Haven: Yale University Press, 1989).

22. Cheetham, "Governer Bent," 361.

23. Carnes, *Secret Ritual,* 31.

24. Ibid., 46.

25. Ibid., 47.

26. Ibid., 32.

27. John Brewer, "Commercialization and Politics," in *The Birth of a Consumer Society: The Commercialization of Eighteenth Century England,* ed. Niel McKendrick, John Brewer, and J. H. Plumb (Bloomington: Indiana University Press, 1982).

28. Ibid., 217.

29. Ibid., 219.

30. Ibid., 219.

31. Ibid., 220.

32. Mircea Eliade, *Rites and Symbols of Initiation* (New York: Harper and Row, 1958), 2.

33. Mircea Eliade, *Myths, Dreams, and Mysteries: The Encounter Between Contemporary Faiths and Archaic Realities* (New York: Harper & Row, 1960), 203.

34. Ibid., 202.

35. Michel Foucault, *Discipline and Punish: The Birth of the Prison* (New York: Vintage Books, 1979), 213.

36. Ibid., 218.

Chapter 8: Victory and Defeat

1. Clifford Geertz, "Deep Play: Notes on the Balinese Cockfight," in *The Interpretation of Cultures* (New York: Basic Books, 1973), 220–221.

2. Mary Douglas, *Natural Symbols* (New York: Pantheon, 1970), 123–140.

3. Roy A. Rappaport, *Pigs for the Ancestors: Ritual in the Ecology of a New Guinea People* (New Haven: Yale University Press, 1968), 29.

4. Ibid., 31.

5. Richard White, *The Middle Ground: Indians, Empires, and the Republics in the Great Lakes Region, 1650–1815* (Cambridge: Cambridge University Press, 1991), ix.

6. Ibid., x.

7. Ibid., xv.

8. Ibid., xiv.

9. Quoted in Elman R. Service, *Profiles in Ethnology* (New York: Harper & Row, 1963), 16.

10. Quoted in Robert A. Trennert, "Indian Policy on the Santa Fe Road: The Fitzpatrick Controversy of 1847–1848," *Kansas History* 1, no. 4 (1978): 245.

11. Ibid., 244–245.

12. Ibid., 248.

13. Ibid.

14. Ibid., 248–250.

15. Donald J. Berthrong, *The Southern Cheyennes* (Norman: University of Oklahoma Press, 1963), 113–114.

16. Ibid., 119.

17. The livestock of emigrants ate the grasses upon which the buffalo depended. Moreover, buffalo were restricted in their range because if they went near trails, they were shot by the newcomers who streamed along them.

18. Ibid., 124.

19. Berthrong, *The Southern Cheyennes,* 129.

20. Ibid., 129–130.

21. Ibid., 131.

22. Ibid., 138.

23. Ibid., 140–141.

24. Although firearms were certainly in use by then, George Bent, the half-breed and renegade son of William and Owl Woman, recalled that they were "very few . . . in those days and most of these weapons were cheap, short-range smooth bores." From George E. Hyde, *Life of George Bent, Written from His Letters,* ed. Savioe Lottinville (Norman: University of Oklahoma Press, 1968), 102.

25. Berthrong, *The Southern Cheyennes,* 132.

26. Quoted in Hyde, *Life of George Bent, Written From His Letters,* 105–107.

27. Quoted in Stan Hoig, Jr., *The Sand Creek Massacre* (Norman: University of Oklahoma Press, 1961), 7–8.

28. Ibid., 19.

29. Ibid., 19.

30. Ray C. Colton, *The Civil War in the Western Territories: Arizona, Colorado, New Mexico, and Utah* (Norman: University of Oklahoma Press, 1959), 49–80.

31. Berthrong, *Southern Cheyennes,* 157.

32. Ibid., 174.

33. Ibid., 190, and Hoig, *Sand Creek Massacre,* 58–59.

34. Ibid., 60.

35. Ibid., 61.

36. Otis B. Spencer, "A Sketch of the Boone-Bent Families," *Westport Historical Quarterly* 8, no. 4 (1973): 102–103.

37. Ralph K. Andrist, *The Long Death* (New York: McMillan Company, 1965), 88–91.

38. Hoig, *Sand Creek Massacre,* 143; Hyde, *Life of George Bent,* 149.

39. Hoig, *Sand Creek Massacre,* 147.

40. Hyde, *Life of George Bent,* 148–168.

41. Hoig, *Sand Creek Massacre,* 145–192.

42. Hyde, *Life of George Bent,* 155.

43. Hoig, *Sand Creek Massacre,* 156.

44. Hyde, *Life of George Bent,* 156.

45. Ibid., 158.

46. Hoig, *Sand Creek Massacre,* 168.

47. Ibid., 172.

48. Berthrong, *Southern Cheyennes,* 224.

49. Hyde, *Life of George Bent,* 179.

50. Berthrong, *Southern Cheyennes,* 228–229.

51. Ibid., 328–329.

52. David Lavender, *Bent's Fort* (Lincoln: University of Nebraska Press, 1954), 389.

53. Mircea Eliade, *The Sacred and the Profane: The Nature of Religion: The Significance of Religious Myth, Symbolism, and Ritual Within Life and Culture,* trans. Willard R. Trask (New York: Harcourt Brace Jovanovich, 1957), 29.

Epilogue: Modern Ritual at Bent's Old Fort

1. Clifford Geertz, "Deep Play: Notes on the Balinese Cockfight," in *The Interpretation of Cultures* (New York: Basic Books, 1973), 122.

2. Ibid., 219.

3. Mark P. Leone, "Time in American Archeology," in *Social Archeology* (New York: Academic Press), 1978.

4. Geertz, "Deep Play," 194.

5. Eric Berne, *What Do You Say After You Say Hello?* (Toronto: Bantam Books, 1972), 148.

6. Ibid., 153.

7. Gramsci developed the idea of cultural hegemony in notebooks he kept while in prison. He attributed the failure of communist revolutions largely to the control over the media, educational systems, advertising, churches, and other means for the propagation of culture by the ruling classes. Two selections of these notebooks have been translated into English and provide a full discussion of Gramsci's theory: Antonio Gramsci, *The Modern Prince,* trans. Louis Marks (London: Lawrence and Wishart, 1957); and *Selections from the Prison Notebooks of Antonio Gramsci,* trans. Q. Hoare and G. Nowell Smith (London: Lawrence and Wishart, 1971).

8. Unless one employs that term even more broadly than I have done here and says that culture is only ideology that has taken various guises. I stop short of this.

9. David M. Pletcher, *The Diplomacy of Annexation: Texas, Oregon, and the Mexican War* (Columbia: University of Missouri Press, 1973), 5.

10. Richard White, *The Middle Ground: Indians, Empires, and the Republics in the Great Lakes Region, 1650–1815* (Cambridge: Cambridge University Press, 1991).

11. David J. Sandoval, "Gnats, Goods, and Greasers: Mexican Merchants on the Santa Fe Trail," *Journal of the West* 28 (1989): 25.

12. Susan Calafate Boyle, "Comerciantes, Arrieros, y Peones: The Hispanos and the Santa Fe Trade," manuscript on file, National Park Service, Denver Service Center, 1992; and Jere Krakow, personal communication, 1993.

13. See, for example, Rhys Isaac, *The Transformation of Virginia, 1740–1790* (Chapel Hill: University of North Carolina Press, 1982), 163–177.

14. Mary Douglas, *Natural Symbols,* 137.

15. Anthony Giddens, *Emile Durkheim: Selected Writings* (Cambridge: Cambridge University Press, 1972), 22.

16. Merrill J. Mattes, "From Ruin to Reconstruction," in *Bent's Old Fort,* ed. Cathryne Johnson (Denver: Colorado Historical Society, 1976), 61.

17. It is of some importance to note here that, as is almost always the case, local and state governments and organizations sought to place the historic site within

the National Park System. The federal government almost never takes the initiative in establishing National Park units. Thus, the federal government is not aggressively pursuing an agenda of "cultural hegemony," at least through such actions. On the contrary, local governments and organizations are typically eager to establish an affiliation with the federal system, thereby legitimating the importance of, or validating, their own history.

18. Mattes, "From Ruin to Reconstruction," 76.

19. Robert F. Berkhofer, Jr., "The Challenge of Poetics to (Normal) Historical Practice," *Poetics Today* 9 (1988): 441.

20. Mary Douglas, *Natural Symbols* (New York: Vantage Books, 1970), 125.

21. Isaac, *The Transformation of Virginia*.

22. Geertz, "Deep Play," 94–95.

23. During the time of Bent's Old Fort, however, this would have been far north of the typical range of the Southern Cheyenne and Arapaho, who were kept to the south by the opportunities offered by the fort.

24. John Eddy, "Astronomical Alignment of the Big Horn Medicine Wheel," *Science* 184 (1974): 1035–1043.

25. Ibid., 1036.

26. George Grinnell, "The Medicine Wheel," *American Anthropologist* 24 (1922): 299–310, discussed on 307ff.

27. Eddy, "Astronomical Alignment," 1036.

28. Ibid.

29. Geertz, "Deep Play," 128.

30. Ibid.

31. Quoted in Joseph Campbell, *Historical Atlas of World Mythology, Volume 1: The Way of the Animal Powers, Part 2: Mythologies of the Great Hunt* (New York, Harper & Row, 1988).

32. Yi-Fu Tuan, *Segmented Worlds and Self: Group Life and Individual Consciousness* (Minneapolis: University of Minnesota Press), 175.

Index

Abenaki, 104

Abert, J. W.: "Journal from Bent's Fort to St. Louis in 1845," 91, 97, 175, 275

Adair, Mary, 139

Adobe Walls, 94

Aldred, Alexandra, 266, 274–277

Algonquin, 64, 71

Alienation: on American frontier, 2, 7; and attraction to religious ritual, 6–7

Alott, Gordon, 259

Althusser, Louis, 105

Alvarez, Manuel, 128, 203, 208

American Fur Company, 27, 96, 202, 203

Anasazi-Pueblo, 102, 193; trade with Plains Indians, 109, 111

Ancestors: ritual reenactment of actions, 24, 138; veneration as result of human neoteny, 23, 83, 164, 246–247, 281–282

Anglo-Americans: alienation, 6–7; conflict with Native Americans in Southwest, 31, 234–238; evangelical religiosity, 6–7, 49; mythology of entrepreneur, 197; mythology of the West, 86; nostalgia for Native American culture, 85–88; trading practices, 28–29, 144

Anomie, 46, 82, 217, 278; among the sub-proletariat, 55; among those excluded from high-grid, low-group societies, 46–47

Anthony, Scott J., 238

Anthropology: cognitive, 70–71

Apache, 9, 14, 81, 120; Mescalero, 81

Arapaho, 8, 9; acquisition of horse, 109; alliance with Cheyenne, 109; ancestral home, 107; benefits of trade with Bent & St. Vrain, 121; difficulty adapting to sedentary life, 234; disenfranchisement by Treaty of Fort Wise, 232; early resistance to American traders, 11, 13, 116–117; 1863 delegation to Washington, 234–235; fictive kinship relation to Bent's Fort traders, 14, 155; hostility toward Anglos after Sand Creek, 31; intertribal conflict of 1850s, 229–230; middleman role in southwestern trade, 111, 155; relocation to Oklahoma, 16, 31, 243; Siberian ancestry of, 65; trade with Pueblo, 109; trade with Spanish, 11, 13; Treaty of Fort Laramie, 227–228

Archaeology, 56–62; and language, 60

Archuleta, Diego, 15, 161

Arikira, 116; Treaty of Fort Laramie, 227–228

Armijo, Manuel, 15, 161–162, 210

Army of the West, 15, 102

Assiniboin, 142; Treaty of Fort Laramie, 227–228

Astor, John Jacob, 114, 202

Auguste, Charles, 199

Australian aborigines, 76

Axis mundi, 3–4, 25–27, 71, 72, 282–283; Sun Dance pole as, 25–26

Babitt, Almon W., 230

Baker, Bob, 255

Baltimore and Ohio Railroad, 190

Compositor: Integrated Composition Systems
Text: Galliard
Display: Galliard
Printer: Haddon Craftsmen, Inc.
Binder: Haddon Craftsmen, Inc.